THE BIRTH OF HEDONISM

THE BIRTH
OF HEDONISM

The Cyrenaic Philosophers
and Pleasure
as a Way of Life

KURT LAMPE

PRINCETON UNIVERSITY PRESS
Princeton & Oxford

Copyright © 2015 by Princeton University Press
Published by Princeton University Press, 41 William Street, Princeton,
New Jersey 08540
In the United Kingdom: Princeton University Press, 6 Oxford Street,
Woodstock, Oxfordshire OX20 1TR
press.princeton.edu
Cover art: Henri Matisse, *Luxe calme et volupte*, 1904, Musée d'Orsay, Paris,
France. © 2014 Succession H. Matisse / Artists Rights Society (ARS), New York.
Photo credit: © RMN–Grand Palais / Art Resource, NY / Hervé Lewandowski.
Cover design by Pam Schnitter
First paperback printing, 2017
Paperback ISBN 978-0-691-17638-3
LIBRARY OF CONGRESS CATALOGING-IN-PUBLICATION DATA
Lampe, Kurt, 1977–
The birth of hedonism : the Cyrenaic philosophers and pleasure
as a way of life / Kurt Lampe.
pages cm
Includes bibliographical references and index.
ISBN 978-0-691-16113-6 (hardcover : alk. paper) 1. Hedonism.
2. Cyrenaics (Greek philosophy) I. Title.
B279.L36 2014   183'.5—dc23
2013039984
British Library Cataloging-in-Publication Data is available
This book has been composed in Minion
Printed on acid-free paper ∞
Printed in the United States of America

PARENTIBUS DILIGENTIBUS,

QUI ME EDUCANDUM CURAVERINT

SOPHIAE HANINA, CUIUS AMORE MAIOR SIM FACTUS

UNIVERSITATIS BRISTOLIENSIS CONLEGIS, QUORUM

CONSTANTIA AUDACIAQUE ME CORROBORAVERINT

CONTENTS

ACKNOWLEDGMENTS

This book began life as a PhD dissertation at the University of Berkeley in 2005–2007. Above all I must thank Tony Long, my lead supervisor, for giving me the latitude to pursue my own interests at that time. The mandate to produce an immediately publishable thesis, thank goodness, was never imposed on me. While this freedom led to many dead ends and complete revisions, the wandering involved has undoubtedly been fundamental not only for this book (notwithstanding its remaining flaws!), but also for my broader development as a scholar.

For the last two years of my PhD I was actually resident either at Cambridge or at the Warburg Institute in London. I am grateful to both institutions for their supportive research environments. In particular I want to thank David Sedley and Malcolm Schofield at Cambridge and Charles Burnett at the Warburg.

Many others have helped with both the PhD and subsequent drafts of this work. First, John Ferrari and Nelly Oliensis read drafts of many chapters at Berkeley. Hans Sluga read the completed dissertation and offered me his comments, as did Margaret Graver. As I revised and re-revised the manuscript, chapters were read by Geoffrey Lloyd, Duncan Kennedy, Charles Martindale, Lee Behlman, and Gillian Clark. Stephen Clark was kind enough to read almost an entire draft. To all of these people I owe my thanks—and indeed my apologies, since I fear I have not always been a gracious recipient of criticism!

I also owe a great deal of gratitude to the Classics & Ancient History Department at the University of Bristol, which has been unfailingly supportive during the long revision process. Indeed, from my first weeks here I was permitted to turn my attention to entirely new and unrelated projects. Without the lapse of time this created I do not think I would have arrived at some of the most important interpretive claims in this book.

Some of this material—often in embarrassingly undercooked form—has been presented at the APA convention in San Diego (2007), the University of Toronto (2007), the University of Cambridge (2010, 2011), and Durham University (2011). I am grateful to those audiences for their criticisms.

Finally, I want to thank Rob Tempio, my editor at Princeton University Press, and the referees. One of those referees—Voula Tsouna—chose to reveal her name to me afterwards. I have benefited from both her detailed report and from subsequent correspondence.

ABBREVIATIONS

My abbreviations for classical authors follow those of LSJ and *The Oxford Latin Dictionary* (ed. P.G.W. Clare, 1982. Oxford: Clarendon Press). For ease of reference I list them here as well. I also give the publication details for works that are harder to find.

All translations are my own unless otherwise noted. There exists no convenient English translation of the collected evidence for the Cyrenaics, although some of it can be found scattered through Boys-Stones and Rowe 2013. Onfray 2002 is currently the only modern-language translation of this evidence of which I know, although another is forthcoming by Mársico. Those wishing to consult English translations of particular Greek or Roman works are advised to check first in the Loeb Classical Library series (Harvard University Press), whose translations of book titles I use in the following list. Translations and commentaries I have cited in the text are given in the bibliography under the name of the translator or commentator.

Ael. = Aelian
- *AH = Animalium Historia* (*On Animals*)
- *VH = Varia Historia* (*Historical Miscellany*)

Aët. = Aëtius, *Placita* (in Diels 1879, 267–444)

Al. Aphr. *De An.* = *Alexander of Aphrodisias, De Anima Liber* (*On the Soul*)

Anecd. Gr. = *Anecdota Graeca*. Ed. J. Fr. Boissonade. 1829–33. Paris: The Royal Press.

Andron. Rh. = *Pseudo-Andronicus of Rhodes: Περι Παθῶν. Édition critique du texte grecque et de la traduction latine médiévale*. Ed. A. Glibert-Thirry. 1977. Leiden: Brill.

Anon. *Comm. in Pl. Tht.* = Anonymous *Commentarius in Platonis Theaetetum* (*Commentary on Plato's Theaetetus*). Ed. G. Bastianini and D. N. Sedley. 1995. In *Corpus dei papiri filosofici greci et latini* vol. 3. Florence: Olschki.

Apul. *Flor.* = Apuleius, *Florida*

Ar. *Av.* = Aristophanes, *Aves* (*Birds*)

Arist. = Aristotle
- *AH = Animalium Historia* (*History of Animals*)
- *De An. = De Anima* (*On the Soul*)
- *EN = Ethica Nicomachea* (*Nicomachean Ethics*)

- *Ph.* = *Physica* (*Physics*)
- *Pol.* = *Politica* (*Politics*)
- *Rhet.* = *Rhetorica* (*Rhetoric*)

[Arist.] *MM* = Pseudo-Aristotle, *Magna Moralia*

Aristocles: See Chiesara 2001

Arius Didymus *Epit.* = *Epitome of Stoic Ethics*, ed. A. Pomeroy. 1999. Atlanta: Society of Biblical Literature.

Arr. *An.* = Arrian, *Anabasis of Alexander*

Athen. = Athenaeus, *Deipnosophistae* (*The Learned Banqueters*)

Aug. *Civ. Dei* = Augustine, *City of God*

Aulus Gellius, *Noct. Att.* = *Noctes Atticae* (*Attic Nights*)

Auson. *Opusc.* = Ausonius, *Opuscula* ("Book III: Personal Poems" in the Loeb)

Bion: see Kindstrand 1976

Callimachus *Ep.* = *Epigrammata*. Ed. R. Pfeiffer, 1953. *Vol II: Hymni et Epigrammata*. Oxford: Clarendon Press.

Cic. = Cicero
- *Fin.* = *De Finibus Bonorum et Malorum* (*On Ends*)
- *Luc.* = *Lucullus* (sometimes called the *Prior Academics*)
- *ND* = *De Natura Deorum* (*On the Nature of the Gods*)
- *Off.* = *De Officiis* (*On Duties*)
- *Tusc.* = *Tusculanae Disputationes* (*Tusculan Disputations*)

Clem. Al. = Clement of Alexandria
- *Paed.* = *Paedagogus* (*The Pedagogue*)
- *Protrept.* = *Protrepticus*
- *Strom.* = *Stromata*

Dem. = Demosthenes, *Orations*

D.H. = Dionysius of Halicarnassus

Diog. Oen. = Diogenes of Oenoanda. 1993. *The Epicurean Inscription*. Ed. Martin F. Smith. Naples: Bibliopolis.

DK = Diels, H. and W. Kranz. 1952. *Die Fragmente der Vorsokratiker*. 6th edition. Berlin: Weidmann.

D.L. = Diogenes Laertius, *Lives of the Philosophers*.

DPhA = Goulet, Richard, ed. 1989–. *Dictionnaire des Philosophes Antiques*. Paris: CNRS Éditions.

Epiphanius: see Holl and Dummer 1980, Williams 1987

Epicurus, *Rat. Sent.* = *Ratae Sententiae*. Also often called *Kuriai Doxai* (*Principal Sayings*).

Eur. = Euripides
- *Ba.* = *Bacchae*
- *Hec.* = *Hecuba*

Eus. *PE* = Eusebius of Caesarea, *Praeparatio Evangelica* (*Preparation for the Gospel*)

FGrHist = Jacoby, F. et al. 1923–. *Die Fragmente der griechischen Historiker.*
Berlin: Weidmann; Leiden: Brill.

Gal. = Galen
- *PHP* = *De Placitis Hippocratis et Platonis* (*On the Doctrines of Hippocrates and Plato*). Ed. Phillip De Lacy. 1978–84. 3 vols. Berlin: Akademie-Verlag.
- *Protr.* = *Protrepticus* (*Protreptic*)

[Gal.] *Hist. Phil.* = Pseudo-Galen, *Historia Philosopha* (in Diels 1879, 597–648).

Gnom. Vat. = *Gnomologium Vaticanum e Codice Vaticano Graeco 743.* Ed.
L. Sternbach. 1963. Reprint. Berlin: De Gruyter.

Heraclitus: Russell, Donald A. and David Konstan, ed. and trans. 2005.
Heraclitus: Homeric Problems. Atlanta: Society of Biblical Literature.

Homer
- *Il.* = *Iliad*
- *Od.* = *Odyssey*

Hor. = Horace
- *Ep.* = *Epistulae* (*Epistles*)
- *Serm.* = *Sermones* (*Satires*)

Jo. Chrys. *Hom. in Mt.* = John Chrysostom, *Homily on the Gospel of St. Matthew*

John of Salisbury
- *Ep.* = *Letters*
- *Policr.* = *Policraticus*

LS = Long, A. A. and D. Sedley, ed. and trans. 1986. *The Hellenistic Philosophers.* Cambridge: Cambridge University Press.

LSJ = Liddell, H. G. and R. Scott. 1996. *A Greek–English Lexicon.* Revised and augmented throughout by Sir Henry Stuart Jones, with the assistance of Roderick McKenzie, and with the cooperation of many scholars. Oxford: Clarendon Press.

Lucian, *Vit. Auct.* = *Lives for Sale*

Lucr. = Lucretius, *On the Nature of Things*

Lys. = Lysias, *Orations*

Marc. Aur. = Marcus Aurelius, *Meditations*

Maxim. Tyr. *Phil.* = Maximus of Tyre, *Philosophical Orations*

Pater, Walter
- *Letters* = 1970. *The Letters of Walter Pater.* Ed. L. Evans. Oxford: Clarendon.
- *ME* I and II = 1909. *Marius the Epicurean: His Sensations and Ideas.* 4th edition. 2 vols. London: MacMillan and Co.
- *MS* = 1895. *Miscellaneous Studies: A Series of Essays.* Ed. C. L. Shadwell. London: Macmillan and Co.
- *PP* = 1910. *Plato and Platonism: A Series of Lectures.* London: MacMillan and Co.

- *R* = 1910. *The Renaissance: Studies in Art and Poetry.* Library edition. London: Macmillan and Co.

Philo, *quod omn. prob.* = *Quod omnis probus liber est* (*Every Good Man is Free*)

Phld. = Philodemus

- *Academica* = *Philodems Academica: Die Berichte über Platon und die Alte Akademie in zwei herkulanensischen Papyri.* Ed. K. Gaiser. 1988. Stuttgart–Bad Cannstatt: Frommann-Holzboog.
- *Academicorum Historia.* In *Storia dei filosofi: Platone e l'Academia : (PHerc. 1021 e 164).* Ed. and trans. Tiziano Dorandi. 1991. Bibliopolis: Naples.
- *De Morte* = *On Death.* Ed. and trans. W. Benjamin Henry. 2009. Atlanta: Society for Biblical Literature.
- *Ind. Sto.* = *Index Stoicorum.* Ed. Tiziano Dorandi. 1982. "Filodemo. Gli Stoici (PHerc. 155 e 339)." *Cronache Ercolanesi* 12: 91–133.
- *On Choices and Avoidances.* Ed. and trans. G. Indelli and V. Tsouna-McKirahan. 1995. Naples: Bibliopolis.
- *On Property Management.* Ed. and trans. V. Tsouna. 2013. Atlanta: Society for Biblical Literature.
- *Rh.* = *Philodemi Volumina Rhetorica.* Ed. Siegfried Sudhaus. Leipzig: Teubner.
- *To The Friends of the School.* Ed. and trans. A. Angeli. 1988. *Filodemo: Agli Amici di Scuola (PHerc. 1005).* Naples: Bibliopolis.

Pindar, *Pyth.* = *Pythian Odes*

PKöln 205 = Cologne Papyrus 205. See M. Gronewald, ed. and trans., 1985. "205. Sokratischer Dialog." In *Kölner Papyri (P.Köln) Band 5,* ed. M. Gronewald, K. Maresch, and W. Schäfer, 33–53. Opladen: Westdeutscher Verlag.

Pl. = Plato

- *Apol.* = *Apology*
- *Chrm.* = *Charmides*
- *Cri.* = *Crito*
- *Euth.* = *Euthyphro*
- *Grg.* = *Gorgias*
- *Hp. Ma.* = *Hippias Major*
- *Phd.* = *Phaedo*
- *Phlb.* = *Philebus*
- *Prt.* = *Protagoras*
- *Resp.* = *Republic*
- *Symp.* = *Symposium*

Plb. = Polybius

Plut. = Plutarch

- *Alex.* = *Life of Alexander*
- *Demetr.* = *Life of Demetrius*

- *Mor.* = *Moralia*
- *Phoc.* = *Life of Phocion*

[Plut.] *Vit. Hom.* = Pseudo-Plutarch, *Lives of Homer*

RE = Wissowa, G. et al. (1894–1978) *Paulys Real-Encyclopädie der Classischen Altertumswissenschaft. Neue Bearbeitung.* Stuttgart: J. B. Metzler.

Scholia in Apoll. Rhod. Argon. = C. Wendel, ed. 1935. *Scholia in Apollonium Rhodium vetera.* Berlin: Weidmann.

Schol. in Hom. Il. E = I. Bekker, ed. 1825–27. *Scholia in Homeri Iliadem.* Berlin: G. Reimer.

S.E. = Sextus Empiricus

- *M* = *Adversus Mathematicos* (*Against the Dogmatists*), which encompasses *Against the Professors, Against the Logicians, Against the Physicists,* and *Against the Ethicists*
- *PH* = *Purrhoneiai Hupotuposeis* (*Outlines of Pyrrhonism*)

SEG = *Supplementum Epigraphicum Graecum*

Seneca

- *Ep.* = *Epistulae Morales* (*Epistles*)
- *Tranq.* = *De Tranquillitate Animi* (*On Tranquility*)

Socr. *Ep.* = (spurious) letters of Socrates and the Socratics. Editions include:

- 1928. *Die Briefe des Sokrates und der Sokratiker.* Ed. L. Köhler. Leipzig: Dieter.
- 1997. *Socratis quae feruntur epistolae.* Ed. and trans. J.-F. Borkowski. Stuttgart and Leibniz: Teubner.

SSR = *Socratis et Socraticorum Reliquiae.* Ed. Giannantoni, G., 1990. 4 vols. Naples: Bibliopolis.

Stob. = Stobaeus. *Anthologium.* Ed. C. Wachsmuth, O. Hense. 1884–1912. 5 vols. Berlin: Weidmann.

SVF = *Stoicorum Veterum Fragmenta.* Ed. Arnim, J. von and M. Adler, 1905–1914. 4 vols. Leipzig: Teubner.

Teles: See Hense 1909

Th. = Thucydides, *History of the Peloponnesian War*

Themist. *Orat.* = Themistius, *Orations*

Xen. = Xenophon

- *Ap.* = *Apology*
- *Smp.* = *Symposium*
- *Mem.* = *Memorabilia*

THE BIRTH OF HEDONISM

CHAPTER 1

Introduction

1.1. A Cyrenaic Parable: The Choice of Pleasure

If we are to believe Xenophon, Socrates did not entirely approve of Aristippus of Cyrene. Xenophon and Aristippus were both among the crowd of young men who passed their leisure time with Socrates. However, Xenophon felt that he and Socrates agreed on the importance of self-control, which was the foundation of responsible management of one's body, soul, household, relationships, and polis. By contrast, he narrates how Socrates "had noticed that one of his companions [i.e., Aristippus] was rather self-indulgent" with regard to food, drink, sex, sleep, cold, heat, and hard work (*Mem.* 2.1.1). So Socrates tries to show Aristippus the error of his ways. His admonishment concludes by recalling the wisdom of the poets Hesiod and Epicharmus, who concur that sweat and suffering are the price of all good things (2.1.20). He then paraphrases Prodicus's story about "the choice of Heracles," in which the hero is confronted with two allegorical figures. The figure of Vice promises every sort of pleasure without effort, while Virtue reiterates that there is no happiness without exertion (2.1.21–34). Socrates does not tell us which choice Heracles made, but we all know he chose the path of suffering and glorious virtue. The question is, which choice did Aristippus make?

Xenophon's way of presenting Aristippus leads most readers to conclude that he chose the path of easy pleasure. Of course, this is not a reliable account of the historical Aristippus's thoughts. It is a fiction colored by Xenophon's opinions of Aristippus and Socrates and his own conceptions of virtue, vice, pleasure, and happiness. But it is a useful parable for thinking about the impetus behind the philosophical movement Aristippus started. That movement is called "Cyrenaic" after Cyrene, the polis in North Africa where most of the movement's participants were born. Although the Cyrenaics do not associate pleasure with vice, Xenophon is right to represent Cyrenaic philosophy as the choice of pleasure. The Cyrenaics reflectively affirm their intuitive attraction to pleasure and commit themselves to working through this decision's life-shaping consequences. This is what I will mean in this book by calling the Cyrenaics philosophical hedonists.

There are two aspects of this hedonism I initially wish to highlight. First, many of the Cyrenaics' fundamental beliefs and arguments revolve around pleasure and pain. In particular, they all agree that either bodily or mental plea-sure is the greatest and most certain intrinsic good. We might call this formal hedonism. Second, they actually indulge in all sorts of everyday pleasures such as food and sex. In other words, notwithstanding disagreements among mem-bers of the movement, in general it is not by sober parsimony or self-restraint that they attempt to live pleasantly. In this they differ (at least in degree) from many formal hedonists, including their competitors and eventual successors, the Epicureans. We might call this everyday hedonism.

In fact we can plausibly think of Cyrenaic philosophy as the first attempt in the European tradition to formalize everyday hedonism with increasingly systematic theories. The Cyrenaics were obviously not the first to claim that pleasure is a good thing; indeed, pleasure's supposedly universal appeal is the foundation of their reflective choice. Nor were they the first thinkers to grant pleasure an important theoretical position. It seems that Democritus, for exam-ple, gave both "pleasure" (*hēdonē*) and "delight" (*terpsis*) thematic prominence in his ethical writings.[1] Moreover, among Aristippus's approximate contempo-raries were Eudoxus of Cnidus, who elaborated his hedonism within Plato's Academy,[2] and the lamentably shadowy Polyarchus, "The Voluptuary" of Syra-cuse.[3] But the Cyrenaic tradition clearly involves a much more sustained inves-tigation of hedonism than any of these.

It is thus with some justice that the Cyrenaics have sometimes been rep-resented as the originators of the tradition of philosophical hedonism in Eu-rope. For example, both Watson's *Hedonistic Theories from Aristippus to Spencer* (1895) and Feldman's *Pleasure and the Good Life: Concerning the Nature, Variet-ies, and Plausibility of Hedonism* (2004) begin by sketching ostensibly Cyrenaic theories, which they then proceed to demolish. Cyrenaicism is thus portrayed as an infantile stage in an evolving theoretical organism. Onfray gives the Cyrena-ics an even more originary status in the resoundingly titled *L'invention du plai-sir: Fragments cyrênaïques* (*The Invention of Pleasure: Cyrenaic Fragments*; 2002), which until very recently was the only translation of the Cyrenaic evidence into a modern language. However, Onfray's narrative is reactionary rather than pro-gressivist: he sees Western civilization as a "historically sublimated neurosis," the causes of which lie in Platonism and its monstrous offspring.[4] The cure for this neurosis is re-engagement with our embodied experience, beginning with the rediscovery of the "philosophical Atlantis" of Cyrenaicism.[5] There, at the histori-cal foundation of the problem, we must reassemble Aristippus's "anti-Platonic war machine" to undermine the corrupt fortress of our unhealthy ideologies.[6]

Watson, Onfray, and Feldman remind us in their different ways that the search for origins—in this case the origin of philosophical hedonism—often comes bundled with trans-historical explanatory and critical agendas.[7] Insofar as those explanations or critiques invoke the chronological primacy of Cyrenaicism, they rely on the historical accuracy of their presentations of this early movement. Yet hitherto there has been no systematic reconstruction of Cyrenaic ethics within its own historical contexts. The most recent monograph, by Guirand, focuses on Aristippus and his reception in European (especially Francophone) literature.[8] Two other monographs, by Antoniadis and Döring,[9] have primarily been concerned with stipulating who thought what and when. The collections of the Cyrenaic fragments and testimonia, by Giannantoni and Mannebach respectively,[10] have furthered this biographical and doxographical work, corroborated it with source criticism, and added essays on many items of philosophical interest. Scattered chapters and articles have addressed Socrates' influence on Aristippus and later Cyrenaicism,[11] Aristippus's relationships with and influence on Xenophon and Plato,[12] the Cyrenaics' putative rejection of "eudaimonism,"[13] the historiography of the schismatic Cyrenaics,[14] and a number of other topics.[15] But none of these attempts to convey an appreciation of Cyrenaic ethics in the round by exploring the developmental history of the movement and the manner in which theories arose from and found expression in principled lifestyles. Moreover, few of these works are in English, and many are hard to come by.

This volume therefore aims to be a complement to Voula Tsouna's monograph on *Cyrenaic Epistemology*, which is the most thorough investigation of Cyrenaic skepticism,[16] and to help make a fuller appreciation of this "original hedonism" available to classicists, philosophers, and cultural historians.[17]

1.2. Methodology

In order to accomplish this project it is necessary to find a method that respects the limitations in the evidence yet still permits us to produce new historical, literary, and philosophical insights. The first challenge is the diversity of our sources, which include hundreds of testimonia from dozens of authors over more than a thousand years. Dealing with these sources has become somewhat easier since Giannantoni's multi-volume *Socratis et Socraticorum Reliquiae* (1990) assembled the ancient testimony for all the so-called "minor Socratic" philosophers. Nevertheless, a great deal of research is necessary to assess the knowledge, generic aims, personal agendas, and lines of transmission of the authors and texts involved. Since the painstaking philology involved in this task would frequently interrupt the flow of my arguments, and some readers may want to skip it entirely, I have relegated much of it to footnotes and appendixes 1 and 2.

The second challenge for the interpreter of Cyrenaicism is to say something philosophically interesting despite the fragmentary nature of these testimonia. It is partly for this reason that I will not restrict myself to tracing the development and relations of beliefs and arguments. Of course I will try to present these ratiocinative structures in the clearest and most accessible fashion possible. But if I were to exclude their practical and cultural contexts, not only would I increase the danger of misunderstanding the evidence, I would also find it impossible to reconstruct what it would be like to mentally inhabit this sort of ethical system.

I have chosen the phrase "mentally inhabit" because its resonances are simultaneously intellectual, practical, and existential. I intend to suggest that we can profitably think of Cyrenaic ethics as involving much more than the theories on which previous scholars have generally focused. This is true of most post-Socratic Greek philosophical ethics, as Anthony Long has expressed in speaking of "philosophical power":

> Try to imagine a single affiliation incorporating your political party, religion, form of therapy, cosmology, psychology, and fundamental values, an affiliation which unified all that might be involved in being, for instance, a Christian, Jungian, socialist, utilitarian, and believer in evolution and the Big Bang. Then you have a loose analogy to one of the leading Hellenistic schools in their most challenging phase and a reason for thinking of them as experiments in philosophical power.[18]

Long is speaking about the schools that succeeded Cyrenaicism, but his lesson applies to the Cyrenaics as well. Here he emphasizes not only the reach of these schools' doctrines, but also their "power" to give shape to entire ways of being in the world. The point is that this kind of philosophy does not simply develop arguments about, for example, the truthfulness of Christian theology or Jungian psychology. It aims to incorporate those truths into its practitioners' attitudes and behavior, for which it requires something loosely analogous to Christian ritual or Jungian therapy.

The scholar who has done the most to chart the analogues for these elements in ancient philosophy is Pierre Hadot. In his inaugural lecture at the Collège de France he said,

> Each school, then, represents a form of life defined by an ideal of wisdom. The result is that each one has its corresponding fundamental inner attitude—for example, tension for the Stoics or relaxation for the Epicureans—and its own manner of speaking, such as the Stoic use of percussive dialectic or the abundant rhetoric of the Academicians. But above all every school practices exercises designed to ensure spiritual progress toward the ideal state of wisdom . . .[19]

In other words, ancient philosophical schools are not simply defined by their doctrines; they are defined by the combination of systematized beliefs, formalized modes of inference, informal ways of speaking and thinking (including patterns of imagery), intentional and affective attitudes, characteristic interpersonal relationships, and the exercises by which members of the school attempt to unify all of these components and channel them into personal transformation. It is this multifaceted breadth that allows these philosophies to pervade their followers' entire ways of being.

My first response to the fragmentariness of our evidence is therefore to spread my investigative and interpretive nets more widely. On the one hand this will

give me a more versatile toolkit for working through the evidence on which previous scholars have already focused. On the other, it will allow me to make use
of testimony that has hitherto seemed "sub-philosophical" or trivial. While these
additional facets of Cyrenaic philosophy are even less well-documented than
Cyrenaic theory, every piece of information we glean contributes to understanding the philosophy as a whole. For example, I have just mentioned the practical
or "spiritual" exercises through which ancient philosophers attempted to bridge
the gap between an understanding of principles and the consistent enactment
of those principles throughout life's manifold circumstances. Such exercises in
other schools include (to name just a few) the memorization of key sayings and
rules of thumb, examination and criticism of each day's actions, meditation on
mortality and other perspective-altering topics, self-testing through hardship
and temptation, cooperative critical inquiry, and exegesis of canonical texts.[20]

Acknowledging that some of our testimony may pertain more to spiritual
exercises than to theory is just one of the specific ways in which this approach
to ancient philosophy will alter my handling of the evidence. The general effect
of this approach will be to make me cautious about separating doctrinal asser-
tions and their justifications from their contexts within the larger enterprise of
philosophizing. I will instead attempt to think of theory as being in dynamic
interaction with pre-philosophical intuitions and the rewarding or disappointing experience of putting doctrines into practice. This begins when a potential
philosopher approaches a teacher. As Hadot writes,

> At least since the time of Socrates, the choice of a way of life has not been
> located at the end of the process of philosophical activity, like a kind of
> accessory or appendix. On the contrary, it stands at the beginning, in a
> complex interrelation with critical reaction to other existential attitudes,
> with global vision of a certain way of living and seeing the world, and
> with voluntary decision itself. . . . Philosophical discourse, then, origi-
> nates in a choice of life and an existential option—not vice versa.[21]

This does not mean that philosophical discourse is merely a rationalization of
what its practitioners are already inclined to do. It means that, faced with an
array of possible teachers, potential philosophers' initial choices depend more
on their reactions to individual personalities and the "existential options" ad-
umbrated by each than on the cogency of their arguments.[22]

Consider, for example, a more sympathetic depiction than Xenophon's of
the inaugural scene of Cyrenaic philosophy. Here Plutarch (perhaps relying on
Aeschines of Sphettus, another of Socrates' followers[23]) permits us to imagine
how Aristippus arrived at what I called the "choice of pleasure":

> When Aristippus met Ischomachus at the Olympics, he asked him what
> sort of things Socrates used to talk about in order to have such an effect
> on young men. When he'd heard just a few starting points and indications

of Socrates' words, he was so profoundly affected he swooned. He became totally pale and weak until, filled with burning thirst, he sailed to Athens, drew from the spring, and investigated the man, his words, and his philosophy. (Plut. *Mor.* 516c = *SSR* 4A.2)

Note that Aristippus had only heard a few "starting points and indications" of Socrates' beliefs and arguments before being filled with impassioned desire. Something in Socrates' words touched Aristippus's own inchoate aspirations and kindled a "burning thirst" to articulate and fulfill them. At this point he turned to rational inquiry, which is what makes this conversion *philosophical.* Aristippus "investigated the man, his words, and his philosophy," and elaborated whatever he took from Socrates as seemed best to him. It has been suggested, for example, that one source of Aristippus's hedonism was the Socratic imperative to critically inspect his beliefs, actions, and character. This inspection led him to harmonize his beliefs and consistently orient his actions toward pleasure and the avoidance of pain. This orientation would then be tested in the laboratory of daily experience, with the expectation that it would slake the "thirst" and ease the "burning" which led him to philosophy in the first place.

Disappointing feedback from experience could therefore provoke changes in theory or even holistic changes in scholastic allegiance. A radical example of this principle is provided by the defection of Dionysius of Heraclea from the earliest Stoics to the latest Cyrenaics. In Lucian's comic dialogue *Twice Indicted,* Dionysius's defection is described like this:

> Until he got sick, [Dionysius] hoped that he would get some benefit from his discourses on fortitude. But when his body hurt, he felt ill, and he really began to suffer, then he observed that his body was philosophizing against the Stoa and holding opposite doctrines. So he trusted it rather than them! (section 21; cf. D.L. 7.166, Cicero *On Ends* 5.94, *Tusculan Disputations* 2.60)

In less humorous terms, Dionysius found a discrepancy between his rational evaluation of his situation, which was based on Stoic doctrine, and his intuitive reaction. As a Stoic, Dionysius knew a battery of arguments demonstrating that pain and suffering were indifferent. His acute illness should not therefore have affected his judgment of his own well-being. But at the level Lucian describes as his "bodily philosophizing," he was profoundly certain that his situation was very unsatisfying indeed. Thus he decided that there was an irreconcilable conflict between his doctrines and the intuitions those doctrines were supposed to clarify and organize. His response was not merely to adjust his belief about pain, but to adopt an entirely new philosophy. As a character in Athenaeus's *Sophists at Dinner* puts it, "He took off the frock of virtue and put on flowery garments" (7.281d).

The interaction of arguments with pre-philosophical intuitions and feedback from experience leads me to two final methodological rules of thumb.

First and most important, we should be extremely skeptical that any Cyrenaic ever adheres to a significant ethical position because of the force of reasoning alone. The core positions of each school frame an existential option which is chosen for its positive features, i.e., the satisfying fit between the world it discloses and the inarticulate aspirations of its followers. It is particularly important to keep this in mind whenever an important doctrine seems, at first glance, to be grounded in feeble arguments or simply unlivable. Our initial assumption should always be that those who commit to Cyrenaicism find something compelling even in its apparently weak positions, and something appealing in its seemingly unpalatable ones. Part of my task in this book is to explore what the power and appeal of such positions might be.

My second rule of thumb is that ambient culture will sometimes help to illuminate this power and appeal. One of the striking features of most Greek philosophy is its aspiration to rebuild its practitioners from the "bare self" up—to determine what is universally good and desirable, and to reorganize life and society based on this determination.[24] But modern philosophers have rightly argued that the bare self is a fantasy; selfhood is largely constituted by libidinal, evaluative, and narrative orientations, which can only be altered gradually and piecemeal.[25] Part of this constitutive orientation is historically specific. For example, one complex of values that will prove illuminating in this study revolves around masculine competition and honor. This complex finds its most influential expression in Homer, whose epics *The Iliad* and *The Odyssey* precede Cyrenaicism by several hundred years. Homer's enormous influence on subsequent Greek culture is well indicated by the claim in Plato's *Republic* that "this poet educated Greece" (606e). The capacity of so-called "heroic values" to shed light on classical Greek culture has recently been demonstrated in studies of both Socratic philosophy and Athenian legal procedure.[26] Closely related to this are other features of Homeric ethics and its descendants in lyric and tragic poetry, which will help to fill in the background behind otherwise puzzling Cyrenaic beliefs or behavior.

In the foregoing I have sketched some considerations that will help me to offer a robust and historically sensitive interpretation of Cyrenaic ethics as it functioned in ancient Greece. Building up this historicized interpretation will occupy me for most of this book. But my final methodological suggestion is that we should also take a broader view of Cyrenaic ethics, not as a set of beliefs and practices confined to a particular time and place, but as a framework for thinking and acting that can be filled out in different ways in different times and places. The gaps in our evidence mean that we will never reconstruct all the key arguments, spiritual exercises, and other important elements of ancient Cyrenaicism. However, at least one author has already undertaken the feat of imaginative sympathy necessary to flesh out these doxographical bones and knit together these anecdotal tissues. I am thinking of the Victorian cultural critic and novelist Walter Pater. Despite the fact that one chapter of his *Marius the Epicurean* is entitled "A New Cyrenaicism," the erudition and profundity of

Pater's engagement with Cyrenaic doxography appears never to have been recognized. In fact almost the entirety of *Marius* can usefully be read as a critical
appropriation of Cyrenaic philosophy, which clarifies the meaning and practical consequences of several of the Cyrenaics' important and otherwise enigmatic doctrines. I will therefore conclude this book with a chapter on Pater's
"new Cyrenaicism." I wish to emphasize that my purpose in doing so is not
to trace the influence of ancient Cyrenaicism on later thought, which would
require a survey of how Cyrenaic ideas—generally in superficial forms—have
appeared in the works of diverse authors over the last 2,400 years. Rather, I will
focus on this single point of reception because in some ways it communicates
what "Cyrenaic ethics" could mean today with greater vivacity than our ancient
sources. This sort of reception study should therefore not be an afterthought to
historicist interpretation, but a complement to it.[27]

I acknowledge that parts of the methodology I have just outlined will be
controversial. My objective here has been to introduce and explain them, not
to defend them against their critics. That would require the sort of extended
arguments elaborated by the authors I have cited in the footnotes. However, I
hope that the following chapters' results will display the merits of this approach,
and perhaps even inspire its application to other little-studied and poorly documented Greek philosophies.

1.3. Overview of the Book

This book might have been organized in two ways. One possibility was to proceed chronologically, devoting a chapter to each of the major figures or stages in
the movement. However, there were two main obstacles to this organizational
strategy. The first is that we do not know enough about most figures in the
Cyrenaic movement to sketch their philosophy in the round. The second is that,
as I argue at length in appendix 2, the mainstream doxography at D.L. 2.86–93
has been interpolated with Annicerean elements. It is sometimes impossible to
ascertain whether a particular doctrine is mainstream, Annicerean, or both. I
have therefore adopted what is primarily a thematic organization. This not only
avoids the obstacles of the diachronic approach, it also permits me to combine
the evidence on each theme from various Cyrenaics. What is lost in exactitude
is more than offset by gains in the evidentiary basis for analysis, which has
resulted in more substantial and philosophically interesting interpretations.
Moreover, it has still been possible to handle the chronological development of
themes wherever the evidence has been strong enough to support it.

I therefore begin with a biographical survey of the movement in chapter 2,
which introduces what we know about all the named Cyrenaics. I also say a few
words there about the culture of ancient Cyrene more generally.

In chapter 3 I address the theoretical foundations of Cyrenaicism, which
are the positive valuation of pleasure, the negative valuation of pain, and the
impossibility of discerning any value independent of pleasure or pain. This is

a good example of a topic where chronological analysis descends almost immediately into pure speculation: it is best to treat Cyrenaic epistemology as the shared intellectual property of almost all the philosophers we will be studying.

In chapter 4 I turn from theoretical foundations to ideals of happiness. First I focus on what Aristippus, the mainstream Cyrenaics, and Annicereans say about education, virtue, and happiness. This permits me to show how their foundational beliefs support a vision of what it means to have a successful life. I then address their formulations of the ethical end, where Anniceris appears to have introduced a position that is strikingly unusual in ancient Greek ethics. Happiness is not the end, he says, nor is there any single end for the whole of life. Rather, each action has its own particular end. I attempt a sympathetic interpretation of this innovation, yet acknowledge the problems it creates for other areas of Cyrenaic theory.

In chapter 5 I address the greatest controversy in existing scholarship on Cyrenaic ethics, which is the school's "anti-eudaimonism." On the basis of Anniceris's formulation of the end many scholars have asserted that Cyrenaics are not "eudaimonists," meaning their ethics does not center on the pursuit of happiness through cultivation of the virtues. In the light of chapter 4 I will suggest that this is incorrect for most Cyrenaics, and misleading even for Anniceris. However, it has led to philosophically interesting speculation about *why* the Cyrenaics would reject eudaimonism. Explanations have focused on personal identity, the subjectivity of value, and prudential reasoning. I try to show that each of these explanations relies on unsustainable interpretations of particular pieces of evidence. However, I introduce Rorty's distinction between "historical reconstruction" and "rational reconstruction" in order to suggest that these are outstanding cases of the latter: a historically indefensible interpretation has permitted the Cyrenaics to become interlocutors in modern debates. I therefore propose that we think of this as an interesting episode in the reception of Cyrenaic philosophy rather than a plausible interpretation of what ancient Cyrenaics actually believed.

In chapter 6 I address Cyrenaic positions on personal and civic relationships, beginning with a short overview of assumptions about positive and negative reciprocity in ancient Greek culture (friendship and enmity, benefaction and injury, intra-polis solidarity and inter-polis war, etc.). I then look at the tension between involvement in these cultural institutions and withdrawal into self-sufficiency, which develops from Aristippus through mainstream Cyrenaicism. This tension is abolished by Hegesias and Theodorus, who repudiate all of the relationships involved and embrace what we might call ethical solipsism. Finally, I analyze how Anniceris opposes Hegesias by reappraising the importance of friendship, filial piety, and civic participation for effective hedonism.

In chapter 7 I focus on the enigma of Hegesias's pessimism. First I summarize and criticize the interpretation of Wallace Matson, according to whom Hegesias's pessimism is the result of his "ruthless deduction" of the consequences of basic Cyrenaic principles. Pessimism is therefore a "gloomy" corner into which Hegesias finds himself coerced by reasoning. After refuting Matson's interpretation of the evidence I develop an alternative, beginning by emphasizing the thematic importance of "indifference" throughout our Hegesiac evidence. Comparison with Pyrrho shows how an attitude of indifference can be valued by Hegesias's philosophical contemporaries. In fact it has heroic or semi-divine resonances, which leads me to propose that several other aspects of Hegesiac ethics lend themselves to analysis as a sort of philosophical heroism. I am therefore able to interpret the bizarre combination of radical self-sufficiency and pessimism as an ideal to which Hegesias and his followers positively aspire.

In chapter 8 I turn to the other provocateur from the final generations of the Cyrenaic movement, Theodorus "the Godless." Previous scholars have noted the profound break Theodorus makes from Cyrenaic tradition, since he declares bodily pain and pleasure "intermediate" between goodness and badness. In order to understand Theodorus I suggest we pay attention to two points: first, the intermediate status of pain and pleasure is closely related to Theodorus's attested attitude of "indifference," which should be interpreted as an evolution from Hegesias's indifference; second, this evolution necessitates a new basis for the joy which Theodorus makes his ethical end. This illuminates the new prominence Theodorus assigns to the virtues, which I suggest are the primary source of his joy. His ideal philosopher lives joyfully because he knows that everything he does is just and wise, and everything other than justice and wisdom is indifferent. But Theodorean virtue cannot be systematized, which is why most of Theodorus's recorded arguments are critical rather than constructive. The main task of his philosophy is to clear away conventional and dogmatic impediments to the sage's extemporaneous moral perception, not to elaborate principles and rules. His so-called "atheism" is one of several cases in point.

With these eight chapters I will have completed my interpretation of the ancient Cyrenaic movement. Before gathering my concluding thoughts, I append a chapter on the only significant re-appropriation of mainstream Cyrenaic ethics (of which I know): Walter Pater's "new Cyrenaicism." In particular, I suggest that Pater casts light on four elements that remain obscure in ancient Cyrenaic doxography: "unitemporal pleasure," the relation of hedonism to traditional virtues, the "economy" of pleasures and pains, and the Cyrenaic argument against the fear of death. I also argue that the narrative framework of Pater's novel communicates how and why Cyrenaicism could attract someone better than arid doxography ever could.

1.4. A Note on Conventions

In formulating my references to ancient texts I have kept in mind the needs of both specialists and readers from other fields. I have therefore assumed that every reader will have at hand (or be able to get hold of) an edition or translation of Diogenes Laertius's *Lives and Opinions of the Eminent Philosophers*, which is by far our most important source. Thus I always cite Diogenes directly, abbreviating his name to "D.L." I have also assumed access to A. A. Long and D. N. Sedley's *The Hellenistic Philosophers* (1986), which I abbreviate "LS." Most of our other texts are assembled in Giannantoni 1990, which I abbreviate *SSR*. However, since *SSR* is only of use to those with strong Latin and Greek reading skills, in every case I also cite the author and work. Where this has made citations lengthy and cumbersome, I have removed them from the main text to footnotes. My abbreviations are listed at the front of this book.

Except where otherwise indicated I follow the textual readings of Giannantoni. All translations are my own except where otherwise indicated.

For the sake of Greekless readers I have transliterated Greek words and phrases in the main text, except where I have found it advisable to quote Greek passages at length (more than five words).

I have adopted the ending -ean for "Aristippean," "Annicerean," and other adjectives whose Greek stems end in epsilon-iota. In this I follow the convention of "Epicurean" and "Pyrrhonean." Other scholars sometimes write "Annicerian," "Theodorian," and so on. I have also adopted endings in -ic for "Megaric," "Hegesiac," and other Greek stems ending in iota-kappa. In this I follow the convention of "Peripatetic," "Academic," and so on. Other scholars sometimes write "Megarian," "Hegesian," and so on.

CHAPTER 2

Cyrene and the Cyrenaics:
A Historical and Biographical
Overview

2.1. Introduction

Now seems the time to introduce the members of the Cyrenaic movement to whom I will frequently allude in the following chapters. The principal figures are Aristippus, their notional founder, who followed Socrates; the mainstream Cyrenaics (Arete, Epitimides, Antipater, Paraebates, the Metrodidact, and probably Aristoteles), who first codified Aristippus's inspirational example; Hegesias, who accentuated the mainstream Cyrenaics' egoistic individualism and introduced pessimism; Anniceris, who opposed Hegesias by reasserting the importance of personal and civic relationships; and Theodorus, an eclectic and flamboyant thinker, who is most renowned for his supposed "atheism." Hegesias, Anniceris, and Theodorus each had their own followers, called the Hegesiacs, Annicereans, and Theodoreans. Finally, there is one significant Cyrenaic whose place in this series is unclear: Dionysius "the Turncoat" of Heraclea. This catalogue takes us from around 435 BCE to around 250 BCE. Most of these philosophers were born in or around Cyrene, though some are known to have been active abroad.

This may be enough biographical information for some readers, who will want to skip ahead now to the philosophical analyses. However, others will want to know more about each of these figures, their relationships to each other and to non-Cyrenaic philosophers, and the state of Cyrene at this time. In the following sections I attempt to answer these questions as clearly and concisely as our highly fragmentary evidence permits.

2.2. Fourth-Century Greek Philosophy

It is worthwhile beginning with just a few words about fourth-century Greek philosophy. It is easy to forget how fantastically diverse the philosophical scene was in the generations after Socrates' death and before the hegemony of the four big Athenian schools was established (Plato's Academy, Aristotle's Lyceum, the Stoa, and Epicurus's Garden). In the first place, descendants of some of the so-called "pre-Socratic" philosophies continued to be active. For example, the last Pythagoreans—e.g., Echecrates and Archytas[1]—were associates of Plato and Aristotle, and Epicurus studied with the Democritean Nausiphanes.[2] Second, Anaxarchus and Pyrrho, who would inspire the "Pyrrhonean" and later "Neopyrrhonean" skeptics, attracted a significant following.[3] Most importantly for my purposes, Socrates' various disciples had scattered to their home cities after his condemnation and execution in 399 BCE, and many attracted followers, who in turn gathered their own students and splintered off. In this way they generated recognizable "schools of thought."[4] Hence while neither Xenophon nor Aeschines of Sphettus had recorded pupils, Phaedo attracted a following at Elis, who would later be called the "Elians," though some were renamed the "Eretrians" after the subsequent leadership of Menedemus in Eretria. Euclid inspired the "Megarics" in Megara, from whom diverged the "Dialecticians."[5] Various "Cynics" took their inspiration from Antisthenes and Diogenes of Sinope. Finally, of course, there was what I have been calling the Cyrenaic movement, which took its inspiration from Aristippus of Cyrene, and developed into four overlapping schools of thought: the mainstream Cyrenaics, Hegesiacs, Theodoreans, and Annicereans. While it is almost certainly true that Plato's Academy and Aristotle's Lyceum were far larger, more institutionalized, and more influential philosophical centers than any of these others, we should bear in mind that the Cyrenaics coexisted with all of these renowned and influential intellectuals in various parts of the Greek-speaking Mediterranean.

2.3. Cyrene and Cyrenaica

Since I will sometimes invoke the influence of literary and popular culture to explain Cyrenaic positions, it will also be helpful to situate Cyrene itself in the Greek-speaking Mediterranean of its time. Of the twenty recorded Cyrenaics (*kurēnaïkoi*), students of Cyrenaics, and philosophers who considered studying with Cyrenaics, fifteen indicate through their geographical names their city of origin.[6] We can make educated conjectures about three of the others. Of these eighteen, twelve hail from what would later be the Roman *provincia Cyrenaica*, which in the period concerning us included Cyrene itself, its rivals Barca and Euhesperides (later called Berenice), the ports that would become Apollonia and Ptolemaïs, and perhaps several hundred thousand Greeks and indigenous "Libyans" settled across the agricultural plateaus or living nomadically in the ravines and deserts.[7] Eleven bear the geographical name "Cyrenean" (*kurēnaios*), which probably means that they were born in Cyrene itself. Another is said to be from Ptolemaïs.[8] Notwithstanding the fact that ancient philosophical schools, like modern religious movements, often recruited through established social networks,[9] and that some of the Cyrenaics certainly spent significant amounts of time abroad, this amounts to strong evidence that the

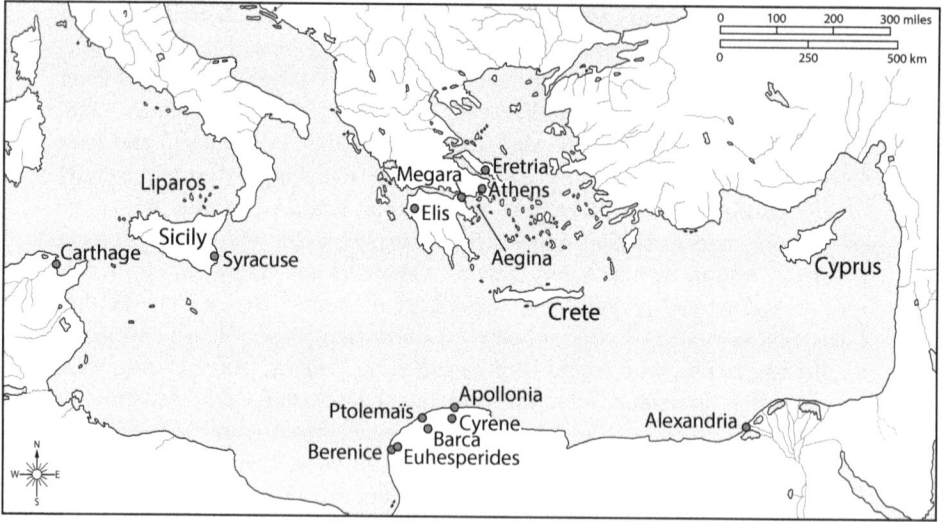

The world of the Cyrenaics.

movement was based in Cyrene. The six from elsewhere in the Greek-speaking Mediterranean show the international influence of the movement.[10]

Cyrene at this time (ca. 420–250 BCE) was a wealthy, cultured, and militarily powerful polis. Legendarily founded in 631 by colonists from the island of Thera (itself a Spartan colony),[11] it was situated amidst arable plateaus between the sea and the desert, the beauty of which Gomperz long ago described in rhapsodic terms:

> Ancients and moderns agree in praising the superb site of this city, and the richness of the surrounding country. . . . Down over the green hills and the deep-cut ravines, overgrown with broom and myrtle, with laurel and oleander, the eye is carried smoothly onward to the blue sea below, over which, in days gone by, immigrants sailed from the island of Thera, from the Peloponnese, and from the Cyclades, to this royal seat, made, one might almost say, for the express purpose of dominating the surrounding country and the Berber tribes that dwell there.[12]

Around the time of Aristippus's birth (ca. 440 BCE), it divested itself of its monarchy and instituted an oligarchical regime that lasted until the time of Anniceris and Hegesias a century and a half later, although not without at least one violent expansion of the governing class.[13] The fourth century was a prosperous one for Cyrene, not only because the region was endowed with significant natural resources (most famously the mysterious spice "silphium"[14]), but also because it escaped the upheavals caused by Macedon in mainland Greece.

Hence between 360 and 330 BCE the Cyreneans were able to construct and dedicate a treasury to Apollo at Delphi, and between 330 and 326 BCE, during a severe famine in the Mediterranean, they delivered immense quantities of grain to other Greek cities.[15] During the first three quarters of the century Cyrene overcame its rival Barca and conquered the tribes who controlled the trade routes into the interior of north Africa.[16] But things became more turbulent in the last three decades of the fourth century, when a war involving Thibron of Macedon, rivalries within Cyrenaica, and revolution in Cyrene itself (324–321 BCE) was succeeded by uneasy subjection to Ptolemy I of Egypt. The Cyreneans revolted against Ptolemy several times, and were led by his regent Ophellas on a disastrous campaign against Carthage (309–308 BCE).[17] The last revolt (ca. 305–301 BCE) was ended by Ptolemy's regent Magas, who later broke with Ptolemy II and ruled an independent and flourishing kingdom of Cyrenaica until his death (ca. 280–250 BCE).[18] Theodorus ended his life under Magas's patronage in Cyrene, which apparently aspired to be a learned capitol like those of other Hellenistic monarchs.[19]

Although Cyrene could not compete with the cultural influence of Athens and Alexandria, Magas' dream was not entirely unrealistic: the city contributed significantly to literature and athletics throughout this period and into the following centuries.[20] Continuing the tradition celebrated by some of Pindar's fifth-century victory odes, Cyrenean competitors were prominently represented at pan-Hellenic games.[21] And Cyrene's intellectual culture in the late fifth century gave birth not only to Aristippus but also to the mathematician Theodorus, who appears prominently in Plato's *Theaetetus*.[22] Plato had contact with at least one other Cyrenean, if we can trust the story that a certain Anniceris of Cyrene ransomed him after one of his ill-fated expeditions to Sicily.[23] This would suggest that Cyreneans' philosophical interests were not restricted to their homegrown Cyrenaics, as is confirmed by the fact that Apollonius of Cyrene (*fl.* 360/330 BCE) studied with Eubulides in Megara and taught the great Dialectic philosopher Diodorus Cronus. In the later third and second centuries, as Cyrenaicism waned and vanished, the skeptical "Middle Academy" drew a number of its most famous members from Cyrene—beginning with Lacydes (ca. 290/270–207 BCE) and ending with Carneades (214/3–129/8 BCE).[24] But more famous than any of these philosophers were the poet Callimachus (ca. 310–240), renowned for cataloguing the library at Alexandria and for his influence on Roman poets, and the polymath Eratosthenes (ca. 276–ca. 195 BCE), who became head of that library.

Cyrene's well-preserved archeological and epigraphical remains would allow me to add a good deal more about their economy, international diplomacy, government and religion, but I have said enough already to establish that the city was a wealthy and powerful metropolis that participated in the mainstream of pan-Hellenic culture.[25] The paucity of literary records for this period means that we cannot speculate about where in Cyrene our philosophers might have met, how they may have interacted with their co-citizens, or how customs or institutions particular to Cyrenaica may have influenced their thinking. At this point I will therefore turn to the Cyrenaics themselves.

2.4. Aristippus

Almost all our ancient testimony names Aristippus of Cyrene as the founder of Cyrenaicism. This must be taken with a grain of salt: ancient doxographers like to package groups of philosophers into neat who-taught-whom sequences descended from founders, to whom they assign (sometimes with demonstrable anachronism) all the principal doctrines of the group.[26] We will see later in this book that that there are powerful reasons for doubting that Aristippus articulated some of the positions ascribed to him by some sources. But we will also see that it makes good sense to think of him as the inspiration for later Cyrenaic ethical doctrine, even if he was not its chief architect.

Aristippus was born around 435 BCE,[27] almost certainly to one of those families in whose hands Cyrene's great power and wealth were concentrated.[28] His father was named Aritades (Suda A 3908 = *SSR* 4a.1);[29] his mother may have been named Mica or Sonica.[30] Given the picture of Cyrene I painted in the last section, he probably received a good Greek education in literature, music, dancing, some sort of athletics and military exercise, and perhaps also in mathematics and the art of speaking. No source says anything at all about Aristippus studying with any of the so-called "sophists" like Hippias or Protagoras.[31] We do not know when and why Aristippus first left Cyrene for mainland Greece, but it is clear that he became one of Socrates' well-known associates.[32]

Aristippus's activities after Socrates' death can only be inferred from scattered references of uneven reliability. If he was indeed in Aegina when Socrates was executed, it is doubtful that he fled to Megara with Plato and the others.[33] There has been a great deal of speculation about Aristippus's personal and literary relationships with Socrates' other followers,[34] but all we can say with any degree of confidence is that he got along well with Aeschines and poorly with Xenophon and Plato.[35] One tradition, probably spurious, relates that he actually spent two months a year in Aegina with the famous courtesan Laïs (Athen. 588e–f = *SSR* 4A.92). Many anecdotes put him in the court of Dionysius I of Syracuse in Sicily, whose patronage Plato and Aeschines also enjoyed. An encounter with a Persian satrap, on the other hand, puts him in Asia Minor (D.L. 2.79–80).

Whatever his precise movements, what is clear is that by this time his intellectual powers and reputation were well established, and he took advantage of both rich patrons and fee-paying students to finance his travels and lifestyle. Some of his reputation for taking money "like a sophist" may be due to debates among Socrates' followers, but there is probably a kernel of truth in it as well.[36] The contemporary comic poet Alexis depicts a slave claiming,

When my master was young he devoted himself to words and had a go at philosophizing. There was a Cyrenean named Aristippus, a noble sophist, they say. In fact, in terms of loose living, he excelled and exceeded anyone past or present! So my master gave him a ton of money. He didn't really learn the art, but . . . (Athen. 544e = *SSR* 4A.9)

Unfortunately, the punch line is missing! Of course we cannot trust a comic poet's representation, but this confirms what the preponderance of our evidence indicates: Aristippus expected those who benefited from his wisdom to compensate him appropriately.[37]

All of this certainly led to prolonged absences from Cyrene, and one curious anecdote records that his father often sent for him, and threatened to sell him into slavery "according to ancestral law" for his refusal to obey the summons. Aristippus replied, "Wait a while: I'll be worth more, and you'll get a better price!" (Gnom. Vat. 743 n. 42 = *SSR* 4A.134) But we also know that Aristippus had a wife and two children, at least one of whom lived in Cyrene.[38] This was his daughter Arete, to whom he taught the fundamentals of his philosophy. Our sources also mention another Cyrenean student named Antipater. So Aristippus probably not only returned to Cyrene intermittently, but also spent a significant period of time there. By this time his ideas and practices must have been fairly stable, so that Arete and Antipater were able to acquire from him the rudiments of what would become the Cyrenaic school of thought. He is estimated to have died around 355 BCE.[39]

Both ancient and modern historians have debated whether Aristippus left any writings behind. Diogenes Laertius testifies that many works circulated under his name, including a history of Libya, dialogues in both Attic and Doric dialect, and twelve "compositions" of various genres (2.83–85). We also have a series of citations from books 1 and 4 of a book called *On the Luxury of the Ancients*, which is ascribed to Aristippus. This work was certainly spurious,[40] as were most of the others.[41] The strongest candidates for authenticity are the "compositions," since the most reliable ancient authorities accepted them but rejected the rest.[42] Their titles are *On Education, On Virtue, Protreptic, Artabazus, Ship-Wrecked Sailors, Exiles, Discourses in Six Books, Sayings in Three Books, To Laïs, To Prorus, To Socrates*, and *On Fortune*. It is possible that some of our anecdotes come from the books of *Sayings*,[43] that the story about the Persian satrap comes from the work *Artabazus*, and that some of the other pieces of evidence come from unidentifiable works.[44] But it is safest to assume that almost all of our evidence is third- and fourth-hand, and derives ultimately either from works of Aristippus's successors or their philosophical antagonists.

Also lost, unfortunately, are two fourth-century dialogues named after him and written by non-Cyrenaics. The first was *Against Aristippus of Cyrene* by Speusippus, Plato's nephew and successor as head of the Academy (D.L. 4.4). This may have been an attack on the lifestyle and ideas of Aristippus and his earliest followers. On the other hand, Aristippus may have been a diplomatic stand-in for Eudoxus of Cnidus, a hedonist who was associated with the early Academy.[45] The other was a dialogue named *Aristippus or Callias* by the Megaric Stilpo (D.L. 2.120). This would be of significant interest, since, as we will see in the next section, Stilpo was personally involved with the Cyrenaics. First, he reportedly competed for students with two of them (D.L. 2.113, 2.134). Second, an anecdote places him in dialogue with Theodorus (D.L. 2.116). Although he is obscure today, Stilpo was renowned in his own time. Among his numerous students were Menedemus of Eretria, who inspired the short-lived Eretric movement, and Zeno of Citium, who founded the Stoa. Kings Ptolemy and Demetrius both paid their respects to him. Sadly, the details of his polemical interactions with Aristippus's legacy can no longer be reconstructed.

2.5. Mainstream Cyrenaicism

Diogenes Laertius begins the first of his Cyrenaic doxographies by saying, "Those who stuck with Aristippus's ways and were called Cyrenaics believed the following things" (2.86). For the sake of convenience I shall refer to this vague grouping as "mainstream Cyrenaics." I intend for this label to extend from Aristippus's immediate followers to whenever their followers' followers ceased to think of themselves as adhering to the same core beliefs and pursuing the same lifestyle as their predecessors. As we will see below, this period probably amounted to around a century. We should therefore be cautious about the homogenizing effect of Diogenes' introduction: we have no reason to expect so many philosophers over so long a period of time to have agreed about every particular. The principal aim of Diogenes' grouping of "those who stuck with Aristippus's ways" is not to imply a strong theoretical continuity between them and Aristippus, nor yet to affirm complete doctrinal concord among them, but rather to distinguish them from those who conspicuously modified Aristippus's ways.[46] The latter group encompasses the Hegesiacs, Annicereans, and Theodoreans. Even this turns out to be a fuzzy distinction, since we will see that the evidence for mainstream and Annicerean Cyrenaics is often amalgamated. Nevertheless, the evidence does not permit any alternative to dealing with this amorphous collective as a group.

Diogenes Laertius and the Suda both divide the Cyrenaics into two neat successions.[47] In the first generation Aristippus taught his daughter Arete of Cyrene, Antipater of Cyrene, and possibly someone named Aithiops of Ptolemaïs (D.L. 2.86). Based on Aristippus's dates, we can estimate that all of these flourished between 370 and 350 BCE. But the name "Aithiops" never appears in inscriptions from Cyrenaica, although the regional onomasticon is otherwise extremely repetitive.[48] Moreover, the city of Ptolemaïs was not built until much later.[49] So it is uncertain what name, if any, lies behind this garbled reminiscence. (Since "Aithiops" simply means "black," perhaps this was a racial moniker for a non-Greek follower of Aristippus.) Arete is credited with teaching her son Aristippus, who was accordingly called the Metrodidact.[50] He probably flourished around 340 BCE. The Metrodidact has often been considered a key figure in Cyrenaic theory, since Eusebius explicitly distinguishes between Aristippus's imprecise way of speaking about ethics and the Metrodidact's formal theories (Eus. *PE* 14.18.32 = *SSR* 4b.5). However, the Metrodidact's only named pupil is Theodorus the Godless (D.L. 2.86), who is also said to have studied with Anniceris and many non-Cyrenaic philosophers. No anecdote explicitly places the Metrodidact in interaction with any of his other contemporaries, so it is unclear how broad his impact really was either within the movement or beyond it.

Alongside the succession running through Aristippus's family and ending with Theodorus's heterodoxy we are given another beginning with Antipater. The existence of two anecdotes regarding Antipater, in one of which he is mocked by the renowned orator and tragedian Theodectes of Phaselis,[51] attests to his notoriety outside of Cyrene (Cic. *Tusc.* 5.112, Gnom. Vat. 743 n. 353 = *SSR* 4c). His student—his only student, according to Theodectes—was Epitimides of Cyrene. We know nothing of Epitimides other than that he taught Paraebates of Cyrene, who in turn was the principal teacher of Hegesias and Anniceris. All of these figures were active in the fourth century BCE, although the rapidity of their succession makes precise dating difficult. For Paraebates, like Antipater, we have evidence of engagement with non-Cyrenean Greek intellectuals: Menedemus of Eretria, who later became an important philosopher in his own right, reportedly "spurned" Paraebates in favor of the renowned Megaric philosopher Stilpo (D.L. 2.134). This suggests that Menedemus considered studying with Paraebates.[52] Since Paraebates' two famous pupils—Anniceris and Hegesias—introduced significant and contrary innovations, it is unfortunate that we know nothing at all about his own philosophy.

Several additional Cyrenaics are known from other sources, though they do not appear in any doxographical successions. The most well-documented is Aristotle of Cyrene, whom I will call "Aristoteles" throughout this book to distinguish him from the more famous Aristotle who studied with Plato and founded the Lyceum. We probably owe two of our best citations of Aristoteles to Istrus, who was the slave of the Cyrenean polymath Callimachus (ca. 310–240 BCE).[53] It may be because of this local connection that Aristoteles' name has escaped oblivion. We know that he had his own students, but like Paraebetes lost at least two of them to the Megaric Stilpo. He may also be the same "Aristoteles of Cyrene" who wrote a *Poetics* (D.L. 5.35).

The other well-known Cyrenaic excluded by the successions is Dionysius of Heraclea, more often called Dionysius the Turncoat (ca. 328–248 BCE). Dionysius's philosophical formation was eclectic: he supposedly studied with the Academic Heraclides at home in his youth, then the Megaric Alexinus, Menedemus of Eretria, and finally the Stoic Zeno (D.L. 7.166). He left the Stoics and joined the Cyrenaics when either an eye infection or kidney stones convinced him that pain was in fact a bad thing.[54] Evidence for both stages of his career, oddly excluded from the collections of Cyrenaic fragments and testimony by Mannebach and Giannantoni, is collected by von Arnim in *Stoicorum Veterum Fragmenta*.[55] Although Athenaeus says that he became an Epicurean (281d), Diogenes Laertius says he became a Cyrenaic (7.66). The latter is more likely to be true, since the obscure label "Cyrenaic" could easily have been replaced by the more well-known "Epicurean." Moreover, Dionysius's association with sex, courtesans, and general self-indulgence in both Athenaeus and Diogenes seems rather more in keeping with the Cyrenaic than the Epicurean lifestyle (D.L. 7.166, Athen. 437e–f). Finally, Philodemus gives "bodily pain" as Dionysius's "end of evils" (*Ind. Sto.* col. 32), which agrees with Cyrenaic rather than Epicurean doctrine. Since he cannot have defected from Zeno until some time after the latter began teaching around 288 BCE, Dionysius belongs to the last known Cyrenaic generation. In fact, were it not for his controversial defection we would not even be certain Cyrenaicism had survived until after the rise of Stoicism. It is possible that Dionysius defected to Annicerean rather than mainstream Cyrenaicism.

The last philosopher deserving mention here is Aristoxenus of Cyrene, who according to Athenaeus "really participated in the national philosophy" (7c). Whether Aristoxenus was actually a Cyrenaic, however, remains unclear. Athenaeus informs us that a particular way of preparing ham had been named after him, and that

> because of his extraordinary luxury, he watered the lettuce in his garden with honeyed wine in the evening. When he picked one in the morning, he would say he had green cakes that were sent to him by the earth. (ibid.)

We are given no indication of his dates or his beliefs, which makes it impossible to say whether he was part of the Cyrenaic movement, a later revivalist, or simply a voluptuary who happened to live in Cyrene.[56]

2.6. Hegesias

Just before the mainstream doxography Diogenes Laertius gives a thumbnail sketch of the different figures in the Cyrenaic movement, beginning as follows: "Since we have written his life, come now, let us go through the Cyrenaics ‹descended› from him, some of whom also called themselves Hegesiacs, some Annicereans, and some Theodoreans" (2.85). That Anniceris and Theodorus indeed gained notoriety and followings is confirmed by a list of philosophical sects reported by Hippobotus:

> In his *On the Sects*, Hippobotus says there are nine sects and ways of life: first Megaric, second Eretric, third Cyrenaic, fourth Epicurean, fifth Annicerean, sixth Theodorean, seventh Stoic, eighth the old Academic, ninth Peripatetic. (D.L. 1.19–20)[57]

Since Hippobotus probably wrote near the end of the third century BCE,[58] within a few decades of the end of the Cyrenaic sects, he is an unusually good witness to their separate identities. It is therefore curious that he does not include a Hegesiac sect in his enumeration. One possible explanation for this is that Hegesias attracted little attention from other philosophers or potential students, so that his philosophy was not prominent enough to merit notice. However, Diogenes twice speaks of "Hegesiacs" (2.85, 2.93), implying a group of students. Moreover, the most famous anecdote concerning Hegesias, which I discuss below, attributes impressive influence to his public discourses. An explanation more in keeping with this evidence is that Hegesias, like Anniceris, claimed to be the heir of mainstream Cyrenaicism. Hippobotus may have been persuaded by this claim and therefore included Hegesias under the generic heading "Cyrenaic."[59]

We know very little about Hegesias's life and writings. We can estimate that he flourished any time between 320 and 290 BCE. Our sparse sources inform us of two further particulars. First, Cicero tells us that Hegesias wrote a book called *The Man Starving Himself to Death* (*Tusc.* 1.84 = *SSR* 4f.4). "In this," Cicero says, "someone who is leaving life by starvation is recalled by his friends. In response he lists the inconveniences of human life." It is also possible that Hegesias (or one of his students) authored Cologne Papyrus 205, which is a dialogue in which Socrates explains to an unnamed interlocutor why he did not propose a counter-penalty when the prosecution at his trial proposed death as his punishment.

Our second biographical datum is an anecdote recorded by Plutarch and Cicero.[60] Cicero tells us that Hegesias rehearsed these same human ills with his students, and was so devastatingly persuasive that, following a number of suicides, he was forbidden to teach by King Ptolemy (Cic. *Tusc.* 1.83 = *SSR* 4f.3). If the anecdote were true, it would suggest that Hegesias was active in Ptolemy's capitol, Alexandria. It is very likely that Hegesias spoke to students about the themes he covered in his book, and not impossible that one or more auditors committed suicide. Certainly his ethics are remarkably pessimistic by the standards of ancient Greek philosophy. However, I argue in chapter 7 that we must treat this anecdote with caution. It may have been inspired partly or wholly by his writings rather than by historical events.

2.7. Anniceris

The first-century BCE geographer Strabo begins his list of famous men from Cyrene as follows:

> Famous Cyreneans include Aristippus the Socratic, who laid the foundations for the Cyrenaic school of thought; his daughter named Arete, who succeeded him in the school; her son Aristippus, the so-called Metrodidact, who also succeeded her in the school; and Anniceris, who seems to

have corrected the Cyrenaic school and introduced the Annicerean in its place. (*Geogr.* 17.3.22 = *SSR* 4a.1 + b.1 + g.1)

The verb I have translated "corrected" actually means "set upright again" (ἐπανορθῶσαι), so Anniceris probably claimed that he was restoring the spirit of Aristippean philosophy to its pristine state.[61] He almost certainly attributed its decadence to Hegesias, whose pessimism and egoistic individualism he vehemently opposed. It is perhaps due to the enthusiasm with which he reasserted the value of friendship that the Suda claims he was an Epicurean: "Anniceris, Cyrenean, philosopher, who became an Epicurean, although he was an acquaintance of Paraebates, who had listened to Aristippus" (A 2466 = *SSR* 4g.2). Anniceris shared with Epicurus the belief that successful hedonism should incorporate caring relationships and membership in a community. But numerous references to the "Annicerean" school, his distinctly un-Epicurean position on ends, and a significant amount of anti-Epicurean polemic make it clear that Anniceris did not defect to the newer hedonism of his Athenian rival. Rather, he found precedents for the positions he wanted to defend in the Cyrenaic tradition itself.

Once again we know almost nothing about Anniceris's life. The Suda goes on to say, "Anniceris had a brother named Nicoteles, a philosopher, and Posidonius was a famous pupil of his. From him came the so-called Annicerean school of thought. He lived in the time of Alexander." While Anniceris was certainly alive during the lifetime of Alexander the Great (356–323 BCE), his tutelage by Paraebates and polemical exchanges with Hegesias and Epicurus make a slightly later *floruit* more likely, something between 320 and 290 BCE.[62] The date of his birth would therefore be between 360 and 340; that of his death is harder to approximate. Based on lexical evidence, we can also say that Anniceris was a native of the region of Cyrene. He shared his name with important Cyrenean nobles, whose importance in the city is documented by numerous inscriptions.[63] In all probability Anniceris belonged to the aristocracy himself.

Theodorus is said to have been a student of Anniceris, in addition to Posidonius and probably Nicoteles (D.L. 2.98). The Suda does not explicitly assert that Anniceris's brother Nicoteles was an Annicerean, the way that Epicurus's brothers are known to have become Epicureans (D.L. 10.3). It is possible, although unlikely, that Nicoteles belonged to a different school. About the supposedly "famous Posidonius" we know nothing further; the famous Posidonius remembered today is the first-century BCE Stoic, who taught in Rhodes. It is worth remarking that if someone named Posidonius did study with Anniceris, he probably came from abroad for that purpose. No one named "Posidonius" appears in the principal collections of Cyrenaic inscriptions until the second century BCE, so the name does not appear to have been in use in the region.[64] This suggests Anniceris possessed a certain renown. If the Annicerean Posidonius was also "famous," then we would expect him to have had his own students. But no record survives of later generations in the Annicerean school, so we cannot say how long it endured. Nor do we have any indication that Anniceris left any writings behind.

2.8. Theodorus

Regarding Theodorus we have the good fortune to be somewhat better informed than we are for Hegesias and Anniceris. This is partly due to his renown for being "godless" or "atheist" (*atheos*). Denying the existence of the gods is a radical position in ancient philosophy, and therefore Theodorus' book *On the Gods* received a lot of attention from both pagan and Christian authors. However, we are also informed that Theodorus "wrote many things pertaining to his own school" (Suda Θ 150). While not even the names of these other works survive, a range of other anecdotes and doxographical passages permit us to develop a more rounded understanding of his life and philosophy.

Theodorus's birth can be very approximately dated to 345 BCE. We know nothing about his family, although his name appears frequently in fourth-century inscriptions among Cyrenean priests, military leaders, and municipal benefactors.[65] So he was probably from an aristocratic family,[66] which would have provided him with the usual military, athletic, and literary education. During his youth he may have studied with some of the sophists, philosophers, or other intellectuals who inhabited or passed through Cyrene. Certainly he studied with the Metrodidact (D.L. 2.86), and possibly also with Anniceris (D.L. 2.98). At some stage he was exiled from Cyrene,[67] although the reason is not clear. Possibly it had to do with political connections and the factional strife following the failed coup d'état of 324–21 BCE, which ended with the imposition of Ptolemaic rule. It could just as well have transpired after the failed revolution against Ptolemy of 313/12 BCE.[68]

In any event, Theodorus made his way to mainland Greece, where he studied with Dionysius of Chalcedon, sometimes said to be founder of the Dialectic offshoot of the Megaric school (D.L. 2.98). The Suda also names three other teachers: "Theodorus, named the Atheist, . . . studied with Zeno of Citium, and learned from Bryson and Pyrrho the Ephectic" (Θ 150 = *SSR* 4h.2). It is very hard to assess the testimony about Bryson, since scholars do not agree how many Brysons there were, with whom they studied, or when they lived.[69] It is plausible that Bryson studied with Euclid of Megara or his follower Clinomachus,[70] in which case his ideas may have been similar to those of Dionysius of Chalcedon. It is chronologically possible that a student of Clinomachus taught Theodorus. It is also chronologically possible for Theodorus to have learned from Pyrrho.[71]

On the other hand, it may be better to take the Suda's testimony as a fabrication inspired by similarities between the ideas of Bryson, Pyrrho, Zeno, and Theodorus.[72] It is extremely unlikely that Theodorus studied with Zeno of

Citium, who was approximately ten years his junior, and who almost certainly did not begin teaching until after Theodorus's exile from Athens (see below). But Theodorus shares with both Zeno and Pyrrho an ideal of indifference and impassivity, as he shares the eristic and parodic use of syllogisms with Bryson. These similarities may have been enough to inspire doxographers determined to discover neat chains of influence among famous philosophers.

While still at Athens Theodorus began to lecture and teach others. There the fascinating and eclectic Bion of Borysthenes heard him "displaying his sophistic ability in every sort of speech," and spent some time studying with him (D.L. 4.52, 54);[73] and Phocus, son of Phocion, heard him completing a syllogism in the Lyceum (Plut. *Phoc.* 38.3 = *SSR* 4h.6). During this period of studying, teaching, and debating Theodorus was probably synthesizing his Cyrenaic education with other influences. But he left Athens before the big Hellenistic schools, Stoicism and Epicureanism, established themselves there. Zeno arrived around 311 BCE, but probably did not begin advancing his own positions until a decade later. Epicurus arrived in 307/6 BCE, but Theodorus was already gone, as is clear from the involvement of Demetrius of Phalerum. Demetrius was both a Peripatetic philosopher and the Athenian regent for Cassander of Macedon until 307 BCE.[74] According to Diogenes Laertius, Demetrius interceded to prevent Theodorus's trial on a charge of impiety (D.L. 2.101). Other sources claim Theodorus was exiled from Athens or even forced to drink hemlock.[75] Precisely what happened—other than that he did *not* drink hemlock—is uncertain,[76] but we can take at least two points from this incident: first, Theodorus's provocative opinions were developed enough and strident enough to attract the attention of the Areopagus court; second, he was cultivating people in high places.

He apparently found shelter under the patronage of Ptolemy I in Alexandria, as a popular anecdote attests.[77] This was the second ruler whose patronage he accepted. Diogenes Laertius testifies to a third: "Eventually he returned to Cyrene, lived with Magas, and continued to be held in high esteem" (2.103). Magas became regent of Cyrene around 301 BCE, declared himself an independent king around 272, and died around 250. Theodorus's return to Cyrene may have occurred at almost any time during this period. If he did not study with Anniceris before his early exile, then his late Cyrenaic formation and the codification of his thought probably dates to this period.[78] But he can just as well have engaged in system-building—to whatever extent he embraced systematicity— in Demetrius's Athens and Ptolemy's Alexandria, and it seems slightly implausible for him to have sought Anniceris's tutelage at this mature age. Again, he may have established a more regular group of disciples at Cyrene, including the otherwise unknown Lysimachus, later a court intellectual under the patronage of Attalus of Pergamum (Athen. 252c = *SSR* 4h.27).[79] On the other hand, his life may have revolved around Magas' court. We simply do not know. Our only clue to his time of death is our estimate of his date of birth, which suggests that he died by 255 BCE at the latest.

Although he is conventionally treated as part of the Cyrenaic movement, and undoubtedly was heavily influenced by his Cyrenaic predecessors, we will see that Theodorus's innovations are more far-reaching than those of Anniceris or Hegesias. He has sometimes been considered half-Pyrrhonean, half-Dialectic, or even half-Cynic. Whatever the genealogy of his beliefs and practices, they make an appropriate coda to the movement begun by the followers of Aristippus. While we cannot say when the last Hegesiac, Theodorean, or Annicerean ceased to be active, the movement probably died out some time in the middle of the third century BCE.

CHAPTER 3

Knowledge and Pleasure

3.1. Introduction

When the great Academic skeptic Carneades was categorizing all possible organizing principles for ethical systems, he most often chose either Aristippus or the Cyrenaics generally as the figureheads for hedonism.[1] More specifically, he said that the Aristippean and Cyrenaic "end" was "obtaining pleasure."[2] "End" (*to telos*) is a technical term in ancient philosophy. It means the goal of all deliberation and action, the best thing in human life, or both. It is important to recognize that this is Carneades' way of slotting the Cyrenaics into his scheme, not an exact report of the Cyrenaics' own presentation of their position. Nevertheless, it is a good indication of the centrality of pleasure to their ethics. Investigating how the Cyrenaics describe pleasure, how they argue for its preeminent choiceworthiness, and how this choiceworthiness is supposed to guide their actions and establish their horizon of care is thus a good way to begin exploring their ethics.

On the one hand Cyrenaic thinking about pleasure is surprisingly underexplored. In their influential book on *The Greeks on Pleasure*, for example, Justin Gosling and Christopher Taylor devote just over two pages to Aristippus and the Cyrenaics.[3] On the other hand, there has been a great deal of research on Cyrenaic epistemology, and the important role of pleasure and pain in that epistemology has always been acknowledged. In fact Voula Tsouna goes so far as to assert (judiciously, in my view) that what we call Cyrenaic "epistemology" is not really a theory of knowledge at all. When discussing knowledge and truth, she says, the Cyrenaics "pursue questions to the point of vindicating their ethical project, and perhaps to the degree of eliminating any substantial opposition (or so they hope), and then they drop them."[4] This "ethical project" is a life organized around the action-guiding truth of pleasure and pain. Cyrenaic epistemology is therefore focused on demonstrating this truth and distinguishing it from the inferior epistemic access we have to all other sources of guidance for action and care. In fact none of the divisions of mature Cyrenaic philosophy corresponds to what we call epistemology. They divide their philosophy into five parts: on what is choiceworthy and worthy of avoidance, on experiences, on actions, on causes, and on arguments (Sen. *Ep. Mor.* 89.12, S.E. *M* 7.11 = *SSR* 4a.168). The further details of this division are unknown to us, but we can reasonably conjecture that what we call "epistemology," although concentrated in "on experiences," also extended into the other parts.

In this chapter my emphasis is on illuminating how the Cyrenaics' theories about the truth of pleasure and pain provide a justification and initial point of orientation for the rest of their ethical theories and attitudes. While I will not work through all the questions scholars have asked about Cyrenaic epistemology, I draw on many of their arguments and conclusions.[5] I will begin by investigating the hedonism of Aristippus and its relationship to Socrates. I will then discuss several aspects of the Cyrenaic theory of the experiences, focusing on the experiences of pleasure and pain. In particular, I will address the manner in which the truth of pleasure and pain is set apart from the epistemic status of other potential values. I will then consider how this truth is capable of guiding action. Finally, I will conclude this chapter by looking at the role of pleasure and pain in Cyrenaic formulations of the end, which will provide a transition to the following chapter.

3.2. Aristippean Hedonism

It is clear from all of our ancient sources that Aristippus enjoys and is inclined to pursue bodily pleasure, freedom from bodily pain, and peace of mind. In *Memorabilia* 2.1 (which we have already met in chapter 1), Aristippus's contemporary Xenophon depicts an extended conversation between him and Socrates. He introduces the conversation as follows:

> Socrates' way of speaking about this sort of thing also seemed to me to encourage his companions to exercise self-control in their desire for food, drink, sex, cold, heat and work. For example, when he noticed that one of his companions was rather self-indulgent concerning these things, he said, "Tell me, Aristippus . . ." (2.1.1 = *SSR* 4a.163)

A series of arguments follows, in which Socrates tries to show Aristippus that he will live better if he exercises moderation in his pleasure-taking and voluntarily exposes himself to pain. For example, Socrates argues that the sort of person destined to rule needs training in self-restraint and endurance, so that he can concentrate on the complex tasks leadership involves. He asks Aristippus whether he assigns himself to the rulers or the ruled. Aristippus agrees that ruling requires this sort of training, and therefore indicates that he does not assign himself to the class of would-be rulers. Rather, he says, "I assign myself to those who want to live as easily and pleasantly as possible" (2.1.9). By "living easily and pleasantly" Aristippus presumably has in mind the sorts of things Socrates has just said a ruler must forego, such as "gratifying the belly" (2.1.2), and avoiding the sorts of things Socrates has just said the ruler must practice, such as "being able to refrain [from drinking] when thirsty" (2.1.2), "being able to go to sleep late and get up early and stay awake," "being in control of sexual appetites," "willingly enduring hard work," and "learning whatever is necessary in order to prevail over your opponents" (2.1.3). These are Socrates' examples, not those of Aristippus. Moreover, Xenophon appears to be a hostile source. Nevertheless, the rest of our evidence confirms the positive value Aristippus places on bodily gratification and the negative value he places on bodily and mental disturbance.

In fact many of our sources go further, and suggest that Aristippus not only values eating, drinking, having sex, and avoiding hard work, but indeed prefers to do so in style. Another relatively early source, the Pyrrhonean skeptic Timon (ca. 310–220 BCE), speaks of "the voluptuous nature [*truphere phusis*] of Aristippus, groping after falsehoods" (D.L. 2.66). This is an excerpt from Timon's *Silloi*, which is a far-ranging satire of dogmatic philosophers.[6] It therefore suggests that Timon believes Aristippus is at the least strongly committed to pleasure, and perhaps even inclined toward "voluptuousness" or "luxury" (*truphē*)—in other words, toward the cultivation of appetite and the refinement of its satisfactions.[7] Dozens of later anecdotes fill out our picture of what this voluptuousness involves: some concern Aristippus's enjoyment of scented oil and fine garments,[8] while many others pertain to his association with expensive courtesans.[9] Two of the lost (and probably spurious) works attributed to him nicely encapsulate this penchant for luxury: *Toward Those Who Blame Him for Having Vintage Wine and Courtesans*, and *Toward Those Who Blame Him for Being Extravagant in His Expenditure on Fish* (D.L. 2.84).[10] The latter may have been concocted out of anecdotes like the following:

> When someone was criticizing him for his extravagant expenditure on fish, he asked, "Wouldn't you have bought this for three obols?" When the other agreed, he said, "So I'm not over-fond of fish, you're just over-fond of money!" (D.L. 2.75)

It was also said that Aristippus's primary reason for visiting the tyrant Dionysius in Sicily was to enjoy the luxuries he could provide. In one anecdote, for example, Aristippus has to explain why he endures being spit on by the tyrant. "'Well,' he said, 'fishermen endure getting wet with sea water in order to catch a gudgeon. Shouldn't I endure getting wet with wine in order to catch a tuna?'" (D.L. 2.67; cf. 2.73, 2.80, Athen. 544c–d = *SSR* 4a.36). None of these anecdotes are reliable on their own or in their specifics, but in the aggregate they paint a consistent picture of someone who enjoys and values refined pleasures.

However, Aristippus clearly balances this taste for refinement with the need to retain his peace of mind. To put it another way, he not only values bodily pleasure and its refined variations, he also values freedom from mental distress. This is why he is careful not to become attached to any particular source of bodily pleasure. Diogenes Laertius puts this most clearly:

> Aristippus was able to harmonize himself with his place, time, and role and perform harmoniously in any circumstance. For this reason he was more in favor with Dionysius than the others, because he always made

good use of whatever happened. For he enjoyed the pleasure of whatever was present, and didn't hunt painfully for the enjoyment of what wasn't present. (2.66)

In other words, Aristippus does not value any particular pleasure so much that he would trouble himself if it were not available. That would be counterproductive: the distress of "hunting painfully" for fine garments, perfume, or some particular courtesan would more than counterbalance whatever enjoyment they could yield. In the next chapter I will consider how this position suggests an attitude toward future experiences and a prudential rule of thumb. For now, I want to emphasize that it implies that the stress and anxiety of a mind filled by unruly desires are significant evils for Aristippus. While one of the goals of his philosophy is to clarify the goodness of pleasure and ensure its regular supply, another is to eliminate mental uneasiness.

A family of sayings and anecdotes testifies to this function. For example, according to Bion of Borysthenes (ca. 325–250 BCE), who himself studied with the Cyrenaic Theodorus, "When his attendant was carrying his silver on the road and was struggling with the weight, Aristippus said, 'Pour off the excess and carry what you can'" (D.L. 2.77).[11] The moral is clearly that neither money nor what money can buy has any hold on Aristippus's mind. He is able to shed anxieties like his slave sheds that onerous silver. Another set of anecdotes shows how easily he loses real estate,[12] while others display his concern to use speech in order to dispel anger and distress.[13] Finally, many sources testify that "confidence" (*tharrein* or *tharsos*) is a product of his philosophy that he particularly values.[14] In practice this means feeling comfortable rather than anxious or fearful in unknown or threatening situations.

All of this suggests that Aristippus tends to perceive the world in terms of opportunities for enjoyment and risks of suffering pain or distress. Moreover, it suggests that he has begun to articulate this existential attitude in a series of evaluative arguments: he consistently argues that actions, experiences, and conditions are laudable or choiceworthy because they are associated with pleasure, and merit avoidance because they are associated with pain or distress. But this does not yet amount to a clear set of doctrines. This may be due to the state of the evidence, but it may also be due to the nature of Aristippean thought. Like his fellow Socratics Xenophon and (arguably) Plato and Aeschines of Sphettus, Aristippus may not have articulated any complete and coherent system.[15]

It is worth expanding briefly on the comparison with Xenophon, since modern philosophers may feel that the "arguments themselves" should have driven Aristippus to stabilize his hedonism with clear axiomatic foundations. Xenophon's works obviously recur to the same themes and values, but they neither present these values as foundational doctrines nor rigorously ground their thematic discussions in them. The values emerge from numerous passages across Xenophon's works. For example, in *Memorabilia* 1.6.3 the sophist Antiphon accuses Socrates of being a "teacher of unhappiness." In reply Socrates defends the merits of the lifestyle generated by his philosophizing: (a) he is free to choose whom he teaches, because he does not take payment; (b) he enjoys bodily satisfactions more, and feels bodily pains less, because of his moderation and endurance training; (c) he enjoys the delight of knowing he is becoming a better man; (d) his bodily and mental conditioning make him capable of helping his friends and his polis; (e) he is as self-sufficient as a human can be; (f) and because he is self-sufficient, he is as divine as a human being can be (1.6.4–10). This defense implies a set of goods that are operative throughout Xenophon's Socratic works: freedom from constraint (a), pleasure and freedom from pain (b, c), virtue and goodness (c), helping your friends and your polis (d), self-sufficiency (e), and godlikeness (f). Elsewhere Xenophon's Socrates also values self-knowledge and knowledge of ethical and political concepts (e.g., *Mem.* 1.1.16, 4.2.24–40, 4.6.1).[16] But the *Memorabilia* show little interest in molding these values into a clearly articulated system. As they wend their way through themes as diverse as the need for self-control, how to attract friends, how to make an armored breastplate, and the nature of dialectic, they draw opportunistically on these values in order to display Socrates' happiness and his tendency to make his companions happier. There is no evidence that Aeschines of Sphettus, substantial fragments of whose dialogues survive, proceeds more systematically.[17] For these contemporaries of Aristippus and fellow students of Socrates, critical reflection upon ethics does not entail establishing clear axiomatic foundations.

It may therefore be true in a sense that Aristippus is not a hedonist, if by "hedonist" we mean someone who unambiguously defines pleasure as the highest good, or the only intrinsic good, or the end of all deliberation and action.[18] But he is certainly a hedonist in the sense that pleasure is central to both his lifestyle and many of his ethical arguments. We can elaborate and corroborate this subtle distinction by reference to an unusually good piece of Cyrenaic doxography:

> Aristippus was a companion of Socrates, and set up the so-called Cyrenaic school of thought, from which Epicurus took the starting points for his exposition of the end. Aristippus was an entirely lush-liver, a real pleasure-lover, but he himself didn't speak openly about the end. Implicitly, however, he said that the essence of happiness lies in pleasures, since he was always talking about pleasure, and this led those who came to him to suspect he was saying the end was to live pleasantly. (Eus. *PE* 14.18.31 = *SSR* 4a.173)

Eusebius is a reliable source. Moreover, his assertion that Aristippus implicitly said that happiness lies in pleasures is entirely consistent with all the evidence we have just seen.[19] And he is surely right to say that Aristippus did not speak openly about the end, since "the end" (*to telos*) only became a regular feature of philosophical ethics after Aristippus's death.[20] Just as important as this negative stipulation, however, is his positive characterization of Aristippean ethics as something expressed in the combination of his lifestyle and his characteristic topics of conversation. Whereas his followers felt an impulse to identify a clear doctrine about the end, Aristippus "was an entirely lush-liver, a real pleasure lover" and was "always speaking about pleasure." Eusebius seems to be saying that Aristippus's lifestyle and conversational themes were all his followers had to go on. He did not subordinate his behavior or arguments to any clearly formulated, foundational doctrines. Nevertheless, that behavior and those arguments made it clear that he took pleasure and the avoidance of pain to be important points of reference for his decisions, aspirations, and inquiries.

Most of the evidence I have surveyed in this section is imprecise and fourth- or fifth-hand. It is therefore best to be diffident about the extent to which Aristippus elaborated any fixed doctrines. But the clearest testimony we have suggests that he left theoretical systematizing to his successors. His own hedonism gained enough stability from its consistent application to his behavior and from its oral presentation in polemics or instruction. As the study of ethics became increasingly specialized over the ensuing century, however, his followers would feel the pressure to stabilize their position with firmer foundational positions and arguments.

3.3. Socrates' Influence on Aristippus's Hedonism

Before proceeding to Aristippus's successors, it is worthwhile digressing to address the possibility that Socrates had some influence on Aristippus's hedonism. Recall once more Xenophon's *Memorabilia* 2.1, in which Socrates attempts to convince Aristippus that his self-indulgence is imprudent. The opposition to immoderate enjoyment throughout the works of Xenophon and Plato might lead readers to feel that Aristippean hedonism is profoundly un-Socratic. But Xenophon's Socrates actually goes on to argue against self-indulgence precisely on the grounds that it leads to pain and distress. This comes across clearly in the story about the choice of Heracles. Here Vice tells Heracles, "If you make me your friend, I'll lead you by *the most pleasant and easiest road*. There's no delight you won't taste, and you'll live out your life without experiencing hardship" (2.1.23, italics mine). The echo of Aristippus's stated preference for living "*as easily and pleasantly as possible*" is obviously deliberate; Socrates is implying that Aristippus's lifestyle is the way of Vice. But that innuendo is tangential to his argument, the heart of which is put in the mouth of Virtue. Virtue argues that Vice is deluding Aristippus: enjoyment does not materialize without the painstaking cultivation of gods, friends, household, and polis. Moreover, immoderate indulgence dulls the capacity for pleasure. So Virtue's way is actually more pleasant in the end.

This could be taken as an ad hominem argument meant simply to persuade Aristippus, which does not commit Xenophon's Socrates to any hedonistic beliefs. However, various passages elsewhere in Xenophon's *Memorabilia* make similarly hedonistic defenses of Socrates' lifestyle (e.g., 1.6.6–9, 2.1.27–34, 4.5.9,

4.8.6; cf. *Symp.* 2.25, *Apol.* 6).[21] Hedonism also occasionally appears as the underpinning of the virtues for Plato's Socrates, most emphatically at *Protagoras* 351b–58b.[22] On this basis some scholars have suggested that far from betraying Socrates' teachings, Aristippean hedonism was actually nourished by them.[23]

The argument can plausibly be made, for example, that Aristippus came to Socrates with a strong predisposition to believe that pleasure is good and pain is bad. He was therefore only too prepared to observe that pleasure was an important criterion for evaluating behavior and character in many of Socrates' conversations. He appropriated this pattern of reasoning and began consistently using pleasure as a criterion in his own arguments—both the sort of pleasure Socrates seemed to approve of, such as intellectual pleasure and moderate satisfactions of appetite, and the sort Socrates denigrated, such as the immoderate enjoyment of refined tastes, scents, and sexual activity. In this way Socratic influence combined with Aristippus's pre-philosophical predisposition to generate his hedonism. Let us call this the "strong argument" about Socratic influence. Such an argument would put us well on our way to Zeller's belief that Aristippus's hedonism, Antisthenes' morally rigorous pragmatism, and Euclid's theoretically abstract investigation of Goodness and Being each developed a genuine but "one-sided" element of Socrates' ethics.[24]

On the other hand, the intense controversies regarding the historical Socratics may incline us to avoid making any assumptions about the relation between hedonistic arguments in Plato and Xenophon and Socrates' own beliefs and arguments.[25] In that case we might advance what I shall call the "weak argument" about Socratic influence on Aristippean hedonism. One thing the depictions of Plato, Xenophon, and Aeschines of Sphettus incontestably share, we might begin, is that in them Socrates urges his interlocutors to consider whether their ethical beliefs are consistent. Furthermore, he asks them whether their actions, abilities, and character are compatible with their beliefs and conducive to their aspirations. Hence Plato's Euthyphro is compelled to examine his understanding of piety, since he aspires to display piety in his prosecution of his father (Pl. *Euth.*). Xenophon's Euthydemus is brought to reflect on the qualities a statesman must possess, since he aspires to a leading role in Athenian statesmanship (Xen. *Mem.* 4.2). In Aeschines' *Aspasia*, Xenophon and his wife are led to ask whether they understand what it is to be lovable, since they aspire to love and be loved by one another (Cic. *Inv.* 1.51–3 = *SSR* 6a.70).[26] Examples could obviously be multiplied. The point is that if we know anything at all about the historical Socrates, it is that he pressed his companions to ask themselves whether their deepest ethical intuitions and aspirations gave them reasons to change both themselves and their behavior.

It could be in this indirect fashion that Socrates, although he was not a hedonist himself, provoked Aristippus to harmonize his thoughts and actions with his aspiration to live pleasantly.[27] An entire series of authors testifies that Aristippus followed Socrates in rejecting the study of nature and focusing exclusively on ethics.[28] This already makes it plausible that Aristippus asked himself the sort of questions on which Socrates focused. A remark made by Aristotle partly confirms this suspicion, although it requires a bit of exegesis to see how. Aristotle lived in the generation after Aristippus, so his information has not been filtered through so many intermediaries. Moreover, he has no obvious reason in this passage to distort Aristippus's position:

> Some of the sophists, for example Aristippus, used to abuse the mathematical sciences. In other crafts (he argued), even manual crafts like carpentry or shoe-making, everything is accounted for as being better or worse. But the mathematical sciences take no account of what is good and what is bad. (*Met.* 996a32–b1 = *SSR* 4a.170)

What is immediately at issue here is whether mathematics is a valuable occupation, something worth studying. The unfavorable comparison between mathematics and carpentry or shoe-making suggests that any valuable body of knowledge helps its possessor decide which actions are better and which are worse. For example, given the desire to re-sole a shoe, a shoe-maker will choose this leather rather than that, hammer in the nails at this angle rather than another, and so forth. What determines these choices is his intention to make a *good* shoe. Aristippus is not only suggesting that mathematics, because it lacks this orientation toward what is good and what is bad, does not merit study.[29] He is also suggesting that his sort of philosophizing is more craftsmanlike than mathematical in this particular: its guiding purpose is to establish which choices and actions are more conducive to certain goals, and therefore good or bad. Socrates draws analogies between philosophy and crafts many times in Plato's early and middle dialogues (e.g., *Chrm.* 170e–175a, *Prt.* 321d–328d, *Grg. passim*),[30] so this way of thinking about ethics may go back to the historical Socrates. But whether or not Aristippus took this analogy from Socrates, the key point is that he probably took from him the necessity of examining his character and actions to ensure that they were *good* rather than *bad* for his goals. And this is where his pre-philosophical hedonism may have coalesced into a consistent and reflective disposition. As he thought critically about the virtues, education, luck, freedom, statesmanship, luxury, and the other topics represented in our evidence, he may gradually have developed a series of positions which both elaborated and vindicated his tendency to pursue enjoyment and avoid pain and distress.

We can return to *Memorabilia* 2.1 to see one example of how this could work.[31] Because statesmanship requires painstaking training, Aristippus disclaims any interest in political office. He recapitulates his point later in the conversation:

> But Socrates, how do the people who are being educated for the art of kingship, which you seem to think is happiness, differ from those who

voluntarily undergo bad things? After all, they'll voluntarily be hungry, thirsty, cold, sleepless, and generally miserable. As for me, I can't see what difference it makes whether being whipped is voluntary or involuntary, since it's the same skin; or generally whether having your body besieged by all these things is voluntary or involuntary—unless the difference is that whoever willingly endures these distressing things also displays his stupidity. (*Mem* 2.1.17)

Here Aristippus clearly grounds his argument in the badness of bodily pain. He eschews the "art of kingship" because it requires what he summarizes as "undergoing bad things" (*kakopathountōn*) and "being miserable" (*mokhthēsousin*). More specifically, he spells out this misery and endurance of bad things in the necessity of experiencing hunger, thirst, cold, and sleeplessness. Finally, he encapsulates all of these problems under the phrase "enduring distressing things" (*lupēra hupomenein*). Elsewhere in the same conversation Aristippus also rejects the political role of subject, since he agrees with Socrates that rulers live "more pleasantly" than those they rule (2.1.9–10). Here again it is mainly the prospect of experiencing pleasure and pain which determines his position.

This leaves Aristippus with no place at all in a polis. Socrates implies that if Aristippus does not choose to rule, by default he will be "subjected" to those who are stronger: "I presume you can see that stronger groups and individuals know how to make weaker ones lament and to treat them like slaves" (2.1.12). The gist of Socrates' argument here and afterwards is that pain is inevitable: our goals must be to minimize it and to retain control over when and where we experience it. But we have just seen that Aristippus rejects this goal: he thinks that whoever chooses to undergo pain is not only miserable, but also stupid. He is able to adopt this disdainful position because he is willing to reject the conventional assumptions that lead Socrates to conclude pain is inevitable. When asked to choose between the hardships of ruling or the distress of serving, he proposes a radical third option: "In order not to experience these things, I don't even enclose myself in a polity: I'm a foreigner everywhere" (*Mem*. 2.1.13).[32] With this rejection of political affiliation Aristippus abandons one of the primary constituents of identity for any free Greek man.[33] Not only that, he also takes himself out of the localized networks in which most Greek men pursue honor and avoid shame, which are the heart of their sense of dignity and happiness. Aristippus takes these radical steps out of fidelity to his ethical intuitions: these are the logical consequences of his preference to pursue pleasure and avoid pain. In other words, this radical position represents the reflective working-through, under Socrates' critical questioning, of his pre-philosophical hedonism. If Aristippus puts this position into practice, and this practice forms part of a satisfying life, then that satisfaction will also vindicate and corroborate his hedonistic intuitions.

Despite initial appearances, then, it is not difficult to make a speculative case for Socratic influence on Aristippus's hedonistic arguments. At the least they probably arose from sustained critical reflection on which beliefs, actions, and states of character are better and which are worse. Even if such reflections led Socrates to thoughts about the intrinsic goodness of certain states of the soul, they probably led Aristippus to thoughts about pleasant or painful consequences of those beliefs, actions, or character traits. But it is also possible that Socrates himself frequently elaborated hedonistic arguments, whether or not he believed them, and that Aristippus expanded and extended these arguments. In the absence of stronger evidence, it is best to suspend judgment about which of these reconstructions is closer to the truth.

3.4. The Cyrenaic Theory of the Experiences

In the previous two sections I have argued that Aristippus was consistently disposed to positively value bodily pleasure and to negatively value bodily pain and mental distress. I then argued that this disposition probably arose from the combination of his pre-philosophical attitudes with the guiding influence of dialectical investigation, which he experienced in the company of Socrates. My assumption is that more or less the same is true of the later Cyrenaics. For example, Antipater joined Aristippus, Epitimides joined Antipater, and Paraebates joined Epitimides largely because they saw in the pleasant lifestyle and hedonistic arguments of their teachers a realization of their own inchoate intuitions. If they had not, other options were available: around the same time Apollonius of Cyrene joined the Megarics, whose philosophy was in many ways contrary to Cyrenaicism (Strabo 17.3.22). Of course, personal connections were also important, as evidenced mostly clearly by the hereditary succession passing from Aristippus to Arete and the Metrodidact. The theoretical activity these philosophers then undertook aimed at justifying their pre-philosophical inclinations and shaping them into a stable and effective system of practical reasoning and behavior.

Unfortunately, very little biographical material survives to document this intermeshing of theory and practice. We would like to know more about the lives and practices of the Cyrenaics, but what doxographers have preserved is primarily their theoretical defense of their hedonistic inclinations and behavior. In this project their most fundamental set of doctrines concerns the division between their experiences (*pathē*) and what causes those experiences.[34] This division seems to have been maintained by all the Cyrenaics except (possibly) Theodorus. We find it expressed already in Eusebius's account of the Metrodidact, which follows immediately from the quotation I gave in section 2 of this chapter. We do not know whether the Metrodidact was the first to expound this theory, as many scholars have supposed. Nor do we know whether the sophist Protagoras, Plato's *Protagoras*, or the skeptic Pyrrho influenced its exposition.[35]

What we can say with confidence is that the Metrodidact is the first Cyrenaic to whom this line of thought is individually ascribed.[36]

Here is the key evidence:

⟨Aristippus's⟩ daughter Arete was among ⟨his⟩ auditors, and she had a son whom she named Aristippus, though he was called the Metrodidact because he was introduced to philosophy by her. He clearly defined the end as living pleasantly and assigned a place to pleasure in motion.[37] He explained that there are three states in our constitution. In one, which is like a storm at sea, we feel pain. In another, which is similar to a smooth undulation stirred by a favorable breeze, we feel pleasure (for pleasure is a smooth motion). The third state, in which we feel neither pain nor pleasure, is in the middle and is like a calm sea. And he used to say we have perception of these experiences alone. (*SSR* 4b.5 = Eusebius *PE* 14.18.32)

We shall return to this passage a number of times in this book. What interests us at present is the doctrine concerning the three "states" (*katastaseis*) of our "constitution" (*sunkrasis*), each of which contains both an apparently physiological element (smooth undulation, violent motion, or stillness) and a phenomenological element (pleasure, pain, or neither).[38] Shifting his terminology in the final sentence, Eusebius reports that "we have perception of these experiences alone." The most straightforward reading of this terminological shift is that by "these experiences" (*pathē*), Eusebius means the experiences of our own states: it is solely of these that we "have perception."[39]

It is possible that originally the Cyrenaic theory of the experiences only encompassed the three states the Metrodidact mentions: pleasure, pain, and stillness. But in the form in which we find it in the rest of our evidence, it comprehends many other subjective states as well.[40] These are always presented as first-person statements about one's own condition, a point which is often emphasized by awkward neologisms. Hence Aristocles says that according to the Cyrenaics, "if they are being burned or being cut they know that they are experiencing something. But they can't say whether what burns is fire, or what cuts is iron" (F5.1 = Eusebius *PE* 14.19.1 = *SSR* 4a.218). When these Cyrenaics know "they are experiencing something," they not only know that their state is, as the Metrodidact puts it, "like a storm at sea." In other words, they not only know that "I am feeling pain." Their experiences encompass far more qualitative detail, as a further source makes explicit: "That I am being burned, they say, I apprehend; but it's unclear whether fire causes burning" (Anon. *Comm. in Pl. Tht.* = *SSR* 4a.214). There is an experience to which I give the name "being burned," and it differs from other painful experiences, such as "being cut." The same holds true for pleasant experiences: while the Metrodidact suggests "I am feeling pleasure" (cf. Cic. *Luc.* 20, 76, 142 = *SSR* 4a.209), Plutarch and Sextus Empiricus both give the more specific "I am being sweetened" (Plut. *Mor.* 1120e, S.E. *M* 7.191 = *SSR* 4a.211, 213). In fact our sources reveal that Cyrenaic experiences are as variable as the sensory qualities non-Cyrenaics say they perceive in the world. Plutarch offers "I am sweetened," "I am embittered," "I am cooled," "I am warmed," "I am lightened," and "I am darkened" (ibid.). Sextus adds "I have been disposed lightly," "I am stirred yellowly," "I am stirred purply," and even "I am stirred as if by two" (*M* 7.192, 198).[41] From this catalog we can discern that experiences correspond to what we usually consider sensations of taste (sweet, bitter), vision (light, dark, yellow, purple, duality[?][42]), and touch (burning, cutting, hot, cold). Cicero attests that hearing was also included: "They deny they know what color or sound anything has, but only sense that they are experiencing in a certain way" (*Luc.* 76). No source mentions the sense of smell, but it probably belongs here as well.

The first thing I want to highlight about the Cyrenaics' theory is that it emphatically differentiates between our superior epistemic access to experiences and our inferior epistemic access to what causes those experiences. I will begin with the former. Several scholars have suggested that the Metrodidact's term "perception" (*aisthēsis*) is the one the Cyrenaics themselves use to denote our privileged access to our own experiences.[43] Like "experience" (*pathos*), it was a word in common usage at the time. Almost all of our testimony replaces this term with the words later popularized by Stoic epistemology: "apprehension" (*katalēpsis*), "apprehensible" (*katalēptos*), and "apprehend" (*katalambanō*).[44] For example:

> The Cyrenaics say that the experiences are our criteria and that they alone are apprehended and happen to be infallible, while none of the things which produce the experiences are apprehensible or infallible. (S.E. *M* 7.191)

> The Cyrenaics say that only the experiences are apprehensible, but things from outside are inapprehensible. (Anon. *Comm. in Pl. Tht.* col. 65 = *SSR* 4a.214)

> Next would be those who say that only the experiences are apprehensible. Some of those from Cyrene said this. (Aristocles F5.1 = Eus. *PE* 14.19.1 = *SSR* 4a.218)

> What do you think of the Cyreneans, not at all contemptible philosophers, who deny that anything from outside can be apprehended? They say they only apprehend what they perceive with their inner sense of touch, like pleasure and pain. (Cic. *Luc.* 76)

Whether the Cyrenaics' own term was "perception," "knowledge," "apprehension," or something else again, its meaning is tolerably clear from our sources. This is that our sensations of vision, hearing, taste, and touch do not vouch for whatever they appear to represent; they only vouch for themselves, and they do so *inwardly, unmistakably, truly,* and *incorrigibly.*

Cicero testifies to their *inwardness* by distinguishing the "inner touch" from all our exterior sensations. We have interior contact with our pleasure and pain, just as we have interior perception of our own yellowing, burning, or embittering. Plutarch employs similar rhetoric in saying,

> These men placed the experiences and appearances in themselves; they didn't think the proof from these sufficed for the confirmation of real things. As if in a siege, they withdrew from what is outside and locked themselves into their experiences. (*Mor.* 1120c–d = *SSR* 4a.211)

Here again the experiences are inside the citadel, as it were, along with the subject. The point the Cyrenaics intend to make may be similar to that of later philosophers who speak of unmediated introspection.

Plutarch goes on to explain that it is the very nature of an experience to reveal itself *unmistakably*: "each of these experiences has in itself its own unshakable self-evidence [τὴν ἐνάργειαν οἰκείαν ἐν αὐτῷ καὶ ἀπερίσπαστον]" (1120e). The word I have translated "self-evidence" can also mean "brilliance" or "distinction."[45] The point is that each experience has its own strikingly distinctive character. To have the experience at all is necessarily to perceive this character.

The Cyrenaics also say that both the experiences themselves and statements about them are *true* and *incorrigible*. For example, they assert, "In all these cases it is true that they are experiencing this thing, such as they are yellowed or they are reddened or they are doubled" (*M* 7.193). In other words, it is true that the experience of one person is "being yellowed," the experience of another is "being reddened," and the experience of a third is "being doubled." Moreover, they seem to argue that beliefs and sincere statements about these experiences are also unmistakable, true, and incorrigible: "if belief abides by the experiences it remains unerring" (Plut. *Mor.* 1120f); "It's possible to say infallibly and truly and firmly and incorrigibly, they say, that we are lightened or we are sweetened" (S.E. *M* 7.191). Although our evidence does not explicitly say so, it is fair to assume that the experiences themselves are incorrigible: because we have unique access to them, no one else is in a position to challenge them (S.E. *M* 7.196). Beliefs and sincere statements about experiences then somehow borrow the characteristics of the experiences they represent.[46]

Our epistemic access to the causes of experience, principal among which are things in the external world (τὰ πράγματα, τὰ ἐκτός, τὰ ἔξωθεν), is profoundly inferior to our access to experiences themselves. First, this access is not inward or unmediated. We do not perceive external objects by "inner touch"; we must rely on our sensory organs. Second and most importantly, the connection between the distinctive character of experiences and the qualities of the objects which cause them is far from unmistakable. The primary argument for this claim is based on the diversity of experiences in different people and animals generated by the same causes. For the purposes of this argument the Cyrenaics apparently grant that we can perceive other people and animals, the objects that are causing their experiences, and some evidence of the nature of those experiences.[47] Their argument is then designed to show that the empirical evidence produced by granting this hypothesis actually undermines it: these people and animals appear to be having different experiences in response to the same causes, so how can we be confident that our experiences of them, or of anything else, accurately represent external reality?

For example, Sextus presents a series of Cyrenaic arguments resembling what later skeptics would call "arguments from circumstances" or "arguments from conditions":[48] the person with jaundice sees everything yellowly, the person with ophtalmia sees everything redly, the man who presses his eyeball sees two suns, and Pentheus—driven mad by Dionysus—sees two cities of Thebes (*M* 7.192). Of course, most of us do not see everything yellow, red, or double, so we are led to suspect that the same object generates different experiences for percipients in different conditions. Plutarch concentrates on Cyrenaic arguments resembling what later skeptics would call "arguments depending on the differences among animals":[49] some people or beasts "dislike honey, like olive shoots, are burned by hail, cooled by wine, blinded by the sun and see at night" (*Mor.* 1121e). Of course, most humans find honey sweet and agreeable, olive shoots bitter and disagreeable, and so on: we disagree with these bestial percipients. This suggests that the qualities of our experiences may be relative to our bodily or mental constitutions, and therefore implies that it is far harder to know external reality than to know our own experiences. If we can in any way know the nature of objects in themselves, it will only be by working through our disagreements about them.

But the Cyrenaics do not believe we can work through these disagreements and thus reveal the truth about external reality. They not only want to argue that we are less certain about the external world than about our own experiences, they want to argue that that we cannot know external reality at all.[50] As we have seen, Plutarch makes this point metaphorically by saying, "As if in a siege, they withdrew from what is outside and locked themselves into their experiences." He also asserts it in less metaphorical terms. Immediately after citing the diverse experiences generated in different percipients by honey and olive shoots, he infers the following conclusion:

> So if belief abides by experiences it remains unerring. However, if it goes beyond them and becomes meddlesome, it disturbs itself and quarrels with others by making judgments and assertions about externals, because those others receive contrary experiences and different impressions from the same things. (*Mor.* 1120f)

Here Plutarch simply assumes that there is no way for us to work through our "contrary experiences" and "different impressions" and so reconstruct the qualities of external reality. The effort to do so can only lead to futile "disturbance" and "quarreling." Even attempting to take a position on external objects is therefore simply "meddling" in a business for which we are not epistemically equipped.

Sextus reports a Cyrenaic argument which may be specifically intended to cut off the possibility of reconciling our divergent experiences. According to him the Cyrenaics argue that our language is already built on our idiosyncratic experiences:

> We all commonly call something "light-colored" or "sweet," but we don't have anything light-colored or sweet in common. Each person grasps their own individual experience, but he cannot say whether this experience comes to him and his neighbor from a light-colored cause, since he doesn't receive his neighbor's experience. Nor can his neighbor say, since he doesn't receive the other person's experience. (*M* 7.196)

In other words, even where there appears to be broad consensus about the experiences generated by an object, this consensus may be illusory: we have no way of knowing whether the words in which we formulate our consensus refer to the same kind of experiences. For example, I cannot perceive the experience which you name "light-colored" any more than you can perceive the experience to which I give the same name. Our experiences may have a different hue, luminosity, or degree of saturation. And whatever words we use to try to explain what we mean by "light-colored" must encounter the same fundamental problem: *all* our descriptive words refer to our own private experiences.[51]

My purpose in summarizing these arguments has not been to communicate their subtleties or evaluate their merits, but rather to show how far the Cyrenaics go in order to contrast the immediacy and infallibility of experiences with the opacity of the external world. This brings me back to the prominence of pleasure and pain within the "citadel" of those experiences. We have already seen that the Metrodidact emphasizes these two affects in Eusebius's report of his doctrine. Here we should note that Diogenes Laertius's doxography reiterates this emphasis:

> They posited two experiences, bodily pain and pleasure, one a smooth motion, pleasure, and pain a rough motion. One pleasure does not differ from another, nor is anything particularly pleasant.[52] Pleasure is good-seeming to all animals, and pain is repulsive. (2.86–7)

This testimony parallels the Metrodidact's exposition of three bodily states, of which alone we have perception. The Metrodidact explicitly agrees with Diogenes' report that pleasure, which is like a gentle undulation at sea, is a "smooth motion." Although he does not explicitly call pain a "rough motion," both the complementarity of pleasure and pain and the fact that he compares pain to "a storm at sea" give us reason to believe that this description goes back to him as well. Diogenes does not mention our perception of the third state, which the

Metrodidact compares to a calm sea. This could be because Eusebius, in eliding the connection between states and experiences, has spoken imprecisely: when a state involves no motion, the Metrodidact would have said there is nothing to perceive, and hence no experience. Earlier in the doxography we are told that the end is "smooth motion delivered to perception" (D.L. 2.85), which suggests that some motions are too gentle to be perceived. *A fortiori*, stillness would not be perceptible.[53] Later in his doxography Diogenes tells us that the state without motion is "the state of someone sleeping" (2.89). Another piece of testimony says that it is "the state of a corpse" (Clem. Al. *Strom.* 2.21.130.8 = *SSR* 4a.4).[54] The former leaves unclear whether there is an experience of stillness, but the latter strongly implies that there is not.

This leaves just pleasure and pain as the experiences at the heart of Cyrenaic ethics. Their capacity to ground choice and action is encapsulated in the technical terms Diogenes ascribes to them: "Pleasure is satisfying [*eudokētēn*] to all animals, and pain is repellent [*apokroustikon*]." These adjectives appear to define the distinctive and unmistakable character of these experiences. To experience pleasure is to perceive "being satisfied" (*eudokein*)[55] and to experience pain is to perceive "being repelled" (*apokrouesthai*), just as to experience "being warmed" is to perceive a certain invigoration of the affected body parts. This comparison also permits us an initial understanding of the claim that "one pleasure does not differ from another." For an experience to qualify as "being warmed," it must possess this particular invigorating phenomenal character. In this respect no experience of being warmed differs from any other. Of course, this is compatible with some experiences being more invigorating than others: the "unmixed wine" mentioned in the Cyrenaic example is significantly less invigorating than boiling oil, for example. It is the same with pleasure: it must have this stamp of "satisfaction," or we would not identify it as pleasure. All pleasures are "satisfying," even though some pleasures may be more satisfying than others.

We are now approaching the principal conclusion toward which the entire Cyrenaic theory of experiences is oriented, which is that our infallible and incorrigible experiences of "satisfaction" and "repulsion" are the best guides for action and concern. The initial argument for this is built right into the self-evident content of "satisfaction" and "repulsion." That which is "repellent" (*apokroustikos*) literally "strikes" (*krouei*) us "away" (*apo*). In other words, it is part of the self-evident character of this experience that it motivates avoidance. That which is "satisfying" involves a perception of what is good for me, as the Greek word communicates etymologically: my experience is "satisfying" (*eudokētē*) because "I appear" (*dokō*) "well" (*eu*) to myself. We will see in a moment that the Cyrenaics' philosophical contemporaries agree that whatever is good necessarily motivates pursuit. But it is worth adding that our Cyrenaic sources also hint at the ability of satisfaction to motivate pursuit by saying that pleasure is intrinsically "choiceworthy" (*hairetē*):

The particular pleasure is choiceworthy for itself; happiness is not choice-worthy for itself, but for particular pleasures. (D.L. 2.88)

Pleasure is good even if it comes from the most unseemly sources, as Hippobotus says in his *On the Sects*. For even if the action is out of place, still the pleasure is choiceworthy for itself and something good. (Ibid.)

Although pleasure is choiceworthy in itself, the sources of some pleasures are opposed because they are disturbing. (D.L. 2.90)

Notwithstanding the fact that the word "choiceworthy" (like the complementary term "avoidance-worthy" [*pheuktos*]) became a standard technical term in later ethics, we have good reason to believe that the Cyrenaics themselves used it.[56] As I have already mentioned, "on what is choiceworthy and avoidance-worthy" is one of the five parts of mature Cyrenaic philosophy. My suggestion is that when the Cyrenaics say pleasure is choiceworthy "for itself" (*di' hautēn*) and "in itself" (*kath' hautēn*), they are thinking of its self-evident phenomenal character: it always motivates pursuit behavior, i.e., choosing.

Admittedly, the word "choiceworthy" is not always used by the Cyrenaics of an experience whose self-evident content motivates pursuit. For example, later in the doxography practical wisdom and wealth turn out to be "choiceworthy" (D.L. 2.91). Neither of these is an experience at all, much less an experience that self-evidently motivates pursuit. But practical wisdom and wealth are both said to be choiceworthy "not for themselves." They are choiceworthy for the sake of the pleasures they generate. By contrast, pleasure is choiceworthy for its own sake and even when, given the circumstances, it ought not to be chosen. This is clear from the second and third quotations above. The second quotation says that pleasure is choiceworthy even when it comes from an "out of place" action. But later in the doxography we read, "The serious man will do nothing out of place because of existing penalties and beliefs" (2.93). The third quotation says that pleasure is choiceworthy even when the effort of obtaining it is distressing and therefore "opposes" the pleasure. In both of these cases pleasure is not choiceworthy *given the circumstances*, since its acquisition involves more than countervailing pains. But it remains choiceworthy *for itself* and *in itself*. In other words, its intrinsic ability to motivate choosing is a matter of its self-evident phenomenal character, which is not altered by prudential circumstances.

The Cyrenaics do not rest their case for the action-guiding capacity of pleasure and pain on the self-evident phenomenology of these affects. They buttress this initial argument with an argument from universal consensus. As we have already seen, they say that "Pleasure is satisfying to all animals, and pain is repellent." This form of argument recalls debates in fourth-century Greek ethics about "the good." For example, Eudoxus, a participant in Plato's Academy and younger contemporary of Aristippus, argued that "pleasure was the good because he saw that all beings desire it, both those with and those without reason" (Arist. *NE* 1072b9–10). Plato's *Philebus* probably reflects Eudoxus' influence when it makes this one of the criteria of the good: "whatever recognizes ⟨the good⟩ hunts after it and desires it, wanting to get it and keep it nearby" (20d7–9). But Plato's formulation adds an important element by noting that we only pursue the good when we in some sense "recognize" it (*gignōskōn*). A big disagreement between hedonists and non-hedonists in subsequent Greek philosophy would be whether what counts as "recognition" is the immediate intuition we share with animals and children, as the Cyrenaics and Epicureans maintain, or rather the educated and rationally informed response of a properly educated adult human, as Aristotle and the Stoics believe.[57]

The Cyrenaics confirm their commitment to a non-intellectual interpretation of recognition when they declare,

> A proof that pleasure is the end is that we are favorably inclined to it without deliberate choice from childhood, and when we have attained it, we seek nothing further, and avoid nothing so much as hurt,[58] which is opposed to it. (D.L. 2.88)

There are two points here which interest us at present. First, human children are inclined toward pleasure (*ōikeiōsthai pros autēn*) without any process of reflective decision-making (*aproairetōs*).[59] The Cyrenaics emphasize this point because they believe that intrinsic desirability should be identified by intuitive reactions, not by a decision that follows ratiocination. Second, this inclination is unmediated by upbringing. This is important, because the Cyrenaics believe that upbringing can "pervert" our intuitive reactions: "They say that some people are able not to choose pleasure, due to perversion [*diastrophēn*]" (D.L. 2.89). The pursuit behavior which the Cyrenaics take to be decisive evidence of intrinsic desirability is therefore that which proceeds directly from children's unreflective and uneducated reactions. In the terms I have been using hitherto, children's behavior attests that desirability is part of the self-evident character of the experience of pleasure. And the converse is true of pain: children "avoid nothing so much as hurt." This brief clause implies an argument which concludes that children universally perceive pain as "avoidance-worthy" and "repellent."

It is worth digressing briefly to note that this argument once again begs the question of how we know about other people and animals. By the Cyrenaics' own arguments, we cannot in fact know when our experiences are caused by any particular sort of external being. Therefore we cannot know when we are in the presence of a human child or another animal, much less investigate how they respond to pleasure and pain. Hence we must assume that the Cyrenaics suspend their doubts on this point for the sake of joining the contemporary debate about what is universally desirable and good. We can think of this as a two-tiered argumentative strategy. First, the fact that pleasure is satisfying and pain is repellent is unmistakably given in the experiences themselves. Second, if you insist on looking beyond your own self-evident experiences and "meddling" in debates about external reality, you will conclude that other percipients universally agree about the motivational properties of pleasure and pain.

One might also object that this argument is incompatible with the Cyrenaics' claim that we cannot know the referents of other agents' descriptive terms. When a child says a lemon is yellow, for instance, we can never know to what phenomenal experience she gives the name "yellow." But pleasure and pain are special cases, because unlike "I am being yellowed," the declarations "I feel pleasure" and "I feel pain" should always accompany particular forms of behavior. We will observe these children pursuing the experiences that they declare pleasing. And if they say that something causes them pain, we will observe them avoiding that experience. So if we grant for the sake of argument that we can perceive other people, then in this case we can also know something about their experiences. We know that by "pleasure" all people mean something that motivates pursuit, and by "pain" all people mean something that motivates avoidance.[60]

We have now surveyed the battery of arguments by which Cyrenaics defend their position that pleasure and pain contain self-evident motivations for pursuit and avoidance, and are therefore of key importance for guiding action and concern. Establishing this thesis is the primary purpose of the theory of the experiences. It remains to add that, despite their skepticism about the qualities of external reality, the Cyrenaics do not recognize any basis for knowledge other than external reality and internal experience. Our sources say very little about this vital point, but it appears that they insist perception must be the basis of knowledge; reasoning can only serve to work through the starting points provided by perception. Hence Sextus tells us that "The school of Plato . . . considered the criterion to be a combination of self-evidence and reason, while the Cyrenaics limit it to instances of self-evidence and experiences alone" (*M* 7.200 = *SSR* 4a.213).[61] Here Sextus has been discussing the criteria espoused by Plato's *Timaeus*, Speusippus, Xenocrates, Arcesilaus, and Carneades. He maintains that according to these philosophers, some form of reason must cooperate with sensory perception for making judgments about perceptible reality. For example, he believes that for Plato, Speusippus, and Xenocrates reason is in contact with imperceptible intelligible beings, and uses its acquaintance with these beings to understand sensory perceptions. By contrasting the Cyrenaics with "the school of Plato" Sextus therefore implies that the Cyrenaics do not attribute an independent criterial role to reason. They deny that reason is in contact with any source of knowledge other than perceptual experience.

In this section we have seen how the Cyrenaics attempt to provide a theoretical foundation for the central importance of pleasure and pain in their thoughts and actions. By way of conclusion, it is important to add that the sharp distinction between our epistemic access to experiences and to external reality could be used to create a sort of firewall between pleasure and pain and any other motivators of action and concern that might be proposed. Since the Cyrenaics deny the power of both sensory perception and intuitive reason to disclose truths about the external world, the goods of their philosophical competitors, such as ethical virtues, will never be as certain as pleasure. How can we ascertain the intrinsic goodness of virtue, if we can trust neither the intuitions nor the perceptions of the universe which lead others to declare that virtue is the greatest good? For that matter, how can we even aim effectively at acting virtuously, if we cannot perceive how our actions affect other people? Similar problems arise for the goods of popular morality, such as helping friends, harming enemies, and enhancing one's honor in the community. We will see in later chapters that the Cyrenaics make room for all of these values in their ethics. However, since their independent goodness or badness cannot be ascertained, Cyrenaics value them for their pleasant or painful consequences.

3.5. The Experiences as a Basis for Action

Given the epistemic chasm between the Cyrenaics' certainty of their experiences and their ignorance of the causes of those experiences, it may have occurred to the reader to wonder how pleasure and pain could actually become the basis for choice and action. It is all very well to say that pleasure is unmistakably choiceworthy, but if we have no perception of the external reality in which we must pursue it, how can its choiceworthiness meaningfully guide our deliberations or actions? As Socrates memorably objects in Plato's *Philebus*, if you had all the pleasure in the world, but not the slightest power of intelligence, thinking, calculation, memory, understanding, or even true opinion, "You wouldn't be living the life of a human being, but the life of a mollusk or a marine crustacean" (21c6–8). Socrates intends this as a knock-down rhetorical punch against pure hedonism, not an attack on Cyrenaic epistemology in particular. But it is easy to see how the metaphor could be turned against the Cyrenaics: with their withdrawal from beliefs about external reality and their careful focus on interior sensations, in what respect could they be more purposeful than limpets?

In fact Aristocles directs a similar attack at them, exclaiming, "It's obvious they don't even understand what we're saying right now! Such people are no better than gnats or flies. Except even those creatures recognize what is natural or unnatural" (F5.7 = Eus. *PE* 14.19.7). The intended point may simply be to compare the Cyrenaics with "crude" animals, but we can easily develop it into a more substantive criticism. Gnats and flies, one might think, have scarcely any awareness of the world. They are rudimentary sensory-response machines: tempt them with a pleasant sensation and they approach; chastise them with pain and they withdraw. But they at least perceive the food whose aroma they pursue, and somehow discern it is "natural" for them. A Cyrenaic cannot even do that: he may enjoy the same aroma as the fly, but unlike the fly, he insists he has no idea what causes this pleasure. So while the fly buzzes toward the warm honey cake, the Cyrenaic does not stir a muscle. As Aristocles says earlier in this passage, "Or how do they know that they should choose this and avoid that? If they don't know these things, they won't have any impulse or desire, and so won't even be animals" (F5.5). In other words, they will be plants.[62]

It is not absolutely clear to what extent the Cyrenaics are aware that their theory of experiences could be construed as undercutting all guidance for action. However, it seems likely that this problem would have occurred either to the several generations of Cyrenaics who held this position or to their contemporary opponents. Moreover, several tantalizing bits of evidence suggest both that they recognized the problem and that they attempted to formulate a solution.

My starting point for reconstructing this solution will be to look at what Neopyrrhonean skeptics later propose when their antagonists confront them with a similar conundrum (e.g., D.L. 9.104–8, S.E. *M* 11.162). Neopyrrhonists insist that they have neither knowledge nor beliefs about external reality; reality simply "appears" a certain way to them, and all their inquiries lead them to the "appearance" (not to say dogmatic conclusion) that they lack the ability to get past appearances to things themselves.[63] In fact they cultivate this suspension of judgment by practicing various "modes" of argument, by which they develop equipollent arguments on either side of every question. This does not imply that they repudiate all standards of judgment. To the contrary, they recognize a standard of judgment "for action, by attention to which we take some actions and not others in life" (S.E. *PH* 1.21). They explain: "For it was necessary for the aporetic philosopher, if he wasn't to end up entirely idle and inactive in the actions of life, to have some standard of judgment for choice and avoidance" (S.E. *M* 7.30; cf. *M* 11.162–68, *PH* 1.23). In fact appearances themselves serve as standards for action. For example, sensory perceptions, thoughts, and appetites simply come to Neopyrrhonists unbidden, and they accept all of them without believing that they represent reality. Furthermore, they observe the customs of their upbringing and the techniques of any trade they practice without questioning whether their normative force has any real foundation. In this manner "they submit to life without having beliefs, in order not to be idle" (*PH* 1.226). But this carefully qualified submission, in which they preserve their doubts about reality, has a vital therapeutic purpose: it weakens the hopes and fears associated with what appears good or bad for them, since it keeps in their minds the possibility that these appearances do not correspond to reality. Thus it diminishes the Neopyrrhonists' stress and brings them closer to tranquility.[64]

Two pieces of evidence suggest that the Cyrenaics proposed a loosely similar solution to the problem of idleness. The first is a passage to which we will return later in this chapter, so I give it here I full:

> What these men say about ends appears to be analogous to what they say about criteria, since experiences extend all the way to ends. Some experiences are pleasant, some are painful, and some are in between. They say

the painful ones are bad, and their end is pain. The pleasant ones are good, and their infallible end is pleasure. The ones in between are neither good nor bad, and their end is what is neither good nor bad, which is an experience between pleasure and pain. So experiences are ⟨our⟩ criteria and ends for all beings, and we live, they say, by submitting and paying attention to self-evidence and satisfaction—self-evidence in the case of the other experiences, and satisfaction in the case of pleasure. (*SSR* 4a.213 = S.E. *M* 7.199–200)

For now I want to focus on the final sentence of this passage: "we live, they say, by submitting and paying attention to self-evidence and satisfaction—self-evidence in the case of the other experiences, and satisfaction in the case of pleasure." Here we recognize the technical terminology of the theory of the experiences: experiences carry their own incontrovertible "self-evidence" in them. In the case of pleasure, this is called "satisfaction." We should undoubtedly supply what this passages leaves out, which is that in the case of pain, this is called "repulsion." We would then have before us the entire informational panoply permitted by the theory of the experiences.

The sentence says that "we live . . . by submitting and paying attention to" just these experiential data. Here it is worth remarking that this testimony regarding the Cyrenaics comes from the same Neopyrrhonist whose formulations of Neopyrrhonean skepticism I have just been quoting. Thus it is not coincidental that the terms "living," "paying attention," and "submitting" occur repeatedly in the Neopyrrhonean passages as well. For example, Sextus says it is by using appearances as a standard of judgment that Neopyrrhonists "take some actions and not others *in life* [*kata ton bion*]" (*PH* 1.21); that "by paying attention to appearances *we live* [*bioumen*] without having beliefs ⟨and⟩ in such a way as *to preserve normal life* [*kata tēn biōtikēn tērēsin*]" (*PH* 1.23); that Neopyrrhonists must not be "entirely idle and inactive *in the actions of life* [*tais kata bion praxesin*]" (*M* 7.30); and that the Neopyrrhonean way of perceiving things to be good or bad is simply a matter of "submitting *to life* [*tōi biōi*] without having beliefs" (*PH* 1.226). In all of these cases "life" and "living" do not mean simply breathing, but going about our lives: making decisions, taking actions, and generally avoiding inactivity and idleness. In the Cyrenaic passage Sextus uses a different verb for "we live" (*zōmen*), which often means "living" simply in the sense of not being dead. But it may also be a synonym for the verb "go about our lives" (*bioō*),[65] and assuming it has that meaning here produces the clearest sense of what Sextus says about the Cyrenaics: "we *live*, they say, by submitting and paying attention to self-evidence and satisfaction." So the topic of Sextus's report is how a Cyrenaic can escape idleness and go about normal life.

This conjecture is corroborated by the fact that the participles "submitting to" (*hepomenoi*) and "paying attention to" (*prosekhontes*) also occur repeatedly in the passages describing how Neopyrrhonists avoid idleness. We have just seen the phrase "submitting to life [*hepomenōn tōi biōi*] without having beliefs" as a description of the way Neopyrrhonists name things good or bad. For example, Neopyrrhonists do not believe that pleasure is good, but if pleasure appeared good to them, they would act on this appearance. In this sense they "submit to life" by accepting a standard of judgment for action. The standard of judgment for action is also the topic of *Outlines of Pyrrhonism* 1.21–3 and *Against the Dogmatists* 7.29–30, in which the verb "pay attention" occurs five times. Here we can understand "attention" as the determinant of what is foregrounded or backgrounded in someone's phenomenal field. For example, when the Olympian Milo is wrestling an opponent, he is acutely aware of his grip, his center of balance, and his opponent's position and muscular tension. These things are foregrounded: he pays attention to them. He is not aware of the judges, the massive crowd, or the blue sky over his head. These things fade into the background. In a similar fashion, when action is at issue a Neopyrrhonist foregrounds whatever simply appears to him—his appetites, his relevant sensory perceptions, his awareness of what is usually done in this culture, or his technical training. He does not ask himself what he *really* ought to do; in situations like this, questions about what is *truly* good or bad remain in the background.

It is likely that Sextus has used the participles "submitting" and "paying attention" with the same meaning in the Cyrenaic passage. This would make good sense of the text: "we live, [the Cyrenaics] say, by *submitting* and *paying attention* to self-evidence and satisfaction—self-evidence in the case of the other experiences, and satisfaction in the case of pleasure." We would then say that Cyrenaics simply "submit to" whatever cumulative impressions their visual, auditory, gustatory, tactile, and olfactory experiences give them. If they have an impression of an obstacle in their path, for example, they act as if there were an obstacle in their path: they deviate in order to avoid it.[66] If the honey tastes sweet, they act as if the honey were sweet: they eat the honey. If the fire feels caustic, they act as if it were caustic: they move away from it. Like the Neopyrrhonists, however, this does not mean that they have forgotten their principles. They remain aware that they cannot know whether the impressions generated by their experiences correspond to real objects. This is important, since it preserves the unique motivational status accorded to pleasure and pain. But they also pay attention to their informational experiences, since these experiences give them the coordinates among which they can attempt to pursue pleasure and avoid pain. This is how they avoid inactivity.

A second piece of evidence supports this speculative reconstruction. This is a sentence in a treatise that has been preserved on a papyrus from Herculaneum, which has plausibly been ascribed to the first-century Epicurean Philodemus. In the opening columns the author appears to be cataloguing rival positions on standards of judgment for choice and avoidance. Fortunately, the sentence which concerns us is extremely well preserved:[67]

> Some people proposed that the experiences of the soul are ends and that they don't need additional judgment based on further things. So they

gave everyone unchallengeable authority to say they enjoy whatever they want, and to do whatever is conducive to it.[68] (*On Choices and Avoidances*, col. III, 6–14)

The editors of this papyrus rightly argue that the Cyrenaics are the most likely candidates for "some people."[69] The passage's identification of experiences with ends is very close to the Cyrenaics' reported beliefs.[70] Moreover, its granting to everyone of "unchallengeable [*anupeuthunon*] authority to say they enjoy [*khairein*] whatever they want" corresponds to the incorrigibility of the Cyrenaics' claims about their own experiences. The Cyrenaics would agree that when someone says "I feel joy" (*khairō*), the rectitude of their statement cannot be "challenged" or "straightened out" (*euthunesthai*) by anyone else.

Parts of this testimony harmonize with and partially corroborate the interpretation of Cyrenaic action I have been developing in this section. For example, experiences "don't need additional judgment" for two reasons: first, the motivational power of the experiences of pleasure and pain is self-evident. Second, the Cyrenaics make no effort to verify that the experiences by which they guide their actions correspond to external reality. Here it is worth noting that the passage under discussion follows a sentence which, though it is extremely lacunose, almost certainly questions the possibility of grasping any standards of judgment for action: "Some people denied that it is possible to know anything. . . ."[71] So it is not a great leap to see in our highly abbreviated sentence the Cyrenaics' solution to this skeptical problem. As Tsouna puts it, the Cyrenaics maintain that "we live in an internal world and we manage as best we can."[72] Yet this does not freeze Cyrenaics in idleness; they are authorized "to do whatever contributes to" their hedonistic goal of enjoyment. The text's Epicurean author may intend this as a criticism of the Cyrenaics: their theory permits everyone to pursue whatever they find pleasant, without due regard for the imprudence of this strategy.[73] If so, we will see in the next chapter that this is a polemical distortion. For now I want to emphasize its implicit epistemological premise, which is that "the experiences of the soul" are sufficient criteria both for diagnosing enjoyment and for taking action. Those experiences give all people "unchallengeable authority" not only to describe their experiences as pleasant, but also to pursue them. This could mean that it is up to each percipient to determine, by submitting and paying attention to his own experiences, how he will pursue pleasure and avoid pain.

The last relevant piece of evidence comes from the Hegesiac sect. The sentence reads: "They rejected perceptions since they don't permit accurate discernment, and said they do everything that appears reasonable" (D.L. 2.95).[74] For the first clause, compare Diogenes' testimony for the mainstream Cyrenaics: "[they said] the perceptions don't always tell the truth" (2.93).[75] In both cases we are obviously dealing with perceptions *of external reality*, not the perception *of experience* which is the gold standard of Cyrenaic truth. Our vision, hearing, and taste do not reliably report the qualities of things themselves. This clearly recalls the Cyrenaic distinction between the certainty of sensory experience (e.g., being sweetened) and the opacity of its relation to the cause of sensation (e.g., honey).

The connection between this first clause and the second is initially puzzling. What does the rejection of perceptions have to do with the basis for action? I suggest that we take the second clause as a solution to a problem generated by the first: although perceptions do not permit discernment of their causes, Hegesiacs still have a basis for decision and action. This basis is compacted into the phrase, "everything that appears reasonable" (tōn t' eulogōs phainomenōn panta).

This phrase raises two sets of questions. The first concerns these "appearances," the logic of which is substantially different than that of experiences. As Tsouna has remarked, whereas experiences "focus on the condition of the affected subject," appearances "are centered on what appears to the subject."[76] In other words, appearances refer to external reality, not internal sensory awareness. For example, I might say that "this honey appears sweet" rather than "I have been disposed sweetly." For this reason Tsouna rightly suspects Sextus Empiricus of misrepresentation when he claims that Cyrenaic experiences *just are* appearances.[77] We should also be wary of Plutarch's vocabulary when he claims,

> These men placed the experiences and appearances [phantasias] in themselves; they didn't think the proof from these sufficed for the confirmation of real things. As if in a siege they withdrew from what is outside and locked themselves into their experiences, positing [tithemenoi] of externals that "it appears" [phainetai] but not declaring in addition that "it is." (Mor. 1120d = SSR 4a.211)

Like Sextus, Plutarch casually associates experiences with appearances. He also says that Cyrenaics "posit" appearances, i.e., make truth claims about them. For example, I might claim it is true that "the honey appears sweet to me." But no such claim occurs in our evidence for the Cyrenaics. Even Plutarch's own reports of Cyrenaic language refer exclusively to how percipients are affected. We should therefore reject the innuendo that Cyrenaic experiences can readily be translated into appearances which share the same epistemic status.

However, the evidence from Hegesias gives us reason to believe that at least some Cyrenaics do speak of appearances. The utility of such language is obvious: it gives them a vocabulary for discussing the impressions of the world generated by their experiences. Thus they can move from "I am being sweetened" to "this appears sweet" and "this appears to be honey." Moreover, the appearances in question are also the direct object of the verb "do": Hegesiacs "do everything that appears reasonable." In this case what appears must be a course of action. For example, "taking the honey" or "eating the honey" may appear reasonable. This could also be expressed as an action-guiding affordance of the honey, e.g., "the honey appears taking-worthy [lēpton or lēpteon]," "the honey appears eating-worthy [edeston or edesteon]," etc. Unfortunately, the further details of this theory are lost to us.

The second question raised by the Hegesiac evidence concerns the word "reasonable" or "reasonably" (*eulogōs*). The answer will be important, since Sextus's language of "submitting to" experiences might lead us to assume that Cyrenaics simply accept whatever impressions reality generates in them without attempting to reason about them. In fact it has been argued that Cyrenaics "cannot perform practical choices on rational grounds."[78] At least for Hegesiacs it seems that this assertion requires qualification.

One possible function for reason here would be to assess whether appearances correspond to reality. A model of how this could work is suggested by comparison with the Stoics. Consider the following anecdote about the Stoic Sphaerus, who lived about two generations after Hegesias:

> There's a witticism from Sphaerus, who studied with Chrysippus alongside Cleanthes, and was summoned to Alexandria by King Ptolemy. When wax birds were placed in front of him and he reached out his hands, he was stopped by the king, who said he'd assented to something false. But he gracefully replied that he didn't assent that they were birds, but that it was reasonable they were birds. For an apprehensible appearance differs from what is reasonable: the former is infallible, but what is reasonable could turn out otherwise. (Athen. 354e; cf. D.L. 7.177 [parts of both at LS40F])

In this anecdote the birds exist in external reality, and the question is whether Sphaerus can perceive that they are made of wax. For the Stoics the fundamental standard for what is true is the "apprehensible appearance" (*phantasia kataleptikē*), an appearance that arises from something that really exists and is stamped with the attributes of its cause in such a way that it could not have arisen from a cause lacking those attributes (LS 40D–E). A Stoic sage is only supposed to give his mental assent to apprehensible appearances. So Ptolemy is mocking Sphaerus for not being able to distinguish apprehensible from non-apprehensible appearances, and perhaps implying that no such distinction exists. Sphaerus's rejoinder is that his action in reaching for the bird was not based on assent to an apprehensible appearance, but only to "what is reasonable" (*to eulogon*).[79] Unlike apprehensible appearances, he explains, what is reasonable can arise from a cause lacking the attributes of the appearance. We read elsewhere in our Stoic sources that a proposition is "reasonable" "when it has many starting points [*aphormas*] toward being true, such as 'I will be alive tomorrow'" (D.L. 7.76). If I am healthy, no personal enemy is threatening me, and my polis is at peace, I have multiple "starting points" for believing I will be alive tomorrow. Similarly, if what Ptolemy puts before Sphaerus is shaped like a baked thrush, has the color of a baked thrush, and perhaps even smells or feels like a baked thrush, then the appearance it presents has many starting points for deriving from a baked thrush. The function of reason here is to collate these starting points and draw an inference from them. Yet this appearance could obviously arise from something other than a genuine baked thrush, since in fact it arises from an artfully designed piece of wax. So the appearance is not yet apprehensible. This would have become obvious to Sphaerus when he tried to eat it, which was actually a great way of determining whether this reasonable appearance merited assent as an apprehension!

Hegesias could have in mind something like this, but with an important difference: he could never assess whether his appearances correspond to reality, but only whether they are the sort of appearances typically generated by their external cause. For example, from a distance he might have a visual experience consistent with a small jar with two handles. Moving closer, he might find this visual appearance confirmed. Picking it up and smelling it, he might receive a floral olfactory experience. Tasting it, he might "be sweetened." The confluence of these experiences could lead him to think, "This *appears* to be a jar of honey." Once again it would be the function of reason to collate these experiences and appraise their consistency. But if Hegesias remained faithful to the Cyrenaic theory of the experiences, he would not say that it was reasonable that this actually *was* a round jar or that its contents were floral-smelling and sweet-tasting. According to his Cyrenaic predecessors, none of these experiences reveals anything about its cause; each merely reveals the way those causes affect him. So what would be reasonable is simply that this is the sort of thing that regularly affects Hegesias in this way—whatever that is, and whichever its actual attributes. Thus it would also be reasonable for Hegesias to eat from the jar, and we would have further refined our understanding of how Cyrenaic experiences provide a basis for action.

One might well object that at this point Hegesias ought to abandon the antithesis between reality and experience/appearance and simply accept that "reality" always means reality-as-it-appears-to-sensory-experience. But there is a good reason to believe Hegesias remains faithful to the Cyrenaic theory. This is that he continues to maintain that pleasure and pain are the targets at which action should aim. As I explained in the last section, the theory of the experiences underpins the foundational role of pleasure and pain in Cyrenaic arguments and attitudes. Therefore if Hegesias were to abandon this theory and permit "reasonable" judgments about the attributes of external reality, he would undercut his core doctrine and the rationale behind his own behavior. So it is best to assume that like Sextus and Philodemus, Hegesias is telling us how Cyrenaics claim to make decisions and take actions without admitting any knowledge of external reality.

3.6. Cyrenaic Formulations of the End

I began this chapter with Carneades' claim that the Cyrenaic end is "obtaining pleasure." We have also encountered various sources reporting the relation of pleasure and pain to the Cyrenaic end or ends. In late classical and Hellenistic philosophy the technical term "end" was used in several distinct but overlapping senses. Therefore I will not exhaust what there is to say about Cyrenaic ends in this section; they will continue to be relevant to next chapter's more detailed exploration of the Cyrenaics' handling of the virtues and their attitudes toward past, present, and future conditions and events. But an initial analysis of these doctrines in light of how the Cyrenaics discuss the ends of different sorts of experiences will help me to complete this chapter's account of the Cyrenaics' attitudes and theories regarding pleasure and pain.

The sense of the "end" which concerns us now is the one implied by the passage from Sextus Empiricus quoted in the last section. I repeat the relevant portion here:

> Some experiences are pleasant, some are painful, and some are interme-
> diate. They say the painful ones are bad, and their end is hurt. The pleas-
> ant ones are good, and their infallible end is pleasure. The intermediate
> ones are neither good nor bad, and their end is what is neither good nor
> bad, which is an experience between pleasure and pain. (*M* 7.199 = *SSR*
> 4a.213; cf. [Plut.] *Strom.* 9 = *SSR* 4a.166)

Here we are presented with not only an end of good experiences, but also an end of bad experiences and an end of those that are neither good nor bad. What, therefore, can "end" mean in this sentence? We will see later that "end" most often means that for the sake of which other actions are performed or possessions and conditions are prized. But this interpretation will not work very well for an "end" of bad experiences, much less for an end of experiences that are neither good nor bad. As several scholars have already perceived, it is therefore best to take "end" in this passage to mean "the fullest, highest, most complete expression" of whatever attributes the adjectives "good," "bad," and "neither good nor bad" connote.[80] We have already seen that the Cyrenaics agree with other philosophers of the period in assuming that what is truly good is intrinsically and universally desirable, while what is bad is intrinsically and universally avoidance-worthy. We can therefore propose that the end of goods is that which is intrinsically desirable to the highest degree, while the end of bad things is that which is intrinsically avoidance-worthy to the highest degree. It is harder to make sense of the end of things that are neither good nor bad. One possibility is that that this phrase denotes "purely informational" experiences like being yellowed, in which case their end is to be yellowed (or reddened, or made salty, or affected with a certain sound, etc.) to the highest degree.[81] An- other is that it simply denotes experiences which are value neutral—"neither good nor bad"—to the highest degree; in other words, experiences which are completely lacking in intrinsic motivational power.

I shall concentrate on the ends of good and bad things. If I am right that when the Cyrenaics speak of "ends" they sometimes mean the "most complete expression" of goodness or badness, then we can resolve a puzzle in Cyre- naic doxography. We have already seen Diogenes' testimony that "They [the Cyrenaics] posited two experiences, bodily pain and pleasure, one a smooth motion, pleasure, and pain a rough motion" (2.86). A little later Diogenes goes on, "They mean pleasure of the body, which is also the end, as Panaetius says in his *On the Sects*" (2.87). This would be puzzling if we took "end" to mean primary object of care and ultimate goal of all action. We have seen that Aristippus is extremely concerned to eliminate mental distress. If the Cyrenaics insisted that mental pain is only avoidance-worthy insofar as it leads to bodily pain, they would be excluding most forms of distress. And if they excluded most forms of distress, they would be jettisoning an important element in Aristippus's thinking and practice. Moreover, mainstream, Annicerean, Hegesiac, and Theodorean sources repeatedly testify to their ongoing concern with purely mental pleasure and pain. It suffices for the moment just to list these passages:

(Mainstream Cyrenaics)

. . . not all mental pleasures and hurts supervene on bodily pleasures and hurts. For joy occurs also for the simple prosperity of the fatherland, as for our own. But they also deny that pleasure is perfected by the memory or anticipation of good things, as Epicurus thought. For the movement of the soul is dissipated by time. They say that pleasures don't occur through mere seeing or hearing, since we listen with pleasure to people mimicking songs of mourning, but with displeasure to those really singing them. Bodily pleasures are actually much better than pleasures of the soul, and bodily disturbances are worse. Hence it is by these that criminals are more often punished. (D.L. 2.89–90)[82]

The wise man will neither feel envy nor erotic passion nor superstitious dread, because these things happen through empty belief. (D.L. 2.91)

. . . whoever has thoroughly learned the account of what's good and what's bad can speak well and be free from superstitious dread and escape the fear of death. (D.L. 2.92)

They say that some people feel more distress than others (D.L. 2.93)

(Hegesiacs)

Happiness is wholly impossible, since the body has been filled with many sufferings, and the soul suffers along with the body and is troubled, and fortune prevents many things we hope for. (D.L. 2.94)

The wise person will not so much excel in choosing good things as choosing to avoid bad things, since he posits as his end not to live painfully in either body or soul. (D.L. 2.95)

(Annicereans)

For we feel joy not only because of pleasures, but also because of other people's company and the love of public distinction. (Clem. *Strom.* 2.21.130/8–9 = *SSR* 4G.4)

(Theodoreans)
Theodorus understood the end to be joy and distress. (D.L. 2.98)

Given this recurrent interest in joy, distress, and other varieties of mental affect, it is hard to understand how the Cyrenaics could posit *bodily* pleasure and pain as the goal of all deliberation and action. For this reason it has even been suggested that we are looking at two stages in the movement: in the first, the Cyrenaics only recognize bodily experiences; in the second, they incorporate mental affects as well.[83] But this hypothesis is unnecessary if "end" in this case means "complete expression." For in that case bodily pleasure can be intrinsically desirable in the highest degree, yet mental joy can be intrinsically desirable as well. And bodily pain can be intrinsically avoidance-worthy in the highest degree, yet mental distress can be intrinsically avoidance-worthy as well. There would not be any contradiction in labeling bodily pleasure and pain the ends while also pursuing joy and avoiding distress for their own sakes.

This explanation prompts us to return to the doctrine that "One pleasure does not differ from another" (D.L. 2.87). Earlier I suggested that this means all pleasures belong to the same phenomenal kind: they are all experiences of satisfaction, and they are all choiceworthy for themselves and in themselves. If they were not, they would not be pleasures at all. There is no reason this doctrine cannot pertain to both bodily and mental pleasure. These do not differ qua being pleasant, but they do differ in terms of how good they are. That is why only *bodily* pleasure and pain are the ends. As we have just read, "Bodily pleasures are actually much better than pleasures of the soul, and bodily disturbances are worse." In other words, bodily pleasure and pain are more completely good or bad than their mental analogues.

Calling bodily pleasure the "end of good things" and bodily pain the "end of bad things" captures and highlights the ethical core of the Cyrenaic theory of the experiences, and both together articulate part of the existential attitude from which Cyrenaicism arises. I have suggested in this chapter that those who became committed Cyrenaics must have had hedonistic inclinations before coming to philosophy. They were already attuned to the ways in which the world could provide them with pleasure or cause them pain. The Cyrenaic theory of the experiences allowed them to articulate and justify their mode of attunement to the world. They could then explain that possibilities for pleasure and pain mattered to them because these experiences are self-evidently satisfying and choiceworthy or repellent and avoidance-worthy. No other experiences possess these attributes. Moreover, even among these experiences some are more satisfying or repellent than others: bodily experiences are more intense than mental ones. So it makes sense to perceive the world above all in terms of opportunities for bodily enjoyment or risks of bodily pain.

CHAPTER 4

Virtue and Living Pleasantly

4.1. Introduction

In the last chapter I attempted to reconstruct how Aristippus and the later Cyrenaics established a rational foundation for their hedonistic intuitions. I argued that Aristippus began with a family of arguments justifying his choices by their capacity to generate pleasure or ward off pain. This is not to say that Aristippus was simply working out rationalizations for choices he would have made even without philosophy. To the contrary, I suggested that Socrates' guidance helped him to reflect critically on his beliefs and behavior and begin to organize them. But there is no reliable evidence concerning whether or how Aristippus argued for the foundational premises in these arguments, namely that pleasure is preeminently good and pain preeminently bad. It is Aristippus's successors who clearly took an interest in providing a theoretical foundation for both their arguments and their lifestyle. This foundation is the theory of the experiences, which culminates in three ethically relevant points: first, pleasure is self-evidently satisfying and therefore choiceworthy in itself and for itself, while pain is self-evidently repellent and therefore avoidance-worthy in itself and for itself; second, nothing else valued by the general public or by the Cyrenaics' philosophical competitors shares this self-evident motivational quality; third, bodily pleasure is the end of goods, i.e., the most complete good, while bodily pain is the end of bad things, i.e., the most completely bad thing.

Cyrenaic ethics does not stop with this establishment of foundations, of course. On these foundations the Cyrenaics attempt to construct a theoretical edifice which organizes and justifies an entire way of life devoted to enjoyment and the avoidance of pain and distress. This is the existential option for the sake of which they have undertaken the intellectual and practical exercise of philosophizing. It requires a commitment to education and habituation, both of which aim at the virtues of character and intellect necessary for obtaining pleasure and avoiding pain and distress. It also assigns an appropriate place to instrumental goods like health, wealth, friendship, and political participation. Finally, it becomes an object of reflection in its own right, prompting the Annicereans to ask how each individual pleasure in its self-sufficiency and finality relates to the entire pleasant life presupposed as a goal by many of their arguments and practices.

The object of this chapter is to work through the evidence for how the Cyrenaics build a system of arguments and practices on the foundation explored in the last chapter. Once again I will begin with the un-systematized thinking of Aristippus, from whom we have a rich variety of sayings and anecdotes but practically no clear positions or extended arguments. Even this evidence will suffice to show that Aristippus once again sets the model that later Cyrenaics codify in theory. I will then pass to the mainstream and Annicerean Cyrenaics, whose ethics are extremely similar. (Hegesias and Theodorus, both of whom introduce substantial changes, are dealt with in other chapters.) I will address the Cyrenaic handling of a range of goods, each of which is valued for the sake of the pleasures it generates. I will focus on wealth and the virtues of practical wisdom and justice. Finally I will return to the mainstream and Annicerean formulations of the end and ask how successful they are in reconciling the particularity of each pleasant experience with the holistic life at which the acquisition of wealth, maintenance of health, and development of the virtues aim.

4.2. Aristippus on Education, Virtue, and Happiness

In the last chapter I explored Aristippus's tendency to ground his arguments in the choiceworthiness of pleasure and avoidance-worthiness of pain. But pleasure, pain, and distress are not the only items of value in Aristippean thinking. The evidence for his commitment to the development of philosophical insight and ethical character is extremely strong.[1] In this section I explore the anecdotal evidence for the value he places on education, wisdom, and virtue.

In many anecdotes Aristippus argues that "education" (*paideia*), and especially the education he himself offers, is a precious thing. Two examples will suffice:

> When someone asked him how much he was asking for the education of his son, [Aristippus] replied, "A thousand drachmas." The other said, "By Heracles! That's an exorbitant demand! I could buy a slave for a thousand drachmas!" "Then you'll have two slaves," Aristippus replied, "your son and the one you buy." (Plut. *Mor.* 4f = SSR 4A.5; cf. D.L. 2.72)

> Aristippus said that he took money from his associates not in order to use it, but so they would know on what they should spend their money. (D.L. 2.72; cf. Gnom. Vat. 743 n. 24 = SSR 4a.7)

The primary reason that numerous anecdotes on this topic have been preserved is because Socrates did not accept payments, so Aristippus's fee-charging arrangements opened him to accusations of "un-Socratic" behavior.[2] Thus it is hardly surprising to find him defending the merit of his product. But there is no reason to doubt that Aristippus genuinely believed the training he offered was excellent value for money. While he may have taught the rhetorical art of "speaking well,"[3] the anecdotes consistently suggest that he provided much more: as he implies above, his students were transforming their "slavish" characters into "free" ones. Having a "free" character might involve not only the capacity to speak with sophistication but also the understanding and self-possession to merit the privileges accorded to free males (as opposed to women or slaves) in the hierarchical world of Greek antiquity.[4] Another saying on this topic corroborates the transformational power of education, but does so rather differently: "When he was asked how those who are educated exceed those who are not, he said, 'In the same way as tame horses exceed wild ones'" (D.L. 2.69).[5] Rather than moving from slavishness to freedom, these pupils move from savagery to civilization. It is unclear precisely how Aristippus believes tame horses exceed wild ones. It is obvious, however, that breaking and training a horse not only gives it the capacity to perform new tasks, but also transforms its attitudes about many experiences and provides it with a new way of life. Aristippus is suggesting that the education of a human being has the same breadth of effect, and therefore is worth every obol.

The content of this character- and life-transforming pedagogy is surely nothing other than Aristippus's own philosophy. Certainly this is the case regarding his daughter: "He instructed his daughter Arete in the best fashion, sharing with her his training in being disdainful of excess" (D.L. 2.72). This description emphasizes the exercises through which Arete accustoms herself to a new mode of thinking and feeling: Aristippus "shared his training" (*sunaskōn*); he taught Arete "to be disdainful of excess" (*huperoptikēn tou pleionos einai*).[6] These exercises would have been underpinned by reasoning about what is good and what is bad, as the anonymous authors of the spurious Socratic Epistles have imaginatively reconstructed.[7]

In the twenty-seventh epistle, Aristippus, who has fallen ill on the way home from Sicily,[8] indicates that he has received a letter from Arete complaining about how the officials in Cyrene are treating her. Aristippus counsels her,

> I instruct you to manage this business with the rulers in such a way that my advice benefits you.[9] That advice was not to desire what is excessive. In this way you'll live out your life in the best fashion, if you're disdainful of every excess. Those men will never wrong you so much that you'll be in want, since you still have the two orchards, and they suffice even for a luxurious life. Even if only the property in Berenice were left, it wouldn't fail to support an excellent lifestyle. (Socr. *Ep.* 27.2)

Here the authors imagine Aristippus in the very act of "instructing" his daughter (*hupotithemai*). It is clear that he has already taught the principles of "not wanting excess" (*mē tou pleonos orignasthai*) and "being disdainful of every excess" (*huperoptikē pantos . . . tou pleonos*). It is now a matter of helping her to see how they apply in this circumstance. Arete already has several properties in and around Cyrene. Aristippus urges her to consider that those properties are more than sufficient for an "excellent" and even "luxurious" lifestyle. Note, therefore, that "disdaining excess" does not entail embracing austerity: excess is defined relative to what is actually good, which for Aristippus is pleasure, not excluding luxurious enjoyment. Aristippus makes this explicit later: "Since you share this pleasant lifestyle with those women, let the officials in Cyrene wrong you as much as they want: they won't wrong you with respect to your natural end" (27.3). The phrase "natural end" (*phusikon telos*) is anachronistic for Aristippus, but we can nevertheless appreciate how this letter recreates his effort, through both teaching Arete principles and training her in their application, to mold her thoughts and feelings with the rational standards of judgment articulated by their shared philosophy. The result at which this kind of education aims is not only understanding of what is good and bad, but also everyday feelings and actions in accord with this understanding. In short, it is a transformation of both belief and desire.

Since it is a behavioral disposition with a rational underpinning, we can usefully think of the ability to disdain excess as one of the virtues of Aristippean philosophy. In fact, we could call it Aristippus's version of "temperance" or "soundness of mind" (*sōphrosunē*).[10] Numerous anecdotes display the value Aristippus attributes to this disposition and the positive consequences he recognizes from it. In one family of anecdotes he is threatened at sea, either by pirates or by his fellow passengers. He ensures his safety by tossing his money overboard (D.L. 2.77, Suda A 3909, Gnom. Vat. 743 n. 39 = *SSR* 4a.79, 82). After all, he needs his life, but not his money. In a saying recorded by Plutarch, Aristippus explains the virtue of disdaining excess with a medical metaphor:

> Anyone who remembers Aristippus would be especially amazed by people who haven't lost anything, have many possessions, but always still need more [*pleonos*]. He used to say, "If someone eats a lot and drinks a lot and is never satisfied, he goes to the doctor and asks what his illness is, what his condition is, and how he can be freed from it. But if someone has five couches and wants ten, or possesses ten tables and buys as many again, or isn't satisfied when plenty of estates and money are available, but remains stressed, sleepless, and insatiable with everything, this man doesn't think he needs someone to care for him and show him why he has this illness." (*Mor.* 524a–b = *SSR* 4a.73)

Those who are always dissatisfied, no matter what they acquire, have an "illness" (*pathos*).[11] The justification for pathologizing this state is not only that it is "unreasonable" or "unnatural," which some might contest,[12] but also—and more importantly from a hedonistic perspective—that it is uncomfortable: its symptoms include stress (*suntetatai*) and insomnia (*agrupnei*). Another Aristippean saying makes a similar point: "It's better to live by sleeping on straw but feeling confident than to have wealth but be strangled by your own thoughts" (Anecd. Gr. ed. Boissonade I p. 36.18–21 = *SSR* 4a.77). Aristippus's philosophy aims to equip its practitioners with the beliefs and attitudes they need in order to be "cured" of their attachment to superfluities, and thus to be freed from their stress, insomnia, and the stranglehold of their own preoccupations.

Aristippean temperance also has a positive aspect. It not only eliminates mental "illness," it also enables enjoyment. Once again there are numerous anecdotes testifying to this function. The most popular concerns an incident in the court of the tyrant Dionysius in Syracuse:

> Once when they were drinking and Dionysius ordered everyone to put on purple robes and dance, Plato refused. "I couldn't put on women's clothing," he said. But Aristippus took the robes and when he was about to dance he gracefully replied, "even in Bacchic celebrations, if a lady is sound of mind [*sōphrōn*], she won't be corrupted." (D.L. 2.78)[13]

Here Plato is quoting the verses of Pentheus, the doomed protagonist in Euripides' *Bacchae* (line 836). Aristippus, by contrast, is quoting the verses of the blind prophet Tiresias, who always perceives the truth that tragic protagonists stubbornly refuse to see (lines 317–18). The moral is obviously that whoever has a truly sound mind can indulge in beautiful clothes, dancing, and bodily pleasure without "being corrupted"—in other words, without beginning to feel that those things are necessary.[14] Such a person will not forget that what really matters is simply to avoid pain and distress and experience some sort of pleasure. The source of that pleasure is unimportant, as a key passage testifies: "[Aristippus] enjoyed the pleasure of what was present, and didn't hunt painfully after the enjoyment of what was not present" (D.L. 2.66). This is why Aristippus can walk away from any particular source of pleasure without even a twinge of regret, as he sometimes demonstrates very conspicuously:

> Once Dionysius ordered [Aristippus] to choose one of three courtesans. Aristippus led away all three, saying, "It didn't do Paris any good to choose just one!"[15] But they say that after he led them away, when he got as far as the gate he dismissed them. That's how strong he was in both choosing and disdaining. (D.L. 2.67; cf. Athen. 544d, Socratic Epistle 9.1 = *SSR* 4a.86, 96, 222)

Aristippus can send away the courtesans because he knows that his night will be none the worse for it. Of course, having sex with three women would be pleasant and therefore choiceworthy. But a display of wit and magnanimity will impress Dionysius and thus secure future enjoyment. And for anyone with an understanding of what is really good and bad, three courtesans are excessive: one sexual partner, or even an alternative source of bodily pleasure, is just as good. This insight provides Aristippus with both the tranquility and the self-mastery to which every ancient Greek sage aspires. It is encapsulated in what may be Aristippus's most famous saying, which refers to his relationship with the renowned courtesan Laïs: "I have, but I am not had" (*SSR* 4a.95–96). In other words, he knows what he wants from this relationship, which is simply pleasure. Unlike so many others, he has not become infatuated with this renowned courtesan; she has no hold over him.[16]

Aristippus's particular interpretation of temperance dovetails with another of his virtues, which is mastery of interpersonal relations. For ease of reference I shall refer to this as "sociability." Aristippus's concern with sociability emerges from the way he reportedly characterizes the product of his understanding and training: "When he was asked what he got out of his philosophy, he said, 'The ability to associate confidently with all people [*pasi tharrountōs homilein*]'" (D.L. 2.68).[17] This saying suggests at least two aspects to Aristippean sociability: first, he can get along with any sort of person whatsoever; second, he can do so without anxiety. It is possible to reconstruct links between both of these and Aristippean temperance. First, because Aristippus understands both cognitively and emotionally that all he really needs is to avoid pain and discover some modicum of pleasure, he feels more relaxed around people. He does not need to impress anyone, since he is not after wealth or political advancement. This is why he feels confident. Second, knowing that just about every situation presents opportunities for enjoyment encourages him simply to accommodate himself to his company at any given moment: "He was able to adapt himself to every place and time and role and to act harmoniously in every circumstance" (D.L. 2.51). This responsiveness could help him to get along with others.

Of course, responsiveness requires versatility and adroitness. That Aristippean sociability encompasses these capacities is corroborated by other sayings and anecdotes. For example, "When he was asked how a wise man differs from someone who is not wise, he said, 'Send them both naked among strangers, and you'll find out'" (D.L. 2.73). The point is not merely that the wise man will be feel comfortable, but also that he will be adroit enough to turn the situation to his advantage. A popular story illustrates this:

> The Socratic philosopher Aristippus was shipwrecked and thrown onto the shore of Rhodes. When he saw geometrical figures drawn there, he reportedly said to his companions, "Cheer up! I see signs of humans," and right away he hurried to the citadel of Rhodes and went straight to the gymnasium. There he was rewarded with gifts for his philosophical disputations, so that he not only equipped himself, he also provided clothes and food for those who were with him. When his companions wanted to return to their country and asked him what news he wanted sent home, he told them to say, "The kind of possessions and traveling provisions free men ought to acquire are those which can swim away from a shipwreck with them." (Vitruvius, *De Arch.* 6.1.1)[18]

This anecdote actually brings together adroitness, confidence, and temperance. Aristippus's adroitness is displayed through his ability to impress the Rhodians with his dazzling wit and wisdom. This adroitness is part of what gives him confidence. (In fact, the word "confidence" appears explicitly in Galen's Greek version: "He became confident [*etharrēse*] when he saw a geometric drawing in the sand" [*Protr.* 5].) And the lesson of the entire anecdote, which Aristippus explicitly communicates to "the folks back home" (nominally the Cyreneans, but more importantly *us* who have not yet completed his philosophical "journey"[19]), is about temperance. In the journey of life, we should only carry the kind and quantity of provisions that could swim away from a shipwreck along with us. Of course, Aristippus has in mind his own philosophical wisdom, which swims as well as he does. That is why a naked sage has everything he needs to flourish among strangers.

These intellectual and ethical virtues lead Aristippus to value both himself and his life as a whole, as a final anecdote attests:

> Once when [Aristippus] was sailing to Corinth and was caught in a storm it happened that he became upset. Someone said, "We common people weren't afraid, but you philosophers acted like cowards!" "Well," he answered, "we aren't contending for the same kind of soul!" (D.L. 2.71)

Aristippus has a lot more to lose than his fellow passengers, because his soul is the repository of his knowledge and capacities. There is an almost heroic grandiloquence in his statement that his soul is not of the same kind as that of his fellow passengers (*ou . . . homoias psuchēs*). In his version of the anecdote, Aulus Gellius brings this out in a slightly different way: "he replied that of course the other hadn't been terribly worried about the soul of a totally worthless loser [*nequissimi nebulonis*], but he was afraid for the soul of *Aristippus!*" (*Noct. Att.* 19.1.1 = SSR 4a.49).

Here we might compare the immense gap in status and worth between the principal characters in Greek epic and tragedy and the common people. Odysseus's ferocious rebuke of Thersites memorably dramatizes this gulf. In book 2 of Homer's *Iliad* King Agamemnon has imprudently tested his Achaean army by encouraging them to give up and go home, and they have eagerly embraced his proposal. Odysseus has salvaged the situation by circulating among the departing men, speaking very differently to the leaders and the commoners: he appeals to the courage of the former, while he tells the latter to

> Sit still and listen to other men's words,
> Who are better than you! You're unwarlike and feeble,
> Of no account in battle or in council.
> There's no way all the Achaeans here can rule like kings.
>
> (*Iliad* 2.200–204)

The bandy-legged, lame, stoop-shouldered, and balding Thersites nevertheless has the gall to criticize Agamemnon for taking the best of the spoils and alienating the Greeks' best warrior. Although Thersites' criticism of Agamemnon is completely accurate, he has spoken out of turn and must be put in his place by Odysseus:

> Stupid Thersites, though you're an audible orator,
> Stop: don't try to be the sort of person who can strive with kings.
> I don't think there's any man here worse than you,
> However many came to Ilium . . .
> I'll tell you something and it will be done:
> If I catch you again acting foolishly like you are now,
> May there no longer be a head on Odysseus' shoulders,
> May I no longer be called the father of Telemachus,
> If I don't take you and strip you of your lovely clothes,
> Your cloak and your tunic, which conceal your shame,
> And send you back to the swift ships in tears,
> Struck from the assembly with shameful strokes.
>
> (*Iliad*, 2.246–64)

Clearly the power dynamics of Aristippus's situation are not like those of Odysseus and Thersites on the plains of Troy. Aristippus and his antagonist are not situated in an explicit military, genealogical, and even ontological hierarchy like Homer's characters.[20] But Aristippus's invocation of his own name is loosely analogous to Odysseus's oath on his own head, just as Aristippus's labeling of his antagonist as a "worthless loser" recalls Odysseus's claim that Thersites is the worst Greek at Troy. These specific parallels aside, the general point is that Aristippus takes seriously what his antagonist tries to turn into a joke: as Odysseus and the other "kings" are set apart from common men like Thersites, the "philosopher" Aristippus is set apart from the class to which this uppity but ignorant critic belongs. And as Odysseus reasserts his status by beating Thersites with his scepter (in the lines immediately following those quoted), Aristippus reasserts his with a put-down witty enough to be remembered throughout antiquity.

It may seem audacious to compare Aristippus with Odysseus, but we will see below that this comparison occurs more than once in our ancient evidence ([Plut.] *Vit. Hom.* 2.150 = *SSR* 4a.55, D.L. 2.79–80 [twice]). Moreover, the shipwreck anecdote we have just encountered recalls Odysseus's shipwreck on Phaeacia, just as the overwhelming impression Aristippus makes on the Rhodians recalls Odysseus's impression on the Phaeacians (whose young men he defeats in athletic competition, and whose king offers him the princess's hand in marriage [*Od.* 7–8]). More generally, heroic posturing is a common element in Greek philosophizing. As Hobbs has convincingly shown, Plato's dialogues contain an extended rumination on the allure and psychology of Homeric heroes and an attempt to represent philosophers like Socrates as alternative role models.[21] Heroic motifs are also scattered throughout many Stoic and Epicurean texts, although no one, to my knowledge, has explored these in detail.[22]

This is something to which I shall remain sensitive in the evidence for the later Cyrenaics, especially Hegesias and Theodorus, for whom the heroic dimension will prove particularly important.

The aim of this section has been to explore how the objects of Aristippus's care and pursuit extend beyond moments of pleasure and pain to comprehend an entire life. The primary concerns which knit together his life are education and the virtues at which it aims. I have not insisted that Aristippean virtues are valued purely as instruments for the generation of pleasure and avoidance of pain, since our evidence does not encourage doctrinal reconstructions, and besides Aristippus may not have favored systematic articulation. But such evidence as we possess suggests that Aristippus tends to view virtues as instrumental goods. It is therefore worth concluding by looking at a third version of the storm-at-sea anecdote. According to Aelian, Aristippus's response to his fellow sailor is, "Naturally [I was afraid]! After all, your concern and risk just now involved an unhappy life, but mine involved a happy one" (*VH* 9.20). In this response what Aristippus values is neither his own heroic superiority nor the virtues contained in his soul. Rather, it is now explicit that Aristippus values those virtues for the sake of the happy life (*biou . . . eudaimonos*) which they will permit him to live in the years to come. Whether or not this wording goes back to Aristippus—and it probably does not[23]—it is entirely plausible that the reason Aristippus prizes the virtues of temperance and sociability is indeed because they support a pleasant life.

4.3. Aristippean Presentism

We have just seen that Aristippus cares about what sort of person he is— whether he is someone with a sound practical understanding of what is really important in life, whether he is someone with the social skills he needs to get what he wants, and perhaps even whether he is one of the "heroes" set apart from the vulgar many. These values strongly suggest that Aristippus also cares about his life as a whole, as Aelian's version of the storm-at-sea anecdote makes explicit. But we must now confront the fact that Aristippus very clearly says that he only cares about what is present; he does not care about what has already happened or what may happen in the future. Furthermore, he exhorts his listeners to adopt the same position. I shall call this Aristippean "presentism."[24] This seems to present an inconsistency in his thinking. However, if we step back and consider analogous statements in another ancient philosophical school, this inconsistency will be greatly diminished.

Let me begin by presenting and analyzing the testimony from Aelian and Athenaeus, which together constitute our key source for this topic. This evidence requires patient unpacking both philologically and exegetically. For convenience of reference I have added numbered and lettered divisions, which do not appear in the original texts.

(1) Even whole schools of philosophers have claimed a lifestyle characterized by voluptuousness. There is, for example, the so-called Cyrenaic school, which took its first principle from Aristippus the Socratic. He embraced pleasant living and declared it was the end and happiness is based on it. (2) Furthermore, he said it was unitemporal. (3) Like wanton people, (4) he thought neither the memory of enjoyments that had happened nor the hope of ones to come were any concern to him. (5) Rather, he judged the good by only one thing, what was present, and thought it was no concern to him that he had experienced enjoyment or would experience it, (6) since one was no longer and the other was not yet and uncertain. (7) This is also how voluptuaries feel when they resolve to get along well just for the present time. (Athenaeus 544a–b, translation adapted from Gulick)

(A) Aristippus seemed to have a very healthy way of putting things (B) when he advised people neither to exert themselves over what is past nor before what is to come. (C) For this sort of thing is a sign of tranquility and a way of showing a cheerful mind. (D) He told ⟨people⟩ to keep their attention on the day, then in turn on that part of the day in which each is thinking or doing something. (E) For he always said that only what is present is ours, neither what has already come nor what is still anticipated. (F) For one has perished, and it's uncertain if the other will happen. (Aelian *VH* 14.6)

We should begin by noting that these are two versions of the same original testimony, as Giannantoni recognizes by grouping them both as *SSR* 4a.174, and not two independent witnesses to Aristippean beliefs. While Aelian may have known and sometimes used the rambling and voluminous work of his older contemporary Athenaeus,[25] the significant discrepancies in these two reports suggests that Aelian had an alternate source in this case.

It is relatively easy to strip away some of what Athenaeus and Aelian or their sources have added to the original core. For example, Athenaeus uses 1, 2, and 7 to situate what he says about Aristippus in the twelfth book of *The Sophists at Dinner*, the topic of which is "people renowned for voluptuousness" (11.509e). The interpolated phrase "like wanton people" in 3 serves the same function. Hence we can exclude 1–3 and 7—none of which occur in Aelian's version—from the shared source. It is also worth noting this anecdote forms the beginning of Athenaeus's miniature biography of Aristippus, which includes a brief doxography and a series of anecdotes (544a–d).[26] Hence the very next sentence begins, "And his life agreed with his doctrine." From this we can see that Athenaeus thinks of 1–7 as having provided "the doctrine" of Aristippus, which in 1 he conflates with the doctrine of the Cyrenaic school as a whole. Thus we will not be surprised to see that he has interpolated quasi-doctrinal elements of Aristippean thought and even Cyrenaic doctrine into the anecdote.

Aelian's version of this passage neither requires any contextualizing within his work nor belongs to a miniature biography, since book 14 of his *Historical Miscellany* progresses from one saying or historical tidbit to another without any apparent plan. What he needs to do instead is concisely establish for his reader what is of interest in this particular intellectual morsel. Section A appears to function in this introductory capacity: "Aristippus seemed to have a very healthy way of putting things . . ." Section C also performs this function: "For this sort of thing is a sign of tranquility and a way of showing a cheerful mind." The first reason to doubt that Aelian means to impute C to Aristippus is that it would make little sense for Aristippus to say that avoiding prospective and retrospective exertion is a "sign" and "way of showing" tranquility. His listeners do not want a way to *display* tranquility; they want to know how to *achieve* tranquility. On the other hand, it makes perfect sense as an explanation Aelian is offering his readers for why he claims in A that Aristippus "had a healthy way of putting things." The second reason to believe C is Aelian's own commentary is that if Aelian had wanted to impute this to Aristippus, he would probably have used an indirect speech construction.[27] So we can also exclude Aelian's A and C, which do not appear in Athenaeus, from the original passage.

What remains still displays significant divergences between the two authors, but it is now becoming far more manageable. For ease of reference, I repeat it here in parallel columns with (loosely) equivalent elements adjacent to one another.

(2) Furthermore, he said it was unitemporal.

(4) he thought neither the memory of enjoyments that had happened nor the hope of ones to come were any concern to him.

  (B) when he advised people neither to exert themselves over what is past nor before what is to come.

  (D) He told ⟨people⟩ to keep their attention on the day, then in turn on that part of the day in which each is thinking or doing something.

(5) Rather, he judged the good by only one thing, what was present, and thought it was no concern to him that he had experienced enjoyment or would experience it,

  (E) For he always said that only what is present is ours, neither what has already come nor what is still anticipated.

(6) since one was no longer and the other was not yet and uncertain.

  (F) For one has perished, and it's uncertain if the other will happen.

We can now see that the core of this testimony is an ethical position—presented either as an exhortation to others or simply as Aristippus's own attitude—and a three-part justification for that position.

Let us begin with the ethical position. First, Aristippus advises against focusing on past and future events. The terminology and emotional tone of this focusing vary between the sources: in Athenaeus, Aristippus refuses to dwell on enjoyable memories or hopes; in Aelian, he discourages others from indulging in backward-looking regret and forward-looking anxiety. Aelian's phrasing is more likely to be original, since the repudiation of enjoyable memories and hopes looks suspiciously like a position the Cyrenaics later adopt in opposition to Epicurus (D.L. 2.89).[28] Aelian's Aristippus then supplements this warning with a positive admonition: his listeners should keep their attention on that part of the day which is circumscribed by their present action or thinking.

The first part of the justification is also presented differently by our two authors. In Athenaeus Aristippus is said to "judge the good by only one thing, what was present" (*heni monōi to agathon krinōn tōi paronti*). We know that he means temporal rather than spatial presence, since he goes on to concretize this phrase in terms of past and future enjoyment: "it was no concern to him that he had experienced enjoyment or would experience it." By contrast, Aelian's Aristippus mentions neither "the good" nor "enjoyment." He simply insists that "neither what has already come nor what is still anticipated" belongs to us. It is not "ours," he literally says. Once again Aelian's reading is probably closer to the original. First, Aelian's version includes some extremely unusual diction, which may go back to the original source itself. Nowhere else in Greek literature, so far as I have been able to determine, does *to phthanon* mean "what has already come."[29] For that matter, the word for "exert oneself after" (*epikamnein*) in B also appears only here in classical Greek literature.[30] Second, Athenaeus's reference to "enjoyment" follows on naturally from his insertion of that term in section 4. I have just suggested that in section 4 it was an interpolation. This is not to deny that language of "enjoyment" is genuinely Aristippean. Enjoyment also appears in other evidence for this topic (see below), some of which Athenaeus probably has in mind. I am merely suggesting that these elements do not belong to this particular saying. So the first part of Aristippus's justification for his attitude would simply be that only what is present is "ours." This claim is more rhetorically powerful than clear, and so must be clarified by what follows.

The second part of the justification is virtually the same in both authors. This is the answer to the question, why does only what is present belong to us? What has gone by "is no longer being" (*ouket' on*), Athenaeus explains; it "has perished" (*apolōlenai*), Aelian says. Athenaeus adds that what is to come "is not yet" (*oupō*). In both cases we are dealing with loosely ontological language. Since what has gone by does not exist, it cannot belong to us or concern us.[31] But it is unlikely, given everything we know about Aristippus, that he intends to commit himself to a metaphysical position. The roots of this argument are not in anything so recondite as the ontology of time. Rather, they lie in commonsensical intuitions. Aristippus is saying that if you define your present by the duration of your current activity or reflection, it seems to possess a reality which what went before and what will follow do not share. If Aristippus is at a symposium with Dionysius, for example, his present is defined by the drinking of wine, sharing of conversation and song, and touching of the courtesan reclining with him on the couch. These things have more vivacity, and therefore more reality, than any memory of the previous day's hardship or any worry about whether he will retain Dionysius's favor tomorrow.[32] Moreover, they are more accessible to action: the connection between Aristippus's decision to reach for more wine and his enjoyment of more wine is more immediate than that between his decision to impress Dionysius and his standing with Dionysius tomorrow.

Both of these interpretations of part two illuminate the third part of the justification Aristippus offers for focusing on the present: the future is "unclear" (*adēlon*). On the one hand, this statement can be understood to reinforce the phenomenological point that future events lack the vivacity of what is present to perception. The future remains hidden; it is "not manifest" (*adēlon*). On the other, it can reinforce the prudential point that future events are less accessible to action, because it is "unclear" (*adēlon*) which factors will intervene between your decision, your action, and the desired outcome.[33]

Now that we have made a careful pass through the key evidence for Aristippean presentism, we are better situated to articulate the potential inconsistency in his thinking. If we are supposed to keep our attention on that part of the day in which we are performing some action or thought, and if future events do not possess enough reality to motivate concern or action, and if future events are in any event inaccessible to action because of the complexity of the causal nexus, then why should we bother educating ourselves? Education may be enjoyable in the present, but it is not always so. Most of its fruits are borne in the future—a temporal domain which supposedly does not concern us. Why, furthermore, should we attempt to develop virtues like temperance or sociability? After all, if we are enjoying ourselves in the present, we have no need of temperance or sociability. And if we are not enjoying ourselves in the present, then we ought to concern ourselves simply with making our present enjoyable: for the future is not yet, and uncertain. Why, finally, should we care about whether our life as a whole will be happy or unhappy? The greater part of each life is either past or still to come, and therefore should not matter to us.

There are at least two texts in which Aristippus more explicitly repudiates care for his life as a whole. The first is sections 1–2 of Athenaeus's testimony, which assert that "pleasant living" is "unitemporal." In metrical texts "unitemporal" (*monokhronos*)—a rare and technical term—means "occupying only one unit of time," which is its probable meaning here.[34] To say that "pleasant living" is "unitemporal" is both initially puzzling and, once understood, oxymoronic.

The Greek word "pleasant living" (*hēdupatheia*) usually denotes habitual behavior, which extends over a long duration.[35] Aristippus may therefore be suggesting, in a deliberately thought-provoking manner, that we think of "pleasant
living" as something to be accomplished within each individual unit of time.

Compare the following passage from Epiphanius:

> Aristippus said that the end of the soul is pleasure, and whoever is expe-
> riencing pleasure, that person is happy [*eudaimōn*], and whoever is not
> experiencing any pleasure is thrice-cursed and unhappy [*kakodaimōn*].
> (*Panarion* VII *de Fide* 9.27 = SSR 4a.177)

Epiphanius is an extremely unreliable source, so we should not put any faith in
his exact wording. However, we can accept the gist of his report, which is that
the present experience of pleasure should be our highest goal. Almost all Greek
philosophers agree that "happiness" (*eudaimonia*), whatever its content, names
the ultimate object of all endeavor. But it was typically thought to be a property
belonging to an entire life, as the historian Herodotus most famously exemplifies in his parable of Solon and Croesus (1.30–32). Count no human happy
(*olbios*), Solon advises the proud king Croesus, until he has died. Plato and
especially Aristotle—who explicitly refers to Solon's advice—adhere firmly to
this conception.[36] Aristippus is therefore suggesting an unusually nonchalant
attitude toward one's own future experiences, although certainly not an unprec-
edented one.[37]

We will see later in this chapter that this tension between caring about one's
life as a whole and caring only about the moment in which one is acting leads
the Annicereans to a radical and problematic formulation of the end. But it
is only by reading Aristippus's statements without any context that we get the
impression that this tension is necessarily a problem for him as well. In fact
these presentist statements probably belong to a form of spiritual exercise that
became nearly universal in Hellenistic philosophy, as Hadot has argued:

> These philosophies were therapies, intended to provide a cure for an-
> guish, and to bring freedom and self-mastery, and their goal was to allow
> people to free themselves from the past and the future, so that they could
> live within the present. . . . This is the true "healthiness of the moment"
> which leads to serenity.[38]

This is particularly clear for the Stoics, whose texts contain several admonitions that resemble that of Aristippus. For example, when discussing the topic
of illness, Seneca writes,

> What good does it do to revisit past suffering and to be miserable now,
> because you have been miserable? . . . So two things should pruned away:
> fear for the future and remembrance of old troubles. The latter no longer
> concerns me, while the former does not yet do so. (*Ep. Mor.* 78.14)[39]

Compare the *Meditations* of the Stoic emperor Marcus Aurelius, who repeatedly speaks of the "gaping of eternity in front and behind" (12.7; cf. 4.3.3, 4.50, 5.24, 12.32) in which "every present time is a point" (6.37). He urges himself to "circumscribe the present time" (7.29; cf. 8.44, 9.25). "If you . . . separate what is hereafter and what is past from time," he elsewhere advises himself, ". . . and you practice living what you are living, that is the present, you will be able to live out whatever remains before death with tranquility, good will, and gratitude toward your guiding spirit" (12.3).[40]

These passages embody a spiritual exercise directed at achieving a particular attitude toward past, present, and future events. The first part of the exercise is to imagine the present moment as a reassuringly manageable segment of the unmanageably vast and complex temporal continuum—whether that be the infinity of cosmic time, or simply the long duration of your own life. This imaginative act sets the foundation for the mental operation Seneca describes as "pruning away" and Marcus describes as "circumscribing" or "separating" what is past or yet to come from what is present. The aim of these operations is to remove the "misery" and "fear" mentioned by Seneca and achieve the "tranquility," "good will," and "gratitude" mentioned by Marcus. The entire exercise constitutes a good example of the "therapy" Hadot has in mind when he says that Hellenistic philosophy aims at serenity in the present moment.[41]

Yet it is clear that neither Seneca nor Marcus intends to commit himself without proviso to the position that only the present matters. Like other Stoics, both believe that what is good for human beings is to perfect their rational natures, which entails living in accordance with ethical virtue (e.g., Sen. *Ep. Mor.* 71.4, 76.9–10; Marc. Aur. 2.16, 3.16, 5.16, 7.67). While the good of perfect rationality and virtue is complete at any single instant (Plut. *Mor.* 1061f = LS 63I), the perfectly rational and virtuous person is unbelievably rare (LS 61N). Stoics like Seneca and Marcus will spend their entire lives trying to achieve this condition through study and habituation. This obviously requires them to look beyond their present condition: they cannot say that future conditions do not concern them, or else they would undercut their own aspirations. Moreover, it is also necessary to consider the future in order to aim at virtue in each action, since one cannot attempt to act like a good son, for example, without considering the future consequences of one's actions for one's mother and father. It is therefore important not to take the spiritual exercise of circumscribing the present moment as a doctrine that would prevent Stoics from valuing future events or taking them into account when deliberating.

In fact both Seneca and Marcus are so far from neglecting the bigger picture that they elsewhere insist every choice must be referred to a single, whole-life-encompassing goal:

> Whenever you want to know what is choiceworthy or avoidance-worthy, look to the highest good, the objective of your entire life. Everything we do should be consistent with that objective. No one can organize his

individual actions except the person who has an ultimate objective for his life. (Sen. *Ep. Mor.* 71.2).

Whoever lacks a single and consistent target for his life cannot be a single and consistent person for his entire life. . . . For if he straightens out all his individual impulses by reference to this ‹target,› he will make all his activities similar and will always be the same person. (Marc. Aur. 11.21)

If the rest of Seneca's and Marcus's writings were lost and only the passages I have quoted were preserved, we might suspect them of maintaining contradictory positions. On the one hand, they urge us to focus only on the present moment. On the other, they exhort us to articulate targets for our entire lives and bear them clearly in mind. But we will not be surprised to hear that the latter exhortation also forms part of a spiritual exercise. This is why Marcus claims that aiming at a single target will turn you into "the same" person, and Seneca goes on to promise, "Let it be clear that only what is fine is good, and all your troubles will rightly be called goods" (71.6). In other words, in these passages a single goal is posited in order to transform our attitudes (troubles become goods) and our selves (we become unified), not as the first step in a theoretical investigation. Theory certainly underpins all these exercises and determines their significance: the Stoics do indeed believe that life has a single target, which is living in accordance with right reason and virtue; and they focus on the present in order more clearly to discern what is reasonable and virtuous in each situation. But these passages are more therapeutic than theoretical, which is why they are speciously inconsistent. At times Stoics find their serenity and moral discernment are increased by visualizing their situation as a punctual moment. At other times, they achieve the same effect by stepping back and thinking about what they want from their lives as wholes.[42]

This digression into Stoic texts allows us to view Aristippus's saying from a different perspective. Like the Stoic admonition to circumscribe the present, I suggest that Aristippus's saying is a spiritual exercise more than a fixed doctrine. In Aelian's version, which I have suggested is closer to the original,[43] Aristippus suggests an effort at progressively increased focus: direct your attention first to the day. Stop worrying about yesterday's embarrassing failure or tomorrow's stressful challenge. Next, pay attention "to that part of the day in which" you are "thinking or doing something." If you are riding a horse or working through a philosophical argument, do not let your mind stray beyond the duration of these activities. In order to aid you in this act of focusing, reflect that what has passed and what is to come are not as fully "real" as what is happening now. The metaphor of ownership pithily reformulates this lesson: past and future events do not belong to you, they are not "yours." If you can accept this, you will both diminish your discomfort and make yourself more receptive to enjoyment.

By saying that this is a spiritual exercise I do not mean to claim that it bears no relation to Aristippus's stable ethical beliefs. To the contrary, there is every reason to suspect that it exemplifies a regular trend in his beliefs about practical reasoning: he prefers to avoid painstaking long-term planning. He puts less faith in his ability to control what happens than in his ability to adapt to it. Presentism as a spiritual exercise thus blends into presentism as a prudential rule of thumb. But in neither case does it amount to a doctrinal strait jacket. That is why Aristippus sees no contradiction between these utterances and his praise for education and virtue.

In fact presentism and care for virtue come together in two more pieces of evidence, the first of which we have already seen several times in this book:

> Aristippus was able to adapt himself to every place and time and role and to act adeptly in every situation. That's why he was more in favor than others with Dionysius, because he always dealt successfully with whatever happened. For he enjoyed the pleasure of things that were present, and didn't hunt painfully after the enjoyment of things that weren't present. (D.L. 2.66)

> And since even Odysseus himself sometimes wore a soft, fleecy mantle, but sometimes rags and a beggar's pouch, and at one time relaxed with Calypso, but at another was treated outrageously by Irus and Melanthius, Aristippus took this as his model for living: he accommodated himself in a healthy way to poverty and pain, but also indulged lavishly in pleasure. ([Plut.] *Vit. Hom.* 2.150 = *SSR* 4a.55; cf. D.L. 2.67, Horace *Ep.* 1.17.12–13 = *SSR* 4a.45; Plut. *Mor.* 330c = *SSR* 4a.56)

The first of these passages speaks clearly to Aristippus's effort to focus on the present. In particular, it explicitly says that he "enjoyed the pleasure of things that were present, and didn't hunt painfully after the enjoyment of things that weren't present." In other words, he directs his attention to current sources of enjoyment, and excludes from his concern things that are not available. Availability is defined not only temporally, but also spatially: he "adapts himself to every place and time." Both texts make the purpose of this exercise more explicit than the passages from Aelian and Athenaeus. First, Aristippus avoids "hunting painfully" (*ouk ethēra ponōi*); he deals with "pains" (*ponous*) "in a healthy way."[44] In short, he reduces his bodily and mental discomfort. Second, he concentrates on "enjoying" what is present. In fact, he gives himself "lavishly" to pleasure.

These passages depict presentism as an exercise at which Aristippus excels *because of his virtues.* The virtues in question overlap with those we have already seen. First, Diogenes speaks emphatically of Aristippus's adaptability: he "was able to adapt himself" (*harmosasthai*) and "to act adeptly [*harmodiōs*] in every circumstance." Pseudo-Plutarch expresses the same idea with a different verb, saying Aristippus "accommodated himself" (*sunēnekhthē*) to poverty and even pain. This ability resembles the virtue I earlier labeled "sociability," the core of which is the capacity get along confidently and effectively with every sort of person. Given the comparison with Odysseus, we might also think of this as an updated form of that hero's "cunning intelligence" (*mētis*).[45] This social cunning blends into temperance as Diogenes' testimony proceeds, beginning with the statement that Aristippus "always dealt successfully with whatever happened." The phrase "deal successfully" (*eu diatithemenos*) implies active manipulation of the situation, which might require charm, quick-wittedness, and courage. But we are also drifting into the domain of temperance, the function of which is to keep before the mind's eye what really matters and what does not. One reason Aristippus makes such good use of available opportunities, this passage hints, is because he knows that most situations offer some pleasures. This hint is corroborated by the very next clause, which says that Aristippus enjoys what is present and does not worry about what is absent.

Far from contradicting the emphasis Aristippus places on education and virtue, his effort to concentrate on the present thus presupposes and helps to justify it. It is only by understanding emotionally and intellectually what matters and knowing that one has the capacity to secure these goods that anyone can really focus on the present. That is why pseudo-Plutarch claims Aristippus learned this by studying Odysseus, who is not only renowned for courage and effectiveness in battle, but more particularly for his temperance and cunning. Paradoxically, it is only a person of firm character and profound insight who can be so malleable, adapting comfortably to every situation.

Like their notional founder Aristippus, the later Cyrenaics are committed to a series of values beyond the experiences of pleasure and pain. In the following three sections I will focus on what the Cyrenaics have to say about wealth, education, and especially virtue. Where it is helpful for reconstructing the reasoning behind their positions, I will introduce additional Aristippean material. Finally, I will consider how these values imply the Cyrenaics are interested in what sort of people they are and what sort of lives they lead. To put it another way, these values show us how the Cyrenaics attempt to construct a way of life on the foundation of the goodness of pleasant experiences and badness of painful ones.[46]

4.4a. The Cyrenaics on Wealth, Justice, and Practical Wisdom

I begin with wealth, since it is a much simpler topic than virtue. Notwithstanding the anecdotes about how Aristippus poured his gold into the sea, told his slave to dump his silver on the road, or advised the Cyreneans to carry only such provisions "as can swim away from a shipwreck," we should not leap to the assumption that he sees no utility in wealth. As we have already seen, his statements are often directed at certain spiritual effects, the achievement of which requires him to imply more radical positions than he would reflectively endorse. In the case of wealth he aims to liberate us from avarice by reminding us that losing money may not mean losing pleasure or incurring pain. But he is very far from advocating the self-imposed poverty of Antisthenes, for example.[47] If he were not, his habit of taking fees from his students would be a little confusing. In fact another source testifies to a much more positive view of wealth:

> Whereas bigger footwear is hard to use, increased property is not so. With the latter great size gets in the way of usage, but you can use the former either in whole or in part as the occasion demands. (Stobaeus 4.31.128 = *SSR* 4a.75)

Here Aristippus is midway between the opinion we might expect from a Cyrenean of his social status, that "wide is the power of wealth,"[48] and Antisthenes' disdain of possessions. The former assumes that wealth is a natural complement to virtue and good birth, which makes it an important component of the good life, while the latter considers wealth a nuisance and an inevitable source of stress. Aristippus's full position seems to have been that wealth is unnecessary: opportunities for enjoyment will always present themselves. However, wealth can be useful for securing diverse pleasures. Thus it is reasonable to devote a modicum of effort to pursuing wealth (e.g., by charging students fees or asking patrons for gifts), but unreasonable to accept any distress for the sake of wealth (e.g., by lamenting the loss of money or property).

A single line in the mainstream Cyrenaic doxography suggests that some of Aristippus's successors hold a similar position: "Wealth is productive of pleasure, although it is not choiceworthy for itself" (D.L. 2.91). This implies that although we should not choose wealth for its own sake, we should nevertheless choose it. The first part of the statement explains this extrinsic choiceworthiness. Wealth is "productive of pleasure": with money one can buy food and drinks, entertain a courtesan, and in other ways obtain what is choiceworthy in itself. In short, wealth is an instrumental good. But the mainstream Cyrenaics' interest in wealth almost certainly remains a moderate one. (It is thus an evolution and not a break from their doctrine when Hegesias declares wealth indifferent [D.L. 2.94].)

This brings me to the topic of Cyrenaic virtues, about which our sources have rather more to say. First, Diogenes' doxography tells us that "Some of the virtues come together even in the foolish. Bodily exercise contributes to the acquisition of virtue" (2.91). It is unclear which virtues the Cyrenaics have in mind here, how they arise from bodily exercise, or how the foolish can possess them. But this at least shows that the Cyrenaics care about ethical character. The same thing is demonstrated by the frequency with which the doxographies for all the Cyrenaic sects mention "the wise man" (*ho sophos*), "the serious man" (*ho spoudaios*), or "the practically wise man" (*ho phronimos*). By convention these are interchangeable ways of denoting the person who has achieved all the intellectual and ethical virtues recognized by any philosophical school. Modern scholars typically refer to this character as "the sage." We will meet Cyrenaic sages throughout the rest of this book, so for now it suffices to quote the doctrine that in a sense underpins all other claims about them: "the wise man exists" (2.93). In other words, the Cyrenaics stipulate that it is possible to achieve the sort of wisdom and virtue at which their philosophy aims, and thus to possess all the capacities they attribute to the sage.[49]

Cyrenaics care about these capacities because they lead to pleasure and the avoidance of pain, as two closely related reports inform us:

> The so-called Cyrenaic and Annicerean philosophers located all good in pleasure and said that virtue was praiseworthy because it was productive of pleasure. When these sects had disappeared Epicurus flourished and defended more or less the same position. (Cic. *Off.* 3.116 = SSR 4a.189).

> Epicurus and the Cyrenaics say that the first thing belonging to us [*to prōton oikeion*] is pleasure, but that virtue, which has emerged for the sake of pleasure, produces pleasure. (Clem. Al. *Strom.* 2.21.128.1 = SSR 4a.199)[50]

This testimony make two things clear. First, the mainstream Cyrenaics and Annicereans consider virtue to be a good. Second, they consider it an instrumental good, like wealth. Exactly why and how will be easier to understand if we investigate the specific virtues mentioned in our sources.

I will first consider the virtue of justice. Several anecdotes suggest that Aristippus is a fair and law-abiding sort of person, but they do not explain the reason for this aspect of his behavior. For example, in one anecdote he hires a speech-writer for a trial, who asks him, "So what good did Socrates do you?" Aristippus answers, "He made the words you've said about me true." (D.L. 2.71).[51] Athenian court speeches often say very little about actual charges, but a great deal about the character of the plaintiff and the defendant.[52] So assuming this anecdote takes place at Athens, it suggests that Aristippus is the sort of person who deserves to win his case: a generally fair and meritorious man. Another saying confirms Aristippus's just behavior: "When he was asked how philosophers excel, Aristippus replied, 'If all the laws are taken away, we'll go on living in the same way'" (D.L. 2.68).[53] This could be taken to mean that philosophers pursue justice for its own sake, but since Aristippus scarcely mentions the words "just" or "justice," this is unlikely. It is more likely that he values justice for the sake of its pleasant consequences.

This would anticipate the mainstream Cyrenaic position, as the following passages reveal:

> Pleasure is good even if it comes from the most unseemly sources. . . . For even if the action is out of place, still the pleasure is choiceworthy for itself and something good. (D.L. 2.88)

> Nothing is just or fine or shameful by nature, but by custom and habit. Yet the serious man will do nothing out of place because of existing penalties and beliefs. (D.L. 2.93)

The second passage clarifies what the Cyrenaics mean by "justice." Justice is not a natural property of actions; the categories "just" and "unjust" are created by the conventions of each community.[54] The two passages together tell us why the Cyrenaics, who are interested in natural rather than conventional goodness, nevertheless behave justly. They believe that actions should be chosen or avoided on the basis of the pleasure or displeasure associated with them. Even "unseemly" and "out of place" actions may be choiceworthy if they are pleasant. However, the Cyrenaics pay careful attention to both the laws and customs of their community, because *other* people believe in these norms. There are therefore both formal and informal penalties associated with unjust behavior, and for this reason the Cyrenaics cultivate justice.

The Cyrenaics' opinion on "practical wisdom" (*phronēsis*) is even more emphatically positive. In fact they say more or less the same thing about practical wisdom in particular as about virtue in general: "practical wisdom is a good, but is choiceworthy because of what arises from it, not for itself" (D.L. 2.91). While no definition of practical wisdom survives, we can approximate its meaning by comparison with the Cyrenaics' philosophical contemporaries. We know that for Aristotle and his immediate successors practical wisdom is intimately involved in the activity of all the other ethical virtues (Arist. *EN* 6; [Arist.] *MM* 1.34). For example, Theophrastus might generally wish to be just. He might also understand that justice involves the distribution of good and bad things according to merit. But unless he can discern what this entails in concrete circumstances, he cannot actualize his desire to behave justly. Practical wisdom is the union of correct goals and the discernment of how they apply in particular circumstances. This is why Aristotle says that the practically wise person deliberates well about what is good and bad for his life as a whole (*EN* 1140a25–28): practical wisdom is both necessary and—barring the effects of luck—sufficient for choosing actions which actually make the agent's life good. Practical wisdom also occupies a central position in the ethics of the Cynics (D.L. 6.13, 6.18), Epicurus (D.L. 10.132), and the Stoic Zeno (LS 61A, C). It is therefore reasonable to conjecture that Cyrenaic practical wisdom underpins whatever other virtues they recognize, and that it combines the understanding of theoretical principles with the ability to apply them in practice.

Practical wisdom will therefore be evident in every reflective decision and purposeful action of the Cyrenaic sage. In order to get a better sense of its operations, in the next section I will turn to two arenas of its activity: skillful speaking and the moderation of emotion.

4.4b. The Cyrenaics on Speaking Well and Freedom from Negative Emotions

One place in the Cyrenaic doxography where we may begin looking for the activity of practical wisdom is in the following passage.

> They refrained from physics because of its obvious inapprehensibility. But they embraced logic because of its utility. Meleager in book 2 of *On Doctrines* and Clitomachus in book one of *On the Sects* says they

believed both the physical and the dialectical parts of philosophy are useless. Whoever has thoroughly learned the rational account about good and bad things can speak well and be free from superstitious dread and escape the fear about death. (D.L. 2.92)

In order to understand the connections of thought in this doxographical jumble we should work backward from the goals announced at its conclusion: speaking well, being free from superstitious dread, and escaping the fear of death. We must also keep in mind the contemporary philosophical interlocutors presupposed by these doctrines.

Let us begin with the goal of "speaking well" (*eu legein*). What exactly this connotes is unclear. It may refer to the philosophical pursuit of truth, whether in cooperative inquiry or polemical debates. On the other hand, it may refer to rhetorical ability: articulacy, quick-wittedness, persuasiveness, and so on. (Of course, these two may overlap.) Either way, it is connected to the embrace of logic and rejection of dialectic earlier in the passage.

"Dialectic" names a practice developed in the fifth and fourth centuries BCE. In both Socratic dialogues and Aristotle's *Topics* this involves one interlocutor eliciting a thesis from the other and then testing the consistency of that thesis with the other's belief set through rigorous questioning. The Dialectic offshoot of the Megaric school clearly engaged in similar exercises, since we are told that Dionysius of Chalcedon "first called them Dialectics because they constructed their arguments through questioning and answering" (D.L. 2.106). The Cyrenaics are therefore denying that this sort of exercise leads to the effective pursuit of truth, rhetorical ability, or both.

While our sources do not tell us why the Cyrenaics make this claim, it is possible for us to make some conjectures. One supposed function of dialectic is to clarify ethical intuitions. In Socratic dialectic, for example, intuitions are the bedrock of ethical reasoning. By contrast, the Cyrenaics believe the only foundation for ethical truths is experience. This could explain why they oppose the emphasis on dialectic in some of their competitor schools. Another function of dialectic is to develop the ability to criticize or defend a thesis. This relates to rhetorical ability.[55] Apparently the Cyrenaics believe that "thoroughly learning the rational account about good and bad things" is a sounder foundation for rhetoric. Of course, this "thorough learning" is not simply a matter of memorizing principal doctrines. The Cyrenaics also study logic, the content of which is suggested by one of the five parts of Cyrenaic philosophy, "on arguments" (*peri pisteōn*; S.E. *M.* 7.11–15 = *SSR* 4a.168). Understanding the available forms of argumentation could help Cyrenaics to apply "the rational account about what is good and what is bad" to particular situations. In fact, this may be part of what "thoroughly learning" means. This would then be one manifestation of practical wisdom.

Let us now turn to the goals of liberation from "superstitious dread" (*deisidaimonia*) and escaping "the fear about death" (*ton peri thanatou phobon*). These goals are connected with the rejection of physics, just as the goal of speaking well was connected with the repudiation of dialectic. This becomes obvious when we reflect that superstition and the fear of death are principal concerns for Epicurean ethics, and that Epicurus claims an understanding of physics is necessary for eliminating them.[56] In order to make an educated guess about how the Cyrenaic sage dispels these fears without understanding physics we must detour into Cyrenaic thinking about the emotions.

While we cannot fully reconstruct Cyrenaic thinking on this topic,[57] we can glean some particulars by combining the foregoing evidence with the following passages:

> The wise man will neither feel envy nor erotic passion nor superstitious dread, because these things happen through empty belief. But he will feel distress and fear, because they happen naturally. (D.L. 2.91)

> They say that some people are distressed more than others. (D.L. 2.93)

> The Cyrenaics think that distress is not caused by every bad thing, but only by an unexpected and unanticipated bad thing. (Cic. *Tusc.* 3.28; cf. 3.52)

It will be easiest to begin with what these passages say about "distress" (Greek *lupē*, Latin *aegritudo*). It is clear that the Cyrenaics, like most other philosophers of the period, analyze emotions partly in terms of their cognitive structure. This is apparent from their assertion that erotic passion and superstitious dread "happen through empty belief."[58] This suggests that beliefs are among the necessary causes of these emotions; thus sages, who lack these "empty beliefs," do not experience these feelings. In Cicero's testimony we can detect the primary belief that is involved in distress, namely, "something bad is happening to me." Unless the person thinking this has sufficiently anticipated the bad thing that is happening, he will feel upset. Prudent people are rarely surprised by what the world throws at them, which is one reason why "some people are distressed more than others." Yet even the sage feels upset sometimes, which we can explain in two ways. First, the Cyrenaics might admit that no one anticipates every accident. Second and more likely, Cicero's source might have over-simplified the Cyrenaic position.[59] The Cyrenaics may want to claim that anticipation eliminates many negative feelings, but not *every* vestige of distress. For this reason they insist that fear and distress "happen naturally": it is natural (i.e., inevitable and appropriate) to be distressed by some things.[60]

Let us now focus on the fear of death and superstitious dread. It is reasonable to assume that as distress involves the belief that something bad is happening now, fear involves the belief that something bad will happen in the future.[61] It might then be objected that the premeditation of future evils, which is recommended in order to mitigate distress, would only exacerbate fear. But this is not necessarily so. In fact the Cyrenaics could argue that firm understanding and lucid anticipation of what is truly bad ameliorate both distress and fear. Failure in either understanding or anticipation increases fear, because you worry about many things that are not truly bad, imagine others that are unlikely to happen, and generally feel unprepared to cope with eventualities. It is *uncertainty* that exacerbates fear. Recall that "confidence" was an Aristippean watchword. Just as confident expectation of bad things mitigates the distress they cause, so too it lessens fear.

Fear of death and superstitious dread are both species of fear. The primary cause of each must therefore be the belief that something bad will happen. A secondary cause may be uncertainty about the bad thing. In the case of death, this could include the process of dying, deprivation of the goods of living, or events in the afterlife. In the case of superstition, it must be punishment by divine and daemonic beings, whether in this life or the afterlife.

We are now in a position to hazard a (very speculative) explanation for how the sage is free from superstitious dread and the fear of death. It is possible that he acknowledges some badness in death, but eliminates fear of this badness through lucid contemplation of death's inevitability. In this way he would attack the secondary cause of this emotion. But it is more likely that he sees no grounds for believing either death or the gods will cause him any harm.[62] Thus he would attack the primary cause of these fears. For example, he might argue that we simply have no idea whether the gods intervene in our lives, whether there is an afterlife, or whether the gods punish or reward people in that afterlife. Fear of divine punishment, whether in life or after death, would therefore be caused by "empty beliefs" about the gods' personalities and powers.[63]

Let us now return to the topic of practical wisdom and consider how the foregoing illuminates its operation. Although the evidence has not permitted a very detailed reconstruction of Cyrenaic theories of the emotions, it suffices to show that once again the sage must not only understand core doctrines, but also be flexible in their application. At the most fundamental level he must understand the "account about good things and bad things." This surely begins with the doctrine that only pleasure is intrinsically good and pain intrinsically bad. It probably also encompasses the theory of the experiences, which justifies this doctrine, and the theory of the end, which encapsulates its relevance to practical ethics. Second, he will need to apply these fundamental theories to superstition and the fear of death. This will involve learning arguments against the painfulness of death or the plausibility of divine punishment. Finally, he will need to select and adjust appropriate arguments when faced with a particular stimulus.

For example, Cyrene's sacred laws prescribe that a woman should visit the temple of Artemis during her pregnancy. If she does not, she may expiate her omission by sacrificing a full-grown animal and keeping pure on the seventh, eighth, and ninth days after birth.[64] Paraebates might therefore experience twinges of anxiety if his pregnant wife could not go to the temple. He might feel vaguely uneasy if he chose to avoid the expense of sacrificing a full-grown animal in expiation.[65] In such a case he would have to reflect that his uneasiness was caused by the judgment that something bad would happen to him: namely, that Artemis, goddess of childbirth, would punish his family for their haughty negligence. He would then need to recall that only bodily and emotional pains are truly bad. Finally, he would need to rehearse a series of arguments against the reasonableness of the belief that Artemis would cause him pain. (For example, he might question the belief that Artemis exists, that she is capable of causing pain, or that she cares about ritual purity, animal sacrifice, or attendance at her temple.) In this way he would attempt to dissolve the unwarranted beliefs underlying and causing his anxiety.

Thus the practical wisdom which applies "the rational account about good things and bad things" is a complex skill. Beginning with assent to Cyrenaic principles and understanding of fundamental Cyrenaic arguments, it must also comprehend the ability to recombine and apply these principles and arguments in the subtle and versatile ways required in order to speak well in particular situations and defuse particular episodes of uncomfortable emotion.

4.4c. The Cyrenaics on Education, Habituation, and Spiritual Exercises

This brings me to the place of education in Cyrenaic thinking. Since we have very little testimony on this topic, I will be brief. Even in the generation of Aristippus's immediate disciples we hear about Antipater "having many seats in his school" (Gnom. Vat. 743 n. 353 = SSR 4c.2).[66] I have detailed the relationships of the Cyrenaics with each other and with non-Cyrenaics in chapter 2. It is safe to assume that the education which was happening in these places of learning and through these relationships involved protracted study and practice. The testimony we have just seen about "thoroughly learning (ekmemathēkota) the rational account of good and bad things" begins to confirm this assumption.

A passage from the Annicerean doxography adds another dimension:

> Reason isn't sufficient for feeling confident and rising above common opinion. It's necessary to habituate ourselves because of the bad disposition that's been nurtured in us for a long time. (D.L. 2.96)

This passage corroborates what I have already argued, that understanding principles and arguments in the abstract is not sufficient for achieving the goals of Cyrenaic philosophy. "Reason" (ton logon) alone cannot cure a "bad disposition" (phaulēn diathesin): it cannot free us from the grip of "common opinion" (tēs tōn pollōn doxēs) or replace our anxiety with the feeling of "confidence" (to tharrēsai). For this we need to supplement abstract reasoning with "habituation" (anethizesthai). "Habituation" is one of the standard ways ancient philosophers describe the effort to internalize abstract principles through spiritual exercises.[67] Aspiring sages require a great deal of exercise in applying Cyrenaic theories; they need to have sound intuitions and persuasive arguments at hand in every sort of situation.

For the most part the details of this training have been lost, but there are three spiritual exercises we can plausibly attribute to the Cyrenaics. One of them is the Aristippean technique of telescoping your attention, shifting from the broad lens of your past and future to the narrow scope of your immediate activity. As we will see in the next section, presentism remains an important element of post-Aristippean Cyrenaicism. The second is suggested by the passing remark that "bodily exercise contributes to the acquisition of virtue" (D.L. 2.91). This could mean that at least some Cyrenaics recommend physical fitness, although the details are not communicated to us.[68]

The third brings us back to the topic of emotions, where the assertion that distress is caused by "an unexpected and unanticipated bad thing" suggests a sort of prophylactic mental training. Cicero himself connects this doctrine with the "premeditation of future evils" (3.29) and "mental foresight and preparation" (3.30). Graver muses that Cicero's discussion

> suggests a regular practice, perhaps daily, in which one looks ahead and tries to imagine each of the terrible things that can happen to a person. It is a sort of visualization technique, intended to soften the impact of those events if any of them should actually come to pass.[69]

Here Graver rightly emphasizes the habit of imagining what can happen to *you* in particular. The exercise probably also involves setting what might happen to you against the backdrop of the regularity and universality of what happens to *everybody*. This is a common palliative strategy in ancient consolation literature. Hence Cicero adds,

> Surely this is that illustrious and divine wisdom, to have thoroughly understood and worked through the human condition, not to be surprised by anything when it happens, and to believe even before it comes to pass that nothing is impossible. (*Tusc.* 3.30)

Understanding that what happens to you has frequently happened to others makes it slightly more palatable, because others have managed to get through it. Moreover, there is no use fighting against the universal human condition.

By increasing their mastery of such exercises and their facility in the application of principles and arguments Cyrenaics gradually approach the ideal of practical wisdom espoused by their school. A final piece of evidence makes this explicit: "They allowed progress both in philosophy and in other things" (D.L. 2.93).[70] In other words, just as someone may become progressively better at riding horses, so too they may become progressively wiser. But just like good horsemanship, philosophical wisdom can only be reached with sustained effort.

4.4d. Interim Conclusion

The foregoing makes very clear that the Cyrenaics care about what sort of people they are and what sort of lives they live. While all of the values we have just seen are grounded in the goodness of pleasant experiences and the badness of painful experiences, they expand the consequences of these fundamental criteria in such a way as to imply long-term projects. I shall defend this claim in some detail, since it has frequently been denied.[71]

First, caring about wealth (even very moderately) implies caring about my future experiences. Sometimes this will be a clearly foreseen future experience. For example, Paraebates might sell a plot of land in order to purchase the favors of a very exclusive courtesan who is going to visit Cyrene. More often, however, wealth is valued for the sake of a vaguely anticipated series of experiences. For example, Paraebates charges fees for his teaching even if he does not immediately need to pay for anything. He assumes he will want to pay for something at some time. In this way valuing wealth begins to knit together Paraebates' life on the basis of his concern for the pleasures and pains money can elicit or allay.

Virtues perform this function much more systematically and effectively. Let us begin with the virtue of justice. If Paraebates had to repay a debt, for example, and the contract for that debt had been lost during the civil war of 320–319 BCE, he would not honor it simply in order to preserve his just character. The Cyrenaics do not believe a just character is an intrinsic good. Rather, he would honor the contract in order to avoid distressing problems with his creditor and his creditor's friends and family. Moreover, he would have in mind that this would give him a better reputation in the community, since most people value fair dealing. And he would rightly anticipate that further civil disturbances could soon follow (as they did in 313–312 and 305–1 BCE), during which the tables could be turned on people who had taken unfair advantage. It would therefore be his concern over future experiences of pleasure and pain, including those far away and not clearly foreseen, that would motivate his just behavior in the present.

The activity of practical wisdom would also project Paraebates' horizon of care into his future. In fact the Cyrenaics would probably classify prudent attention to customs and laws, which I have just been discussing, as a manifestation of practical wisdom. Among the tasks of practical wisdom must be to foresee the consequences of actions and avoid disaster.[72] If practical wisdom encompasses all the techniques I have surveyed in the preceding sections for securing pleasure and diminishing pain, then we can also include here the premeditation of future evils. Clearly the Cyrenaics only practice this exercise because they care about the impact future misfortunes will make on their future selves.

Perhaps the most important way in which Cyrenaic philosophy knits together an entire life with connections of caring, planning, and effort is through education. While studying and practicing may be pleasant in themselves, it is largely for the sake of progress that they are undertaken. Progress, in turn, is valued for the sake of the pleasures it will generate and the pain and distress it will alleviate. Commitment to studying and habituation thus implies caring about those future pleasures and pains. In the long term the life which emerges is at least an approximation of how Cyrenaics would describe overall happiness: an existence with little pain or distress and plenty of pleasure and joy.

4.5. Cyrenaic Presentism

As with Aristippus, with the later Cyrenaics there is an apparent inconsistency between caring about one's life as a whole and striving to focus on the present moment. Unfortunately, the doxographical passage which contains our primary evidence on this topic is extremely difficult to construe. Parts of it are clearly corrupt beyond exact reconstruction. It is therefore necessary to work through it carefully in order to grasp the combination of attitudes it conveys.

Here is the passage in full:

> Bodily pleasures are actually much better than mental ones, and bodily disturbances are worse. Hence it is by these that criminals are more often punished. For they held that experiencing bodily pain is harder, and experiencing ⟨bodily⟩ pleasure is more comfortable for us. Hence they exercised more economical management concerning one of these. For this reason, although pleasure is choiceworthy in itself, the disturbing sources of some pleasures are often opposed. The result is that the accumulation of pleasures, which does not produce happiness, appears to them very troublesome. They think that the wise man does not live pleasantly in every detail, nor does the fool live painfully in every detail, but for the most part. It's enough if someone pleasantly [*text corrupt*] as each one happens. (D.L. 2.90–91)

I will begin by taking the first five sentences as a group, which concludes with the assertion that "the disturbing sources of some pleasures are often opposed." What interests me in this section is the notion of "economical management" in the fourth sentence: "Hence they exercised more economical management concerning one of these" (ὅθεν καὶ πλείονα οἰκονομίαν περὶ θάτερον ἐποιοῦντο). The antecedent for "one of these" is mysterious. One possibility is that it refers to bodily pleasure as opposed to bodily pain. The other is that it refers to bodily rather than mental experiences. Either way, what is important for my current argument is that the Cyrenaics exercise some "economical management" regarding agreeable and disagreeable experiences, whether bodily or mental.

This isolated but important word has attracted surprisingly little attention from commentators.[73] It may simply denote some sort of organized and purposeful activity. In this case we would probably be dealing with prudential planning; the Cyrenaics would be "economically managing" pleasure and pain by weighing up the pain and distress involved in obtaining any given pleasure, the value of that pleasure itself, and the value of its consequences. Another possibility is that we are dealing with "economics" in the technical sense it developed in late classical and Hellenistic philosophy. Treatises on "economic management" survive from Xenophon, Aristotle's student Theophrastus, and (with some lacunae) the Epicurean Philodemus.[74] In that case we would be dealing with the husbandry of household resources. In other words, we would be talking about the instrumental value of property and wealth.

These first five sentences once again suggest that the Cyrenaics care about their own future experiences, not merely about immediately available pleasures and pains. That is why they engage in prudential planning or husbandry of resources. But the rest of the passage communicates a different attitude. The sixth sentence reads, "For this reason, although pleasure is choiceworthy in itself, the disturbing sources of some pleasures are often opposed" (διὸ καὶ καθ᾽ αὑτὴν αἱρετῆς οὔσης τῆς ἡδονῆς τὰ ποιητικὰ ἐνίων ἡδονῶν ὀχληρὰ πολλάκις ἐναντιοῦσθαι). Once again the meaning of this sentence and the sequence of thought leading up to it are obscure. Why does this sentence begin with the conjunction, "For this reason?" It is possible that this is simply an error: in the transmission and truncation of the doxographical material, something has become confused. If the conjunction has any sense, it must be that this sentence explains (at least in part) the "economical management" of the previous sentence. It would be saying that in the course of prudential planning, the wise Cyrenaic will recognize that the sources of many pleasures are themselves unacceptably painful or distressing.

This would be similar to what Epicurus expresses in strikingly similar language: "No pleasure is bad in itself, but the sources of some pleasures bring with them disturbances many times greater than the pleasures" (*Rat. Sent.* 8).[75] The difference is that Epicurus appears to be thinking about the consequences of actions undertaken for the sake of pleasure. For example, in classical Greece the consequences of seducing your neighbor's wife may be imprisonment or even murder.[76] We have already seen that Cyrenaics will avoid this sort of "out of place" action. But their focus in our passage seems rather to be on the difficulty of bringing about future pleasures; it is the sources of pleasure they call disturbing, not what pleasures bring in their wake. A better example of what worries them might be the toil involved in pursuing power. As Xenophon's Aristippus argues, training for leadership requires much more suffering than leadership itself can counterbalance with compensatory pleasure (*Mem.* 2.1).

This interpretation of the sixth sentence is confirmed by the seventh sentence, which reads, "The result is that the accumulation of pleasures, which does not produce happiness, appears to them very troublesome" (ὡς δυσκολώτατον αὐτοῖς φαίνεσθαι τὸν ἀθροισμὸν τῶν ἡδονῶν εὐδαιμονίαν μὴ ποιοῦντα). This sentence has received a broad array of translations from scholars, some of which are incompatible with one another.[77] It is important to make note of this disagreement, since it will prevent us from putting too much weight on its precise wording. That said, I believe that my translation preserves and reconciles the insights of most previous translators. On my reading, the lesson of this sentence follows on naturally from the sentence before it. The foregoing had warned against toiling today for tomorrow's pleasure; this sentence warns against striving to accumulate enough pleasures to constitute a happy life, since the effort will be counterproductive. The problem is that such an accumulative endeavor "does not produce happiness." In other words, there are strict limits to the utility of prudential planning. Trying to plan for your entire life simply leads to wasted effort and anxiety.

The upshot is expressed in the final two sentences. The penultimate sentence reads as follows: "They think that the wise man does not live pleasantly in every detail, nor does the fool live painfully in every detail, but for the most part." (Ἀρέσκει δ᾿ αὐτοῖς μήτε τὸν σοφὸν πάντα ἡδέως ζῆν, μήτε πάντα φαῦλον ἐπιπόνως, ἀλλὰ κατὰ τὸ πλεῖστον). In other words, filling every moment with pleasure is beyond human power. Even the Cyrenaic sage cannot accomplish it. For that matter, even the vulgar person—the unenlightened commoner—manages to live pleasantly some of the time. In other words, there is a troubling modicum of luck involved: pleasure does not always follow merit. This means that anyone who tries to arrange for a thoroughly pleasant life is bound to fail. Not only that, but he will compound the badness of his ineluctable misfortunes with frustration and disappointment.

The ultimate sentence therefore recommends that Cyrenaics restrict their prudential planning, although the text here is desperately corrupt: "It's enough if someone pleasantly [*text corrupt*] as each one happens" (ἀρκεῖ δὲ κἂν κατὰ μίαν τις προσπίπτουσαν † ἡδέως ἐπανάγῃ †).[78] Whatever the verb and direct object missing from this sentence, it nevertheless communicates roughly how the sage copes with the impossibility of planning for a thoroughly pleasant and painless life. Like Aristippus, he concentrates on individual activities or events. In other words, he manages to live pleasantly on the whole precisely by not making a systematic effort to guarantee his future pleasures.

The question with which we are once again left is whether there is a contradiction between this passage, which mandates letting go of the future, and all the ways in which Cyrenaics manifestly care about and try to manage their futures. This problem is more pressing than it was for Aristippus, because his successors commit themselves to an explicit doctrinal system. However, the way I have presented the material should already suggest that I think this contradiction can be avoided. There are many ways of caring about the future, and foreswearing one does not entail foreswearing all of them. Nevertheless, it is clearly important for the Cyrenaics to articulate their doctrines in such a way as to avoid self-contradiction. It is the task of the following section to see how they address this task.

4.6. Cyrenaic Formulations of the End

In section 3.6 I began discussing the Cyrenaic formulations of the ends. There I was considering the Cyrenaic use of "ends" (*telē*) to denote the most complete expressions of goodness and badness. It is in this sense that ancient philosophers often speak of an "end of good things" and an "end of bad things." In the current section I will be focusing instead on the use of "end" to denote the ultimate object of desire and endeavor. The classic exposition of this sense of the end appears in the opening of Aristotle's *Nicomachean Ethics*:

> So if what is done has some end that we want for its own sake, and everything else we want is for the sake of this end; and if we do not choose everything for the sake of something else (because this would lead to an infinite progression, making our desire fruitless and vain), then clearly this will be the good, indeed the chief good. Surely, then, knowledge of the good must be very important for our lives? And if, like archers, we have a target, are we not more likely to hit the right mark? (1094a18–24, trans. Crisp)

There are three interlocking formal criteria for the ultimate end and "chief good" about which Aristotle is speaking.[79] First, it is "final": it is the ultimate explanatory principle and motivator for desire, choice, and action. Aristotle uses a military example: during war we choose to make bridles for the sake of riding horses, but we choose to ride horses for the sake of fighting, and we choose fighting for the sake of victory. Victory is therefore the end which explains and motivates bridle-making in this context. Aristotle believes human life is full of such subordinate and superordinate ends, but one single end stands alone at the top of the pyramid. Because all choices and desires can be traced back to this end, which is choiceworthy for its own sake, desire is not "fruitless and vain." Second, the end is "comprehensive": it subsumes and organizes all the subordinate ends. This is why the end can serve as a "target" for all our purposeful activity, because while each activity has its own end, these ends only become choiceworthy due to the role they play in realizing the ultimate end. The third criterion remains implicit in this passage, but is clearly expressed later (esp. 1097b). The end is "sufficient": when we have it, we desire nothing further.

Our evidence testifies to two different formulations of the end by the mainstream Cyrenaics. Each of these formulations deals differently with finality, comprehensiveness, and sufficiency. Moreover, each represents a slightly different way of resolving the potential contradiction between caring about your life as a whole and attempting to focus on immediate activities and experiences. I will collect and analyze the evidence for each of these formulations separately.

I begin with the formulation of the end ascribed both to Aristippus's grandson the Metrodidact and to the Cyrenaics as a group. Here are the two principal pieces of evidence for this formulation:

> Both the Cyrenaics and Epicurus are among those who take their start from pleasure. These explicitly say that the end is living pleasantly, and that only pleasure is an end-like good. (Clem. Al. *Strom.* 2.127.1.1–2 = SSR 4a.198)

> Aristippus was an entirely lush-liver, a real pleasure-lover, but he himself didn't speak explicitly about the end. Implicitly, however, he said that the

essence of happiness lies in pleasures, since he was always talking about pleasure, and this led those who came to him to suspect he was saying the end was to live pleasantly.

⟨Aristippus'⟩ daughter Arete was among ⟨his⟩ auditors, and she had a son whom she named Aristippus, though he was called the Metrodidact because he was introduced to philosophy by her. He clearly defined the end as living pleasantly, assigning a place to pleasure in motion. (Eus. *PE* 14.18.31–32 = *SSR* 4a.173 + 4b.4).

Since Clement conflates the Cyrenaic and Epicurean positions, it would be imprudent to put much faith in the details of the first of these passages. In particular, we cannot know what Clement means by "end-like good" (*teleion agathon*) or whether this designation even goes back to the Cyrenaics.[80] However, it is true that for Epicureans the end is living in a state of tranquil pleasure.[81] It is therefore plausible that "living pleasantly" is at least a fair approximation of the Cyrenaic end as well.

This plausibility rises to probability in the light of Eusebius's testimony in the second passage. I have given enough context to illustrate the exactitude of his report, since some scholars have suggested that Eusebius is confused in his presentation here.[82] Eusebius is generally an excellent source, and in this case asserts that the Metrodidact "clearly defined" (*saphōs hōrisato*) the end (as living pleasantly). Moreover, there is no need to seek an excuse for assimilating the Metrodidact's end to the second formula, which we will encounter below. Even if that alternate formula is correctly assigned to the mainstream Cyrenaics— rather than originating with Anniceris, as I will suggest—we have seen in section 2.3 that mainstream Cyrenaicism encompasses a large number of philosophers operating over at least three quarters of a century. It would hardly be surprising if there were some doctrinal disagreements and inconsistencies.

Thus we can accept that "living pleasantly" (*to hēdeōs zēn*) is at least a good paraphrase of a genuine mainstream Cyrenaic end. The next question is how this formulation bears on finality, comprehensiveness, and the tension between presentism and caring about life as a whole. In order to answer we should begin by noting that "living + adverb" is a very common way for ancient Greek philosophers to formulate the sort of end Aristotle proposes in the *Nicomachean Ethics*. In fact Aristotle himself says that everyone agrees that this end is named "happiness," "doing well," or "living well" (*EN* 1095a18–20). That is why his own complex and subtle treatment of the end is later summarized by doxographers as "the use of virtue in a complete life" (D.L. 5.30) or even simply "living according to virtue" (Clem. Al. *Strom.* 2.21.128.3).[83] Among the Stoics, Zeno reportedly says the end is "living in agreement with nature" or "living according to virtue"; Chrysippus says it is "living according to experience of what happens naturally" (D.L. 7.87); and Posidonius says it is "living while studying the truth and organization of the universe and contributing to that organization insofar as is possible, while in no way being led by the irrational part of the soul" (Clem. Al. *Strom.* 2.21.129.1). We know that all these philosophers espouse comprehensive final ends. One reason they use the formula "living + adverbial phrase" is because it captures the comprehensive force of these ends, which give shape to lives in their entire synchronic complexity and diachronic duration. We therefore have an initial reason to expect that this Cyrenaic end is also comprehensive.

This chapter has provided all the materials we need for explaining how the Cyrenaic end can be not only comprehensive, but also final and sufficient. Let us start by making more explicit that "living pleasantly" is a synonym for "happiness." The Cyrenaics define happiness as "the composition [*sustēma*] of particular pleasures, among which are numbered both those that have gone by and those that are to come" (D.L. 2.87). We have already seen the ways in which Cyrenaic choices and values can be taken to presume this as their target. To recall just a few examples, it can be argued that it is for the sake of some such composition of pleasures that we choose wealth, avoid unjust behavior, and pursue practical wisdom by studying theories and practicing spiritual exercises. Wealth, justice, and wisdom are all ends, but none of them is a final end; the ultimate explanation for the Cyrenaics' desire for wealth and virtue is the pleasant life they help to create. These goals are comprehended and given meaning by the larger project of living pleasantly. Thus living pleasantly is a final and comprehensive end. Moreover, if we could accomplish the goal of living pleasantly, there would be nothing further to desire.[84] So living pleasantly is also a sufficient end.

Given this formulation of the end, it is relatively easy to harmonize the Cyrenaics' interest in their entire lives with their advice to focus on present activities and experiences. When the Cyrenaics say that their sage simply takes each opportunity as it comes, trying to find the pleasure in each moment, we could explain that this does not imply disinterest in his long-term happiness. Rather, he avoids long-term planning precisely because this is part of his strategy for securing long-term happiness: directing too much of his care and attention to the future is self-defeating.

Next let us turn to the second Cyrenaic formulation of the end. Variations on this formula are attributed to both the mainstream Cyrenaics and the Annicereans. I argue in appendix 2.2–3 that the relevant passage in our mainstream doxography has been interpolated with Annicerean material. In the following I therefore assume that both pieces of evidence go back to Anniceris. However, it remains possible that one of the mainstream Cyrenaics introduced this innovation. Fortunately, it is not necessary to take a firm position on this historical question in order to interpret the philosophical significance of this strand of Cyrenaic thought.

I will once again begin by presenting the evidence.

They also think that the end differs from happiness, since the particular pleasure is an end, but happiness is the composition of particular pleasures, among which are numbered both those that have gone by and those that are to come. The particular pleasure is choiceworthy for itself; happiness is not choiceworthy for itself, but for particular pleasures. A proof that pleasure is the end is that we are favorably inclined to it without deliberate choice from childhood, and when we have attained it, we seek nothing further, and avoid nothing so much as hurt, which is opposed to it. (D.L. 2.87–88)

Those called the Annicereans from the Cyrenaic succession put no definite end in place for the whole of life, but said that the pleasure arising from each action is the private end of that action. (Clem. Al. *Strom.* 2.21.130.7 = SSR 4g.4)

It is best to look at these passages as presenting three complementary arguments for the same radical thesis, which is that happiness is not the end. In the first part of the first report Diogenes appears to be aiming at the finality criterion for the end on the basis of the theory of the experiences. He begins by distinguishing between "the particular pleasure" (*hē kata meros hēdonē* or *hē merikē hēdonē*) and happiness, which is the composition of particular pleasures. The Cyrenaics declare the former to be the end because it is choiceworthy for itself. The easiest way to explain this claim is by noting that according to the theory of the experiences, each individual pleasure is unmistakably choiceworthy for itself and in itself.[85] Because happiness is an abstraction generated from many experiences, it is not unmistakably choiceworthy in the same way. Since one of the formal criteria for the end is that it be the final explanatory principle for what is choiceworthy, this implies that particular pleasures rather than happiness are ends.

The second part of Diogenes' testimony clearly invokes the sufficiency criterion. The Cyrenaics say, "A proof that pleasure is the end is that . . . when we have attained it, we seek nothing further . . ." This is designed to show that pleasure is sufficient for satisfying desire. It could also be the basis for another argument against the status of happiness as the end. Rather than thinking of the end as something sufficient for an entire life, the Cyrenaics would be arguing that satisfaction and need are necessarily cyclical: we obtain the sufficient end with each particular episode of pleasure, but then must replenish that sufficiency as the "smooth motion" of pleasure returns to stillness.[86]

Clement's testimony in the second passage takes aim at the comprehensiveness criterion for the primary end. In this passage the Annicereans deny that there exists "a definite end for the whole of life" (τοῦ μὲν ὅλου βίου τέλος . . . ὡρισμένον). This claim must be explained in light of the Annicerean alternative, which is that the pleasure arising from each action is its private end (ἴδιον ὑπάρχειν τέλος τὴν ἐκ τῆς πράξεως περιγινομένην ἡδονήν). If this testimony is to be compatible with that of Diogenes, then we must once again be dealing with particular pleasures. So the claim would be that while particular actions take aim at particular pleasures, there is no overarching "definite end" that subordinates and organizes all these particular ends.

However, note that an enormous problem appears if we take Anniceris to mean that each action must take as its end just *one* episode of pleasure. Many of the Cyrenaic practices I have discussed earlier in this chapter are valued for the sake of a series of potential episodes of pleasure or pain. The exercise of meditating on future evils is a case in point: its aim is to mitigate an array of potential distressing episodes, not just one episode. Obtaining wealth and realizing the virtues are further examples. If each action must aim at only one episode of pleasure or avoidance of pain, none of these pursuits will be justifiable.

It may be for this reason that Annas declares, "We have no evidence to suggest that the Cyrenaics thought through the extent of the changes they were recommending, or seriously examined their possibility."[87] But the very fact that this interpretation leads to such an obvious conundrum is a good reason to doubt that it is correct. Perhaps Anniceris's point is that, even granted that an action frequently aims at a series of particular pleasures, no action can aim at all the pleasures and avoidances of pain in an entire life. For example, he would admit that today's meditation on illness aims to lighten his distress in many future episodes of bodily infirmity. But he would deny that it makes sense to look beyond these particular alleviations of distress to some whole-life-encompassing end. Such an end would be hopelessly nebulous. Moreover, he could argue that accepting this helps him to relax his efforts to control his entire life. Anniceris can even continue to claim that his philosophy nonetheless leads to happiness (D.L. 2.96), with the proviso that he does not directly choose or desire happiness—he only chooses and desires the particular pleasures and avoidances of pain at which any of his actions aims. Happiness is the unintended consequence.

This interpretation eliminates the impression that by making individual episodes of pleasure the ends, Anniceris undercuts many of his own ethical commitments. Yet it remains open to a number of challenges. The first is that, as Aristotle says, the comprehensive end works like a target: it helps an agent to orient his actions. To put it another way, sometimes you must step back in order even to perceive a choice. This is one reason that ancient philosophers often meditate on death: they ask themselves what sort of life they will want to have lived, so that they can see what they should do in the present in order to bring about such a life.[88] Without such a perspective studying philosophy might never even appear as an option. They will remain engrossed in their own idiosyncratic compulsions or in the pursuits valued by their culture, never asking themselves the Socratic question: "What sort of life should I lead?" Denying the existence of a comprehensive end could thus prevent the enterprise of philosophizing from getting off the ground.

A second objection is closely related to the first. There are some Cyrenaic practices whose ends are hard to articulate as anything other than a pleasant life as a whole. A good example is the practice of studying fundamental Cyrenaic theories, such as those regarding the experiences, logic, or causation.[89] The most plausible object for such studies is to become practically wise, and the most plausible object for practical wisdom is to live like a sage—"pleasantly most of the time" (D.L. 2.91). This looks like a comprehensive end.

To these objections the Annicereans might offer a provocative but in some ways plausible answer. They could simply admit that the philosophical life rarely arises from any weighing up of different lifestyles. Rather, it often coalesces from more specific goals. Much as patients seek psychoanalysis because of a particular "satisfaction crisis," but end up redressing their entire psychological configuration, an Annicerean philosopher's general conversion may arise from the desire to eliminate a particular sort of displeasure or achieve a particular sort of enjoyment.

For example, let us imagine that Anniceris's future student Posidonius has experienced tremendous disappointments in his home polis before coming to Cyrene as an exile.[90] Perhaps members of his political faction were even dispossessed and killed. Witnessing Anniceris's steady good humor, Posidonius could conceive the definite end of eliminating his particular distress through Annicerean philosophy. Eating, drinking, and conversing with Anniceris for a day, Posidonius might think, "I want to enjoy *this* again tomorrow." After a series of similar decisions, each taken with a view to particular pleasures or avoidances of pain, Posidonius might find his distress greatly lessened, his theoretical and practical command of Annicerean philosophy progressing, and his desire to return to Anniceris every day firmly entrenched. His general transformation of lifestyle and character would thus have occurred accidentally, as it were, through specific decisions.

This account would give Anniceris a coherent way of explaining the inception of the philosophical life. Moreover, it would acknowledge that conversion to philosophy, rather than being the result of a distinct choice to aim at a singular target, is often a piecemeal and accidental process. It would therefore have some plausibility as a response to the first objection, that philosophy needs an overarching end. But as a response to the second objection, that the Cyrenaic project implies a comprehensive end, it would be disingenuous. Even if Posidonius genuinely enjoyed studying Cyrenaic theories, it would be odd to claim that it was only for the sake of that enjoyment that he ought to study them, and not for their potential to transform the rest of his life. What Anniceris promises is a new mode of existence for his followers. All of the activities of Annicerean philosophy cooperate to transform its practitioners' characters and the way they experience the world. In abandoning the comprehensive end Anniceris has effectively staked out his own territory in the crowded arena of contemporary philosophical hedonisms (e.g., Hegesias, Theodorus, Nausiphanes, Epicurus). But he has also obscured and disavowed the radically transformative aspiration of his philosophy.

CHAPTER 5

Eudaimonism and
Anti-Eudaimonism

5.1. Introduction

In the previous chapter I attempted to show how Aristippus, the mainstream
Cyrenaics, and the Annicereans build entire ways of life on the basis of their
fundamental commitments regarding pleasure and pain. I also acknowledged
that presentism is a consistent element in Cyrenaic ethics, which I interpreted
in two ways. First, I suggested that it belongs to a family of spiritual exercises shared by many Hellenistic philosophers. The aim of this exercise for the
Cyrenaics is to reduce your anxiety, increase your sensitivity to pleasure, and
sharpen your focus on making the best possible use of available resources.
It therefore overlaps with the second interpretation I offered of Cyrenaic
presentism, which is as a prudential rule of thumb. Cyrenaics advise against
investing too much energy in planning for the future, preferring to follow
Aristippus's example and trust their ability to adapt to whatever happens. I call
this a "rule of thumb" in order to emphasize that it is not a doctrinal strait-
jacket: it would be ludicrous to claim that Cyrenaics make no effort at all to
influence their future experiences. In fact I showed that their stance on justice
implies they avoid many actions because of their unpleasant consequences.
Their positions on wealth, practical wisdom, education and progress, and the
premeditation of future evils all attest that they care not only about their futures, but about their entire lives. Admittedly Anniceris disavows this with his
radical formulation of the end, but even that formulation can be interpreted so
as to permit his followers to pursue complex and long-term goals. Moreover,
it is arguable that Annicereans do care about happiness, although they never
posit it as their goal.

The foregoing interpretation puts me in disagreement with the majority of
recent scholars working on Cyrenaic ethics, who argue that the Cyrenaics as a
group are not "eudaimonists."[1] In other words, it is believed that the Cyrenaics
do not emphasize virtue or care about having a certain sort of life as a whole.
This has led to a number of ingenious explanations for why the Cyrenaics reject
eudaimonism. For example, Terence Irwin and Tim O'Keefe have grounded

their answers in Cyrenaic epistemology. Irwin proposes the Cyrenaics do not believe in personal identity, and therefore have no reason to care about the experiences of their future selves.[2] O'Keefe suggests their theory "radically subjectivizes the good to what I desire at present," and therefore provides no basis for criticizing the whim of any given moment.[3] On the other hand, Fred Feldman and James Warren believe the Cyrenaics have prudential grounds for focusing only on the present and immediate future.[4]

Clearly I disagree with all of these interpretations of Cyrenaicism, since I believe they begin from a false premise about the Cyrenaics' disregard for their own long-term welfare. Yet their prevalence requires a more direct answer than I have been able to make hitherto. Moreover, I wish to acknowledge that they are of philosophical interest in their own right. In fact, it might be better to think of them as working toward what Richard Rorty has called a "rational reconstruction" more than a "historical reconstruction" of Cyrenaic ethics. A historical reconstruction, in the words Rorty borrows from Quentin Skinner, obeys the rule that "No agent can eventually be said to have meant or done something which he could never be brought to accept as a correct description of what he had meant or done."[5] This means that the historian should try to avoid describing the thoughts or actions of her subjects using conceptual frameworks with which they were unfamiliar, or with reference to goals that were not among their concerns. In a "rational reconstruction," by contrast, modern philosophers "re-educate" thinkers of the past in order to allow them to engage in contemporary debates. The leading question for a rational reconstruction would not be what Aristippus himself meant to say or do, but what an "ideally reasonable and re-educable" Aristippus might eventually be brought to say, using a conceptual vocabulary with which he was unfamiliar, about issues that were not necessarily on his agenda.[6] As Rorty persuasively argues, both sorts of reconstruction are valuable, because we want both to appreciate the otherness of bygone ways of questioning human experience and to have conversations with "the mighty dead" about contemporary concerns.[7] But we should be careful about making historical claims for rational reconstructions, and we do not need to limit rational reconstructions to what is historically plausible.

In this chapter I will address each of the explanations for the Cyrenaics' putative rejection of eudaimonism independently. I suggest that we locate them toward the rational end of the reconstructive continuum: they are more interested in putting isolated pieces of Cyrenaic evidence into conversation with modern debates than with holistic understanding of Cyrenaic ethics and its original contexts. As will be apparent from the ensuing discussions, this is not always a bad thing. It often puts the Cyrenaic evidence to philosophically interesting work. On the other hand, it can also lead to uncharitable depictions of Aristippus and company as benighted primitives, too befuddled by their own arguments to see how ridiculous their conclusions were.

5.2. Personal Identity

Terence Irwin's 1991 article, "Aristippus Against Happiness," has been thoroughly discussed by prior scholars, who generally agree that it is both philosophically interesting and implausible based on existing evidence.[8] So I will be brief in summarizing what seem to me to be its principal claims and evidentiary shortcomings, adding a few remarks about the conception of philosophy it implies.

Irwin takes Aristippean, orthodox Cyrenaic, and Annicerean testimony as evidence for a single body of theory, which he attributes to Aristippus.[9] Based on swift but sensitive analyses of Socrates' treatment of hedonism in Plato's *Protagoras*, *Gorgias*, and *Philebus*, Irwin then argues that both Socrates and Plato base their attack on hedonism on the assumption that humans are "temporally extended rational agents" who value their life-long happiness. This is the point, he suggests, which Aristippus cleverly assaults. Because Aristippus believes only self-evident experiences are knowable, he doubts the existence of anything that is not the object of a self-evident experience. In particular, he will not affirm the existence of anything that can only be grasped via an "accumulation" (*hathroisma*) of experiences. One such thing is happiness, which the Cyrenaics call a "composition" (*sustēma*) or "accumulate" (*hathroismos*) of pleasant experiences. Another is the temporally extended numerical identity of any human being.

Irwin admits that there is no direct evidence that any Cyrenaic calls the existence of collections into doubt, but he invokes several points of indirect evidence. First, Plato's *Theaetetus* 157a–59c and *Symposium* 207c–8b provide precedents for doubting the existence of both collections and temporally persisting individuals.[10] Second, according to Plutarch the Cyrenaics do not refer to objects in describing their experiences; they affirm "I am sweetened" but not "I am walled" (*Mor.* 1120 = *SR* 4a.211). This could imply that they refuse on principle to assert the existence of things like walls, because such things can only be grasped through a collection of experiences. Third, this makes better sense of the Cyrenaics' rejection of memory and hope as sources of pleasure. It is understandable not to enjoy memories if you are both an egoist and insist that memories are always of *someone else's* experience. Fourth and most importantly, this provides Aristippus with a powerful reason for rejecting eudaimonism. It is downright foolish to worry about your overall happiness if you seriously doubt the reality of both happiness and your own temporally extended identity.

As Tsouna and O'Keefe have shown, the evidentiary basis is weaker even than Irwin concedes.[11] Most importantly, not only is there no direct evidence that Cyrenaics doubt the existence of collections, but there is abundant indirect evidence that they take the existence of such collections for granted. Based on testimony for Cyrenaic epistemology, Tsouna persuasively concludes that the analysis of perception in terms of the *pathē* of the perceiver is effected at the level of single empirical properties, not of three-dimensional objects, and leaves untouched the fundamental ontological assumptions that real objects exist and that real people exist and have *pathē*.[12]

Against this backdrop, Irwin's reading of Plutarch's testimony seems "tendentious"; Plutarch does not say the Cyrenaics infer anything about the existence of collections or external entities from their fashion of describing their experiences.[13] Moreover, I have argued in detail in the previous chapter that many of the values and practices of Aristippus and the mainstream Cyrenaics require commitment to the long-term happiness of a rational agent. Irwin confronts these problems only with regard to the doxographical statement that happiness is choiceworthy for the sake of its constituent pleasures (D.L. 2.88), which he admits is incompatible with his reading. On his interpretation, there is no single agent for whom happiness—the temporally extended composition of pleasures—is choiceworthy. He therefore suggests we should not take this "as a description of an enlightened Cyrenaic, but as the product of 'empty belief.'"[14] But there is nothing at all in this passage to support such a reading.

These evidentiary objections strike me as decisive, but it is also worth questioning the conception of philosophy implied by this way of grounding ethics in subtle ontological arguments. Such a procedure is entirely at home in Plato's Academy, as the *Philebus* especially demonstrates. More recently, it is fundamental to the work of Derek Parfit, whose intricate arguments about the relation of personal identity to ethics in *Reasons and Persons* (1984) made this a hot topic for Anglo-American philosophers. Interpreting the Cyrenaics in this way thus permits us to put them into dialogue with philosophers today. But the Cyrenaics' documented hostility to physics and mathematics gives us an initial reason to doubt they would employ such arguments; they generally use their epistemology to undercut elaborate ethical arguments, not to support them. Admittedly, Aristippus is willing to flirt with metaphysics for persuasive purposes, as I myself suggested when interpreting the same testimony Irwin invokes.[15] But there is no evidence the Cyrenaics were willing to pursue the implications of these ways of speaking. From the perspective of the academic history of philosophy, such thoroughness and systematicity might make them better interlocutors. But from the perspective of ancient debating and the implementation of practical ethics, such arguments would only back them into an impractical corner. "One wonders," Graver notes,

> how this sort of hedonist can find room for even a short-term interest in one's future well-being—the sort of interest one would need in order to get dressed in the morning, or to order thoughtfully from a menu.[16]

Whether or not some Cyrenaic wandered into this cul-de-sac at some point, there is no evidence that the movement as a whole committed itself to such an unnecessarily ingenious defense of their concentration on present experiences.

5.3. Radical Subjectivism

Tim O'Keefe offers two interpretations of the Cyrenaic position on happiness. His "conservative interpretation" is that we are permitted to value happiness, because all its constituent episodes of pleasure will have value when they become present. But O'Keefe shares Irwin's belief that Cyrenaics reject future-concern, and he wonders whether Aristippus's conviction that future-concern is "self-stultifying" and "self-defeating" suffices to explain this rejection.[17] Could Aristippus justify "jetting to Las Vegas,"[18] for example, on the premise that worrying about his expenses, gambling losses, and liver failure would cause more pain than it would obviate? This seems like an idiotic position to take. For this reason O'Keefe prefers his "radical interpretation." The heart of this interpretation is that, according to Diogenes (2.87–88) and Clement (*Strom.* 2.21.130.7–8 = *SR* 4g.4), Cyrenaics believe each action possesses its own end; and according to Sextus Empiricus (*M* 7.199–200 = *SR* 4a.213), Cyrenaics believe ends are determined simply by what we "approve of" or "prefer" at any given time. Like Irwin, O'Keefe relates this position to Cyrenaic epistemology. This "preference" or "approval" (*eudokēsis*), he suggests, is an unquestionable datum of my experience; until I experience a contradictory preference, I have no basis for disregarding it. So "what is valuable for you at some time is a function of your desires [i.e., approvals] at that time,"[19] even if your desire is to spend all your money on a ruinous trip to the casinos.

Like Irwin's arguments from personal identity, O'Keefe's radical subjectivism has an evidentiary problem. The key passage is from Sextus Empiricus. Though I discussed the passage in question at length in sections 3.5 and 3.6,[20] I reproduce it here for ease of reference:

> What these men say about ends appears to be analogous to what they say about criteria, since experiences extend all the way to ends. Some experiences are pleasant, some are painful, and some are in between. They say the painful ones are bad, and their end is pain. The pleasant ones are good, and their infallible end is pleasure. The ones in between are neither good nor bad, and their end is what is neither good nor bad, which is an experience between pleasure and pain. So experiences are the criteria and ends for all beings, and we live, they say, by submitting and paying attention to self-evidence and satisfaction—self-evidence in the case of the other experiences, and satisfaction in the case of pleasure. (*SSR* 4a.213 = S.E. *M* 7.199–200)

O'Keefe is obviously right that this passage expresses the dependence of Cyrenaic hedonism on Cyrenaic epistemology. We "live by following" the self-evidence and "satisfaction" or "approval" (*eudokēsis*) of our experiences. But it is not the case that this phrase "radically subjectivizes the good to what I desire at present."[21] On O'Keefe's reading, Sextus is saying that we should simply do "whatever we approve of" or "whatever we find satisfactory" (e.g., *hotōi an eudokēsōmen*).[22] The reason is that the experience of "approval" or "satisfaction" is the only criterion for choice Cyrenaic epistemology recognizes. But it is far more plausible that the technical term *eudokēsis* does not pick out *an experience of action-guiding desire*, but rather *the satisfaction that motivates such desires*. To put it another way, the term does not indicate that everyone should choose whatever path of action seems "preferable" to them. Rather, it indicates that everyone naturally "prefers" pleasure, because pleasure is "preferable" to everyone. That is why "preferable" or "satisfying" (*eudokētē*) is the Cyrenaics' technical description of pleasure, which they oppose to their technical description of pain as "repulsive" (*apokroustikos*, D.L. 2.86). As I argued in section 3.4, these terms belong to a foundational argument for the goodness of pleasure and the badness of pain.[23]

Between the incorrigible experience of satisfaction and the formulation of action-guiding intentions lies the terrain of practical wisdom. I have argued in section 3.5 that Cyrenaic epistemology permits the questioning of experiences,[24] and in 4.4a–d that Cyrenaic ethics actually requires this critical reasoning. So O'Keefe's assertion that every desire is an unquestionable criterion for action is not convincing.

5.4. Aprudentialism

Fred Feldman and James Warren differ from Irwin and O'Keefe in not taking explicit positions on Cyrenaic eudaimonism.[25] They are not particularly interested in whether the Cyrenaics preserve some commitment to their lives as wholes at the level of theory. But they both believe that at the level of practical reasoning, the Cyrenaics refuse to concern themselves with experiences beyond their immediate present. Feldman and Warren agree that this is a prudential strategy: like O'Keefe in his conservative interpretation, they think the Cyrenaics believe it is more expedient to focus on available experiences than to go through the hardship of making and carrying out long-term plans. This interpretation allows Warren and Feldman to involve the Cyrenaics in modern philosophical debates, but it is based on very thin evidence.

I shall begin with Warren, whose article compares ancient and modern philosophical debates over the time-relativity of the value of experiences. Unlike Irwin's account, Warren's is explicitly indebted to Parfit and other modern theorists of the relation between personal identity and ethics (especially prudential reasoning).[26] In the modern debate, Warren notes, arguments about the rationality of future-concern often intersect with arguments about the rationality of other-concern. In other words, philosophers feel the need to address whether the indexical "I" (opposed to "you" or "s/he") operates differently than the indexical "now" (opposed to "then").[27] But in the disagreements of Epicureans and Cyrenaics, Warren argues, egoism is simply assumed, so the rationality of treating my experience and others' experiences differently is not an issue. Furthermore, these philosophers do not invoke interpretations of personal identity in debating the value of future-concern. Rather, they focus on the *reliability* of planning for the future.

Warren's interpretation of the Epicurean position is subtle and persuasive, but does not concern us here. I am only interested in what he says about the Cyrenaics. Based largely on evidence about Aristippus—the same evidence Irwin emphasizes—he argues that the Cyrenaics reject planning for the future in favor of concentrating on the present.[28] The only reason he can find for this "aprudentialism" is Aristippus's assertion that it is "unclear" whether future enjoyment will happen (*SSR* 4a.176). He expands upon this as follows:

> Aristippus is simply not able to state definitively, or indeed with the degree of certainty which would be required for some system of prudential future-planning, whether things will be one way or another. In that case the best we can do is focus on the moment and make sure that we make the best of it we can.[29]

In fact, Warren extrapolates from the Cyrenaics' negativity toward "accumulating" pleasures for happiness (D.L. 2.88) and admission that even the wise man only lives pleasantly "for the most part" (D.L. 2.91) that Cyrenaics believe a good measure of pain is unavoidable.[30] "Assume and expect that pain will come," he elsewhere summarizes their position; "enjoy the present while you can."[31] This pessimism about achieving future pleasures or avoiding future pains leads to a further corollary: "the Cyrenaics . . . have no interest in asking us to reduce or examine our desires."[32] In other words, Warren proposes that the Cyrenaic rejection of prudential reasoning extends to disclaiming *any* foreseeable connection between indulging present desires and missing future pleasures or experiencing future pains.

Before responding to Warren, let me address Feldman's briefer and simpler account. Feldman does not bother to cite any exact sources for his claim that "Aristippus is alleged to have said that we should go for near-term pleasures rather than long-term ones."[33] Accepting this alleged rejection of future-concern, he contemplates the explanation that Aristippus thinks the value of pleasures is time-relative. But he concludes instead that "though future pleasures are just as valuable in themselves as same-size present pleasures, the future ones are so uncertain that it would be more prudent to go for the near-term ones."[34] This allows him to reduce Aristippean hedonism ("AH") to the following scheme:

i. Every episode of pleasure is intrinsically good; every episode of pain is intrinsically bad. (But physical pleasures tend to be much more intense, and hence tend to contain more hedons of pleasure, than mental pleasures. And since near-term pleasures are more certain than far-off ones, it is prudent to pursue them instead of their temporally distant cousins.)

ii. The intrinsic value of an episode of pleasure is equal to the number of hedons of pleasure contained in that episode; the intrinsic value of an episode of pain is equal to –(the number of dolors of pain contained in that episode).

iii. The intrinsic value of a life is entirely determined by the intrinsic values of the episodes of pleasure and pain contained in the life, in such a way that one life is intrinsically better than another if and only if the net amount of pleasure in the one is greater than the net amount of pleasure in the other.[35]

This schematization of (some of) the Cyrenaic evidence allows Feldman to make Aristippus his first—and weakest—dialectical partner in constructing and defending his own quantitative hedonistic axiology. This is why he puts the prudential rule about near-term pleasures in parentheses: he believes that hedonism is essentially an axiology, which can and should be separated from prudential questions. Yet he cannot resist commenting on this point:

> Suppose you are given a choice of two pleasures. Suppose you are told on unimpeachable authority that the first pleasure would occur within the next five minutes, and would contain exactly 300 hedons. On the other hand, the second pleasure would occur tomorrow and would contain 10,000 hedons. Neither pleasure will lead to further pleasure or pains. Each is guaranteed. You cannot have both. AH, as I have formulated it, implies that you should pursue the much smaller near-term pleasure. This seems to me to be foolish. I am inclined to say, "Grow up. Learn to defer gratification."[36]

In other words, Feldman not only argues that Aristippean hedonism is inadequate as a theory of value, he also implies it is downright childish as a practical ethics.

The main problem with both these reconstructions is that, having focused exclusively on the presentist aspect of Cyrenaic (and especially Aristippean) statements and doctrines, they then go looking for a single clear reason for it. But as I have argued, this aversion to future-concern is only one aspect of Cyrenaicism; it exists in tension with concern for enduring dispositions and long-term states of affairs. Even within its own remit, it is only a rule of thumb, not a rigid doctrine. Moreover, the evidence that the Cyrenaics accounted for their concentration on the present by claiming that the future is "uncertain" comes down to a single phrase from a single Aristippean source.[37] Elevating this into a doctrine and the foundation of prudential reasoning leads to the sort of patronizing sequence of reasoning Feldman imputes to Aristippus. Especially given the weakness of the evidence, the ludicrousness of Feldman's conclusions should not be taken as a point against the Cyrenaics; it should be taken as a point against the historicity of these reconstructions.

Against Feldman's reconstruction in particular we should add that a precise quantitative axiology in "hedons" and "dolors," divorced from practical ethics, is inconceivable for the Cyrenaics. Like other ethical philosophers of their time, the Cyrenaics did not begin with axiology and then build practical ethics around it; different aspects of their theory evolved together and through interaction with their practices. Greater subtlety and exactitude than daily practice and interscholastic debate demanded would not have been a strength but a weakness.

Warren's interpretation is noteworthy for its erudite juxtaposition of ancient and modern discussions and particularly attractive as a justification for Aristippus's legendarily voluptuous lifestyle. But he overstates the (non-Hegesiac) Cyrenaics' pessimism about achieving pleasures and avoiding pains. The sentence about the wise person's merely preponderant happiness, for example, is actually more positive than negative: "They don't think that the wise man lives pleasantly in every detail, nor that the fool lives painfully in every detail, but for the most part" (D.L. 2.90). This looks more like qualified optimism than pessimism. The other sentence on which Warren relies (concerning the "accumulation" of pleasures for happiness) is textually corrupt, and therefore of little weight. Moreover, I have argued that Warren's translation is probably incorrect.[38] Finally, his assertion that Cyrenaics "have no interest in asking us to reduce or examine our desires," while it makes partial sense of Aristippus's luxurious lifestyle, does not stand up well to comparison with the evidence I analyzed in sections 4.2 and 4.4a–d. In particular, I argued that one of the benefits of Aristippean temperance and Cyrenaic practical wisdom is that it reveals the fungibility of pleasures, and thus reduces desire for any particular source of pleasure. This emphasis on "indifference" develops into an important theme in the ethics of Hegesias and Theodorus, as we will see in chapters 7 and 8.

CHAPTER 6

Personal and Political Relationships

6.1. Introduction

In the previous two chapters I have argued that Aristippus and the mainstream Cyrenaics, like all other ancient Greek philosophers, care about their lives in their entirety. Their end is a form of happiness or *eudaimonia*. Moreover, while Anniceris denies that happiness should be designated the end, I have suggested that this denial is disingenuous; his philosophy nevertheless positions happiness as its implicit goal. We will see further evidence for that assertion in this chapter, where Anniceris argues that Hegesias makes two enormous errors. First, Hegesias rejects the dominant forms of interpersonal solicitude in ancient Greek culture. Second, because of this ethical solipsism, he restricts the number of pleasures available, and therefore wrongly concludes that happiness is impossible. This disagreement between Hegesias and Anniceris demonstrates that the intra-Cyrenaic debate about interpersonal relationships is a disagreement about the constituents of the ideal life. It therefore provides further confirmation for my thesis that the Cyrenaics are not so radical as is often supposed.

By way of introduction it is worth surveying the conceptual and practical frameworks governing these topics in Greek popular and philosophical morality. The primary subtopic for this chapter will be friendship. By "friendship" I mean an enduring relationship of mutual affection and reciprocal support (financial, practical, emotional, etc.). The Greek words with which we are concerned in our evidence—*philia* and *phílos*—do not have precisely the same extension as their nearest modern English equivalents. For example, the noun *philia* denotes family relationships as well as political solidarity and voluntary bonds of affection. The noun *phílos* is arguably narrower in its usage, although still probably broader than the English "friend."[1] However, it is clear that the Cyrenaic debate about *philia* does not concern whether we can or should have blood relatives or co-citizens, but whether we can or should have enduring voluntary relationships of mutual affection and support.

Two other terms in our evidence that overlap with the debate about friendship are *euergesia* and *kharis*. The first can be straightforwardly translated as "good deed" or "benefaction."[2] One meaning of the second is "gratitude."

Gratitude and benefaction obviously belong together, since part of what defines "gratitude" is that it arises in response to someone doing something good for us. More specifically, what arises here is a sensation of "joy" (*kharis* is related to *khairō* and *khara*).[3] When Greeks say, "I know gratitude" (*kharin oida*),[4] they express both this feeling and their cognizance that it should lead to a reciprocal good deed. Hence *kharis* may also mean "favor," and one may "give," "do," "accomplish," or "repay" a "favor" (*kharin dounai, prattein, dran, tinein*).[5] This reciprocation of good deeds or favors is a core component of Greek assumptions about friendship, though it is not entirely rules-based or mechanical; people choose when and how to reciprocate, and sometimes even help spontaneously or "gratuitously."[6] This connects the dynamics of reciprocity with the final translation of *kharis*, which is "charm" or "grace."[7] The deeds of friendship are "gracious" because they are presumed to arise from good will and generosity, even when there are powerful expectations of mutual assistance. To put it another way, the exchange of favors is supposed to be embedded in a relationship of genuine mutual good will, and that good will is embodied by the favors exchanged.[8]

Although it rarely receives much attention in the scholarship on ancient philosophy, it should be noted that an important dialectical partner for friendship in Greek thinking is enmity (*ekhthra, misos*). As Dover comments, "a man [today] who spoke of 'my enemies' could fairly be suspected of paranoia. Athenians took enmity much more for granted. . . ."[9] In ancient Greece mutual hatred and harm between enemies are the correlates of mutual affection and assistance between friends. In fact, a common way of summarizing the whole field of interpersonal ethics is "doing good to your friends and bad to your enemies" (Pl. *Resp.* 332a, Lys. 9.20, Ar. *Av.* 419–20, Xen. *Mem.* 2.6.35, etc.).[10] Succeeding in either of these endeavors brings honor (*timē*) and a good reputation (*eukleia*), which are important motivators. Even contemplating failure—especially through negligence—triggers the sentiment of "shame" (*aidōs*), which motivates its agent to avoid doing anything "shameful" or "ugly" (*aiskhron*).[11]

Two more relationships deserve a brief mention. The first is the parent–child relationship. In our evidence we will encounter an implicit debate about honoring one's parents. Here it suffices to say that Greek literature is almost unanimous in insisting that children must obey and honor their parents, and that not doing so is very shameful.[12]

Closely related to this is duty to the polis. Plato's Socrates argues that the polis is a sort of super-parent, since, like our parents, it is responsible for our existence, nourishment, and upbringing (*Cri.* 50c–51c). In Athenian forensic oratory speakers configure the relationship slightly differently; they discuss how "useful" they have been to the polis, and call upon the jurors, as representatives of the polis, to display gratitude (*kharis*).[13] Thus the polis is treated rather like a friend. In Thucydides' funeral oration Pericles tries a third analogy: he calls on the citizens to fall passionately in love with Athens (2.43.1). Whatever the metaphorical configuration, the point is that ancient Greeks tend to think of their relationship with the polis as a tremendously important one for their welfare and identity. Hence Aristotle famously says that the polis is prior by nature to each of its inhabitants, and that "if someone is unable to be part of a community or does not need to because he is self-sufficient, he is by no means part of the polis, and so he is either a beast or a god" (*Pol.* 1253a25–29).

Friendship with co-citizens and hatred for the citizens of opposing cities is a natural extension of the polis relationship. Thus Aristotle suggests that "there is some form of justice in every community, and also friendship. For people call their fellow sailors and fellow soldiers friends, and the same goes for other communities" (*NE* 8.9 1159b26–29). He goes on to correlate types of friendship with types of political constitution. This troping of politics as personal relationships finds its most emphatic expression in military contexts. For example, in the funeral oration Pericles says that even if the fallen were bad people during their lives, "it is right to place before this their courage against the enemy on behalf of the polis" (Th. 2.42.3). He goes on to praise them for "yearning to take vengeance on their opponents" more than to enjoy the benefits of their present or future wealth (2.42.4). This "yearning for vengeance" clearly implies that these men viewed the polis's enemies as their own.

These relationships—friendship and enmity, benefaction and gratitude, and relations to parents and polis—enmesh most ancient Greeks in a network of motivations, satisfactions, and disappointments, which does a great deal to give their lives structure and meaning. The question we will see the Cyrenaics debating in this chapter is how this network lines up with their philosophical hedonism.

6.2. Aristippus

As usual, I will begin with the example set by Aristippus. Annas claims that "The tradition about Aristippus also shows him as quite strikingly uncaring about others."[14] She goes on,

> [Aristippus] coarsely refuses responsibility for fathering a courtesan's child, and when reproached for exposing his infant son 'as though it had not been produced by him' replies, with stunning brutality, that phlegm and vermin are also produced by us, but we throw them away as far as we can, since they are useless.

I will return to Aristippus and courtesans momentarily. While infanticide (especially of girls) was an accepted practice in classical Athens,[15] Annas's interpretation of this anecdote, in which Aristippus compares babies to lice and phlegm, would make him unusually heartless.

However, the evidence does not support Annas's interpretation. She cites the following text:

Someone blamed him for throwing away his son [*ton huion aporrip-tounta*] as if it didn't come from him. And he answered, "We know that phlegm and lice are begotten by us too, but we throw [*rhiptoumen*] them as far as possible, because they're useless." (D.L. 2.81)

In fact the verb "throwing away" is not generally in use for the exposure of children, so it is unclear whether an ancient Greek would take this to refer to infanticide.[16] The reason this verb was chosen becomes clear if we compare this with other versions of the same anecdote, which appears in five other sources. Three of them more or less agree on the following reading:

[Aristippus] locked out his son because he had become irredeemable [ἄσωτον γενομένον τὸν υἱὸν ἐξέκλεισεν]. When his wife complained because he wouldn't let him in, and repeatedly said that this boy came from him, Aristippus spat and replied, "This comes from me too, but I throw it away [*aporriptō*] because it distresses me!" (Gnom. Vat. 743 n. 25 = Cod. Vat. Gr. 1144 f. 216r; cf. Cod. Neapol. 2D.22 n. 35 = SSR 4a.136).

In both versions someone blames Aristippus for rejecting his son, that person asserts that the son comes from him, Aristippus compares his son to spit, and he uses the verb "throw away" to express the appropriate response. However, it is clear in the extended version that we are dealing with a son old enough to have "become irredeemable." In the abbreviated version this important detail is omitted, and the verb "throw away" has displaced the verb "locked out." It is this abbreviation which generates the mistaken impression that we are dealing with callous infanticide, rather than with Aristippus's intransigence in the face of his grown-up son's bad character.

Note that in Greek popular morality the relationship between parents and children is not a symmetrical one. While children are expected to obey and honor their parents almost no matter what, parents have greater latitude in the way they treat their children.[17] It is far from clear that Aristippus is being any more callous about his son than Socrates, for example, is when in Plato's *Crito* he puts his own commitment to principle above any support he might offer his children (and wife and friends) by preserving his own life.[18] Moreover, we should bear in mind that Aristippus was renowned for having educated his daughter Arete in philosophy, solid evidence that he was capable of expressing very different attitudes toward his offspring.[19]

Aristippus's relationship with Aeschines of Sphettus, another renowned disciple of Socrates, attests that he could also be a caring and supportive friend.[20] One anecdote relates that when Aeschines, like Plato and Aristippus, came to the court of Dionysius in Syracuse, "He was neglected by Plato, but embraced by Aristippus" (D.L. 2.61, Suda S 1684 = SSR 4a.22). The tenth, eleventh, and twenty-third Socratic Epistles imagine this triangle of Socratic disciples at Syracuse in greater detail.[21] At some point Aristippus and Aeschines seem to have quarreled. One anecdote suggests that Aristippus even accused Aeschines of stealing the material for his dialogues (D.L. 2.62).[22] However, Aristippus is also said to have initiated their reconciliation:

> Once Aristippus was angry with Aeschines. After a little he said, "Aren't we going to make up? Will we stop this nonsense, or will we wait for someone else to reconcile us over drinks?" Aeschines said, "I'm happy to stop." "Remember then," said Aristippus, "that even though I'm older than you, I was the first to extend my hand." Aeschines responded, "By Hera, you're right, and a much better man than I. I took the lead in enmity, but you are leading in friendship." (D.L. 2.82–83; cf. Plut. *Mor.* 462d = *SSR* 4a.24)

In a culture where men are touchy about their honor and consider anger and retaliation appropriate reactions to perceived insults, this magnanimity may be more impressive than it appears to many readers today. The fact that Aristippus is older, and therefore could expect Aeschines to yield first, accentuates his magnanimity. Overall we are left with the impression that Aristippus is not only high-minded, but also genuinely committed to this friendship.

On the other hand, Annas is right that some of the evidence testifies to a coolness in Aristippus's attitudes toward the practical and emotional connections created by relationships. For example, Aristippus's repudiation of his son, even if he was not an infant, still gives some impression of coldness. If Xenophon's depiction of Aristippus has any historical value, it reveals a striking withdrawal from civic participation and detachment from civic identity (*Mem.* 2.1).[23] Finally, there is the issue of his callous treatment of courtesans. However, that is a trend which continues through the mainstream Cyrenaics. Moreover, the historically specific valence of courtesans in Greek literature merits discussion in an independent section.

6.3. Cyrenaics and Courtesans

When Annas claims that Aristippus "coarsely refuses responsibility for fathering a courtesan's child,"[24] she has in mind the following anecdote:

> When a courtesan said to him, "I'm pregnant by you," he answered, "You're no more certain of that than if you were walking through a field of clubrushes and you said, 'I've been pricked by *this* one!'" (D.L. 2.81)

Most readers today will agree that Aristippus appears strikingly unconcerned with this courtesan's welfare or any responsibility he should bear for it. However, especially since anecdotes typically convey an attitude as much a historical truth, it is important to historicize the meanings conveyed by representations of courtesans in Greek literature.[25] In fact it has been argued that there are two competing trends in this representative tradition. The first belongs to a minority discourse among aristocrats, who distinguish "courtesans" (*hetairai*) from "whores" (*pornai*) as a corollary to distinguishing themselves from the common people and their mode of exchange from the egalitarian free market. The second is a more widespread and phobic discourse, which represents courtesans as an enormous threat to the self-possession of male citizens and therefore also to the financial integrity of their households. Neither of these traditions should be taken to exhaust the meanings of the various representations of courtesans with Cyrenaics. However, the latter in particular has some bearing on our discussion.

Let us return to the evidence. I have already argued that Aristippus's ability to walk away from any courtesan, including the legendary Laïs, is supposed to be an expression of his temperance.[26] What is involved here is both a prudent strategy for non-committal enjoyment and a performance of virtuous character. The former is nicely communicated by another anecdote concerning Laïs: "When someone spoke to Aristippus, accusing Laïs of not loving him, Aristippus answered that he didn't think wine or fish loved him, but he made use of both with pleasure" (Plut. *Mor.* 750d–e = *SSR* 4a.93). The implication is obviously that Aristippus relates to Laïs as he relates to a fine wine or a beautiful tuna steak. What he values in any of these is simply the enjoyment it offers; he is not invested in an ongoing relationship with any of them. Being able to relate this way to a renowned courtesan (or even to fine food and wine) requires strong character: a lesser man could develop an uncontrollable and debilitating attachment. Hence another anecdote about Aristippus: "When he was going into a courtesan's house and one of the youths who were with him blushed, he said, 'It's not going in that's the problem, it's not being able to get out!'" (D.L. 2.69) Not every man has the wherewithal to pay for a courtesan like Laïs. It is an elite privilege.[27] Even of those who do, many end up investing more money, time, and emotion than they intend.

Later Cyrenaics as well display their ability to "use" courtesans without losing self-possession. For example, one anecdote relates how at the Athenian "Pitchers" festival (which involved heavy drinking) Dionysius the Turncoat, too old to enjoy a courtesan, adapts a line from the *Odyssey*: "I can't stretch it; let another take it" (Athen. 437e = *SVF* 1.428).[28] This conveys some of the same instrumentalizing attitude as Aristippus's retort about fish and wine: this anonymous courtesan is simply an occasion for Dionysius's sexual pleasure—or, failing that, for a display of wit. Where another man might have been embarrassed and frustrated, he remains entirely composed. Another source tells us that Dionysius frequently visited public prostitutes when he was younger. "Once," the story goes, "he was on his way with several acquaintances and happened to pass the brothel he had visited the previous day, where he owed money. Since he had the money at the time, he reached out and paid with everyone looking" (Athen. 437e–f)! Our source intends to castigate Dionysius's shamelessness, but for a sympathetic reader the point is precisely that Dionysius is neither flustered nor compromised.[29] Most striking of all is an anecdote in which Aristoteles

> was the only one to despise Laïs when she was passionate about him. He swore to take her back to his homeland if she'd help him against his antagonists. But when she'd done it, he had a charming way of fulfilling his oath: he had a statue made as similar to her as possible, and set it up in Cyrene. (Clem. Al. *Strom.* 3.6.50.4–51.1 = *SSR* 4e.2)

Aristoteles' treatment of this second Laïs (not the same one with whom Aristippus had a relationship[30]) dramatizes in its most extreme form the Cyrenaics' ability to enjoy without commitment or attachment. Even though Laïs is in love with Aristoteles, he is not in love with her. Even though she helps him, he does not exert himself on her behalf. Rather, he goes serenely on his way, ready to enjoy another pleasure elsewhere.

Since we have now seen how the Cyrenaics' treatment of courtesans is meant to display a sort of virtue, I shall return to the accusation that this involves coarseness or callousness. There is clearly some justice in these charges. First, some aspects of these anecdotes suggest that the Cyrenaics deny courtesans autonomy or treat them as inert objects.[31] For example, we have already witnessed Dionysius's comparison of a prostitute to Odysseus's bow.[32] We have also seen Aristippus's famous claim that "I have, but I am not had," and his comparison of Laïs to fish or wine. In another anecdote he compares a courtesan to a house or a boat: it makes no difference, he says, whether many have used any of them before you (D.L. 2.74, Athen. 588f = *SSR* 4a.92). All of these comparisons figure courtesans as the passive recipients of the Cyrenaic's activity.

On the other hand, there may be another facet of the analogy between a courtesan and a house or a boat. One of its implications is that Aristippus does not care how many other men sleep with Laïs. In other words, he is not possessive or controlling. Compare another anecdote, in which Aristippus explicitly says, "I pay Laïs a lot of money so I can enjoy her, not so no one else can" (Athen. 588e). This could be taken to imply that Laïs is free to view Aristippus precisely as he views her: each gets what he or she wants from the other.

Yet even this mutual instrumentality, while it acknowledges autonomy, threatens to undercut any stable motivation for caring about courtesans' points of view or feelings. This comes across in both Aristippus's response to the pregnant courtesan and, most strikingly, in Aristoteles' treatment of Laïs. Aristippus simply does not care what the courtesan thinks about her child's parentage. The difficulties this pregnancy will cause her are none of his concern. Aristoteles is not worried about the trouble Laïs has gone to on his behalf. Her belief that they have a relationship of emotional and practical reciprocity does not matter, except insofar as it helps him against his enemies. Whatever feelings of intimacy or betrayal she experiences are unimportant to him.

An instrumental attitude also makes courtesans fungible: ceteris paribus, one courtesan is as good as another for the sexual pleasure she can provide. (In this the Cyrenaics appropriate the perspective often attributed, rightly or wrongly, to courtesans themselves: one patron is just as good as another for the support he can offer) This threatens to dehumanize the courtesan, denying any importance to her personality.

In short, even after we have taken account of their historically specific contexts, Cyrenaics' relationships with courtesans are still distant and cold. They speak of courtesans as inert recipients of action; they ignore their feelings and thoughts; they disregard their personality or individuality; and they consider them exempt from norms of reciprocity and gratitude. This is the clearest example of an attitude and behavioral pattern established in mainstream Cyrenaicism, and taken to radical extremes by Hegesias and Theodorus.

6.4. Mainstream Cyrenaics

Relationships with courtesans aside, there are two other items in our mainstream evidence which merit attention. The first is a position attributed to Aristoteles:

> Aristoteles of Cyrene used to say we shouldn't accept any good deed [*euergesian*] from anyone, because either we'd have difficulty in trying to repay it, or we'd appear ungrateful [*akhariston*], if we didn't repay it. (Ael. *VH* 10.8 = *SSR* 4e.3)

This statement shares a certain tone with the anecdote about Aristoteles we encountered in the last section. Without regard to the particular relationships in which good deeds take place, this doctrine already indicates wariness toward the networks of solicitude and the material give-and-take involved in active engagement with others. The unspoken premise here is that the wise person can provide for his own happiness, meaning his own emotional and bodily pleasure, without the exchange of favors. He therefore has nothing to gain by accepting help, while he clearly has something to lose: he could experience "difficulty" in repaying the good deed, or risk censure if he fails to reciprocate. More specifically, he could appear "lacking in *kharis*"; in other words, he would be in violation of the informal rules of emotional and practical reciprocity which are supposed to structure personal relationships. There could be distressing or painful consequences for such ungraciousness. Aristoteles' solution is simply to avoid this element of human relationships entirely.[33]

The other item which concerns me is the mainstream position on friendship itself. This is preserved only in a frustratingly abbreviated form: "a friend is for the sake of use [*tēs khreias heneka*], for we also cherish a body part for as long as it's there" (D.L. 2.91). The brevity of this notice makes it hazardous to read too much into it. However, we can gain some traction by attending to the notion of "usefulness" and to the comparison with body parts.

I shall begin with the former. While modern readers may find it tasteless to cherish friends for their utility, or even suspect this is incompatible with meaningful friendship, we must bear in mind two points from the introduction to this chapter. First, Greek authors almost universally assume that mutual assistance is at the heart of friendship. Second, they see this assistance as the natural expression of mutual good will and affection, not as an alternative to those things.

It should therefore come as no surprise that "usefulness" is a regular element in Greek philosophical discussions of friendship. For example, usefulness is one of the criteria of friendly love (*philia*) canvassed in Plato's *Lysis*, where Socrates suggests that the Lysis's parents cannot love him (*philein*) or be his friends (*phíloi*) unless he is useful to them (210c–d; cf. 214e–15b).[34] Aristotle also assumes that usefulness is one of three fundamental objects of friendly love, although he stipulates that what is useful is always useful for something else—either pleasure or goodness.[35] He famously argues that not only do friends in the fullest sense wish each other well for the other's own sake (*EN* 1155b31, 1156b9–10, 1166a2–5, etc.), but they see one another as "other selves" (*EN* 1166a31–32, 1169b6–7, 1170b6–7, 1171b33–34). Yet notwithstanding this blurring of identity, he asserts that they continue to be "useful" to one another (1157a2–3).[36] Finally, Epicurus too argues that it is for the sake of assistance and the confidence this creates that we cherish friendship (*Sent. Vat.* 23, 34, 39 = LS 22F).[37] Certainly we should not hastily infer that the Cyrenaics approve the same sort of usefulness as Aristotle and Epicurus, or approve it for the same reasons.[38] However, these contexts should stop us from leaping to the conclusion that the Cyrenaics are taking a radical position. Epicurus is a particularly illuminating parallel: despite valuing friendship for the sake of the pleasure it generates, he insists that his sage will endure great pains and even death for the sake of a friend (Plut. *Mor.* 1111b, D.L. 10.120 = LS 22H, Q).

On the other hand, the mainstream Cyrenaic position on friendship still appears at least a little aloof. There is no sign of Epicurus's extravagant enthusiasm when he says, "Friendship goes dancing around the world announcing to all of us to wake up to its blessing" (*Sent. Vat.* 52 = LS 22F). The comparison of a friend with a body part is instructive. Clearly limbs are very important for people who believe that bodily pleasure is the highest good. To that extent this comparison supports the view that Cyrenaics have a fairly robust concern for their friends.[39] However, the metaphor also raises a troubling question.[40] Although I care very much about my legs, I in no way care about them for their own sake; I completely subordinate their interests to my own. (In fact, I would find it odd to think of my legs having independent interests!) If we applied this part of the metaphor to friends, we would infer that the Cyrenaics are as detached from their friends' perspective and feelings as they are from those of courtesans. This is probably an over-reading of the analogy, but it should be ac-knowledged that a certain detachment in friendship would dovetail with much of the rest of our evidence for the Cyrenaics.

6.5. Hegesias and Theodorus

This brings us to the apogee of one trend in Cyrenaic thinking about relation-ships, which is articulated in the ethics of Hegesias and Theodorus. A good starting point for understanding this trend is the middle of the Hegesiac doxography:

> There is no such thing as gratitude or friendship or benefaction, because we don't choose these things for themselves, but for their uses. When the uses are absent, these things too do not exist. (D.L. 2.93)

Here Hegesias goes a step further than Aristoteles, his most obvious predeces-sor in mainstream Cyrenaicism. Aristoteles advises against getting involved in the system of favors, gratitude, and benefaction. Hegesias does not even coun-tenance the possibility of getting involved; he denies that the system genuinely exists. Though Hegesias lumps together gratitude, benefaction, and friendship, I shall begin with the last item in this list and then return to gratitude and bene-faction later in this section.

My initial question will be why Hegesias denies the very existence of friendship. He explains, "we don't choose these things [gratitude, benfaction, and friendship] for themselves, but for their uses. When the uses are absent, these things too do not exist." From this it is obvious that he appropriates the mainstream Cyrenaic doctrine that friendship exists—or would exist, were it possible—for the sake of usefulness. Presumably this means that each person would initiate, accept, or maintain a friendship for the sake of its usefulness to himself. If two people were useful to one another, then a friendship could be sustained between them. The mainstream Cyrenaics make it clear that friends are reliably and enduringly useful, since they compare them to body parts. Two mainstream Cyrenaics would therefore be willing to initiate and maintain a friendship. But Hegesias disagrees with his predecessors. When uses are absent, he stipulates, people cannot be friends. Since he infers from this that people cannot be friends, he clearly believes that usefulness is not a reliable or endur-ing aspect of any human relationship.

One way we can explain this belief is by adducing a complementary passage in the Theodorean doxography:

> He eliminated friendship, because it neither exists among fools nor among wise people. The friendship of fools is removed whenever use is elimi-nated. The wise are self-sufficient, and so don't need friends. (D.L. 2.98)

Theodorus's argument begins with the exhaustive division of all people into "wise people" (*sophoi*) and "fools" (*aphrones*).[41] He then proceeds to show that neither class can sustain friendship. The wise are "self-sufficient" (*autarkeis*), meaning that they achieve happiness with little or no dependency on others.[42] Beyond happiness there is no further good to acquire. It is therefore impossible to be useful to the wise, since they have everything they could want.[43] Common fools, by contrast, may indeed be useful to one another. However, when that usefulness ends, so does their so-called friendship. The implicit argument must be that such transient relationships do not merit the name of "friendship."[44]

Hegesias may share this argument with Theodorus. Indeed, Theodorus may have derived the argument from him.[45] But Hegesias's doxography also supports another, complementary explanation for why the wise man will have no friends. The relevant passage runs as follows:

> The wise person will do everything for his own sake, because he considers no one equal to himself in worth. For even if he seems to receive the greatest profit from someone, it isn't equivalent to what he himself provides. (D.L. 2.95)

Here the emphasis is not on the wise man's self-sufficiency, but rather on the impossibility of an exchange of benefits between him and anyone else. Aristotle reports that "people say equality is friendship" (*EN* 1157b36; cf. 1159b2–4), and makes it one of the marks of complete friendship that its participants make equal contributions (1156b35–36). He admits that in many cases the friends cannot contribute the same benefits, but he devotes a fair amount of attention to determining how the contributions of such friends can be equalized. Hegesias, by contrast, simply denies that such equalization is possible for the sage: even if the sage "seems to receive the greatest profit from someone" (μέγιστα δοκῇ παρά του καρποῦσθαι), he himself necessarily contributes something of much greater value. Once again the idea is probably that the sage has few or no needs he cannot supply himself, and therefore stands to gain very little from whatever someone gives him. Generous gifts of money, for example, may seem great to the unenlightened, but are indifferent to a Hegesiac (D.L. 2.94). By contrast, the sage offers wisdom, which is inestimably precious. Hence the sage can be extraordinarily useful to another person, but that person is of little or no use to the sage. This is why the wise man cannot form friendships, because he cannot engage in meaningful reciprocity.[46]

This brings us back to gratitude and benefaction. Neither of the Hegesiac arguments I have reconstructed rules out individual useful actions. For example, two non-sages can still trade money for goods, services, or political influence. Any of these things can be useful, since they bring their recipients bodily or emotional pleasure. It might even be possible for sages to receive a modicum of pleasure from non-sages, although not enough to be the basis for a meaningful exchange. These considerations could lead us to infer that gratitude or favors and benefaction are still possible, notwithstanding the absence of friendship.

Hegesias's argument must therefore be that these useful actions do not deserve the names "gratitude/favor" (*kharis*) or "benefaction" (*euergesia*). As I explained in the beginning of this chapter, the ideology of *kharis* resists reduction to discrete exchanges of goods by exclusively self-interested individuals. If I buy milk from a convenience store, for example, I am happy to have the milk, and the owner is happy to have the money. But I would not say that I am grateful to her for the milk, or that she is grateful to me for the money. We are both aware that each of us has simply followed the rules of exchange. Furthermore, because this exchange lacks any personal dimension, neither of us will feel obliged to benefit the other further. There is thus no *kharis* involved.

Hegesias is saying that all exchanges are essentially like this one. Non-sages accept benefits from others and reciprocate in accordance with expectations. They may have the impression that they are friendly with their exchange partners, but this illusion is shattered whenever the basis for their relationship is disturbed—for example, when one partner ceases to be able to offer the goods, or when they disagree about the relative value of the items exchanged. Meanwhile sages cannot even participate in meaningful exchanges. We will see in a moment that they nevertheless benefit others. However, they "do everything for [their] own sake." In other words, at the very moment of helping another, a sage is reflectively aware that his motivation is only to benefit himself (*euergetein*). It is merely incidental that the other person benefits.

We can now explain why Hegesias denies that gratitude and benefaction exist. He means to suggest that the actions we usually denote with these names do not in fact answer to the associated connotations. No one "benefits" another except incidentally; whether unreflectively (like non-sages) or reflectively (like sages), all people are really aiming to help themselves.[47] As for the rhetoric of "gratitude" and "favors," it is just a veil we cast over our naked self-love. It is a deceptive way of representing how interpersonal exchanges actually work.

With the foregoing doctrines Hegesias knocks out one column of the cultural edifice I outlined in the introduction to this chapter. No one who adopts this Hegesiac perspective will be able to participate wholeheartedly in the various forms of reciprocal assistance and affection that structure his society. Though he may go through some of the motions, he will remain emotionally aloof.

It should now be added that Hegesias also undermines the other column of reciprocity, which is reciprocal harm and all the negative emotions associated with it. According to our doxography,

> They said that errors receive forgiveness.[48] For a person does not err voluntarily, but because he is coerced by some passion. And ⟨they⟩[49] won't hate, but will rather share ⟨their⟩ teaching. (D.L. 2.95)

What interests me here is the injunction of forgiveness and sharing and the prohibition of hating. Notwithstanding some textual problems, it is clear that this passage presents the behavior to which Hegesiacs should aspire, not a description of how people behave in general. In other words, this is how a Hegesiac sage feels and acts. He neither retaliates when someone "errs" against him nor hates the errant individual. Rather, he keeps in mind that no one errs voluntarily; the offender must have been driven into error by an inaccurate understanding of what is good, what is bad, and what should have been done in that situation.[50] The Hegesiac therefore attempts to instruct his offender and show him why he was wrong.

This is a very important passage for appreciating Hegesias's ethics, and one to which I shall return in the following chapter. For now I want to emphasize that this does *not* demonstrate any philanthropic motivation on the sage's part.[51] After all, the sage rejects gratitude and benefaction, and does everything for his own sake. Far from compensating for his withdrawal from friendly relationships, this doctrine compounds the sage's voluntary isolation: rejecting hatred and retaliation amounts to eschewing what Hegesias's contemporaries considered normal human relations. It is not only Homeric heroes like Achilles who react with rage and hatred when they think they have been dishonored. "He cheated me and he did me hurt," Achilles fumes when Agamemnon attempts to end their feud. "Let him of his own will be damned. . . . I hate his gifts. I hold him as light as the strip of a splinter" (*Il.* 9.375–78, trans. Lattimore). Compare the peroration from a late fourth-century Athenian prosecution speech:

> So I ask you, gentlemen of the jury, . . . that just as each of you, if you are injured, would hate your assailant, that you feel the same anger at this man Conon for my sake; and I ask you not to regard any affair of this sort as a private matter, even if it should happen to another man, but no matter who the victim is, to help him and give him justice and hate those men who before they are accused are brash and reckless but at their trial are wicked, have no shame, and give no thought to opinion or custom or anything else, except for escaping punishment. (Dem. 54.42, trans. Bers)

The speaker of this peroration assumes that every member of the jury hates and feels anger toward anyone he perceives to have wronged him. Furthermore, he hopes that they will join him in solidarity against the defendant, whom he has portrayed throughout the speech as not "one of us"—an impious, shameless, hubristic aristocrat who thinks he is above "our" customs and laws. Thus he hopes to provide the jurors with a motivation for hating Conon and returning a verdict against him. Private enmity thus becomes corporate hatred between different groups and classes. This is the system Hegesias is opting out of: he will no more exchange insults and attacks than favors and benefactions. He has neither personal enemies nor class enemies. In short, he has no strong relationships of any kind with anybody.

The notion of corporate enmity brings us to the final topic of this section, which is political participation. We have seen that the Hegesiac sage deliberately alienates himself from key forms of reciprocity between individuals, both cooperative and destructive. We do not have any information about Hegesias's attitude toward politics, but it is once again plausible that on this topic Theodorus has preserved an echo of his predecessor's position. Theodorus "used to say it was reasonable for the good man not to give his life [*exagein heauton*[52]] on behalf of his country, since it isn't reasonable to throw away wisdom for the sake of helping fools" (D.L. 2.98).

The argument in this piece of evidence is elliptical and admits of several reconstructions. From whose perspective is it "not reasonable" to "throw away" the sage for the sake of helping his foolish co-citizens? To put it another way, who is doing the throwing away? This could be the sage's own perspective. The point could be that nothing any group of fools can offer a sage could begin to compensate him for giving away his life. It would therefore be imprudent for him to sacrifice himself. On the other hand, Theodorus could be speaking from the polis's perspective. The point would be that it is both imprudent and unjust for the polis to send the sage to his death for the sake of his co-citizens. It is imprudent because the fools on whose behalf he gives his life cannot possibly contribute as much to the polis as he does. The polis therefore stands to lose by sacrificing the sage. It is unjust because the sage is being asked to give up something much more valuable than his fellow citizens, since his life is worth more.

However we reconstruct Theodorus's explanation for this position, the important point for now is that he rejects the ideology of patriotism. I discussed the representation of the polis as a parent, friend, and beloved in the introduction to this chapter. I also discussed the representation of co-citizens as friends and citizens of hostile cities as enemies. Like Aristippus, Theodorus repudiates all of this. This is hardly surprising, since he was reportedly exiled from both Cyrene and Athens.[53] His co-citizens are not his friends, since he denies friendship exists. Nor are the enemies of Cyrene his enemies. This is more than a theoretical point, since Cyrene was frequently at war during the years when Theodorus was of an age to fight. He was probably born around 345 BCE, and Cyrene was at war—at the least—from 324–21, 312–11, 309–8, and 305–1 BCE.[54] In fact nearly constant warfare swept through the entire Greek-speaking Mediterranean in the wake of Alexander the Great's death in 323 BCE. Some of this became disconnected from the civic or even pan-Hellenic foundations in which wars of the classical period were usually embedded. Thus, his specific historical context lent plausibility to Theodorus's challenge to people's military "friendship" with their co-citizens and "enmity" with other cities' citizens.

Whatever their theoretical or historical rationale, the point I want to emphasize is that Theodorus defends radical positions on civic participation and friendship. Together with Hegesias, whose perspective may have influenced him, he represents the culmination of one trend in Cyrenaic thinking about relationships and society. This trend leads to the sundering of those bonds of affection and assistance which organized social interaction and aspiration for the Cyrenaics' contemporaries. It draws inspiration from Aristippus's coldness toward his son, impersonal relations with courtesans, and rejection of civic identity. But Aristippus was also a caring father to Arete and friend to Aeschines.

That side of his philosophy bears fruit in the doctrines of Anniceris, to which I will now turn.

6.6. Anniceris

The greater part of Diogenes Laertius's Annicerean doxography concerns friendship, gratitude, and relationships with parents and polis. In order to make this graphically obvious, I print the entirety here with the parts that do *not* concern friendship in italics.

> In other respects the Annicereans agreed with these. But they left friendship in life and gratitude and honor towards parents and taking action on behalf of the fatherland. Hence through these things, even if the wise person experiences disturbances, nonetheless he'll be happy, even if few pleasant things happen to him. A friend's happiness isn't choiceworthy for itself, since it isn't perceptible to his neighbor. *And reason isn't self-sufficient for feeling confident and rising above common opinion. It's necessary to habituate ourselves because of the bad disposition that's been nurtured in us for a long time.* ⟨The wise person⟩ doesn't embrace his friend only because of his uses, and if these run out, fail to care for him. Rather, he ⟨embraces and cares for him⟩ in accord with his established good will, and for the sake of this will even endure pains. Even though he posits pleasure as his end and is annoyed to be deprived of it, still he'll willingly endure for the love of his friend. (D.L. 2.96–97 = SSR 4g.3)

It is clear that the heavy emphasis on friendship results from the desire to contrast Anniceris with Hegesias. This is why the doxography begins, "In other respects the Annicereans agreed with these. But they left friendship in life and gratitude and honor towards parents and taking action for one's country." The antecedent for "these" are the Hegesiacs, whose doxography immediately precedes the Annicerean doxography. Diogenes probably means that the Annicereans share many of their doctrines with both the Hegesiacs and the mainstream Cyrenaics. But the opposition between "in other respects" and "but they left friendship and gratitude" highlights Hegesias's rejection of friendship and gratitude as the specific point of contrast. The fact that Diogenes includes "taking action on behalf of the fatherland" in the contrast confirms that Hegesias, like Theodorus after him, was estranged from political participation. Moreover, the assertion that Annicereans preserve "honor towards parents" implies an element absent from both Hegesiac and Theodorean doxographies: in addition to all his other forms of self-isolation, Hegesias apparently distanced himself from the child–parent relationship.

While Diogenes communicates a fair deal of information about Anniceris' position, its overall configuration requires reconstruction. I will first offer what I believe to be the most straightforward interpretation of the evidence, which raises an obvious problem. I will then outline an alternative that would help to solve the problem.

Annas has aptly said that, at least on a straightforward reading, Diogenes' evidence imputes a sort of "double-mindedness" about friendship to Anniceris.[55] On the one hand it seems that friendship, gratitude, honoring your parents, and acting on behalf of your polis are valued for instrumental reasons. This is the implication of the second sentence in the doxography: "Hence through these things, even if the wise person experiences disturbances, nonetheless he'll be happy, even if few pleasant things happen to him" (D.L. 2.96). Anniceris is not saying that happiness can be achieved even without pleasure. After all, we have already seen that he insists each action takes as its end the pleasure at which it aims.[56] Here too we read that the Annicerean sage "posits pleasure as his end." Rather, the idea must be that through his relationships with friends, parents, and polis, an Annicerean will be happy—i.e., accumulate a certain volume of pleasures across his life—even if few pleasant things happen to him *other than those arising from these relationships.*[57] Thus Anniceris overturns Hegesias's doctrines about human relationships in order also to refute Hegesiac pessimism.

Note that at this level Anniceris seems to agree with the mainstream, Hegesiac, and Theodorean Cyrenaics that friendship exists, if at all, for the sake of usefulness. The sage chooses it because it supports *his* happiness, not for the sake of his friend. The doxography makes this explicit: "A friend's happiness isn't choiceworthy for itself, since it isn't perceptible [*aisthētēn*] to his neighbor." This sentence appears to invoke the theory of experiences, according to which I only have "perception" (*aisthēsis*) of my own experiences, and the satisfaction provided by those experiences is the only thing that is intrinsically choiceworthy for me. It follows that the experiences making up my friend's happiness are not intrinsically choiceworthy for me.

The problem is that the second half of the doxography implies a contradictory position. Here my friend's well-being seems to be choiceworthy to me for its own sake:

> ⟨The wise person⟩ doesn't embrace his friend only for his uses, and if these run out, fail to care for him. Rather, he embraces him in accord with his established good will, and for the sake of this will even endure pains. Even though he posits pleasure as his end and is annoyed to be deprived of it, still he'll willingly endure for the love of his friend.

This section opens by conspicuously rejecting the prior Cyrenaic consensus about friendship: "⟨The wise person⟩[58] doesn't embrace his friend only for his uses, and if these run out, fail to care for him." While admitting that friendship is partly chosen for the sake of usefulness, this sentence clearly denies that friendship can be reduced to instrumentality. This is signposted as an attack on the arguments of Hegesias and Theodorus, as comparison with the Hegesiac and Theodorean doxographies reveals:

[W]e don't choose these things for themselves, but for their uses. When the uses are absent, these things too do not exist. (Hegesias, D.L. 2.93)

The friendship of fools is removed whenever use is eliminated. (Theodorus, D.L. 2.98)

Hegesias and Theodorus both attempt to undermine friendship by arguing that usefulness is necessary for it, and that relationships of utility are unstable. Anniceris admits that usefulness may "run out," but insists that friendship endures.

He suggests two alternate reasons why the sage maintains his friendships even when they are not useful to him. The first is "established good will": "[the sage] embraces [his friend] in accord with his established good will [*para tēn gegonuian eunoian*], and for the sake of this will even endure pains." Aristotle too places "good will" at the heart of friendship, saying,

They say one must wish good things for a friend for his own sake. [But] those who wish good things in this way merely have good will [are *eunous*], unless the same is true of the other. For friendship is good will experienced on both sides. (*EN* 8.2 1155b31–34)[59]

Aristotle claims it is characteristic of friends to wish one another well for the other's own sake. The mainstream Cyrenaic doctrine clearly challenges and attempts to qualify this commonsensical position. Anniceris's assertion that a sage will help his friend because of good will, and *even in the face of pain*, thus represents a return to "common sense."[60] The sage will even ignore his own interests for the sake of his friend's benefit. To put it another way, good will becomes an independent source of motivation, which is occasionally permitted to overrule the pursuit of the sage's own pleasure.

The second alternative to utility proposed by Anniceris is love. "Even though [the sage] posits pleasure as his end and is annoyed to be deprived of it," the doxography says, "still he'll willingly endure for the love of his friend." This is the sort of "love" [*storgē*] tutelary gods feel for their favorites, dogs for their masters, and parents and children for one another.[61] Once again this love constitutes a motivation which is independent from the desire for pleasure, since it causes the sage to willingly forego pleasure.

I have now completed my initial interpretation of Anniceris' theory of friendship. On this interpretation the contradiction in his ethics is obvious. On the one hand the sage remains uniquely motivated by his own satisfying experiences, for the sake of which he makes and keeps friends. On the other hand he is willing to forego pleasure and experience pain because of his good will and love toward his friend. In other words, he is directly motivated by his friend's well-being without reference to his own experiences.

Of course it may be that Anniceris either does not perceive this contradiction or, since he feels committed to both the theory of the experiences and genuine friendship, he cannot resolve the contradiction. "Like a tender-minded utilitarian," Annas writes, "Anniceris denies that his theory really does conflict with common sense, as it clearly seems to do."[62] But it is worthwhile hazarding a more charitable interpretation. After all, the doxographers may have misrepresented Anniceris's position, giving prominence to his vociferous defense of friendship while obliterating its subtler nuances.

In order to eliminate the contradiction what we require is an interpretation of the sage's good will and love which subordinates them to the unique motivational force of the sage's own experiences of pleasure and pain. Here we can take as our starting point a suggestion by Theodor Gomperz:

> [The social feelings] are rooted and grounded in selfishness; they derive their force from praise and blame, from rewards and punishments, from regard to the good opinion and the good will of others, from solidarity of interests; gradually they acquire such strength that they are enabled to break loose from their roots, and exert an entirely independent influence over the soul.[63]

The scenario envisaged may be something like this. An Annicerean sage resolves to enter into and maintain each relationship because he anticipates it will benefit him. For example, he anticipates enjoying his friend's company and allaying his pain through his friend's support. To this extent friendship is indeed "for the sake of its uses." But Anniceris could argue it is a fact of human psychology that sharing your activities and emotions with a like-minded person gradually leads to good will and love. Moreover—and this is the key point—it is a psychological fact that when you wish someone well and love him, you feel pleasure when he is joyful and thriving and distress when he is upset and struggling. In fact it is often the case that the distress you would feel on account of abandoning your friend and seeing him suffer would be greater than the pain you would endure in order to help him. This is all the more true in a culture which places a premium on loyalty, where your peers' disapproval would constantly reawaken your sadness and guilt. The sage could therefore claim that it is ultimately for the sake of cultivating his own joy and avoiding his own distress that he takes pains to help his friends.[64]

While the wording of the doxography does not require this interpretation, it does not rule it out. The biggest problem might be thought to be the final sentence: "Even though he posits pleasure as his end and is annoyed to be deprived of it, still he'll willingly endure for the love of his friend." Earlier I interpreted this to mean that the sage's love for his friend causes him simply to suspend his desire to experience pleasure and avoid pain. This would be the point of saying the sage is "annoyed to be deprived of it" (ἀχθόμενον ἐπὶ τῷ στέρεσθαι αὐτῆς): he regretfully ignores his hedonistic impulses.[65] But this sentence is also compatible with my alternate interpretation of Annicerean friendship, as the following scenario illustrates.

Let us imagine that Anniceris's friend were arrested by Ptolemaic forces following one of the failed revolutions. As one of Cyrene's most famous inhabitants Anniceris might have some influence, but he would have to leave his
symposia and criss-cross Cyrenaica seeking Ptolemy's officers. In this scenario
he might well be "annoyed" at having to exchange his comforts for a dangerous
and uncertain errand. He might even think his friend was downright stupid
to get involved in the political fighting. He might wish he had not started this
relationship. But it would be too late to undo the psychological effects of years
of friendship. In this situation his only options would be to endure the pain of
helping his friend or to endure the worry and guilt of abandoning him. If he
reasonably believed the latter would be worse, it would be rational for him to
"be deprived of pleasure" in order to help his friend.

On this interpretation it seems to me that Anniceris's doctrine is not only
consistent, it is a great improvement on the doctrine of his mainstream predecessors. It preserves the fundamental role of each individual's experiences of
pleasure and pain while simultaneously acknowledging the real psychological
force and importance of normal human relationships.

Yet a worry still remains. Although Anniceris denies the existence of any
comprehensive end such as happiness, his defense of friendship seems to invoke just such an end.[66]

On the one hand this problem is less serious than it might at first appear. In
this section I have been able to reconstruct Anniceris's position without having
recourse to the choiceworthiness of happiness. In each case I have assumed
that an Annicerean chooses particular pleasures or avoidances of distress,
not happiness as a whole. Happiness enters the picture because Anniceris not
only wants to attack Hegesias's ethical solipsism, he also wants to attack his
pessimism. These are separate anti-Hegesiac arguments, which I suspect our
doxographical sources have run together. First, Anniceris attacks Hegesias's repudiation of friendship. Second, he cites the benefits of friendship in order to
attack Hegesias's claim that happiness is impossible.

On the other hand, the reason our doxographers have conflated these positions is undoubtedly because they are closely linked in Anniceris's own thought.
Although he himself denies that he chooses an entire life, it seems natural to say
that he reflectively dismisses Hegesias's entire existential vision and calls upon
his followers to build their lives around a different vision. In other words, his
debate with Hegesias presupposes a comprehensive evaluative and aspirational
framework. Once again, then, his idiosyncratic definition of the end forces
him to disavow a perspective that seems to be built right in to his goals and
arguments.

CHAPTER 7

Hegesias's Pessimism

7.1. Introduction

In *The Birth of Tragedy* Friedrich Nietzsche, who was a professor of classical philology and wrote his doctoral dissertation (in Latin) on the sources of Diogenes Laertius, laments the "senile joy in existence and serenity" of Greek culture after Euripides and Socrates.[1] He argues that Socrates' hypertrophied critical intellect was the paradigm for an attitude which destroyed the archaic Greeks' capacity for both profound suffering and profound artistic creation. "The Greeks knew and felt the terror and horrors of existence," Nietzsche writes,[2] but men like Aeschylus were able to tolerate their sensitivity to the horror of "Dionysian" nature by superposing on it beautiful "Apollonian" forms.[3] In this way they were able to remain open to the other side of Dionysus, which is intoxicating joy. Alas, this talent for both suffering and jubilation, this profound and courageous insight, was done to death by Socratic rationality and its fundamental optimism.[4] Thereafter the Greeks refused to perceive what they could not understand, and thus became decadent and superficial.

I have opened this chapter with the young Nietzsche's *Geistesgeschichte* for two reasons. The first is that, despite his over-generalization and projection of his own ideals onto archaic Greece, Nietzsche is right that post-Socratic Greek philosophy—leaving aside the rest of Greek culture—is essentially optimistic. Nussbaum has written eloquently about the effort of Greek philosophers to reduce "the fragility of goodness," so that the happiness of the wise man becomes nearly impervious to the blows of fortune.[5] By comparison with the Stoics and Epicureans, both of whom claim that the sage remains happy even under extremes of bodily torture and misfortune, it is rather timid for the Cyrenaics to say that "the wise man does not live pleasantly in every detail, . . . but for the most part" (D.L. 2.91). Hegesias's claim that happiness is "entirely impossible" and "non-existent" is another huge leap away from the mainstream. In fact he is arguably the *only* unambiguous philosophical pessimist of Greek antiquity.

The second reason I have begun with Nietzsche is that he provokes us to think about the "life-affirming" uses which pessimism may serve. Nietzsche opens the *Birth of Tragedy* by asking,

Is pessimism *necessarily* the sign of collapse, destruction, of disaster, of the exhausted and enfeebled instincts . . . ? Is there a pessimism of *strength*? An intellectual inclination for what in existence is hard, dreadful, evil, problematic, emerging from what is healthy, from overflowing well being, from living existence *to the full*? (*BoT* §1)

For Nietzsche the willingness to look upon the pain and meaninglessness of the human condition goes hand in hand with the capacity for joy, creativity, and wisdom. This is the "pessimism of strength." Of course, it would be foolish simply to read any of this back into Hegesias's philosophy. However, it would be equally foolish to assume that Hegesiac pessimism arises from either cold calculation or depressive resignation rather than, as in Nietzsche's case, some kind of aspirational vision.

In this chapter I will begin by summarizing Hegesias's formulation of the end, which will establish the doctrinal scaffolding for his pessimism. Next I will introduce the analysis of Wallace Matson, which reduces Hegesiac pessimism to rational calculation and "gloomy" resignation. I will then outline three overlapping frameworks which reveal an aspirational side of Hegesiac ethics. The first is the doctrine of indifference, which is never signposted as an important element in his philosophy (or attributed much importance by scholars), but which runs throughout the doxography. This doctrine expresses an empowering ideal of self-sufficiency and freedom, which must be spelled out in terms of the second and third frameworks. The second is magnanimity, which is a highly gendered, competitive, and essentially heroic attribute. I will argue that Hegesiac magnanimity belongs to a Socratic tradition of appropriating and transforming heroic manliness. This leads into the third framework, which is autonomy. Cologne Papyrus 205, which has plausibly been ascribed to Hegesias, shows how pessimism enables Socrates—and, by implication, anyone who shares Socrates' pessimistic wisdom—to say and do what seems appropriate to him without worrying about the consequences. These three frameworks collectively allow us to understand not only the allure of Hegesias's pessimism, but also how it relates to his repudiation of personal and civic relationships. Finally, I will conclude by returning to Nietzsche's association of the "pessimism of strength" with the beauty and profundity of tragedy, and ask whether there is anything tragic about Hegesias's existential vision.

7.2. Hegesiac "Targets" and the Hegesiac "End"

Diogenes Laertius's Hegesiac doxography opens by informing us that "Those called the Hegesiacs maintained the same targets [*skopous*], pleasure and pain" (2.96). It is not immediately clear to which element earlier in the text the phrase "*the same* targets" refers, since the mainstream Cyrenaics do not nominate any "targets." However, the mainstream doxography begins by informing us that the Cyrenaics "posited two experiences, bodily pain and pleasure." I therefore presume that Hegesiac targets play more or less the same role as these two experiences do in mainstream Cyrenaicism. In other words, Hegesias agrees that pleasure is the only unmistakable and complete good, and therefore the primary point of guidance for what we should choose; and he agrees that pain is the only unmistakable and complete bad thing, and therefore the primary point of guidance for what we should avoid. Thus Hegesiac targets possess some of the features normally attributed to ends.

However, Hegesias draws a clear terminological distinction between "targets" and "the end." The latter is withheld until the very end of the doxography, which reads as follows:

> The wise person will not so much excel in choosing good things as in avoiding bad things, since he posits as his end living neither painfully nor distressingly. This is the advantage gained by those who do not differentiate among the sources of pleasure. (D.L. 2.95)

In section 4.4 I argued that the different ends attributed to the mainstream and Annicerean Cyrenaics are both authentic. The Metrodidact makes "living pleasantly" his comprehensive end. The doctrine that each action takes as its end the particular pleasures arising from it probably originates with Anniceris, who also denies the existence of any comprehensive end. The text I have just quoted shows that Hegesias follows the Metrodidact rather than Anniceris in this regard. "Living neither painfully nor distressingly" (τὸ μὴ ἐπιπόνως ζῆν μηδὲ λυπηρῶς) does not refer to any particular experience of pleasure or avoidance of pain.[6] Moreover, it is unlikely to be taken as the discrete goal of any single action. It looks rather like an attribute of an entire life, which is produced by an entire system of thoughts, attitudes, and behavior. In other words, it is a comprehensive end.

It is odd, of course, for Hegesias to declare pleasure the only complete good and then to make "living neither painfully nor distressingly" his comprehensive end. We would expect him to follow the Metrodidact in aiming to "live pleasantly." However, on this point Hegesias agrees—at least superficially—with the Cyrenaics' critics. A surviving argument by the Cynic Crates (ca. 365–285 BCE) begins, "If we must put together the happy life from an abundance of pleasures . . . no one would be happy. Rather, if you want to calculate all the periods in an entire life, you'll find many more pains" (Teles fr. 6 = SSR 5h.45).[7] It is possible that Crates intends this as an attack on the Cyrenaics in particular.[8] It would be fair to spell out the Metrodidact's goal of "living pleasantly" as achieving an "abundance of pleasures." But even if this were an attack on the Cyrenaics, it would have no impact on Hegesias. "Happiness is wholly impossible," he admits, "since the body has been filled with many sufferings, and the soul suffers along with the body and is troubled, and fortune prevents many things we hope for. For these reasons, happiness is non-existent" (D.L. 2.94). Here he agrees with Crates that suffering preponderates over pleasure, and that this means happiness is unattainable for a hedonist. But he does not follow Crates in concluding that pleasure and pain must not, after all, be the basis of happiness. Rather, he infers that human beings should cease pursuing happiness.

This does not mean that the Hegesiac sage resigns himself to *un*happiness. Between happiness, a life in which good feelings preponderate, and unhappiness, a life in which bad feelings preponderate, there remains the life in which the two balance out. This is the life at which the sage aims: "he posits as his end living neither painfully nor distressingly." There are two essential points to make about this end, which are often overlooked. First, the sage will actually achieve this end: "This is the advantage gained [*ho dē periginesthai*] by those who do not differentiate among the sources of pleasure." Further information about this achievement is provided slightly earlier: "The wise person will not so much excel in choosing good things as in avoiding bad things." Notice that the verb I have translated "excel" (*pleonasein*) corresponds to the noun I translated "abundance" (*pleonasmos*) in Crates' argument. While even the Hegesiac sage cannot achieve an "abundance" of pleasures, he *can* achieve an "abundance" of pain-free moments.

The other point I want to make is that Hegesiac philosophy is not simply an analgesic. To put it another way, it is not the case that the Hegesiac sage aims exclusively to avoid pain and distress and eschews any pursuit of pleasure. To the contrary, sages "do not differentiate among the sources of pleasure." So it is obvious that sages are enjoying pleasures. Indeed they must do so if they are to live neither painfully nor distressingly, since both body and mind are vulnerable to ineluctable disturbances. Only through counterbalancing these with pleasure and joy can they live a life which is, on the whole, neither painful nor distressing. They accomplish this by freeing themselves from moral or aesthetic squeamishness ("they do not differentiate"), which permits them to enjoy themselves without incurring any more pain and distress than is strictly necessary.

7.3. Ruthless Rationalism?

The foregoing gives us the doctrinal core of Hegesiac pessimism, but we are still a long way from understanding it as a theoretical, practical, and attitudinal whole. The closest thing to a recent effort to do so is Matson's article, "Hegesias the Death-Persuader; or, the Gloominess of Hedonism." In fact I believe Matson is deeply wrong about Hegesias, but his errors are instructive.

According to Matson, "To many—readers of Lucretius and *Playboy* alike—hedonism is a liberating and joyous philosophy. Nevertheless, it is a logic that smooths the slope to suicide. . . ."[9] Matson attempts to document this claim by showing that Hegesias "ruthlessly deduced the consequences of [Aristippus's] basic [hedonistic] principles" in a way that leads to the embrace of suicide.[10] The first principle in question is that only our own experiences have intrinsic value for us. Second, pleasures can only differ quantitatively, not qualitatively. Third, "the hedonic calculus always yields a negative bottom line."[11] In other words every agent will experience more pain than pleasure. On the basis of these three principles Matson imputes the following conclusion to Hegesias: "Death, which is the absence of consciousness, is neither good nor bad, hence better than life, which is bound to be bad; so, suicide is rational, and 'whatever is rational should be done.'"[12] Matson believes that Hegesias "positively advocated suicide" as the rational solution to the condition of living.[13] He goes on to suggest that choosing suicide, as some of Hegesias's auditors supposedly did, is precisely what modern game theory dictates: ". . . if forced to gamble where the odds are unknown, a rational player will adopt the strategy designed to maximize the minimum payoff."[14]

Matson thus envisages Hegesias as a "game-theoretical" gambler, whose pessimism arises from a combination of two factors: first, his "ruthless" rationalism; and second, the fundamental wrongness of hedonism, which leads any perspicacious rationalist to look at life as a game he must lose. It emerges at the end of Matson's article that his attack on Hegesias is a skirmish in a larger war on the "game-theoretical" approach to ethical reasoning. Hence Matson also attacks Rawls' theory of justice, since it too is based on a "maximin" strategy.[15] He prefers some form of virtue ethics, concluding that "It was Aristotle, as usual, who got it right."[16] This trans-historical agenda lies beyond the scope of my argument. Insofar as it relies on interpretations of historical hedonisms, however, it merits skepticism. Certainly it is wrong for Hegesias. What I particularly want to criticize is Matson's idea that Hegesiac pessimism is the expression of a scrupulously rational character bound by the wrong-headed principles of the Cyrenaic tradition.

I shall begin by arguing that the "deduction" Matson imputes to Hegesias is not in fact Hegesiac. Its first premise is genuinely Cyrenaic: it follows from the theory of the experiences that only an agent's own experiences have intrinsic value for him. The second premise is also genuinely Cyrenaic, and probably genuinely Hegesiac. That pleasures can only differ quantitatively is suggested by both the theory of experiences, which stipulates that an experience is pleasant if and only if it is "satisfying," and by the Hegesiac sage's strategy of non-discrimination among sources of pleasure. Moreover, it is confirmed by the mainstream claim that "one pleasure does not differ from another" (D.L. 2.87). However, Matson's third premise, that the hedonic calculus always yields a negative bottom line, is not found in our evidence. Matson may be thinking of Hegesias's emphasis on the suffering of body and mind. But I have just finished arguing that the Hegesiac sage, although he cannot achieve happiness, at least manages to avoid unhappiness. Indeed, it is precisely because living pleasantly is impossible that Hegesias nominates this less ambitious end, "living neither distressingly nor painfully"—*because it is possible.*[17] This is probably one reason that Hegesias never puts forward the conclusion that Matson ascribes to him; he never says that suicide is choiceworthy for every agent.

Matson's primary exhibit for the contention that Hegesias advocates universal suicide is a passage by Cicero. There is also a parallel passage in Plutarch, of which Matson may be unaware. I quote both here in full.[18]

> So death takes us away from bad things and not from good ones, if you want the truth. In fact this is so abundantly argued by the Cyrenaic Hegesias that he is said to have been prohibited by Ptolemy from giving this lecture in the schools, because many people were killing themselves after hearing it. Moreover, there is an anecdote by Callimachus about Cleombrotus of Ambracia. Callimachus says that although nothing bad had happened to him, after reading Plato's book he threw himself from the wall. This Hegesias whom I mentioned has a book called *The Man Starving Himself to Death*,[19] in which a man who is departing from life by fasting is recalled by his friends. In response he enumerates the discomforts of human life. I could do the same, although less than he, who believes that living is advantageous for absolutely no one. (*Tusc.* 1.83–84 = *SSR* 4f.3–4)

> Or shall we not even say that people cherish themselves, since many slaughter themselves and throw themselves from precipices? Oedipus "Struck out his eyes, and at once his crimson eyeballs wet his cheeks." And when Hegesias spoke he persuaded many of those listening to starve themselves to death. (Plut. *Mor.* 497c–d, part of which = *SSR* 4f.6)

Matson infers Hegesias's advocacy of suicide from the first passage above and from that fact that at D.L. 2.86 Hegesias is called "the Death-Persuader." He does not explain how this constellation of evidence leads to his inference, but I presume he believes that the way Hegesias persuades his listeners to kill themselves is by explicitly arguing that they should do so. He may also believe that the perspective of the protagonist in *The Man Starving Himself to Death* should be identified straightforwardly with Hegesias's own point of view. But both of these beliefs are dubious.

Let us begin with Hegesias's book. We are fortunate that Cicero has preserved a brief summary of its primary contents:

> [A] man who is departing from life by fasting is recalled by his friends. In response he enumerates the discomforts of human life. I could do the same, although less than he, who believes that living is profitable for absolutely no one.

Obviously it is true that the protagonist of *The Man Starving Himself to Death* makes an argument for the very suicide he is in fact undertaking. It seems that his argument is universal and not based on personal circumstances, since he justifies his decision by "enumerat[ing] the discomforts of human life." However, it is hasty to leap from this fictional framework to Hegesias's own authorial perspective. First we must ask ourselves what protreptic, persuasive, or therapeutic purpose could motivate this fiction. One plausible answer is that Hegesias is trying to make the point as emphatically as possible that most people delude themselves about the goodness of living and the badness of dying. Hence the protagonist directs his argument to a gathering of friends, who obviously believe that dying and death are bad. However, notice that Cicero does not ascribe to this book or Hegesias the position that death is good. Rather, he says that he "believes that on the whole, living is advantageous for no one" (*omnino vivere expedire nemini putat*). It does not follow from this that living is disadvantageous or dying is profitable. It may be that living and being dead are both indifferent. This is what Hegesias's presentation of the end would lead us to expect, since it implies that the sage manages to live neither pleasantly nor painfully, neither joyfully nor distressingly. It would be reasonable to call such a life indifferent.

At this point we must digress to attend to the doxography's statements about the choiceworthiness of living, life, and death, since they are clearly relevant to the question of suicide. First we read that "Life and death are both choiceworthy" (D.L. 2.94). Choiceworthy for whom, we would like to know, and on what basis? One possibility is that the sage, to whom living is indifferent, is authorized simply to follow his whim. It makes no difference whether he lives or dies, so he may choose either. However, the sage's whim would be a very feeble basis for calling an action "choiceworthy." A better interpretation is that for all people the choiceworthiness of living or dying depends on circumstances. For example, a healthy young person living in a peaceful and flourishing polis has good grounds for hoping that he can, in the short term, at least break even in the balance of pleasures and pains. By contrast an ill person living in times of war and famine has good grounds for expecting to experience more pain than pleasure. Thus life would be choiceworthy for the former, who should choose to go on living, and death would be choiceworthy for the latter, who should choose to die.[20]

The other relevant part of our doxography is more enigmatic: "And living is advantageous for the fool, but indifferent for the wise man."[21] The second clause confirms what I have already argued about the indifference of life for the sage. The first clause is trickier: it appears to contradict what Cicero ascribes to *The Man Starving Himself to Death*, since it names a class of individuals for whom living is, after all, advantageous. There are once again two ways we might resolve this contradiction. The first is to translate the sentence differently: "And the fool thinks living is advantageous, but the wise man thinks it is indifferent." This neatly solves the problem, but requires us to accuse our source of almost willfully misleading Greek. Moreover, there is a good reason for Hegesias to claim that living is advantageous for those who have not yet achieved his sort of wisdom. The alternative is to admit that, since fools are less able to avoid pain than sages, they should simply commit suicide. In this case Hegesias would be urging all his potential followers to kill themselves rather than study his philosophy. The second and better solution is that Hegesias thinks fools stand to benefit precisely by becoming wise.[22] Unfortunately, our doxography has not preserved enough information for us to understand on what basis Hegesias could make such a claim.[23]

Notwithstanding the murkiness of Hegesias's reasoning about fools, the foregoing demonstrates that Hegesias does *not* recommend suicide for absolutely everyone. Yet Matson might object that this does not explain why so many of Hegesias's auditors committed suicide, and why Hegesias bore the moniker "Death-persuader." Here we must point out that the biographies of ancient Greek philosophers are filled with fabrications based on the author's written works, not on actual records of their lives. Modes of death in particular tend to reflect later generation's reactions to philosophers' doctrines and lifestyles—illustrating a feeling that they are ludicrous, mortifying, or both. Hence Heraclitus reportedly came down from his lonely mountain when he was suffering from edema—i.e., the accumulation of fluid beneath the skin—and "asked the doctors if they could turn heavy rain into a drought." Since they said no, he buried himself in dung and died after two days in the hot sun (D.L. 9.3–4).[24] This bizarre story fits with the perception that Heraclitus's work was riddling, eccentric, and misanthropic, and thus that its author must have been so as well. Zeno of Citium, the founder of Stoicism, reportedly stubbed and broke his toe when leaving his school at an advanced age. Quoting Euripides' *Niobe*—"I'm coming, why do you call me?"—he choked himself to death (D.L. 2.28). This reflects Zeno's ideal of impassivity, his claim that death is neither good nor bad, and his emphasis on following God's rational logos. As a final example, note that Cicero inserts into his testimony on Hegesias the suicide of Cleombrotus of Ambracia: "after reading Plato's book he threw himself from the wall." The book in question, of course, is Plato's *Phaedo*, which famously describes philosophy as "practice for dying" (64a–6). After Callimachus (*Ep.* 23) the story was often embroidered, becoming a literary and philosophical commonplace for discussing the disdain of earthly goods and the aspiration to immortality.[25] It is the desire to comment on the *Phaedo* which drives the repetition and evolution of the anecdote, not the historicity of Cleombrotus's motivations or mode of death.

Thus the story of Hegesias' suicide-inducing lectures may have been concocted on the basis of his book, *The Man Starving Himself to Death*. This gives us an initial reason to be skeptical about it. There are also two more specific reasons. First, Cicero avoids vouching for its accuracy: "the Cyrenaic Hegesias . . . *is said* [*dicitur*] to have been prohibited by Ptolemy from giving this lecture in the schools, because many people were killing themselves after hearing it."

Cicero reports the existence and contents of Hegesias's book as a fact, but this anecdote about suicides as a mere rumor. Second, Plutarch's report conflates the title of Hegesias's book with the events in the anecdote: "when Hegesias spoke he persuaded many of those listening *to starve themselves to death* [*apokarterēsai*]." The fact that the listeners take their lives in the same way as the protagonist of *The Man Starving Himself to Death* [*Apokarterōn*] deepens our suspicion that the literary fiction has given birth to a biographical fiction. Of course, it remains possible that one or more of Hegesias's listeners actually did commit suicide. This could explain the nickname "death-persuader." But the evidence is by no means strong enough to support the conviction that many of Hegesias's auditors committed suicide, much less that Hegesias was "positively advocating" that they do so.

Matson's reconstruction of Hegesias's position thus looks rather hasty. Not only does Hegesias not claim that death is always choiceworthy, he explicitly states that living is advantageous for the fool and indifferent for the sage. Moreover, the claim that Hegesias urges his listeners to commit suicide stands on shaky ground. With its conclusion lacking and its third premise explicitly contradicted by the evidence, Matson's "ruthless deduction" can no longer be ascribed to Hegesias. His pessimism does not arise from a game-theoretical speculation about the human condition. In order to reconstruct the meaning of Hegesias's pessimism we must therefore investigate the remainder of that evidence more carefully, drawing on the historical contexts which can help to illuminate its meaning.

7.4. Indifference

The concept of "indifference" has occurred several times in the foregoing sections.[26] In fact, words with the root "(in)differ-" ([a]diapher-) appear four times in a doxography that is less than a page long. In order to bring out the importance of this theme for Hegesias's pessimism I shall begin with a quotation by Bernard Williams, who makes the following observation in the course of an article entitled "Unbearable Suffering":

> Various traditional counsels have suggested that the way to make life bearable lies in the direction of *ataraxia*, the refusal of identifications and projects (except, of course, that project itself). . . . [W]hat is the sage who is dedicated to *ataraxia* going to make of the sufferings he cannot avoid? What will help him bear them with equanimity is not the blankly negative idea that they are meaningless. What will help, him, rather, is the idea, so far as he can keep it going, that they are *unimportant*, and this implies that something else is more important: notably, the conception of the self as something to which attachments and contingencies, even the contingency of its own existence, are indifferent. . . . If such an idea helps

to make suffering bearable, it does so by indeed providing meaning, if not to suffering itself, to a life that contains such suffering as one cannot oneself eliminate from it.[27]

The majority of Williams' article concerns Nietzsche, which explains why he associates *ataraxia* or "tranquility" with pessimism about the inevitability of suffering. *Ataraxia* is well known as an Epicurean term, and Nietzsche represents Epicureanism as a response to the problem of suffering.[28] But the particular theory Williams has in mind, whether it be Epicureanism (through Nietzsche's eyes) or some Eastern philosophy, does not concern me here. What is germane to my investigation is the nexus encompassing belief in the ubiquity of suffering, indifference, and a meaningful project for living. We have already seen that Hegesias believes both body and soul are vulnerable to many sufferings. In the remainder of this chapter I will argue that this emphasis on suffering is connected to indifference and a meaningful project for living in the way Williams suggests.

The argument can be made that the entire central block of the Hegesiac doxography is organized around the theme of indifference:

> They claimed that nothing is pleasant or unpleasant by nature, but that some are pleased and others displeased because of lack or strangeness or satiation. Poverty and wealth are irrelevant to the account of pleasure, since rich people do not feel pleasure *differently* than poor people. Slavery is just as *indifferent* as freedom to the measure of pleasure, as are noble birth or humble birth, fame or ignominy. And living is advantageous to the fool, but *indifferent* to the wise person. (D.L. 2.94–95)

The emphatic message of this passage is that the things which Hegesias's contemporaries generally pursue or avoid are actually indifferent. In each case this indifference is spelled out in terms of the hedonic consequences of these specious goods or evils. First, it does not matter how much money you have, "since rich people do not feel pleasure differently [*diapherontōs*] than poor people."[29] We can undoubtedly add that rich people do not feel pain differently than poor people, either. The same goes for another fundamental value in classical and Hellenistic Greek societies: "Slavery is just as indifferent [*adiaphoron*] as freedom to the measure of pleasure [*pros hēdonēs metron*]." This clause makes it clear that we are dealing with the quantity rather than the quality of pleasure; the point is that rich, free people experience no more pleasure than poor slaves, and no less pain. Finally, the passage adds that noble birth and reputation are equally indifferent to the quantity of pleasure one will experience. Hegesias has thus concisely eliminated four key preoccupations of his contemporaries, two hereditary or otherwise given (noble birth and freedom), two partly acquired (wealth and reputation). In short, he argues that it does not matter into what status you have been born or driven, so your status should neither inflate you with pride nor embitter you with envy; and the things you think cause happiness or unhappiness are in fact irrelevant, so you should stop yearning for them or fearing them.

Of course, Hegesias cannot adopt the position that absolutely everything is indifferent. That may be the belief of his slightly older contemporary Pyrrho of Elis (ca. 365–275 BCE), who reportedly claims that "things are equally undifferentiated, unstable, and indeterminate."[30] Our source goes on,

> Therefore neither our sense perceptions nor our opinions are true or false. So for this reason we should not trust them, but should rather be without belief, inclination, or disturbance, saying about each single thing that it no more is than is not, or that it both is and is not, or that it neither is nor is not. (Eus. *PE* 14.18.3)

In short, Pyrrho not only believes that things are unknowable to human intellects, he also thinks that they are in themselves undifferentiated. This leads him to a state of absolute tranquility, as Eusebius goes on to report: "To those who are in this condition, Timon says, will come first speechlessness, and then impassivity" (*PE* 14.18.4). Timon is Pyrrho's most famous disciple. Surviving fragments of his philosophical poetry repeatedly and emphatically address the extraordinary disposition which arises from Pyrrho's metaphysical and epistemological insights:

> Such was the man I saw, not puffed up or broken
> by whatever has broken the well-known and unknown alike,
> the fickle races of people, who are weighed down on all sides
> with passions, opinion and futile legislation.
> (Quoted in Eus. *PE* 14.18.19, translation adapted from LS 2B)

> Pyrrho, my heart yearns to hear
> how, though you are a mortal man, you live so easily and tranquilly,
> forever without concern or commotion, always in the same state,
> . . . .
> alone among mortals you show humans the path of god.
> (quoted in D.L. 2.65 + SE *M* 11.1 + *M* 1.305,
> translation adapted from LS 2D)

For Pyrrho, understanding the indifference of things in the world leads to tranquility about what he does and what happens to him. While there is no evidence that Hegesias has been influenced by Pyrrho, he probably aims to achieve a similar result through his indifference.[31] However, unlike Pyrrho, Hegesias is committed to the dogmatic positions that pleasure and joy are good, while pain and distress are bad. How, then, can he approach this sort of impassivity?

This question provides the clue to understanding the first sentence in the paragraph I quoted above: Hegesiacs "used to claim that nothing is pleasant or unpleasant by nature, but that some are pleased and others displeased because of lack or strangeness or satiation." This doctrine begins with a commonsensical intuition, but ends on a more radical note. It is commonsensical that our tendency to experience pleasure has something to do with familiarity/strangeness and satiation/lack. For example, an almond croissant first thing in the morning, when you are in a state of "scarcity" or "want" (*spanis*) regarding food, may be very agreeable. However, an almond croissant after a large dinner, especially if all the week's meals have consisted exclusively of almond croissants, may be nauseating. The reason would be your state of "satiety" or "excess" (*koros*) both with food in general and almond croissants in particular.[32] Similarly, someone accustomed to Western pastries may find a dessert of candied lotus root around a salted egg yoke disgusting. The reason would be the "strangeness" (*xenismos*) of this eastern delicacy. Our doxography does not explicitly say that we enjoy things through "familiarity," but some such complement to "strangeness" has probably fallen out. The claim would then be that we can habituate ourselves to enjoy things. For example, very spicy foods are intolerable to those who are unaccustomed to them, but pleasant to those who eat them every day.[33]

This part of the sentence already goes some way toward resolving the tension between aspiring to indifference and being committed to pursuing pleasure and avoiding pain, since it gives each agent a fair degree of control over the way he experiences things. But the latter part of the sentence is more radical. It claims that "nothing is pleasant or unpleasant by nature" (φύσει τ᾽ οὐδὲν ἡδὺ ἢ ἀηδὲς). In fact a forerunner for this claim appears already in the mainstream doxography, albeit in a sentence which may be textually corrupt: "One pleasure does not differ from another, nor is anything particularly pleasant" (μὴ διαφέρειν ἡδονὴν ἡδονῆς, μηδὲ ἥδιόν τι εἶναι).[34] If the reading "nor is anything particularly pleasant" is sound, one plausible interpretation of the mainstream Cyrenaics' claim is that particular sources are not *necessarily* connected with either pleasure or pain.[35] Hegesias would then be saying the same thing: for example, honey is not necessarily connected with pleasure, though we mistakenly believe it is so. Even more radically, fire is not necessarily connected with pain, although once again we mistakenly believe it is. Of course Hegesias can point out that some people dislike and are allergic to honey. The Greeks also believed that "green honey" was sickening and intoxicating.[36] Moreover, he could point out that fire is warm and agreeable when enjoyed from a safe distance. Perhaps this is as far as his indifference goes: he argues that every object can be used in such a way as to cancel whatever pleasure or displeasure it might offer. In that case this part of the sentence would merely weaken the connection between particular types of *objects* and the experiences they generate. In this way it would strengthen the sage's control over his own experiences.

On the other hand, Hegesias may intend the more radical claim that particular types of *events*, such as putting your hand in a fire or being struck with a sword, are neither pleasant nor unpleasant by nature. But in the absence of well-developed consciousness-altering practices in late classical Greek philosophy, it is hard to imagine how Hegesias could defend this position. There are certainly anecdotes about the superhuman bodily control of Greek philosophers. For example, it is said that Pyrrho underwent medical treatment—"septic drugs and cutting and burning"—without raising his eyebrows (D.L. 2.67).[37] If there were any truth to this anecdote, we might conjecture that Pyrrho had learned some of the meditative practices of the Indian "gymnosophists" he met when accompanying Alexander the Great (D.L. 9.61). Among these gymnosophists was one Calanus, who had himself immolated with a memorable show of impassivity (Str. 15.1.64–65, Plut. *Alex.* 69.3–4, Arr. *An.* 7.3). There was also an earlier tradition of bodily endurance in Greece. This is most famously represented by Socrates' ability to go barefoot in the depths of winter, stand motionless in contemplation for twenty-four hours, and drink all night without becoming intoxicated (Pl. *Symp.* 220a1–d5, 223c2–d12). Several scholars have connected this to the shamanic tradition most prominently represented by Empedocles' *Purifications*.[38] These contexts could help make sense of a radical interpretation of the claim that "nothing is pleasant or unpleasant by nature." However, they could only make that interpretation plausible if the Hegesiac sage were a master of meditative or ecstatic trances. In the absence of even a hint of evidence pointing in this direction, I prefer to interpret Hegesias's claim more cautiously: no object in the world is necessarily pleasant or unpleasant; habituation and satiety make a great difference in how we experience events; but some events, like being cut or burned, are still unavoidably painful.

The upshot will be that a Hegesiac sage cannot be quite as nonchalant about what happens to him as Pyrrho supposedly is, although he can be much more impassive than his average contemporary. This cautious interpretation harmonizes with Hegesias's insistence that many bodily and mental sufferings are inevitable, so that even the sage cannot achieve happiness. Moreover, it fits with the sage's strategy for achieving his end of "living neither painfully nor distressingly." As we have already seen, such an end can be achieved "by those who do not differentiate [*tois adiaphorēsasi*] among the sources of pleasure" (D.L. 2.96). If nothing at all were necessarily painful or distressing for the sage, there would be no intelligible motivation for this behavior. He could be as picky or imprudent as he wished, since no consequences would necessarily be painful and therefore bad. The assumption in this doctrine seems rather to be that some things are painful even to the sage, so that indifference to the sources of pleasure is important: it allows him to choose pleasures which do not lead to pain or distress. Hence he does not treat events as utterly indifferent, since they are differentiated by their association with pleasure and distress. Rather, as with wealth, noble birth, and fame, he treats the *non-hedonic* aspects of events as indifferent.

Before concluding this section I should emphasize that the sage's attitude of indifference, which corresponds to the "natural" indifference of most objects and events, is an extraordinary accomplishment. Normal Cyreneans not only think of honey and figs as pleasant, they also think of honor and political power as enjoyable. They not only think of surgery as painful, they also think of dishonor or slavery as distressing. These beliefs lead both to uncomfortable emotions and to imprudent actions, which in turn generate further pain and distress. Escaping this cycle is almost impossible, which is why Timon praises Pyrrho so extravagantly. Pyrrho has arrived at what Williams calls "the conception of the self as something to which attachments and contingencies, even the contingency of its own existence, are indifferent." The Hegesiac sage cannot become quite so detached, since *some* contingencies, especially those which may cause pleasure or necessarily cause pain, continue to matter to him. But from a broader perspective even those are reasonably unimportant, since if he were not experiencing *this* pleasure, he would find another, and if he did not yield to *this* pain, another would come along. Because these even out over time, his own existence is indeed indifferent: "living is . . . indifferent to the wise person." Really understanding this intellectually, emotionally, and practically is central to the sage's wisdom and thus to Hegesiac philosophy.

We have now seen how the prevalence of pain and distress in human life is connected to the sage's ability to perceive the indifference of most things, adopt a corresponding attitude of impassivity, and thus at least neutralize the "unbearable suffering" to which he would otherwise be exposed. But we have only begun to see how this attitude fits into the projects which make a Hegesiac life satisfying and meaningful. That is the task of the next two sections.

7.5. Magnanimity and Philosophical Heroism

In sections 4.2 and 4.3 I discussed Aristippus's heroic posturing and some of the parallels between the anecdotes about him and Odysseus. Among the features to which I drew attention was the status gap between the philosopher and other men, which loosely recalls the gap between Homer's "kings" and their followers. Demonstrating such elevated status is an important component of what has sometimes been called "the heroic code," which is the network of values governing Homeric life.[39] In Homer, and to a significant extent in classical Greece as well, such elevation is necessarily embodied in "good reputation" (*eukleia*) and tokens of "honor" (*timē*). These tokens include a range of gifts and prerogatives, from golden tripods to civic offices. But as Achilles magnificently exemplifies, the pursuit and defense of reputation and honor is tightly connected to competition, self-assertion, and violent anger. Angela Hobbs' book *Plato and the Hero* explores in compelling detail how this social and psychological complex makes sense of characters like Callicles and Thrasymachus, and how Plato's integration of the *thumos* into his tripartite psychology finally permits him to understand it, criticize it, and propose a persuasive alternative.[40] The philosopher emerges as a man whose *thumos* is not stifled, but rather trained to behave in the way that leads to the happiest life. In this section I will argue that we can profitably think of Hegesiac indifference as an alternate philosophical way of appropriating and domesticating heroic ethics.

Let me begin by recalling the Hegesiac sage's extraordinarily high self-estimation and relating it to the heroic tradition. Hegesias believes that

> The wise person will do everything for his own sake, because he considers no one equal to himself in worth. For even if he seems to receive the greatest profit from someone, it isn't equivalent to what he himself provides. (D.L. 2.95)

The sage believes he is without peer: "he considers no one else equal to himself in worth" (οὐδένα γὰρ ἡγεῖσθαι τῶν ἄλλων ἐπίσης ἄξιον αὐτῷ). This sort of claim is common in heroic ethics as well, where it is entangled in the competitive pursuit of honor. Compare Achilles' repeated claim to be "the best of the Achaeans" in Homer's *Iliad* (1.244, 1.412, 18.105–6), since he is the greatest warrior, and Agamemnon's opposing claim that *he* is the best of the Achaeans (1.91, 2.83; cf. 1.87), since he leads the largest army. When Achilles objects to Agamemnon's behavior, Agamemnon responds, "I won't beg you to stay. There are many others who will honor me [*timēsousi*], and above all Zeus of the high counsels" (*Il.* 1.174–75). But Agamemnon sends his men to take Achilles' woman Briseïs, "so that you'll know how much greater I am than you" (1.185–86). In response Achilles withdraws from battle, prophesying that "some day a yearning for Achilles will come to all the sons of the Achaeans. . . . And you'll tear your heart out, enraged that you showed no honor [*ouden etisas*] to the best of the Achaeans" (1.240–44). Of course, this quarrel is the source of the "countless sufferings of the Achaeans" related in the *Iliad* as a whole (*Il.* 1.2). An alternate tradition has it that "the beginning of suffering for the Trojans and the Danaans" was "a quarrel of Odysseus and Achilles," who are once again named as "the best of the Achaeans" (*Od.* 8.72–82).[41] Nagy persuasively suggests that in this tradition, there is a different basis for the argument about preeminent worth: Achilles' brute force is opposed to Odysseus's cunning.[42] Finally, a similar drama is played out in Sophocles' *Ajax*, where the titular character's giant strength is contrasted with Odysseus's temperance. Once again a nearly disastrous quarrel arises from Ajax's insistence that he is the most worthy of honor (in this case the arms of Achilles), because *he* is the best of the Achaeans (*Ajax* 636).

These plot summaries show both that the sage's claim to superlative worth is a familiar one from the heroic tradition and that it tends to be associated with anger, quarreling, and suffering. But it need not always be so, as we can see by considering Aristotle's virtue of "magnanimity" (*megalopsukhia*). Commentators have rightly associated this virtue with heroic ethics. In the *Nicomachean Ethics* Aristotle defines the "magnanimous man" as someone "who thinks himself worthy of great things, being worthy of them" (*EN* 1123b1–2). In other words, magnanimity combines extraordinary worth with accurate assessment of that worth. Aristotle later adds that the principal "great things" with which the magnanimous man concerns himself are "honors and dishonors" (1124a4–5). So the magnanimous man will expect to receive honors commensurate with his own great worth. So far it looks like Aristotle is describing men such as Achilles, Agamemnon, Odysseus, and Ajax.[43]

However, Aristotle also recognizes an alternative paradigm for magnanimity. Later in the same chapter he adds that the magnanimous man

> will show moderation with regard to wealth, power, and every good or bad fortune, whatever happens, and will neither be overjoyed by good fortune nor severely distressed by bad fortune. For he's not disposed to think that even honor is very important. . . . For this reason [magnanimous people] seem disdainful. (*EN* 1124a13–20)

Here the demand for honor commensurate with worth is counterbalanced by the tendency of the magnanimous person to rise above whatever happens. The implicit logic seems to be that if the magnanimous person really is "great," then neither chance events nor the actions of other people should really affect him. In fact Aristotle explicitly formulates these two competing facets of magnanimity in the *Posterior Analytics*:

> I mean, if we're asking what magnanimity is, we must investigate what single thing some magnanimous people we know share insofar as they're magnanimous. Like if Alcibiades is magnanimous or Achilles and Ajax, what single thing do they all share? They can't endure being treated insultingly. That's why one went to war, one was filled with rage, and one killed himself. In turn we must investigate other cases, like Lysander or Socrates. Since ⟨what they share is⟩ being indifferent to good or bad fortune [τὸ ἀδιάφοροι εἶναι εὐτυχοῦντες καὶ ἀτυχοῦντες], taking these two features, I ask what impassivity with regard to fortune and the intolerance of dishonor share in common. If there is nothing, there would be two forms of magnanimity. (95b15–25)

Whether Aristotle succeeds in reconciling these two features of magnanimity is not my concern here. The important point for Hegesias is that Aristotle recognizes indifference and impassivity as manifestations of this virtue. He associates this form of the virtue with Socrates, which suggests that it was already part of the *philosophical* appropriation of heroic greatness. But he also associates it with Lysander, who was the Spartan counterpart to Alcibiades: a controversial but powerful politician and a renowned general, who finally brought Athens to capitulation in the Peloponnesian War. This suggests that the connection between indifference to good or bad fortune and greatness had broader cultural currency as well.

I have now established that the nexus of great worth, accurate assessment of that worth, and an attitude of indifference constitutes one paradigm for the heroic virtue of magnanimity. Of course, the Hegesiac sage exemplifies this nexus of attributes. Moreover, these are not the only elements of magnanimity which he displays. Aristotle also suggests that the magnanimous man "isn't mindful of wrongs, because it isn't proper to the great-souled man to remember things, especially wrongs, but rather to overlook them" (*EN* 1125a3–5). This casts further light on Hegesias's doctrine that "errors receive forgiveness. For a person does not err voluntarily, but because he is coerced by some passion. And ⟨they⟩ won't hate, but will rather share ⟨their⟩ teaching" (D.L. 2.95).[44] While it is often remarked that this passage recalls Socrates' insistence that no one errs voluntarily,[45] no one seems to have remarked on the magnanimity of the Hegesiac sage in responding to "errors" by "sharing his teaching." First, this refusal to retaliate suggests that the error was insignificant to him. Even if his antagonists intended to harm him, it was not in their power to do so. Second, the sage goes beyond high-minded nonchalance and actually benefits his antagonists. This too has a (partial) parallel in Aristotle, who says that the magnanimous person "is the sort to do good for others, but is ashamed to have good done for him. For the one belongs to the superior person, the other to the inferior" (Arist. *EN* 1124b9–10).[46] Following this logic we might propose that the sage shares his wisdom simply for the joy of expressing his superiority. This combination of disdain and condescension is more befitting and therefore more agreeable for him than retaliation.[47]

Hegesias's version of magnanimity appropriates the satisfactions of heroic greatness without the ruinous concomitants of this status in literature and contemporary society. By declaring that "fame" is equivalent to "ignominy" (*doxan adoxiāi*), since both are indifferent for pleasure and pain, Hegesias removes the principal ground for quarreling and anger. The sage does not require other people to recognize he is the most worthy and to honor him accordingly, especially since he does not believe they have the intelligence to judge. It suffices that he himself perceive his preeminent excellence. In this way his philosophy provides scope for the agonistic impulse to "be the best," and permits its followers the satisfaction of believing that their insights make them better than their co-citizens. At the same time it eliminates the tempestuous conflicts in which both epic protagonists and the most ambitious of Hegesias's contemporaries are often embroiled.

7.6. Autonomy and Cologne Papyrus 205

It is not coincidental that Aristotle names Socrates among those who, like Hegesias, exemplify magnanimity through their indifference to good or bad fortune. The example of Socrates will help us to explain the second way in which indifference fits into a meaningful project for life: being able to perceive the indifference of most things empowers the sage to remain faithful to his own inclinations and deliberations. In order to demonstrate this I will examine a hitherto under-utilized source for Hegesiac thinking, Cologne Papyrus 205. I will argue that Hegesias or a Hegesiac is the most likely author of the fragmentary dialogue preserved on this papyrus. Although this attribution cannot be considered certain, my arguments in the rest of the section do not rest on it: even if the dialogue is not Hegesiac, it still provides a concrete scenario for considering the sorts of things a Hegesiac *would* say in a situation where a philosopher might be tempted to compromise his autonomy.

Papyrus 205 from Cologne (PKöln 205 = *SSR* 1c.550) consists of eight fragments, substantial parts of the first and second of which are legible, from a Socratic dialogue used to wrap a mummy in Ptolemaic Egypt.[48] Since this dialogue has never—to the best of my knowledge—been translated into English, I provide a complete translation here. Where the papyrus is badly damaged and either the lettering or the meaning is uncertain, I have put my translation in italics. Note that the division of the text between speakers is not marked in the papyrus.[49]

(column I)
> [papyrus illegible for 13 lines[50]]
> "*. . . we have digressed* to this topic of inquiry . . .
> ". . . to the wise man . . ."
> [illegible for 7.5 lines]
> ". . . for life . . . because . . . life . . ."
> [illegible for 3 lines]
> ". . . who's going to die won't be disturbed, if he's leaving a life that's both pleasant and upright. Or don't you remember **(col. II)** *that it was because of this that we digressed to this topic of inquiry?*"
> "Certainly I remember. I know it perfectly well."
> "So up until now we haven't in any part of our discussion been able to find that the life of a sensible person is more pleasant [approximately eight characters missing] *than* distressing?"
> "Well, certainly not, by Zeus!"
> "So then the sensible person wouldn't be grieved to leave *these not-so-pleasant things* behind, if he were going to die?"
> "It seems not, I *tell* you."
> "And he certainly won't shrink from dying in order to avoid anything disagreeable happening next in Hades. I think we've shown in the foregoing that it's not possible for anything disagreeable to happen to anyone in Hades."
> "I certainly think that you've adequately shown this as well."
> **(col. III)** [5 lines mostly illegible]
> ". . . why I offered no defense to the Athenians about the death penalty?"
> "No, by Zeus! I don't think so anymore! To you and me, Socrates, and to anyone who thinks that pleasure is the best end of life, and distress the worst, you would appear to have defended yourself well in all these matters, because you offered no defense regarding the death penalty."

"[one or two words illegible] other people, who posit that the fine and the fine life are the best end, and that the shameful and the shameful life are the worst, won't want to agree with us. They'll argue that, since in pleasure and distress . . . by no means . . . less . . ."
[the rest mostly illegible[51]]

Notwithstanding the many lacunae, it is clear that in his dialogue Socrates explains to an unnamed interlocutor why he did not try harder at his trial to preserve his life. As we know from many sources, the outcome of this trial was that he was condemned to die. The fragmentary opening lines suggest that Socrates' explanation here is framed in terms of how the "wise man" (*tōi phronimōi*) feels about life (*ho bios*). Socrates reminds his interlocutor that he has already argued that no sensible person is upset by the prospect of leaving life, since even a sensible person's life has no surplus of pleasure. Moreover, he has also argued that nothing bad will happen after death. His interlocutor remembers these conclusions, and infers from them that "to you and me and anyone who thinks that pleasure is the best end of life, and pain the worst, you would appear to have defended yourself well." Either Socrates or his interlocutor then appears to begin arguing that dying will, however, be upsetting for those who believe that "the fine and the fine life is the best end, and the shameful or the shameful life is the worst." Here the fragment ends.

Given its dating and subject matter, scholars have repeatedly thought of Cyrenaics as the most plausible authors of this dialogue. Gronewald dates the papyrus itself to the third century BCE based on its script and orthography, and remarks that it belongs to that body of Socratic dialogues, of which only Plato's *Phaedo* and *Crito* survive, which depict Socrates conversing about his trial and death during the month he spent in prison.[52] Barnes plausibly suggests that it was "written in polemical vein against the more severe accounts of Socrates' final thoughts which had been published by Antisthenes and Plato."[53] Gronewald and Barnes think of Aeschines and Aristippus as the most likely authors of such a polemic.[54] The hedonistic tone of the papyrus makes Aristippus the more tempting alternative, although we cannot be certain that Socrates is supposed to be representing his own beliefs here rather than adopting hedonism for the sake of argument.[55] Moreover, it was contested already in antiquity whether any of the dialogues and compositions ascribed to Aristippus were genuine; in any event, none of thirty-one titles given by Diogenes Laertius 2.84–85 seems a likely source for our passage. The subject matter fits no better with the substantial fragments and testimonia of the seven dialogues confidently ascribed to Aeschines in antiquity.[56] However, among the so-called "headless" Aeschinean dialogues, of which both the authenticity and the quality have been repeatedly questioned, we find one called the *Phaedo*.[57] It is possible, though by no means certain, that the coincidence of title indicates a coincidence of subject matter with Plato's *Phaedo*. So both Aeschines and Aristippus remain possible authors, but there are problems with ascribing the dialogue to either of them. It does not fit with Aristippus's known literary output, and it does not fit with Aeschines' known ethics.[58]

The most plausible solution to this aporia is to admit that the dialogue belongs to neither Aeschines nor Aristippus, but to some later Socratic philosopher. This later dating is supported by the phrases "best" and "worst end in life" to describe pleasure and distress (ἡδονὴμ[59] μὲν εἶναι [τέ]λος ἄριστον βίου, λύπην δὲ κάκισ[το]ν, III.15–19) or moral beauty and shame (ἄλλοι γε τέλος τιθέμενοι τό καλόν τε καὶ τὸν καλὸμ βίον ἄριστο[ν εἶ]ναι καὶ τὸ αἰσχρὸν [κ]αὶ τὸν αἰσχρὸμ β[ίο]ν κάκιστον). Notwithstanding the appearance of the word "end" in Plato's *Gorgias* with the meaning "the good for the sake of which other things are done" (499e6–500a1),[60] the formulation of "ends" as ultimate reference points of positive and negative value, by which ethical systems could conveniently be encapsulated and compared, dates to a time after the debate among Socrates' immediate followers.[61] It is for this reason that this word appears only incidentally in the *Gorgias* with this sense. It does not appear at all in Plato's comparison of the lives of cognition and pleasure in his *Philebus*.[62] The casualness with which Socrates' interlocutor uses it in PKöln 205 suggests a date some time after this technical term became central to ethical philosophy, as we first find it in Aristotle's *Nicomachean Ethics*.[63]

Given that this terminological consideration makes the middle of the fourth century BCE the *terminus post quem* for PKöln 205, while the end of the third century BCE remains the *terminus ante quem* for papyrological reasons, we now have to think of Socratic schools rather than of Socrates' immediate followers. We know that Plato's successors continued writing Socratic dialogues, since many of their works were ascribed to the master and have survived as the *spuria Platonica*.[64] It would hardly be surprising for rival schools, such as the Cyrenaics, to express their alternate conceptions of Socratic philosophy by also writing Socratic dialogues. It is even possible that these dialogues were sometimes fathered on Aristippus just as Academic dialogues passed under Plato's name. This could account for some of the spurious Aristippean works circulating in the Hellenistic period. Whatever authorship it claimed, PKöln 205 is certainly a plausible candidate for a later Cyrenaic work: the distinctive antithesis between "best" and "worst" ends, though not foreign to other philosophies, is well represented for the Cyrenaics;[65] the organization of life around pleasure is consonant with Cyrenaic ethics; and with the exception of the Epicureans, who were not known to write Socratic dialogues, it is hard to think of anyone else who would have polemicized against the attachment to "moral beauty and the morally beautiful life" espoused in different ways by Megarics and Dialectics, Cynics and Stoics, and Academics and Peripatetics.

We can be more specific than this: as Spinelli plausibly suggests, Hegesias or a Hegesiac is the Cyrenaic most likely to have authored this work.[66] The main argument for this ascription depends on the strikingly unusual combination of doctrines in this papyrus: first, the "best end of life" is pleasure, and the "worst end" is pain; second, a pleasant life is impossible. Of course, in our doxography Hegesias therefore proposes the compromise end of "living neither painfully nor distressingly." This compromise may also be represented in the papyrus, where Socrates says that "up until now we haven't in any part of our discussion been able to find that the life of a sensible person is more pleasant [. . . . .] *than* distressing" (οὐκοῦν ἄχρι γε τοῦ νῦν κατ᾽ οὐθένα τῶν λόγων δυνάμεθ᾽ εὑρεῖν ὡς ὁ τοῦ νοῦν ἔχοντος βί[ο]ς ἡδίων ἐστὶ [. . . . . .] ἢ ἐπιλυπότερος; I.12–13).[67] On Spinelli's reconstruction, this would read,

> ". . . will not be more pleasant."
> "[What do you mean?] Would it be more distressing?"
> "Certainly not, by Zeus!"[68]

In other words, Socrates would be arguing that the "sensible person's" life is neither pleasant nor distressing. But even without this conjecture, the convergence between Socrates' position in the dialogue and Hegesias's very unusual beliefs is remarkable. Although no source tells us that Hegesias wrote Socratic dialogues, either he or his followers certainly could have done so; our sources very rarely record the works of minor Socratic authors. Moreover, Hegesias's activity in north Africa (and possibly in Egypt) also favors the Egyptian origin of this papyrus.[69] Therefore I agree with Spinelli that the most plausible author for this dialogue is Hegesias or a Hegesiac, although the fragmentary nature of the evidence prevents certainty.

This brings me to the connection between Hegesiac pessimism, indifference, and autonomy. We know from the apologetic works of Plato and Xenophon that what Socrates must explain to his followers—and what his followers must explain to one another, Socrates' detractors, and the general public—is why Socrates did not mount an effective defense at his own trial. Plato puts the most trenchant criticism of Socrates' handling of the affair in the mouth of Crito:

> Moreover, Socrates, your current undertaking doesn't even seem just to me. You're betraying yourself even though you could save yourself, and you're eagerly bringing upon yourself precisely the things your enemies would bring and have brought upon you, since they want to destroy you. Moreover, I think you're betraying your sons as well, since you're abandoning them, although you could raise them and educate them. As far as you're concerned, they'll have to take their chances, and chances are that they'll experience exactly what orphans usually experience without parents. Either you shouldn't have children or you should see through their upbringing and education. But you seem to me to choose the easiest path. You should make the choice that a noble man would make, especially since you always say that you cultivate virtue throughout your life. So I'm ashamed on your behalf and on behalf of your friends. It'll look like this entire affair has been steered by our cowardice: the charge came to trial,

although it didn't need to; the trial was managed as it was; and finally, as the ridiculous end of the whole affair, this opportunity has escaped us through our cowardice, since neither did we save you nor did you save yourself, although it's feasible and possible if we're any use at all. So take care that these things not be bad and shameful for both you and us. (*Cri.* 45c5–46a4)

As Beversluis in particular has appreciated, although Crito's objection may not be philosophically sophisticated or rigorously defended, it is principled and significant.[70] Socrates is permitting his life to be ended, although he could escape death. He is permitting his enemies to have their way with him, although he could frustrate them. He is abandoning his children, although he could raise and educate them. And he is bringing upon his friends as well as upon himself the shame of failing in all these ways. It is not only by refusing Crito's offer to help him escape that he is doing these things. The problems began when he permitted his case to come to trial, although there were ways of avoiding it, and it continued with his incompetent management of his defense. The average observer might think that Socrates' behavior throughout has been ignoble and embarrassing.

While it is doubtful that the author of our papyrus raised precisely these accusations against Socrates, they constitute a useful list for thinking about how Hegesiac pessimism and indifference could help provide an answer. We should start with the key issue in our fragment of the papyrus, which is the death penalty. Trials in the Athenian popular courts generally involved both a guilt phase and a penalty phase. During the latter the prosecutor proposed a penalty, then the defendant proposed a counter-penalty, and the jurors decided between the two.[71] In Plato's *Apology* the prosecution proposes the death penalty, and Socrates famously suggests that the appropriate "penalty" for his deeds would be free meals for life in the Prytaneion. Eventually Plato and some others convince him to propose a modest financial penalty (*Apol.* 32b3–38b9). In Xenophon's *Apology*, by contrast, Socrates refuses to propose a counter-penalty, saying that "to propose a counter-penalty is the part of someone who admits acting unjustly" (*Apol.* 23). Our papyrus clearly sides with Xenophon rather than Plato in this regard, since Socrates says that "I offered no defense to the Athenians about the death penalty" (οὐκ ἀπελ[ογ]ησάμην Ἀθη[ν]αίοις περὶ τῆς τοῦ θανάτου δίκης, III.6–9; cf. III.21–4). In Xenophon this decision is explained by the opposition of Socrates' daemonic sign and his inference that "death was more choiceworthy than life" for him (*Apol.* 1).[72] If old age were to take away his mental acuity, Xenophon's Socrates asks, "how would I still live pleasantly?" (*Apol.* 6). In our papyrus the argument is similar,[73] but the hedonism is more self-conscious and systematic. Socrates argues he was right not to oppose the death penalty because pleasure is the best end in life and distress the worst, and even the wise man's life is no more pleasant than distressing. Furthermore, nothing "disagreeable" (*duskheres*) will happen after death. Hence Socrates will neither be deprived of any positive balance of pleasures nor experience any increase in pains by dying.

It is worth noting briefly that a Hegesiac could answer Crito's other charges as well, although they do not come up in the surviving part of the papyrus. Yielding to his "enemies" would not discomfit a Hegesiac Socrates, since Hegesias does not recognize any enemies. Reputational damage to his "friends" would also be insignificant, since Hegesiacs have no friends. Moreover, they believe that reputation is indifferent, so Socrates' own disrepute would not bother him either. The Hegesiac doxography does not pronounce on children, but given its blanket rejection of human relationships Hegesias probably repudiates anything other than utilitarian relations with offspring as well. So if Socrates were a Hegesiac, the posthumous suffering of his orphaned children would not matter to him.

None of this paints Hegesias in a very flattering light, and I shall consider in the next section whether we ought to think of his sage as a sort of anti-heroic monster. Before coming to that, however, I should emphasize what a Hegesiac would consider the positive side to this disregard for everything normal people care about. Because the sage is indifferent to enmity, friendship, kinship, and even his own death, he is able to defuse all of Crito's charges. For Plato, Xenophon, and the author of our papyrus the big question is why Socrates did not alter his habitual ways of thinking and speaking for the sake of the trial. If we read this papyrus as a Hegesiac document, the answer it provides is that Socrates had no motivation for altering his habits. Socrates was not guilty: he had lived a life of gratuitous beneficence, helping his followers and co-citizens even though they could do practically nothing to increase his well-being. Why should he not tell them precisely this at his trial? The "penalty" he really deserved they would never approve, and what they might approve he did not deserve. So why should he propose any penalty at all? In fact, if he had given any weight to the sort of criticisms Crito makes, he would have been unfaithful to his own beliefs about what is good and bad in life. It is precisely this sort of moral compromise which magnanimous impassivity allows a Hegesiac to avoid.

7.7. Pessimism and Heroism Revisited

I began this chapter by highlighting how unusual Hegesias's pessimism is in the ancient philosophical tradition, which made the question of its motivation all the more pressing. What led Hegesias to accept such a radical doctrine? Was it, as Matson suggests, a series of "ruthless deductions" from Aristippean principles, the "gloomy" conclusions of which Hegesias was powerless to resist? In the foregoing I have not only challenged Matson's interpretation of individual pieces of evidence, I have also tried to build a picture of Hegesiac philosophy in which hedonism, pessimism, indifference, magnanimity, and autonomy fit together as a whole, the sort of whole which someone could intelligibly choose as a way of thinking and behaving with its own (very idiosyncratic) allure. While each of these elements is grounded in arguments, for those predisposed to find

Hegesiac philosophy attractive it is the allure of the entire package which makes each of those arguments persuasive. Thus I suggest that Hegesias is very far from resigning himself to pessimism. To the contrary, he positively embraces it as one aspect of a radical but coherent existential choice.

With this conclusion in mind it is worth returning to Hegesias's doctrines about interpersonal relationships, which constitute another part of the same existential vision. In section 6.5 I reconstructed two overlapping arguments for the sage's inability to befriend fools. First, usefulness is the primary basis for friendship, the sage is self-sufficient, and therefore no one is useful to him. It follows that he cannot form friendships on the basis of usefulness. Second, reciprocity is the mode of usefulness appropriate to friendship, and the sage cannot engage in meaningful reciprocity. It follows that even if someone could be useful to the sage, the sage could not be his or her friend.

However, I left in abeyance the question why, granted that the Hegesiac sage cannot befriend fools, he cannot befriend *another sage*.[74] Since two sages would each already possess wisdom, their modest contributions to one another would be equal: particular enjoyments, resources for the mitigation of pain, etc. Hegesias might respond that the sage has no real use for these little pleasures or analgesic devices, since he is self-sufficient. But the details of this self-sufficiency are entirely lacking. Surely we are not to imagine that the sage grows his own food, makes his own clothes, and generally withdraws from the civilized division of labor?[75] If not, then why cannot two sages, granted that they are indifferent to almost everything, still benefit one another in those basic necessities which are *not* indifferent? And even if Hegesias has a convincing answer to this question (which I doubt), we would still want to ask why he has constructed a theory of friendship that rests solely on the psychologically crude and theoretically rigid basis of utility.

The answer I would like to suggest is that Hegesias is predisposed to find isolation attractive, just as he is predisposed to embrace pessimism. That is why he is drawn to this kind of theory, which rules out the possibility of friendship. Moreover, that is why, although Stoic and Aristotelian (and, to a lesser extent, Epicurean) theories of friendship are oriented toward relationships between like-minded virtuous people, the Hegesiac doxography never even mentions the possibility of a relationship between sages. It is as if the Hegesiac sage were necessarily a solitary genius.

This brings me back to Nietzsche's vision of a "pessimism of strength," which we can apply to Hegesias by thinking further about his appropriation and transformation of tropes from heroic literature. Both pessimism and isolation are regular elements of Greek heroism. Regarding the former Hobbs notes,

> Yet the toughest challenge that Socrates faces is the fact that Achilles does not, as it were, come alone. I wish to argue that the thumoeidic characteristics that Achilles embodies, both good and bad, arise directly from the

Iliadic world-view that he represents—a world-view that is, furthermore, essentially tragic.[76]

One need only cite Achilles' words to Priam in *Iliad* 24, when the elderly king has come alone to supplicate the killer of his sons. Achilles and Priam both weep, and then Achilles begins to speak:

> There is not
> any advantage to be won from grim lamentation.
> Such is the way the gods spun life for unfortunate mortals,
> that we live in unhappiness, but the gods have no sorrows.
> There are two urns that stand on the door-sill of Zeus. They are unlike
> for the gifts they bestow: an urn of evils, an urn of blessings.
> If Zeus who delights in thunder mingles these and bestows them
> on man, he shifts, and moves now in evil, again in good fortune.
> But when Zeus bestows from the urn of sorrows, he makes a failure
> of man, and the evil hunger drives him over the shining
> earth, and he wanders respected neither of gods nor mortals.
>
> (*Il.* 24.523–33, trans. Lattimore)[77]

As Achilles puts it, there are two possibilities for mortals: either they oscillate between happiness and misery, or they experience only misery. Pindar (ca. 522–443 BCE), who was often considered the greatest of the lyric poets, both expresses the survival of this perspective into classical Greece and articulates one of its ethical consequences:

> If you rightly and deeply understand the crown of my words, Hiero, you have
>   learned and recognize this old wisdom:
> For every good the immortals allot two sufferings
> to mortals. Childish people cannot endure this with decorum,
> but the good can, turning what is beautiful outward.
>
> (*Pyth.* 3.80–83)

In other words, the darkness of human life presents strong souls with the opportunity to shine all the more brightly.[78] This interconnection of suffering and heroic virtue in Greek literature is unquestionably among the inspirations for Nietzsche's own "pessimism of strength." It is surely also among the heroic resonances Hegesias aims to appropriate, since he and his contemporaries were steeped in Homer from their earliest childhood.

Hegesias would also be aware that isolation is a common trope in Greek epic and tragic poetry. Consider the lonely end of Hector outside the walls of Troy, where Athena has tricked him into believing his brother Deïphobus is with him (*Il.* 22.225–301). As his wife Andromache had predicted in their poignant final meeting, "your own great strength will be your death, and you have no pity / on your little son, nor on me, ill-starred, who must be your widow" (6.406–8). In

other words, Hector's determination to display his virtue and win honor, combined with the intoxication of his manly confidence and enjoyment of battle,
has placed him in a position where he cannot help his family or Troy. At the
moment of death he can only set his sights on his own glory:

> But now my death is upon me.
> Let me at least not die without a struggle, inglorious,
> but do some big thing first, that men to come may know if it.
>
> (*Il.* 22.304–5)

Compare the alienation of Sophocles' Ajax as he approaches his suicide. He
has been dishonored by Agamemnon and Menelaus, who have given Achilles' armor to Odysseus rather than to him; and he has been shamed in front
of the entire army, since Athena took away his wits and drove him to torture
and kill livestock instead of his enemies. In a deliberate echo of Hector and
Andromache, when Ajax recovers from his madness Tecmessa begs him to
consider her and their son (*Ajax* 485–642).[79] Ajax chooses death instead, which
he calls his "salvation" (*Ajax* 691–92). Both Hector and Ajax recognize the consequences of their intended actions for their loved ones (*Il.* 6.461–65, *Ajax* 650–
53), but neither can reconcile his intense concern for honor, shame, and battle
with investment in these personal relationships.[80]

This conflict among values, which the most brilliant individuals set in the
clearest relief, is one of the reasons why human life in epic and tragic poetry is
full of suffering. Heroic isolation and heroic pessimism are closely connected.
But Hegesiac philosophy, though it appropriates both aspects of heroism, does
so in a way that continues the Socratic project of harmonizing human goods
and so eliminating tragedy.[81] In the *Crito* and *Phaedo* Plato puts Socrates in the
position of Hector and Ajax. In the *Crito*, as we have seen in the previous section, Crito objects that Socrates is abandoning his children, and that they will
be treated badly like all orphans: precisely what Andromache tells Hector, and
Tecmessa tells Ajax. In the *Phaedo* Socrates' wife Xanthippe and their son are in
the prison with him before the execution, and when Xanthippe starts weeping,
Socrates tells Crito, "get someone to take her home" (*Phd.* 60a7–8). This might
be compared with Hector's final words to Andromache:

> *Go therefore back to our house*, and take up your work,
> the loom and the distaff, and see to it that your handmaidens
> ply their work also; but the men must see to the fighting,
> all men who are the people of Ilion, but I beyond others.
>
> (*Il.* 6.490–93, italics mine)

Is Socrates removing Xanthippe so that he and the other men can focus on
their philosophical "battle" with the fear of death? Regardless of how we read
Socrates' gesture, the fact is that Plato has gone out of his way to replicate this
vignette of the hero caught between incompatible priorities. But Socrates, in

a series of arguments that many readers find deeply unsatisfying, insists that there is no conflict here: his sons will be no worse off after his death than they would be if he escaped to Thessaly (*Cri.* 54a1–b5).[82] This is one of the scenes in which Socrates most merits Nietzsche's charge that his optimism is both superficial and monstrous.

My concluding suggestion is that Hegesias's response to this kind of conflict is more consistent than that of Socrates, which is why he is both less tragic and less human. For a Hegesiac sage has seen through the delusions of happiness which make other people cling to possessions, aspirations, and so-called friends. His overall project is tightly circumscribed, focusing on the avoidance of his own misery. Unlike Socrates, he does not have meaningful relationships. He does not believe that either the well-being of others or the way he treats them is important for his own well-being. He can therefore pursue his extraordinary lifestyle without the poignant sacrifices which Hector, Ajax, and arguably even Socrates must make. He typically benefits others, but he does not aim to do so; if it becomes advantageous to abandon them, he will not regret it. This purity of vision and freedom from cognitive or emotional dissonance, though both ancients and moderns might find it inhuman, can on the other hand be seen as a form of heroic transcendence of ordinary limitations. It is to this transcendence that Hegesiac philosophy aspires.

CHAPTER 8

Theodorus's Innovations

8.1. Introduction

Theodorus "the Godless" introduces at least three significant innovations to the Cyrenaic tradition. All three of these are concisely outlined by Diogenes Laertius:

> He understood the end to be joy and distress. One follows practical wisdom, the other foolishness. Good things are practical wisdom and justice, bad things are the opposite conditions, bodily pleasure and pain are intermediates. (2.98)

The first and most striking innovation here is Theodorus's demotion of bodily pleasure and pain from the status of ends to that of "intermediates." The second is the corresponding promotion of joy and distress to the status of ends. Third is the newfound prominence of the virtues, and especially of justice. Previous Cyrenaics had certainly valued practical wisdom, which they considered an instrumental good for the acquisition of pleasure and alleviation of pain.[1] However, they had never given it such prominent billing as it acquires here: joy "follows" or "depends on" practical wisdom (it is *epi phronēsei*). As for justice, the noun does not even appear in the mainstream doxography. The adjectives "just" and "unjust" appear only when the doxography insists that the distinctions between just and unjust, fine or shameful exist only by convention. By contrast, justice is one of only two goods named by Theodorus. It is obviously a central component of his philosophy.

The principal thesis of this chapter is that practical wisdom and justice are the key to understanding how Theodorus's innovations fit together. They should also illuminate his many provocative, paradoxical, or parodic positions and arguments. Among these are the assertion that the sage will steal, rob temples, and commit adultery "under the right circumstances"; the advocacy of shamelessness in sexual relations; and, of course, his renowned godlessness. My assumption is that all of these elements constitute an intelligible whole. However, that is not to say that we should attempt to reconstruct a clear, thorough, and rigorous theoretical system on Theodorus's behalf. In many respects he resembles Aristippus: he spent his life roaming the Mediterranean, teaching for pay, and enjoying the patronage of regents and kings. Moreover, he also resembles Cynics like Diogenes and Crates, since he engages in a provocative and radical critique of ethical beliefs.[2] Like Aristippus, Diogenes, and Crates, Theodorus was probably not a system builder. His philosophy consisted rather of the combination of programmatic ideas, which he expressed in diverse ways, and the dialectical criticism of his opponents. Thus we should expect to find consistent and intelligible relations within his program, but we should not expect to discover an articulate theory behind every piece of evidence.

8.2. Ends, Intermediates, and Indifference

A good place to start our investigation of Theodorean philosophy is with the relation between ends and bodily experiences, which will bring us back to one of the themes from the last chapter: indifference. We have just read that Theodorus "understood the end to be joy and distress." Although Diogenes uses the singular "end" (*telos*) here, this is probably just sloppy wording. The most plausible interpretation is that Theodorus names joy and distress his ends (*telē*) in approximately the same sense as the mainstream Cyrenaics name pleasure and pain their ends. In other words, Theodorus believes that joy and distress are the most completely good and bad things for any human being. In the terminology I developed earlier in this book, that would make joy and distress "complete" ends.[3] It is also plausible that Theodorus thinks the pursuit of joy and avoidance of distress should provide the ultimate explanation for every decision or action. Thus joy and distress would be "final" ends. Finally, he may believe the goal of living a joyful life should be used to organize all our plans and endeavors. Thus living joyfully would be a "comprehensive" end. However, it is not clear that Theodorus has all these senses of "end" in mind. In order to be cautious, let us simply assert that Theodorus believes joy and distress should be the primary points of reference for ethical reasoning.

In contrast to the goodness of joy and badness of distress Theodorus posits that bodily pleasure and pain are "intermediates" (*mesa*). This term recalls what the Metrodidact calls "the intermediate condition [*mesēn katastasin*], in which we are neither hurt nor pleased" (Eus. *PE* 14.18.32 = *SSR* 4b.5). Since this intermediate condition is without pain and pleasure, it is clearly neither satisfying nor repellent, and therefore neither good nor bad in itself. Compare the Cyrenaic partition of experiences into those which are hurtful, those which are pleasant, and those which are intermediate (*ta metaxu*) and therefore neither good nor bad (SE *M* 7.199 = *SSR* 4a.213). This tripartite scheme of goods, evils, and things which are neither good nor bad also plays an important role in Stoicism, where the middle class is sometimes called "indifferents," sometimes "things which are neither," and sometimes "intermediates."[4] It is therefore reasonable to assume that Theodorean "intermediates," which are situated between goods and evils, are indifferent.[5]

This helps to explain an isolated bit of Theodorean doxography. According to the Suda, Theodorus "[b]elieved in and taught indifference [*adiaphorian*]"

(Θ 150, Σ 829 = *SSR* 5h.2). In this matter, as in his repudiation of friendship and political participation,[6] Theodorus may be following Hegesias. We saw in section 7.3 that Hegesias's sage aspires to perceive the indifference of most of the things his contemporaries value, including freedom or slavery, noble or humble birth, fame or ignominy, wealth or poverty, and life or death. Although we are not told that Theodorus considers these things indifferent, nothing in our evidence conflicts with this hypothesis. I also discussed Hegesias's effort to make what happens to the sage's body indifferent. We can now observe that Theodorus is able to argue this point more effectively than his predecessor. Whereas Hegesias has to negotiate the apparent contradiction between valuing bodily experience and claiming that most of what happens to the body is unimportant, Theodorus has jettisoned the commitment to bodily experience. He can therefore more easily disdain sensory temptations and physical dangers. Thus his sage is able to realize more perfectly the condition of godlike impassivity, which is the subjective corollary to the objective indifference of things.

It is through the lenses of indifference and impassivity that I would prefer to begin my interpretation of what Winiarczyk has called Theodorus's search for "inner freedom and self-sufficiency."[7] Winiarczyk follows Zeller and von Fritz in arguing that Theodorus was troubled by the dependence of bodily experiences on events outside of his own control.[8] By locating the end entirely in mental joy, and making joy dependent on practical wisdom rather than on external events, he secures the happiness of his ideal philosopher. But nowhere in our evidence are the words "free" (*eleutheros*) or "freedom" (*eleutheria*) mentioned. If they were central to Theodorus's ethics, we would expect them to appear in the surviving anecdotes or doxography. I therefore suggest that we try to understand Theodorus's search for independence through his own terms. The first of these is indifference. The second, as Winiarczyk rightly highlights, is self-sufficiency (*autarkeia*).[9] What synthesizes these terms is not freedom, but the virtues of practical wisdom and justice. My task in the next two sections will therefore be to explore how these virtues interact with the ends and with the attitude of indifference.

8.3. Theodorus the Pyrrhonist?

In my discussion of Hegesias I introduced Pyrrho of Elis as one philosophical model for incorporating indifference and impassivity into thought and action.[10] Aldo Brancacci goes much further than this in his article on "Theodorus the Atheist and Bion of Borysthenes between Pyrrho and Arcesilaus." As the title indicates, his larger project is to trace a line of influence from Pyrrho to Arcesilaus, who initiated the skeptical period in the Academy. In the process he makes an extended defense of the Suda's report that Pyrrho was among Theodorus's teachers (Θ 150).[11] On his interpretation Theodorus is a full-blooded Pyrrhonist, whose wisdom is to perceive that reality is indeterminate and unknowable, and whose indifference is a response to this indeterminacy.[12] This interpretation bears close inspection, since it is chronologically possible that Theodorus studied with Pyrrho. Moreover, it has the merit of binding most of the Theodorean evidence into a coherent network of thoughts and behaviors. However, I will argue that the evidence does not support this interpretation.

I will begin by laying out Brancacci's principal arguments as I understand them. First, he believes that Theodorus agrees with Pyrrho about the indeterminacy and consequent unknowability of reality. He further suggests that this belief is based on a perception of the "mutability" and "corruptibility of everything which exists."[13] This leads to a suspension of judgment not only about the nature of the gods,[14] but also about stable ethical values. That is why Theodorus asserts that by nature nothing is just or unjust, fine or shameful.[15] Moreover, when Diogenes Laertius reports that Theodorus "understood the end to be joy and distress" (D.L. 2.98), Brancacci takes the singular "end" very seriously. He interprets Theodorus to mean that the end is the antithetical pair joy-and-distress, the two elements of which "are placed on the same plane of moral worth."[16] In the absence of natural distinctions the sage himself becomes "the source of all values":[17] "only the most capable human, the *sophos*, can make himself the standard: in each circumstance he'll establish what has value and what does not, making this determination on the basis of the axiological irrelevance of reality."[18] Brancacci argues that it is because the sage is the source of all values that he disdains friendship, politics, pleasure, pain, and even death. It is for the same reason that he is permitted to steal, rob temples, and commit adultery.[19] Yet the sage does not invent these transient, ad hoc values from whole cloth:

> Everything is possible for him because he can discern the *kairos*, an absolute and incommunicable value that assures the universal synthesis of a reality considered inexhaustible in its aspects precisely because it is not necessary, and to which the *sophos* is capable of corresponding with an immediate and absolute adequation.[20]

If I understand Brancacci correctly, he is saying that there is *something* in the flux of reality to which the sage's judgments correspond. However, because reality is "inexhaustible in its aspects," that something cannot be said to determine those judgments, much less to ground any stable and universal ethical scheme.

All of this is thought-provoking, but it rests on some implausible interpretations of the evidence. Let me begin with the claim that Theodorus suspends judgment about gods and ethical values because of the indeterminacy of reality. This claim is based on a single piece of rather imprecise testimony, which has been taken out of context:

> At least, these men who have been called "godless," Theodoruses and Diagorases and Hippos [*sic*], haven't dared to say that divinity is perishable. Rather, they didn't believe that anything imperishable exists, and so didn't leave the existence of anything imperishable, but preserved their preconception of god. (Plut. *Mor.* 1075a = *SSR* 4h.16)

Brancacci infers from this passage's denial "that anything imperishable exists" (*hōs esti ti aphtharton*) a Theodorean doctrine that reality is so "corruptible" and "mutable" that nothing is determinate. Moreover, he takes the phrase I have translated "preserved their preconception" (*tēn prolēpsin*[21] *phulattontes*) as "technical terminology used by Theodorus, which reveals a relatively old formulation of the theme of suspension [of judgment]."[22] Thus he infers that Theodorus refuses to commit to any conception of god because everything, including god, is too mutable to be known.

But this interpretation takes too little account of the context of this passage in Plutarch's *On Common Conceptions: Against the Stoics*. Here Plutarch is arguing that Stoic theology, which holds that all gods except Zeus are perishable, contradicts our common conception of the divine. It is this anti-Stoic context, and not any Theodorean belief in universal flux, which explains the passage's emphasis on perishability. Moreover, "preconception" (*prolēpsis*) is a technical *Stoic* term; Chrysippus says that a "preconception is a natural conception of universals" (LS 40A). It is most likely that Plutarch is turning this Stoic term against its masters, not using an otherwise unknown technical Theodorean phrase that anticipates Arcesilaus's "suspense of judgment." Finally, even if these objections could be overcome, it would be hazardous to infer specifically Theodorean beliefs from a report that runs together "Theodoruses and Diagorases and Hippos."

In fact it is unclear whether Theodorus subscribes to any form of skepticism, including the Cyrenaic theory of the experiences. The inspiration for Brancacci's article is a statement which goes back to the otherwise unknown Diocles of Cnidus, which might be taken to support the ascription of skepticism to Theodorus.

> I am not convinced by what Diocles of Cnidus says in the work entitled *Discourses*. He says that it was through fear of the Theodoreans and the sophist Bion, who were attacking philosophers and not shrinking from refuting anything by every means possible, that Arcesilaus took care to avoid trouble, and appeared not to utter any doctrine openly, thrusting suspension of judgment before him like the ink of the cuttlefish. (Numenius, quoted by Eus. *PE* 14.6.6 = *SSR* 4h.29)

Since Bion of Borysthenes was Theodorus's most renowned student,[23] it is reasonable to take Arcesilaus's ostensible wariness of "Theodoreans and the sophist Bion" as evidence for Theodorus's own behavior. This behavior is described as "attacking philosophers and not shrinking from refuting anything by every means possible" (τῶν Θεοδωρείων. . . ἐπεισιόντων τοῖς φιλοσοφοῦσι καὶ οὐδὲν ὀκνούντων ἀπὸ παντὸς ἐλέγχειν). This pugnacious critical activity could be motivated by skepticism, but the connection is far from secure. There is no evidence that Theodorus or any other Cyrenaic puts the theory of the experiences to any such use. Insofar as we can reconstruct Theodorus's attempts to "refute" popular and philosophical ethical beliefs, several of which I will analyze later in this chapter, they are not grounded in epistemology or metaphysics. Rather, they aim either to reveal latent contradictions or to reduce the positions in question to absurdity. This procedure could be motivated by Pyrrhonean skepticism, but it resembles at least as strongly the antinomian provocations of early Cynics.

In sum, there are no good grounds for attributing to Theodorus a belief in the mutability, corruptibility, and consequent indeterminacy of reality, and only weak grounds for claiming that Theodorus is a skeptic of any variety.

Next let us consider Brancacci's claims about Theodorus's rejection of absolute ethical values. In order to document that Theodorus agrees with Pyrrho in denying that anything is good or bad by nature, Brancacci presents a quotation from Theodorus's doxography as follows:

> In this matter let us consider the passage in which the Cyrenaic claims that "no . . . thing is shameful [*aiskhron*] by nature, once the empty opinion which has been created to restrain the foolish has been removed."[24] (ellipsis in the original)

This quotation obscures the meaning of the evidence by not only ignoring its context, but also removing the word that should stand in the ellipsis. Here is my translation of the sentence in full:

> The wise man will both steal and commit adultery and rob temples under the right circumstances, because none of these things is shameful by nature, once the opinion which exists to restrain the foolish has been removed. (D.L. 2.99)

Brancacci's elliptical quotation ("no . . . thing is shameful by nature") now looks misleading. One could perhaps conjecture that if Theodorus denies *these* acts are shameful by nature, then he believes *nothing* is shameful by nature. But the sentence does not necessarily imply that. Theodorus may believe that other types of behavior are naturally shameful, even though these three are not. Alternatively, his point may be that the masses fail to appreciate the complexity of ethical judgment. In other words, many *token* actions may be naturally shameful, although no *type* of action is consistently so. I will return to this suggestion later in this chapter.

The claim that Theodorus's end encompasses both joy and distress, which have "equal moral dignity," also collapses under closer investigation. Brancacci observes that to the pair joy/distress "corresponds, on the level of intellectual virtues, the other pair *phronēsis/aphrosunē*."[25] But here we must add that Theodorus explicitly asserts that "good things are practical wisdom and justice, bad things are the opposing dispositions" (D.L. 2.98). It is hard to imagine how this could be squared with the claim that nothing at all is good or bad by nature. In fact, it is hard to see how a Pyrrhonean interpretation can make any sense at all of Theodorus's strong commitment to justice. Moreover, it is difficult to escape the conclusion that practical wisdom is good precisely because "joy follows practical wisdom," just as foolishness is bad precisely because "distress follows foolishness." In that case, it is likely that joy is the primary good, and distress the primary evil, as I have already argued. It is therefore unsustainable that Theodorus, following Pyrrho, denies anything is naturally good, bad, just, or shameful.

I hope it is now clear that the interpretation of Theodorean ethics as a form of Pyrrhonism is indefensible. Yet we may still find a use for Brancacci's elegant and slightly mysterious description of "the *kairos*, an absolute and incommunicable value that assures the universal synthesis of a reality considered inexhaustible in its aspects precisely because it is not necessary, and to which the *sophos* is capable of corresponding with an immediate and absolute adequation." Setting aside the metaphysical postulate that reality is "inexhaustible in its aspects precisely because it is not necessary," Theodorus may well believe that the complex and constantly shifting ethical demands of real situations cannot be reduced to consistent rules. He may also believe that the sage's virtue lies in his ability to synthesize these complex demands. The trick for us now will be to understand why Theodorus holds these beliefs without recourse to the indeterminacy or unknowability of reality. Moreover, we will need to supply an answer that, like Brancacci's account, explains Theodorus's commitment to indifference. For this we will need to turn away from Pyrrho and consider another comparative model.

8.4. The Extemporaneity of Ethical Value and Judgment

In this section I will offer an alternate interpretation of how the elements we find in the Theodorean doxography fit together, for which I will draw inspiration from the examples of Bion of Borysthenes and especially Aristo of Chios. It is possible to draw a line of influence connecting these figures. Diogenes Laertius records the educational background of Bion (ca. 325–250 BCE) as follows:

> At first he chose Academic philosophy, at which time he listened to Crates.[26] Then he took up the Cynic way of life, the ragged cloak and leather sack. What else clothed him in impassivity?[27] Then he switched to Theodorean philosophy and followed Theodorus the Godless, who was practicing sophistry in every kind of speech. After him he followed the Peripatetic Theophrastus. (D.L. 4.51–52)

Diogenes also tells us that Bion "made many rather godless suggestions to those who spent time with him, which was a Theodorean habit he enjoyed" (4.54). The Theodorean features of Bion's philosophy are therefore unlikely to be coincidental.[28] Aristo of Chios (ca. 310–235 BCE) studied with Zeno of Citium and the Academic Polemo (D.L. 7.162, Phld. *Ind. Sto.* 10.2). He was renowned and influential in his own time, but afterwards considered heterodox by the Stoic successors of Chrysippus. He is also said to have been an "emulator of Bion" (Strabo 10.5.6).[29] It is thus possible to construct an intellectual genealogy running from Theodorus via Bion to Aristo. However, I do not want to place much weight on the hypothesis of direct influence. My primary intention is simply to demonstrate that some of Theodorus's near contemporaries espoused ethical positions similar to those I will attribute to him.

Let me begin with Theodorus's triangulation between the goodness of practical wisdom and justice, the badness of foolishness and injustice, and the indifference of other things in general. Theodorus may have been influenced in the formulation of this position by his teacher Dionysius of Chalcedon,[30] since our fragmentary evidence about Megaric/Dialectic ethics suggests that it includes both a strong commitment to virtue and knowledge and an aspiration to impassivity.[31] But we know too little about the Dialectic school to make this useful as a comparative model.

In order to imagine how this triangle functions it is more helpful to turn to Aristo of Chios, for whom the following formulations of the end are given:

> Aristo "the Bald" of Chios, who was also called "the Siren," said that the end is living indifferently toward the things between virtue and vice, leaving no distinction among them, but maintaining the same disposition in all cases. (D.L. 7.160)

> Aristo, though he was Zeno's follower, approved in reality what Zeno approved only in words: nothing is good except virtue, nothing is bad except what is contrary to virtue. He repudiated those discriminations among intermediates which Zeno wanted. His end is to be moved in neither direction in these matters, which he himself calls indifference. (Cic. *Luc.* 130)

Here, first, we have a clear statement that only virtue is good, only vice is bad. If we set aside the Theodorean ends (to which we shall necessarily return), this recalls the fact that the only goods Theodorus explicitly mentions are practical wisdom and justice, the only evils foolishness and injustice. The core of virtue for Aristo is understanding, which resembles Theodorus's emphasis on practical wisdom. Aristo says that the cardinal virtues—temperance, practical wisdom, courage, justice—are all varieties of a single condition of the soul, the "understanding of goods and evils," which is differentiated by the material with which it is concerned (D.L. 7.160, Plut. *Mor.* 440f, Gal. *PHP* 7.2.1–4). For example, justice is the understanding of goods and evils "when you need to distribute things according to merit," and temperance is the same understanding "imposing order on desire and defining measure and appropriateness in pleasures." In each instance the key is to perceive that the material involved is indifferent; only the principles of virtue matter, such as "distribution according to merit" or looking for "order," "measure," and "appropriateness" in pleasures.

Sextus Empiricus puts this clearly when presenting Aristo's opinion about how to educate someone: "The discourse which makes virtue a part of someone, makes vice alien to him, and denounces the things in between . . . suffices for living blissfully" (*M* 7.12). Aristo's sage is someone who has internalized virtue, ejected vice, and thoroughly understood that most of the things normal people value are unimportant. Like Theodorus's sage, he therefore becomes impassive with respect to those things: he "maintains the same disposition in all cases," and "is moved in neither direction in these matters."

Another point of convergence between Theodorus and Aristo concerns the emphasis placed on the sage's extemporaneous judgment. The primary objection leveled at Aristo by our sources is that, having denied any distinctions among intermediates, he leaves no material for virtue to act upon. For example, how can you "distribute according to merit" if the items to be distributed are indifferent? How can you then distinguish between what the good person and the bad person deserve?[32] This is part of a larger problem in Aristo, who also refuses to elaborate detailed ethical rules. As Seneca paraphrases his position, we could never match the complexity of ethical life with any quantity of admonitions, but "the laws of philosophy are concise and bind everything together" (*Ep. Mor.* 94.15). Moreover, even the rules we can articulate are useless, as he explains in the case of justice:

> "Treat your friend like this, your co-citizen like that, and your ally like this." Why? "Because it's just." The doctrine of justice told me all those things. There I find that fairness should be chosen for its own sake; we're not coerced into it by fear or allured by reward; whoever likes virtue for anything other than itself isn't just. When I'm persuaded of this and have imbibed it, what do those precepts accomplish, since they're teaching someone who has already learned? Giving precepts to someone who knows is superfluous, but it's inadequate for someone who doesn't know. He should hear not only what is being prescribed to him, but why. (94.11)

So detailed rules are superfluous to the sage, and useless to an ignorant and vicious person. The latter needs to understand the motivational structure behind each of these instructions; he must "be persuaded and imbibe" the sole goodness of virtue. Aristo seems to believe something similar about the laws of the state, which "don't make us do what we should. What are they other than precepts mixed with threats?" (94.34) In other words, like detailed ethical instructions, the laws say "treat your co-citizen like this," but they are both too simple to match the complexity of real ethical demands and unable to motivate anyone except through "threats."[33] The alternative to rules and laws is the sage's understanding, but this begs the question how, though he understands that "fairness should be chosen for its own sake," he can determine what is fair in each situation.

In fact Aristo purports to solve both the problem of indifferent materials and the problem of the absence of detailed rules simultaneously with his doctrine of "situation" (*peristasis*) and "the right circumstance" (*kairos*). Sextus reports this doctrine as follows:

> Just as in the writing of words we begin with different letters at different times, making fresh arrangements for different situations, and write a delta when we write the name of Zeus [*Dios*], an iota when we write the name of Ion, and an omega when we write the name of Orion, not because some characters are preferred to others by nature, but because the right circumstances require us to do this—: just so in matters between virtue and vice there is no natural preference of some things over others, but rather according to the situation. (*M* 11.63)

The letters delta, iota, and omega are not "naturally preferable" to other letters; in fact, they have no "natural value" at all. They are simply the best letters for beginning the names specified. In the same way things in the world are without value, but should be manipulated in certain ways "because the right circumstances require" it (*tōn kairōn . . . anankazontōn*) and "according to the situation" (*kata peristasin*). This is Aristo's solution to the problem of indifferent materials: although letters are semantically indifferent, they are not without phonetic attributes, and these phonemes should be configured in certain ways in order to express certain meanings. Similarly, although things in the world are ethically indifferent, they are not without attributes, and these attributes should be configured in certain ways in order to express justice, temperance, and so on.[34]

It has also been argued that the analogy suggests a solution to the problem of the absence of detailed guidance: although a child must deliberate about spelling on the basis of the sounds made by combinations of letters, literate people generally write without any deliberation at all. Similarly, though fools deliberate about their actions on the basis of their false beliefs about goodness and badness, the appropriate thing to do simply appears to anyone who has thoroughly digested the simple doctrines of virtue.[35] As Cicero dismissively reports, "Aristo . . . didn't dare to leave no [choiceworthy] thing. As the means by which the sage is moved and makes a choice he introduced whatever comes into his mind and whatever, as it were, occurs to him" (*Fin.* 4.43). What Cicero elides is that "whatever occurs to him" (*quodcumque tamquam occurreret*) must not be just any random action, but precisely the just, temperate, courageous, or practically wise thing to do.[36]

This brings me back to Theodorus, who also seems to criticize general rules and define "justice" and "practical wisdom" only by the sage's supple and extemporaneous judgment. Here is the key passage in which we see the sage's justice in action:

> The universe is ⟨our⟩ fatherland. The good man will steal and commit adultery and rob a temple in the right circumstance, since none of these

things is shameful by nature, if one removes the opinion regarding them which exists for the sake of controlling the foolish. (D.L. 2.99)

As in Aristo, here we have an attack on law and common opinion as guides for correct action: formal and informal penalties for theft, sacrilege, and adultery exist for the sake of the foolish, who cannot be trusted to perceive the right thing to do.[37] But for the sage these norms are either erroneous (because they occlude exceptions) or superfluous. This is not because he thinks nothing is shameful or fine, just or unjust. When Theodorus says that the good man's fatherland is the universe, he implies that he does follow "laws," but they are "cosmic" or "natural" laws rather than the positive laws of any given polis. Yet Theodorus is either an agnostic or an atheist, so he cannot discover these natural laws by researching the providential intentions of Zeus. Moreover, there is not even a whisper in our evidence of any interest in physics, which suggests that Theodorus follows his Cyrenaic predecessors in repudiating the study of nature. Thus he cannot discover natural laws by studying the cosmos, either.

Theodorus's sage is therefore left with only himself as a guide to what is "natural" and "lawful." Aristo, too, repudiates physics and suspends judgment about the nature of god (D.L. 7.160, SE *M* 7.12, Cic. *ND* 1.37), yet refers to a "natural" norm (Sen. *Ep.* 94.8). It has been plausibly suggested that Aristo's "nature" is nothing other than his own constitution and intuitions, which have been clarified and harmonized and to which he is uncompromisingly faithful.[38] Along the same lines, I suggest that Theodorus's "natural" law-abidingness is nothing other than complete commitment to his own perception of what is just in every situation, undistracted by false evaluations of indifferents. This takes us back to Brancacci's idea that the sage makes decisions through "an immediate and absolute adequation" to the complex and shifting features of each situation. That is why it is permitted to him to steal, rob temples, or commit adultery "under the right circumstances" (*en kairōi*): he simply intuits in each case what is natural, just, and wise, for him and at the time.

I will have more to say about Theodorus's polemical provocations in the following section. For now it is important to acknowledge that Theodorus, unlike Aristo, subordinates this machinery of virtue, indifference, and extemporaneous judgment to the end of achieving joy and avoiding distress. My suggestion is that when Theodorus says that distress "follows" or "depends on" foolishness (is *epi aphrosunēi*), he means that the false beliefs of fools are the cause of their unhappiness. This is a ubiquitous position in ancient Greek philosophy, but for a particularly snappy formulation we can turn to Theodorus's pupil Bion:

> Bion says that just as with wild animals the bite comes from the way you grip them, and if you grip the snake in the middle, you'll get bitten, but if you grip the neck, nothing bad will happen to you—: in the same way with things in general the distress comes from the way you grasp them, and if you grasp them like Socrates, you won't be distressed, but if you

grasp them otherwise, you'll get hurt, not by things themselves but by your own ways and by false belief. (Teles fr. 2 = Bion F21 Kindstrand)

So it is the "false belief" that indifferents have value that causes people distress. In much the same way, when Theodorus says that joy "follows" or "depends on" practical wisdom, he means that the sage's true beliefs give him reason to feel cheerful. After all, he knows that everything he does is wise and just, and therefore good, and anything else that happens to him is indifferent. Naturally this is gratifying. Once again this is a common principle in Greek philosophy, going back at least to Xenophon's Socrates:

> Surely you know that people who think they're not doing well are not cheerful, while those who think that farming, shipping, or whatever occupies them is going well for them, and that they're doing well, are cheerful. So do you think that any of these yields as much pleasure as thinking that you yourself are becoming better and possessing better friends? (*Mem.* 1.6.9)

In other words, the perception of your own increasing wisdom and virtue is itself the most potent source of good cheer (*euphrainesthai*) and pleasure (*hēdonē*). Compare Bion: "Bion rightly said that we should not acquire our pleasures from the table, but rather from the activity of practical wisdom [*apo tou phronein*]" (Athen. 421e–f = F15 Kindstrand). In Theodorus's case, this must be true not only of wisdom, but also of justice: the sage feels joy in perceiving his own just activity—and all the more so if "fools" think it is imprudent or unjust!

I therefore take issue with the predominant interpretation, according to which Theodorean justice is a prudential strategy to avoid painful consequences.[39] This is obviously true of previous Cyrenaics, but it is not consistent with Theodorus's beliefs or lifestyle. Theodorus thinks bodily pain is of no importance, constantly provokes authorities with the power to persecute him, and cheerfully accepts exile from both Cyrene and Athens (or at least claims to do so). These are not the beliefs and activities of someone who thinks that other people have any meaningful power over him. In what sense could their "punishments" hurt him? Thus when he embraces justice, it must be because he intuits that this is the right thing for him to do, and simply enjoys knowing that he is doing it.

In this section I have attempted to provide a more consistent and plausible interpretation of how the elements in our meager Theodorean doxography fit together. What emerges is precisely the sort of eclectic synthesis of Cyrenaic and other influences we might expect from someone with Theodorus's educational history. His emphasis on sensitivity to circumstances takes us back to the Aristippean inspiration of the Cyrenaic movement. His commitment to indifference and self-sufficiency recalls Hegesias. But he takes both of these further than his predecessors. Meanwhile his downgrading of bodily experience and elevation of justice may owe something to Dialectic or Cynic ideas, or may be largely his own. And I have yet to comment in any detail on Theodorus's godlessness or his other polemical provocations, to which I will now turn.

8.5. "Atheism" and Other Polemics

Earlier in this chapter we saw the testimony of Diocles of Cnidus, who makes the ludicrous suggestion that it was "through fear of the Theodoreans and the sophist Bion, who were attacking philosophers and not shrinking from refuting anything by every means possible" that Arcesilaus introduced suspension of judgment into the Academy (Eus. *PE* 14.6.6 = *SSR* 4h.29). Setting aside Arcesilaus, we can take from Diocles' report the idea that "Theodoreans" were well known for their polemical attacks on other philosophers. I suggested earlier that the surviving examples of Theodorus's polemics are at least as compatible with the radical anti-conventionalism of the Cynics as with anything we find in early Pyrrhonism. In this section I will attempt to back up that suggestion, looking at Theodorus's attacks on the Stoics, on religion, and on sexual ethics. At the same time, I will try to integrate my analysis into the interpretation of Theodorus's core positions that I developed in the previous section. The conclusion toward which I will argue is that this combative and provocative behavior is connected to Theodorus's repudiation of positive law and systematic ethics and emphasis on the sage's extemporaneous judgment.

Let us begin with the tamest of Theodorus's polemics, which appears to be an attack on the Stoics:

> Theodorus the Godless used to say there was no sufficient pretext for the sage to take his life. He accordingly asked the following: If someone has said that only what is fine is good, and only what is shameful is bad, how is it not contradictory for him, who disdains human accidents, to be driven from life? (Stob. 4.52.16 = *SSR* 4h.26)

While Theodorus himself "disdains human accidents," it is unlikely that he would accept that "only what is fine is good, and only what is shameful is bad." This would exclude the goodness of joy and the badness of distress. It is therefore probable that this is a polemical fragment. The position under attack is associated most famously with the Stoics. Theodorus might have encountered one of Zeno's scions in the courts of Ptolemy, Lysimachus, or Magas, or he might have known Stoicism only by its growing reputation.[40] The Stoics claim that suicide is appropriate for the sage whenever he perceives that he cannot continue to live "according to nature."[41] Life according to nature is generally defined by the availability of "preferred indifferents" such as health and a modicum of resources (LS 58A–E). Theodorus's reply is that according to the Stoics, the sage is happy even without those things (since they are indifferent). It therefore makes no sense for him to give up his life, since it is a happy one.[42]

Here we should also recall Theodorus's assertion that it is not "reasonable" (*eulogon*) for the sage to "give his life" or "make an exit" (*exagein heauton*) on behalf of the polis.[43] The Stoics describe the sage's suicide with precisely the phrases "make a reasonable exit" (*eulogōs exagein heauton*) and "reasonable exit" (*eulogos exagōgē*).[44] It is therefore probable that this assertion, even if it emerges from Theodorus's sincere commitment to self-sufficiency, is also part of his polemic against the Stoic position on suicide. This could be part of a larger critique of the orthodox Stoic notion of "preferred" and "dispreferred" indifferents, which many of their antagonists—including, of course, Aristo (LS 58F)—claimed to be inconsistent with their doctrine that only virtue is good, while only vice is bad. This harmonizes with my earlier suggestion that Theodorus is opposed to any endeavor to elaborate a system of correct behavior: in this case, his opposition would be to the Zenonean elaboration of "appropriate behavior" through general rules about what merits "selection" and what merits "disselection."[45]

Next let us consider Theodorus's attacks on religion, which clearly made him notorious. This is evident already from the report that "he nearly risked being taken to the Areopagus court, had Demetrius of Phalerum not shielded him" (D.L. 2.101). It is confirmed by the fact that he is very frequently given the epithet "godless" in our evidence, even in sympathetic anecdotes that make no mention of his critical theology.[46]

Notwithstanding his notoriety, it is not easy to determine precisely what Theodorus said about the gods. Diogenes reports having seen his book *On the Gods* first-hand:

> Theodorus was someone who entirely removed beliefs about the gods. I've encountered his book entitled *On the Gods*, which is by no means contemptible. They say that Epicurus took most of what he said from it. (D.L. 2.97)

Scholars have debated whether, when Theodorus "entirely removed beliefs about the gods" (παντάπασιν ἀναιρῶν τὰς περὶ θεῶν δόξας), he went so far as to affirm that no gods exist.[47] It is possible that Theodorus simply made a radical critique of both popular and philosophical beliefs about the gods. The claim that Epicurus was influenced by the book might be taken as evidence for this interpretation, since Epicurus certainly does not challenge the existence of gods.[48] Here we could also cite two anecdotes which suggest Theodorus does believe in gods. The first is of dubious attribution: "When Lysias the apothecary was asking him whether he believed in gods, 'How can I not,' [Diogenes] answered, 'since I assume you're hateful to them?' But some claim Theodorus said this" (D.L. 6.42).[49] The second relies on a play on words which cannot be reproduced in English:

> Theodorus seems to have been called 'god,' because Stilpo asked him, "Theodorus, what you say you are, are you that?" [ὃ φὴς εἶναι, τοῦτο καὶ εἶ;] When Theodorus nodded, Stilpo asked, "Do you say god exists?"

[φὴς δ᾽ εἶναι θεόν;] When he agreed, Stilpo said "So you're a god." He received this happily, but Stilpo laughed and said, "But, you scoundrel, by this logic you'd admit to being a jackdaw and a million other things!" (D.L. 2.101)

These anecdotes have very little evidentiary value, but they seem to suggest Theodorus admits the existence of god or gods. On the other hand, the later tradition is almost unanimous in asserting that Theodorus denies gods exist at all.[50] Sextus Empiricus relates both that Theodorus denied the existence of the gods and that "in his composition *On the Gods* he demolished what the Greeks say about gods in numerous ways" (διὰ τοῦ περὶ θεῶν συντάγματος τὰ παρὰ τοῖς Ἕλλησι θεολογούμενα ποικίλως ἀνασκευάσας) (*M* 9.50–55; cf. *PH* 3.218 = *SSR* 4f.23). So the truth may be that in *On the Gods* Theodorus made arguments both against Greek religion in particular and against the very existence of gods, notwithstanding what he may have said in conversation with Stilpo.

We can explain both the breadth of this critique and the confusion about Theodorus's beliefs if we propose that his purpose was not to defend any position of his own, but rather to clear away the fears, hopes, and constrictive norms created by both popular and philosophical theology. This agenda would explain the connection Diogenes makes with Epicurean theology, which also attacks popular religion as a source of fear, unrestrained desire, and vice (e.g., LS 23B–C, Lucr. 1.44–109). Diogenes Laertius preserves an example of Theodorus's critique of popular religion:

> Once Theodorus sat down next to Euryclides the Hierophant [of the Eleusinian mysteries] and said, "Tell me, Euryclides, which people are impious with regard to the mysteries?" He answered, "Those who disclose them to the uninitiated." "Then you're impious," Theodorus answered, "since you recite them to the uninitiated!" (D.L. 2.101)

If we took this anecdote in isolation, we would say that Theodorus has done no more than catch Euryclides in an imprecise statement. But that would be to miss the Socratic resonances of the vignette. Ancient sources frequently imply a comparison between Theodorus and Socrates, even claiming that the Theodorus followed his predecessor in being condemned to drink hemlock at Athens (Athen. 611a, D.L. 2.101 = *SSR* 4h.11, 13). This is obviously wrong: Theodorus went on to Alexandria and died at the court of Magas in Cyrene, so he cannot have been put to death at Athens.[51] But we can retain for Theodorus the Socratic suspicion that so-called religious "authorities" have never really reflected on their own rituals and prohibitions. In this Euryclides the Hierophant resembles Plato's Euthyphro, who also claims to be an expert on "impiety."

Theodorus would also have been confronted with well-developed and influential philosophical theologies. The clearest example is that of the Old Academy, of which Theodorus cannot have been entirely ignorant, since he probably spent several years in Athens between 320 and 306 BCE.[52] It has recently been argued that the theology and ethics of Polemo, who was scholarch of the Academy 314/13–270/69 BCE, anticipated in important ways those of his student Zeno.[53] Of course, Zeno later equated his Stoic system of appropriate behaviors with fidelity to the Reason of Zeus, which guides all activity in the universe (LS 54). We have just seen Theodorus's attack on a particular Stoic position. It is easy to see why he would be opposed to theological ethics in general, since it would further entangle its adherents in a system of abstract norms that impede perception of each unique situation and what it requires of each agent. Unfortunately, no further evidence on this topic has survived.

This brings me to the last of Theodorus's attested polemics, which regards sexual ethics. According to our doxography, Theodorus said that "the wise man will treat his beloveds openly and without jealousy" (D.L. 2.99). It has been remarked that the idea of "treating" or "using beloveds openly" (*phanerōs . . . khrēsthai*) recalls Cynic shamelessness, exemplified by the claim that Hipparchia had sex with Crates in public (*en tōi phanerōi sunegineto*; D.L. 6.97).[54] The vagueness of Theodorus's wording makes it hard to say whether he means to go this far, but it is certainly possible; he undoubtedly aims to shock his listeners and call sexual norms into question. We have already seen that he claims the sage will commit adultery "under the right circumstances."[55] His explanation for this claim is lost, but two syllogisms survive which conclude by justifying provocative sexual choices.

The first takes us back to the Cyrenaics' renowned association with courtesans.[56] Once again it relies on a play on words which is hard to reproduce in English:

> They say that Phocion's son was rotten in many ways. When he was in love with a young prostitute who was being raised by a brothel-keeper, by chance Theodorus was around expounding the following syllogism in the Lyceum: "If it's not shameful to ransom [*lusasthai*] a male friend [*philon*], neither is it shameful to ransom a female friend [*philēn*]; and if not a male companion [*hetairon*], then neither a female 'companion' [*hetairan*]. (Plut. *Phoc.* 38.3)

As with Theodorus's mockery of Euryclides, at first blush the syllogism has little substance. As the words were normally used, there is some degree of equivocation in the use of *lusasthai* applied both to paying for the release of a friend and purchasing the contract of an enslaved prostitute. There is some too in the word *hetaira*, which must mean both "female friend" and "courtesan." But if the meanings and values conventionally associated with words are out of sync with listeners' intuitions, this sort of equivocation can provoke reflection on those conventions. Notwithstanding prevalent scaremongering about the manipulative and money-grubbing character of courtesans, a sympathetic listener might say to himself, "This particular courtesan, whom I love, is not like that. Why shouldn't I treat her like a friend?" An even more daring thinker might ask,

"Does this courtesan merit her enslavement any more than my friend, who has been caught by pirates during a voyage? So why shouldn't I use the word 'ransom' in both cases?" This is roughly how Phocion's son supposedly responded: "He decided the argument was a good one (since it was in tune with his desire), and bought the courtesan's contract."

The second syllogism concerning sexual ethics aims to challenge squeamishness about intercourse in general. It runs as follows:

> "Isn't a literate woman useful insofar as she's literate?"
> "Yes."
> "And a literate boy or young man is useful insofar as he's literate?"
> "Yes."
> "So wouldn't a beautiful woman be useful insofar as she's beautiful, and a beautiful boy or young man would be useful for that for which beauty[57] is useful?"
> "Yes."
> "And it's useful[58] for intercourse."
> When these points had been granted, he concluded, "So if someone were using intercourse insofar as it's useful, he doesn't make any mistake. Nor if someone were to use beauty insofar as it's useful will he make any mistake." (D.L. 2.99–100)

It is unlikely that this syllogism is directed against popular ethics, since Greeks were relatively comfortable with intercourse per se. As classicists have recently explored, the sexual preoccupations revealed by Greek oratory, law, and even magic revolve around the masculine display of self-mastery and control of households more than around bodily purity.[59] But Platonic philosophy is well known for combining the exaltation of erotic passion with the claim that ideal lovers will not have sex, because "what beauty is useful for" is not sex, but rather self-purification and recollection of Truth.[60] Sex is a "mistake" and an impediment to purification and recollection. The Academy of Theodorus's time seems to have been particularly committed to spiritual and educative eros.[61] In the same period Zeno defended a version of philosophical eros in the early Stoa, though later Stoics abandoned it.[62] Finally, Menedemus of Eretria, who founded the short-lived Eretric sect, had an extremely intimate (and possibly erotic) relationship with Asclepiades of Phlius.[63] In short, if Theodorus meant this as an attack on philosophical idealizations of erotic passion, he would find plenty of targets.

Theodorus's goal in these provocations is not to recommend purchasing prostitutes and having sex with every beautiful person you see. He no more grants everyone license to do these things than to commit adultery and rob temples. This may be how he was sometimes understood, as he himself complained: "Theodorus the so-called Godless used to say that he offered his arguments with his right hand, but his listeners received them with their left" (Plut. *Mor.* 467b; cf. 378a = *SSR* 4h.10). I take this to mean that his auditors failed to

grasp that his antinomian arguments were intended critically rather than con-
structively. His intention is to shake off the blinders of convention so that people can begin to reconsider their own intuitions about what they should do. But
this does not mean that anything goes: in each case the question must become
whether an action is wise and just in these circumstances and for this agent. No
normative system can answer such questions; each person must answer in each
case for himself or herself. Theodorus's attack on popular and philosophical
prejudices about sexual relationships, like his attack on religion and theology,
aims to clear the ground for this independent reflection.

8.6. Heroism

By way of conclusion it is worth remarking that Theodorus takes the motif of
philosophical heroism to its furthest expression in the Cyrenaic movement.[64]
This is hardly surprising in a philosopher who challenges all conventional and
philosophical norms, setting in their place his extemporaneous judgment. In this
section I will explore the heroic resonances of his philosophy through an anecdote which has done as much as his atheism to guarantee his posthumous fame.
For the sake of this exploration I will once again make use of Aristotle's presentation of the virtue of "magnanimity," which is our clearest ancient analysis of one
of the forms heroic ethics takes in late classical Greek culture. The features on
which I will focus are Theodorus's exercise of freedom of speech, his contempt
for death (in the right circumstances), and above all—as with Aristippus and
Hegesias—his striking sense of his own extraordinary preeminence and worth.

 The anecdote in question concerns a diplomatic mission Theodorus undertook to King Lysimachus of Thrace on behalf of King Ptolemy I of Egypt.[65] The
two became firm allies in 299 BCE, when Ptolemy wedded one of his daughters to Lysimachus and another to Lysimachus's son Agathocles. At this point
Theodorus had left Athens and not yet returned to Cyrene. As Diogenes reports, Theodorus "was staying with Ptolemy the son of Lagus, and was sent
as an ambassador to Lysimachus. There he spoke very freely, and Lysimachus
said . . ." (D.L. 2.101). There are three discrete versions of the exchange of words
that followed. Oddly enough, these versions always appear separately: while
some authors know more than one (e.g., Cicero and Plutarch), no author combines them in any single passage. Thus the degree of historical truth in any of
them cannot be established with confidence. Nevertheless, taken as a group
they clearly say something about Theodorus's behavior and self-conception.

 It will be convenient to take the first two versions of the conversation together. I give only Cicero's renditions here, although variants appear in several
other Greek and Latin authors and anecdotal miscellanies:

> [VERSION 1] When Lysimachus was threatening Theodorus with death,
> he said, "It's really a mighty thing you've accomplished, if you've acquired
> the power of the *cantharis* beetle!"[66] (Cic. *Tusc.* 5.117 = SSR 4h.7)

[VERSION 2] Shouldn't we admire Theodorus of Cyrene? When king Lysimachus threatened him with torture, he replied, "Direct your threats to these luxuriously dressed friends of yours; it makes no difference to *Theodorus* whether he rots under ground or above it!" (Cic. *Tusc.* 1.102 = *SSR* 4h.8)

Theodorus's daring words constitute a final disproof of the claim that his "practical wisdom" and "justice" are simply prudential strategies for avoiding painful consequences. To the contrary, this incident above all exemplifies Theodorus's "indifference" to what other people can do to him. Here he is very much in a tradition of sages speaking truth to power. As we have read in Diogenes' report, Theodorus "was speaking very freely" (*parrēsiazomenou*; cf. Gnom. Vat. 743 n. 352 = *SSR* 4h.7). One might compare Solon and King Croesus (Her. 1.29–33), Socrates and the Athenian jury (Pl. *Apol.*), Diogenes and Alexander the Great (Arr. *An.* 7.2.1–2 = *SSR* 5b.33), or Stilpo and King Demetrius (Plut. *Demetr.* 9.9–10 = *SSR* 2o.15). While these sages have different beliefs about what is good and bad, their stories communicate a common lesson: the leaders think they have power over the sages, but the sages understand the impotence of wealth, prestige, and political might. As the Stoics would put it, the sage is the only true king.

This tradition about the superiority of the sage overlaps with motifs about the superiority of epic and tragic heroes. Notice the way Cicero chooses to present version 2: "Direct your threats to these luxuriously dressed friends of yours; it makes no difference to *Theodorus* whether he rots underground or above it!" First, Theodorus differentiates himself from the sort of people who think that luxurious clothing is worth something. Second, he invokes his own name (*Theodori nihil interest . . .*), just as we saw Odysseus and Aristippus invoking their own names to punctuate their elevated self-conception.[67] Compare also a curious passage in Plato's *Apology* about why Socrates will not beg for the jury's pity:

> For my fame and yours and that of the polis it seems ignoble for me to do these things at my age and with my reputation, whether that reputation is true or not. Because it's believed, in any event, that Socrates is better than [*diapherein*] most people. If those of you who seem to excel [*hoi dokountes diapherein*] in wisdom, courage, or any other excellence behaved this way, it would be a disgrace. (34e1–35a1)

Although Socrates hints that his exceptional reputation may be unmerited, he makes explicit what Theodorus only implies: normal people can be swayed by threats of death or posthumous outrage, but exceptional people owe it to themselves to behave differently.[68] This willingness to face death is another typical component of both philosophical and epic heroism. Finally, Aristotle specifically associates free speech with magnanimity: the magnanimous man "must be open in his friendship and enmity . . . and speak and act openly (he's a free-speaker [*parrēsiastēs*] because he tends to be contemptuous [*kataphronētikos*])" (*EN* 1124b26–29). That Theodorus is "speaking freely" has already been shown.

That he holds Lysimachus in contempt is clear from version 1, where he compares him to the *cantharis* beetle or "Spanish fly." The Spanish fly is highly caustic when ground up, and was therefore commonly used in poisons. Whatever its chemical properties, however, the point is that Theodorus compares Lysimachus *to an insect.*

This brings us to the third and most striking component of the anecdote, which finds its fullest expression in the variant of Philo:

> The story goes that when Theodorus, nicknamed the Atheist, had been exiled from Athens and came to Lysimachus, an official mocked him for his flight and listed its causes: that he had been exiled on account of condemnation for atheism and corruption of the youth.[69] "I wasn't exiled," he replied. "The same thing happened to me as to Zeus' son Heracles. He too was offloaded by the Argonauts, not because he did anything wrong, but because all by himself he was a full load and ballast and weighed them down. So he made his fellow sailors afraid the boat would fill with water. I changed residence for the same reason. The citizens of Athens couldn't keep up with the profundity and magnitude of my thought, and they also envied me." Then Lysimachus asked, "And were you also exiled from your own country because of envy?" And he answered, "Not because of envy, but because of the excesses of my nature, which my country couldn't accommodate. Just like when Semele was pregnant with Dionysus, she couldn't carry him for the defined time until his birth; but Zeus, struck with fear, extracted the fruit of her womb before its time, and made him equal in honor to the gods. In the same way some deity or god raised me up and decided to send me as a colonist to a better place, Athens, because my own country was too narrow to receive such a mass of philosophical wisdom." (*Quod omn. bon. lib.* 127–30 = *SSR* 4h.9)

There is more than a hint of audacious wit in Theodorus's response here, which once again exemplifies his "contemptuous" freedom of speech. Humorous taunts are a regular element of Homeric warfare, and Greek authors in general are well aware that laughter is always close to derision.[70] But this does not mean Theodorus is entirely insincere in likening his condition to those of Heracles and Dionysus. Both of these children of Zeus were born to mortal women, and their persecution on earth spurred them to memorable accomplishments. Eventually, both were elevated to fully divine status. Theodorus "the godless" therefore suggests that he too is a sort of demi-god, and that he will inevitably overcome the challenges imposed on him by his antagonists.

Setting aside his use of myth, what is most noteworthy is how Theodorus turns his expulsion from Cyrene and Athens into proof of his extraordinary nature. The mention of Theodorus's exile is intended to shame him and silence his audacious free speech, as another variant of the anecdote makes clear: "When Theodorus was speaking very freely, Lysimachus said, 'Tell me, Theodorus, aren't you the one who was exiled from Athens?'" (D.L. 2.102) The implication is that even Theodorus's home polis could not tolerate him. But Theodorus re-describes the expulsion in order to present himself as a titanic prodigy, not a run-of-the-mill agitator. The passage bristles with metaphorical expressions of his prodigious character: parochial Cyrene could not endure the "excesses of his nature" (*phuseōs . . . huperbolais*) and "mass of his philosophical wisdom" (*philosophou phronētos onkon*). Even the "ship" of Athens struggled under the "full load" (*plērōma*), "ballast" (*herma*), and "profundity and magnitude of his thought" (ὕψει καὶ μεγέθει τῆς ἐμῆς διανοίας). It might still have been big enough to handle them, but his co-passengers were stricken with "envy." To the best of my knowledge, nowhere does an ancient Greek philosopher give more forceful expression to the feeling that he is a higher and greater being than his fellow humans.

8.7. Conclusion

At the outset of this chapter I suggested that an understanding of Theodorean practical wisdom and justice, which have attracted almost no scholarly attention, could help to unify the evidence for this final, eclectic Cyrenaic. To recapitulate, I have suggested that the goodness of these virtues and badness of the corresponding vices should be taken closely with the report of Theodorean indifference. This tripartite axiology can then be related to the ends, joy and distress, in such a way as to sketch Theodorus's moral psychology. Foolishness and injustice are both networks of false belief about indifferents, which lead to distress. Practical wisdom and justice are not only networks of correct beliefs, which eliminate distress; the sage's perception of his virtue is also his primary source of joy. Yet Theodorus's polemics and provocations suggest that his thinking about virtue tends to be critical rather than constructive. Having posited the importance of justice and wisdom, his primary concern is that conventional and philosophical norms will constrain their free exercise. Once these obfuscations have been removed, the sage can determine on a case-by-case basis what ought to be done. This radical independence of judgment, combined with his repudiation of personal and civic relationships, helps to explain Theodorus's turbulent history: he who neither participates in normal relationships nor subscribes to any conventions of behavior is as troubling for society as the heroes of Greek poetry and history.

CHAPTER 9

The "New Cyrenaicism"
of Walter Pater

9.1. Introduction

In the previous eight chapters I laid out my interpretation of the ancient Greek Cyrenaics. Before pulling together my thoughts, however, I want to look briefly at the only (to my knowledge) significant recrudescence of Cyrenaic ethics in subsequent intellectual history.[1] This is the "new Cyrenaicism" of the nineteenth-century critic, novelist, and Oxford academic Walter Pater. Pater's Cyrenaicism merits investigation for several reasons. First and most importantly, it develops in fascinating detail some elements of Cyrenaic philosophy which are clearly important, but are left tantalizingly vague by the ancient evidence. Among these are the idea of "unitemporal pleasure," the nature of the "education" and "exercises" valued by the Cyrenaics, the details of how skeptical hedonism actually supports ethical behavior, and how it attempts to eliminate the fear of death. The second strength of Pater's new Cyrenaicism is that it subjects these and other elements of Cyrenaicism to a searching critique. Finally, the third is that it situates this critique in the narrative of one particular person's quest for meaning and satisfaction. It therefore exemplifies precisely what I argued in chapters 1 and 3, and assumed throughout this book: Cyrenaic ethics arises from the interaction of particular individuals' pre-philosophical inclinations with critical reasoning, and develops through the dynamic interaction of these two elements with the satisfying or dissatisfying feedback from experience. The protagonist of Pater's *Marius the Epicurean* hence begins with orthodox Cyrenaicism (as Pater understands it), but gradually incorporates other influences into this Cyrenaic foundation as he comes to terms with the events in his life.

9.2. Walter Pater: From the *The Renaissance* to *Marius the Epicurean*

In 1873 Walter Pater, who was a fellow of Brasenose College at Oxford, published a series of essays entitled *Studies in the History of the Renaissance*.[2] To these he affixed, as their "Conclusion," some thoughts he had previously published in an essay on the poet William Morris (1868). Pater's "critical notions always had existential implications," as Wolfgang Iser has put it;[3] and these are expressed in a famous passage of the Conclusion:

> The service of philosophy, of speculative culture, towards the human spirit, is to rouse, to startle it to a life of constant and eager observation. Every moment some form grows perfect in hand or face; some tone on the hills or the sea is choicer than the rest; some mood of passion or insight or intellectual excitement is irresistibly real and attractive to us,—for that moment only. Not the fruit of experience, but experience itself, is the end. A counted number of pulses only is given to us of a variegated, dramatic life. How may we see in them all that is to be seen in them by the finest senses? How shall we pass most swiftly from point to point, and be present always at the focus where the greatest number of vital forces unite in their purest energy?
>
> To burn always with this hard, gemlike flame, to maintain this ecstasy, is success in life. (*R* 236)

Pater goes on to say that we cannot "burn with this hard, gemlike flame" unless we liberate ourselves from those "habits" and "systems" with which we have no impassioned sympathy:

> The theory or idea or system which requires of us the sacrifice of any part of this experience, in consideration of some interest into which we cannot enter, or some abstract theory we have not identified with ourselves, or of what is only conventional, has no real claim upon us. (*R* 237–38)

In place of what is "only conventional," Pater proposes just the sort of exquisite attention to beauty he has been displaying throughout the volume. "For art," he explains in the final sentence, "comes to you proposing frankly to give nothing but the highest quality to your moments as they pass, and simply for those moments' sake" (*R* 239).

These rather "antinomian"[4] passages belong to an ongoing debate in nineteenth-century England, and particularly at Oxford, regarding the relation of higher education and the arts to religion, morality, and (what we would today call) gender and sexuality.[5] Pater's stance places his works in what is now known as the "aesthetic movement," a network of ideas and modes of expression with which are associated painters such as J. M. Whistler and writers such as A. C. Swinburne and Oscar Wilde. Pater shared with many of these figures the ideal of education and self-cultivation freed from the moralizing purposes espoused not only by the church, but even by progressive thinkers such as the critic John Ruskin and the philosopher and translator Benjamin Jowett. For Pater, as we will see below, the study of literature, art, and philosophy all pertain not only to transforming individual lives, but also to lifting Victorian culture out of what he saw as a spider's web of conflicting impulses. It was for these purposes that he, like many of his contemporaries, reassessed the educational value of the works of Greco-Roman antiquity, medieval Europe, and the Renaissance. The broad outlines of his agenda were familiar enough that most reviews of *The Renais-sance* are strikingly positive, and many ignore the provocations of the Conclu-sion, failing even to mention it. Even those opposed to its ethical implications generally adopt a tone of remonstration or condescension rather than outrage.[6]

On the other hand, the Conclusion apparently caused enough disturbance to motivate Pater to excise it in the second edition of 1877. In restoring it (lightly edited) for the third edition in 1888, he added an explanatory footnote:

> This brief "Conclusion" was omitted in the second edition of this book, as I conceived it might possibly mislead some of those young men into whose hands it might fall. On the whole, I have thought it best to re-print it here, with some slight changes which bring it closer to my origi-nal meaning. I have dealt more fully in *Marius the Epicurean* with the thoughts suggested by it. (*R* 233)

Pater's explanation for the Conclusion's omission in the second edition recalls the concern Sidney Colvin had raised in his 1873 review of the first edition,[7] and precisely reiterates the plea of John Wordsworth, then chaplain of Brasenose, in a letter to Pater: "Could you indeed have known the dangers in which you were likely to lead minds weaker than your own, you would, I believe, have paused" (*Letters* 20–21). Pater's tutor at Queen's College, the Reverend W. W. Capes, also criticized him in a sermon delivered that November; and the Bishop of Oxford, J. F. Mackarness, singled out the Conclusion in a lecture on religious unbelief two years later.[8] Moreover, in 1874 the fellows of Brasenose passed over Pater for a Junior Proctorship at the university. Further professional snubs would fol-low in 1876 and 1885.[9] While the reasoning behind these setbacks has not been preserved, Pater's controversial ideas may have been involved.

This and other criticism undoubtedly influenced Pater's expurgation of the second edition of *The Renaissance*, but it is also worth noting that his profes-sional disappointment in 1874 closely coincided with a personal scandal. It may not be accidental that his explanatory note about "misleading . . . young men" recalls the prosecution of Socrates for "corrupting the youth."[10] As was common in the aesthetic movement, Pater's idea of transformative culture involved the sort of homoerotic psychagogy Plato's Socrates memorably dis-cusses in the *Symposium* and especially the *Phaedrus*.[11] And some time in early 1874 Pater's friendship with a nineteen-year-old student, William Hardinge, led to the intervention of Jowett (then Master of Balliol College).[12] Among the whistleblowers for this incident may have been one of Pater's own sisters. Hardinge was sent home, Pater had a very uncomfortable meeting with Jowett, and the incident was hushed up. But it probably got out to the fellows of Brase-nose, whose decision not to promote Pater was taken during this same year. Even if it did not, the disturbance surely contributed to Pater's growing aware-ness that freely expressing and acting on his radical notions could have serious consequences.

This brief account of the early reception of Pater's Conclusion, with its exhortation to shed desiccated conventions and savor each vital "pulse," constitutes the necessary background for understanding his treatment of Cyrenaicism. For among the hostile critics of the first edition of *The Renaissance* is one who titles his review "Modern Cyrenaicism."[13] This anonymous reviewer displays acquaintance with several Aristippean anecdotes and sayings, emphasizing in particular Athenaeus's report of Aristippus's commitment to "unitemporal pleasure" (Athen. 544a–b = *SSR* 4a.174).[14] He allows that neither Aristippus nor Pater make this a license to debauchery, but this strategic concession sets the stage for insinuating that Pater's philosophy is emasculating:

> Get your self-contained pleasure, cried Aristippus; get your "pulsation," cries Mr Pater. Yet, we surely need a criterion of "pulsations." . . . Life, said Aristippus, is so dull, so dreary, so stupid, that I prefer to lie on the seashore watching the gulls overhead, and throwing pebbles into the waves. And in a similar spirit Mr Pater, apostle of the artistic apotheosis of lotus-eating, finds life so dull and hopeless, and in a word "Philistine," that he prefers to wile [*sic*] his moments away with the joys of shape, and sound, and colour.[15]

The problem with Cyrenaic philosophers in every period, this reviewer goes on to object, is that they willfully neglect the investigation of truth and goodness implied by the vocation of philosophy, and the duty actively to shape their lives based on these investigations. "The writer of this article knows," he concludes, ". . . that Pater is an *industrious, energetic,* and *self-sacrificing* College tutor, and that his theories about life are the relaxation of a life *sternly devoted to duty*" (emphasis mine).[16] The words I have italicized outline an ideal of Victorian masculinity—energetic but temperate; hard, self-sacrificing, and dutiful—which Pater himself is visibly concerned to transform, but which, his viewer implies, aestheticism is too languid to sustain.[17] Hence also the comparison with Homer's "lotus-eaters" (*Od.* 9.82–104), who allegorically represent hedonism, according to an interpretation already attested in antiquity,[18] and whose "honey-sweet fruit" makes Odysseus's crew "want to remain with the lotus-eating men, battening on lotuses, and forgetting their journey home." In Odysseus's case, of course, this would mean failing to reclaim his family possessions and wife by killing the suitors infesting Ithaca. The accusation that Pater abdicates such Odyssean duties is a specifically gendered criticism, adding to the religious, educational, and sexual objections we have already seen to Pater's style of writing and living.

By aligning Paterian aestheticism with Aristippean Cyrenaicism, this reviewer enriches his criticism with the same historical resources Pater (and many of his contemporaries) used. Throughout his critical and fictional treatments of antiquity, the middle ages, and the Renaissance, Pater discovers "prefigurations" of nineteenth-century cultural phenomena. The method behind these

discoveries, which combines Hegelian *Geistesgeschichte* with Pater's characteristic emphasis on immediate sensation, is certainly not that of modern historiography.[19] In fact, Pater's sensuous "subjectivity" even elicited criticism in his
own time, leading him to drop the term "history" from the title of the second
and third editions of *The Renaissance*.[20] But for Pater, as for his critic in the last
paragraph, vivacity and relevance to contemporary life and society were more
important than pedantic scruples. It is hard to imagine, for example, a serious defense of that critic's reconstruction of Aristippus's premises for Cyrenaic
ethics: "Life . . . is so dull, so dreary, so stupid." And it is anachronistic for him
to make "ly[ing] on the seashore watching the gulls overhead, and throwing
pebbles at the waves" a vignette of Aristippean pleasure. Beach vacation scenes
belong to the modern European imaginary; in ancient Greek literature, beaches
are typically scenes of anguish and death. But this is beside the point: by making Cyrenaicism a recurrent, intellectually dishonest, and inevitably transient
phenomenon in human history, the reviewer ornaments and corroborates his
moral or religious objections.

As scholars have frequently observed, many of Pater's writings after the first
edition of *The Renaissance* in 1874 display his sensitivity to the setbacks and
criticism that followed it, culminating with his apologia in *Marius the Epicurean* (1885). We have already seen his claim that he "dealt more fully . . . with
the thoughts suggested" by the Conclusion in *Marius*. More specifically, as
Pater explains in a letter to Vernon Lee, this historical novel aims to express
a "sort of religious phase possible for the modern mind" (*Letters* 78). In other
words, through *Marius* Pater aims to address the charges of irreligion made
against him and his work by showing how his aesthetic philosophy introduces
a new "phase" of religiosity, one more in harmony with the currents toward
which he believed modern culture was converging.[21] Because of his belief in
the continuity of alternating historical problems and resolutions, and the subtle
persistence of transcended phases in later periods, he chooses to situate this
"new" nineteenth-century religiosity in second-century Rome. In fact, he intended *Marius* to be the first part of a trilogy "dealing with the same problems,
under different historical conditions" (*Letters* 96; cf. 98, 212). The third part of
this trilogy, which was never begun, would probably have been set in Pater's
own time.[22] The unspecified "problems" include not only religion, but the entire interlocking array of educational, sexual/erotic, gendered, and moral issues
raised by and since the Conclusion of *The Renaissance*.

Since Pater's apologetic project is situated during what Gibbon famously
considered the apogee of classical culture (and the beginning of its "Decline
and Fall"), Pater anchors it in his protagonist's critical encounters with what,
following Iser, we can call Greek "existential" positions. For these he turns especially to Greek philosophy—more specifically, to middle (Apuleian) Platonism,
Roman (Aurelian) Stoicism, and Cyrenaicism. (Notwithstanding the title and

frequent quotations of Lucretius, Marius does not engage seriously with Epicureanism.[23]) Significant parts of the novel are actually direct translations from Marcus Aurelius's *Meditations*, Apuleius's *Golden Ass*, Lucian's *Hermotimus*, and the pseudo-Lucianic *Halcyon*. Others are heavily influenced by Apuleius's *On the God of Socrates* and Cicero's Stoicizing *On Obligations*.[24] Aurelius, Apuleius, and other famous intellectuals also meet and personally influence Marius. Of course, no Cyrenaic texts survived for Pater to translate and weave into his novel, but chapters 8, 9, and 16 contain explicit and sustained engagements with Cyrenaic doxography, which are more well-informed and detailed than has been recognized hitherto. (In fact, I am not aware of any existing treatment of Pater's engagement with Cyrenaicism.) In chapter 9, entitled "A New Cyrenaicism," Pater takes up the gauntlet flung by his critic, and refers to the Aristippean ideas Marius is digesting as "this 'aesthetic' philosophy" (*ME* I.149). In other words, he assimilates Aristippean philosophy to his own aestheticism. These ideas become a vital element in Marius's attempt to resolve the problems of second-century Roman culture, and therefore convey how aestheticism can lead to flourishing religiosity, moral integrity, and loving happiness, rather than to seagull-watching and lotus-eating.

The full complexity of *Marius'* treatment of these ethical and religious issues, including their relations to the cultures of Antonine Rome and Victorian England, are beyond the scope of my investigation. Moreover, the development of Marius's "sensations and ideas" (the novel's subtitle) is sufficiently nuanced to have generated a range of different but persuasive interpretations of its trajectory and meaning.[25] In the following, therefore, I will focus on how the novel enriches and critically explores several aspects of Cyrenaic doxography; the development of Marius's ethical intuitions will interest me only insofar as they shed light on these Cyrenaic elements.

9.3. Unitemporal Pleasure

As we saw in the previous section, one of Pater's hostile critics argues that his outlook in the Conclusion to *The Renaissance* is merely reheated Cyrenaicism: "Memories and hopes Aristippus refused to estimate. What we possess, he taught us, is that which now *is*; that which now is, is the moment; and the pleasure of the moment—the *monokhronos hēdonē*—is all that man has."[26] This critic is obviously thinking of Athenaeus 12 544a–b:

> [Aristippus] embraced this pleasant living and declared it was the end and happiness is based on it. Furthermore, ⟨he said⟩ it was unitemporal [*monokhronos*]; like men of profligate life, he thought neither the memory of enjoyments that had happened nor the hope of ones to come were any concern to him. Rather, he judged the good by only one thing, what

was present, and regarded the fact that he had enjoyed or would enjoy as not concerning him, since one was no longer, and the other was not yet and uncertain.[27]

Strictly speaking the phrase "unitemporal pleasure" does not appear in this passage. It is either "pleasant living," or "happiness" which is "unitemporal." But Pater's critic is more concerned with the deleterious consequences of Cyrenaic presentism than with exact quotation. Aristippus's focus on "self-contained pleasure[s]," he goes on to assert, disincentivizes development of the virtues he charitably admits Aristippus possesses; and since Pater's "pulsations" are identical with Aristippus's pleasures, focusing on them has the same pernicious effect.

Pater appears to have considered this critique carefully. When he introduces "unitemporal pleasures" twelve years later in chapter 9 of *Marius*, it is to situate them in an ongoing ethical investigation that is vastly more complex and dynamic than the crusading manifesto of the Conclusion. In the first three chapters of the novel readers have become acquainted with Marius's foundational concerns and commitments, among which are certain moral intuitions (including innate religiosity and scrupulous distaste for causing pain), empiricist "idealism" (fidelity to his immediate experiences, cultivation of "vision," and skepticism about objective and communicable truths),[28] and "a certain vague fear of evil" (*ME* I.22). His father dies when he is young, and the death of his mother at the opening of chapter 4 sharpens an intellectual curiosity already glimpsed in earlier chapters: "the death of his mother turned seriousness of feeling into a matter of the intelligence: it made him a questioner" (*ME* I.43). Hence intellectual integrity begins to emerge as another foundational commitment. For the rest of the novel Marius will make recurrent efforts to harmonize his ethical intuitions and idealism in a manner that also resolves his "vague fear of evil."

He begins by going to school in Pisa, where he falls under the influence of one of his co-pupils. The narrator[29] describes Flavian as "The brilliant youth who loved dress, and dainty food, and flowers, and seemed to have a natural alliance with, and claim upon, everything else which was physically select and bright" (*ME* I.51). His initial impact on Marius is sensual and erotic more than intellectual, as Marius reflects long afterward:

> From Flavian in that brief early summer of his existence, he had derived a powerful impression of the 'perpetual flux': he had caught there, as in cipher or symbol, or low whispers more effective than any definite language, his own Cyrenaic philosophy, presented thus, for the first time, in an image or person, with much attractiveness . . . :—a concrete image, the abstract equivalent of which he could recognise afterward, when the agitating personal influence had settled down for him, clearly enough, into a theory of practice. (*ME* I.234–35)

In other words, the "agitating personal influence" of Flavian impresses itself upon Marius without any deliberation on his part, much less any critical understanding of the principles of Flavian's lifestyle. Together the two adolescents discover the exquisite artistry of Apuleius's *Golden Ass*,[30] which spurs Flavian to compose a poem in the pursuit of fame. "In him," the narrator comments, "a fine instinctive sentiment of the exact value and power of words was connate with the eager longing for sway over his fellows" (*ME* I.94). Marius already half-senses Flavian's selfish ambition, "spirit of unbelief," and "the extent of his early corruption" (*ME* I.52–53), but only much later—after intellectually digesting Flavian's behavior and formulating it as a "theory of practice"—will he begin to weigh its pros and cons. This intellectual digestion will be a long process, and only begins after Flavian's death in the plague. Stricken with grief, Marius begins his renewed studies with the nature and fate of the soul:

> [T]here came a novel curiosity as to what the various schools of ancient philosophy had had to say about that strange, fluttering creature; and that curiosity impelled him to certain severe studies, in which his earlier religious conscience seemed still to survive, as a principle of hieratic scrupulousness or integrity of thought, regarding this new service to intellectual light. (*ME* I.124)

Here the intellectual seriousness stimulated by his mother's death is redoubled and explicitly connected with his innate religiosity, of which it is an expression. Marius sublimates his love and grief as "hieratic scrupulousness or integrity of thought."[31] His "severe studies" quickly extend into metaphysics and ethics more generally, which help him to work toward the first (partial) accommodation among his foundational commitments. Not coincidentally, this accommodation takes the form of a theoretical reincarnation of his lost friend.

Thus when Cyrenaic philosophy enters Marius's consciousness, it provides answers to questions arising from some of his deepest concerns. More specifically, through Cyrenaic theory Marius attempts to integrate the passions Flavian's beauty and untimely death have elicited with his continuing sentiments of evil, "scrupulous" fidelity to his own experiences, and intellectual integrity. Cyrenaicism is not the first theoretical framework he encounters in this endeavor. His survey of philosophical psychology begins with the "*Arcana Celestia* of Platonism," which he finds unsatisfying, since "the various pathetic traits of the beloved, suffering, perished body of Flavian, so deeply pondered, had made him a materialist" (*ME* I.125). In other words, the inarticulate evil he is attempting to mitigate is currently instantiated by Flavian's beautiful, suffering, and now perished body. Platonism's faith in immortal souls, which does not address this body, cannot mitigate this sentiment of evil. Moreover, it seems intellectually dishonest to him, because it is not compatible with his "exact estimate" of "the actual feeling of sorrow in his heart" (*ME* I.126–27). It would be an act of bad faith to paper over his sorrow with assurances that Flavian, because his immortal soul lives on, has not really died. His immediate experience of sorrow, which he trusts more than any argument about immortal souls, belies this attempt at therapy. What appeals to Marius instead is a "Cyrenaic" philosophy of which, as we have already seen, Flavian will appear to have been the "cipher," the "symbol," and the "concrete image."[32] He arrives at this by combining (parts of) Heraclitean metaphysics with (a particular interpretation of) Cyrenaic epistemology and ethics.

From Heraclitus Marius takes the idea of "the swift passage of things, [and] the still swifter passage of those modes of our conscious being which seemed to reflect them," both of which pass "too swiftly for any real knowledge of them to be attainable" (*ME* I.131). This doctrine of radical flux clearly harmonizes with Marius's raw sentiment of mortality as a principle of change, which has created "this alienation, this sense of distance" between him and his friend—first through Flavian's delirium, then as his corpse is transformed into an inhuman and frightening object, and finally when "Flavian had gone out as utterly as the fire among those still beloved ashes" (*ME* I.120–23). In this respect it is more faithful to Marius's experiences than Platonism's transcendental psychology. This helps to explain why Marius focuses on the "negative" aspect of Heraclitean philosophy. On Pater's interpretation, Heraclitus himself progressed from purgative skepticism to an effort to perceive "the sleepless, ever-sustained, inexhaustible energy of the divine reason itself, proceeding always by its own rhythmical logic, and lending to all mind and matter, in turn, what life they had" (*ME* I.130–31; cf. *PP* 18–21). But Marius is not interested in this "large positive system of almost religious philosophy" (*ME* I.130). Like Platonism, its contact with his experiences, sensations, and emotions is tenuous; he prefers to focus on "the lowlier earthy steps nearest the ground" (*ME* I.132).

Marius therefore uses Heraclitean metaphysics primarily to justify his withdrawal of interest from pursuing objective and communicable knowledge, which validates his constitutional idealism:

> He was become aware of the possibility of a large dissidence between an inward and somewhat exclusive world of vivid personal apprehension, and the unimproved, unenlightened reality of the life of those about him. As a consequence, he was now ready to concede, somewhat more easily than others, the first point of his new lesson, that the individual is to himself the measure of all things, and to rely on the exclusive certainty to himself of his own impressions. (ME I.133)

From the Heraclitean doctrines of physical and phenomenal flux, Marius infers a "first lesson" that Heraclitus, with his overwhelming emphasis on "shared" or "common" Logos, does not mean to "teach": Marius refocuses his attention on the "inward and somewhat exclusive world of vivid personal apprehension," and deliberately disconnects from the "unenlightened reality of the life of those about him." In this way he makes Heraclitean epistemology "almost identical with the famous doctrine of the sophist Protagoras, that the momentary, sensible apprehension of the individual was the only standard of what is or is not" (*ME* I.130–32). This sets the stage for his incorporation of Aristippean ideas.

Pater attributes the Cyrenaic theory of the experiences to Aristippus, whom he believes to have deduced it from Heraclitus's beliefs about the radical instability of consciousness and of objects in the world.[33] But this (historically implausible[34]) assumption is inessential to Marius's pairing of Heraclitus with Aristippus, since the reduction of Heraclitean metaphysics to Protagorean relativism already prepares him for Cyrenaic epistemology. The key point in this epistemology is what the narrator calls

> the opposition between things as they are and our impressions and thoughts concerning them—the possibility, if an outward world does really exist, of some faultiness in our apprehension of it—the doctrine, in short, of what is termed "the subjectivity of knowledge." (*ME* I.137)

This is a faithful representation of the core of Cyrenaic epistemology, which the narrator goes on to support with arguments taken from good doxographical sources.[35] The terminology of Cyrenaic skepticism, which is grounded in *pathē* (which I have translated as "experiences," but which may also mean "feelings") may also influence Marius's slide from "impressions" and "thoughts" to "feelings": "Our knowledge is limited to what we *feel*, he reflected: we need no proof of what we *feel*. But can we be sure that things are at all like our *feelings*?" (*ME* I.138; italics mine) And this, in turn, further authorizes Marius's grouping of sensations, ideas, and emotions as equally foundational elements in his own epistemology.

Aristippus thus helps Marius to elaborate the epistemological consequences of his interpretation of Heraclitus, but his key impact is in revealing the "ethical," "practical," and "sentimental" equivalents for these metaphysical and epistemological positions. The narrator's exposition of this idea of "equivalents" in different domains of philosophy, which recurs in Pater's later work (e.g., *PP* 48), is worth setting out at length:

> The difference between [Aristippus] and those obscure earlier thinkers . . . was the difference between the mystic in his cell, or the prophet in the desert, and the expert, cosmopolitan, administrator of his dark sayings, translating the abstract thoughts of the master into terms, first of all, of *sentiment*. It has been sometimes seen, in the history of the human mind, that when thus translated into terms of sentiment—of sentiment, as lying already half-way towards practice—the abstract ideas of metaphysics for the first time reveal their true significance. The metaphysical principle, in itself, as it were, without hands or feet, becomes impressive, fascinating, of effect, when translated into a precept as to how it were best to feel and act; in other words, under its sentimental or ethical equivalent. (*MM* I.135)

For Pater, sentimental and ethical rules—"precept[s] as to how it were best to feel and act"—encapsulate the "true significance" and the end, as it were, of philosophy. His hostility to metaphysics and abstraction (nearly a hendiadys in his usage) begins with his rejection in *The Renaissance* of "the abstract question what beauty is in itself, or what its exact relation to truth or experience—metaphysical questions, as unprofitable as metaphysical questions elsewhere" (*R* ix). It perseveres through his discussion of Plato's Eleatic predecessors in *Plato and Platonism*, regarding whom he says, "It was the beginning of scholasticism; and the philosophic mind will perhaps never be quite in health, quite sane or natural, again" (*PP* 31).[36] But his conception of the "healthy" side of philosophy evolves over the intervening decades. In *The Renaissance* he had claimed that "The service of philosophy, of speculative culture, towards the human spirit, is to rouse, to startle it to a life of constant and eager observation" (*R* 236; cf. 230). Here philosophy seemed exclusively to serve the "quickening" of sensation. As we have seen, an anonymous critic lampooned this goal as lotus-eating and seagull-watching. Pater never disavows this philosophical purpose, but in *Marius* philosophy works also on sentiment (including moral sentiment) and behavior.[37]

This brings us finally to Pater's revised conception of unitemporal pleasures as the core of Aristippean ethics. Pater signposts his response to his critic with a paraphrase of the passage from Athenaeus to which that critic alludes:[38]

> And so the abstract apprehension that the little point of this present moment alone really is, between a past which has just ceased to be and a future which may never come, became practical with Marius, under the form of a resolve, as far as possible, to exclude regret and desire, and yield himself to the improvement of the present with an absolutely disengaged mind. (*ME* I.139)

For Pater's Marius, this "resolve to yield himself to the improvement of the present" is the ethical equivalent of Heraclitean metaphysics for at least two reasons. First, in its Aristippean reception, that metaphysics has led "almost [to] the renunciation . . . of metaphysical enquiry itself" (*ME* I.140). As we have just seen, for Pater metaphysics is the paradigm of systematic and abstract theory—in short, of every way in which the human impulse to understand outreaches human cognitive abilities. Marius' mind is therefore liberated from an entire array of dubious systems and abstractions in the wake of this "anti-metaphysical metaphysic." In effect, this implosion of metaphysics allows Marius to relax his effort to project his understanding both imaginatively and temporally beyond what is present to his sensations or emotions. From this relaxation emerge his practical efforts to become "absolutely virgin towards . . . experience" (*ME* I.141), i.e., toward the sensations and feelings happening in each moment.

The second connection between Heraclitean metaphysics and Aristippean presentism is the principle of flux, which also demonstrates how this ethics responds to Marius' deepest concerns. Among the most important of these, we recall, is his enduring sentiment of inarticulate evil. This sentiment has become closely bound to the fragility of all things mortal, such as his father, mother, and Flavian. As Flavian lay dying, Marius had observed how

> he would set himself . . . to fashion out . . . still a few more broken verses of his unfinished work, in hard-set determination, defiant of pain, to arrest this or that little drop at least from the river of sensuous imagery rushing so quickly past him. (*ME* I.117)

Flavian's anguished and futile attempt to arrest "the river of sensuous imagery," which will soon leave him behind, exemplifies the problem of mortality. In choosing to focus only on *present* sensations, Marius attempts to solve this problem by "'throwing himself into the stream,' so to speak" (*ME* I.139). In other words, contemplating both physical and phenomenal flux, and reflecting also on his painful attachment to some of those vanishing physical objects, Marius resolves to embrace rather than fight this ubiquitous mobility.[39] He will collude in the fluidity of his consciousness. At the same time, this decision to identify with each passing experience justifies in theory and somehow re-animates part of Flavian, who was vividly sensitive to "select and beautiful" things. Finally, it reinforces and coheres with Marius's innate tendency to cultivate his sensory capacities.

By making Cyrenaic presentism the solution to a family of personal concerns for Marius, Pater has already enriched and clarified the lines of thought preserved in our ancient evidence. There presentism is a prudential and emotional attitude, which is justified by universalizing claims about value and moral psychology, cultivated by a series of spiritual exercises, and recommended to anyone seeking to be happy.[40] Pater admits what the ancient Cyrenaics cannot, that different people have different predispositions, and that Marius is simply predisposed to prioritize immediate experiences. Moreover, he replaces the tangle of poorly preserved arguments around ancient Cyrenaic presentism with Marius's personal struggles against some ineffable evil, his passionate attachment to Flavian, and his poignant sentiment of mortality. In this way he concretizes the motivations for his new Cyrenaic presentism by grounding them in the interplay of historically attested arguments with individual psychological development. Cyrenaicism does not thereby become irreducibly idiosyncratic, but it does abandon its pretension to be the One True Ethical Theory. Anyone interested in Pater's new Cyrenaicism must ask herself not only whether she assents to Marius's metaphysical and epistemological arguments, but also whether she shares some of his basic concerns.

These same considerations also provide the beginning of a response to Pater's critical reviewer. Contrary to the reviewer's caricature of aesthetes, Marius does not "find life so dull and hopeless, and in a word 'Philistine,' that he prefers to wile his moments away with the joys of shape, and sound, and colour." His problem is not that life lacks interest, but that what is precious in life always slips away. He focuses on vivid experiences not in order to mitigate ennui, but in order to capture something fugitive. And we should note that Pater avoids the word "pleasure" throughout his presentation of this new Cyrenaicism. "Really," the narrator tells us,

> to the phase of reflection through which Marius was then passing, the charge of "hedonism," whatever its true weight might be, was not properly applicable at all. Not pleasure, but fullness of life, and "insight" as conducting to that fullness—energy, variety, and choice of experience, including noble pain and sorrow even, loves such as those in the exquisite old story of Apuleius, sincere and strenuous forms of the moral life, such as Seneca and Epictetus—whatever form of human life, in short, might be heroic, impassioned, ideal: from these the "new Cyrenaicism" of Marius took its criteria of values. (*ME* I.151–52; cf. I.142])

The narrator admits that Cyrenaicism may be "pernicious for those who have any natural tendency to impiety or vice" (*ME* I.150),[41] of which Flavian's selfish ambition is a case in point. But he insists that it allows for diverse modes of fulfillment, including not only love and "noble sorrow," but even "strenous forms of the moral life." Hence it is compatible with those manly virtues with which Pater's critic denies it can coexist, and may even help to motivate them, although it does not mandate them.

At this stage we can already begin to see how Marius's personalized journey through classical philosophies augments the doxographical framework for Cyrenaicism. But in order more fully to appreciate Pater's effort to harmonize aestheticism with morality, as well as what it means for Marius to live in the moment, we need to turn to his appropriation of Cyrenaic "education."

9.4. From Education to Morality

When we say that Aristippus strives to be "receptive" or "sensitive" to the enjoyment available in each moment, our mode of speaking tends to imply that "enjoyablness" exists out there in the world, and that Aristippus merely concentrates on "receiving" or "sensing" it as vividly as possible. Marius's aspiration to be "absolutely virgin towards . . . experience" implies something similar, although his goal has shifted from enjoyment to "energy, variety, and choice of experience." From this perspective, the function of philosophy is simply to remove impediments to the purest and most immediate reception of those experiences. Among these impediments are anxiety, regret, and unjustified (merely conventional) compunctions, all of which we have seen both the ancient Cyrenaics and Marius concerned to eliminate.

But this manner of speaking can be misleading. It may be true that some enjoyable or otherwise "choice" experiences cannot be augmented, only sensitively received. An example might be the sensation of slaking my thirst with cool water. But most valuable experiences admit some form of connoisseurship, which is not simply a matter of receiving them without preoccupation. For example, I enjoy an exquisite ribeye steak more if I know the difference between a ribeye and a porterhouse, between free range and factory-farmed beef, and between rare and medium or well-done. Knowing the range of possibilities for aging and preparing the raw meat can also enrich my experience, because I can literally *taste* all of these things in the steak: my palate is practiced in discerning them, and my mind can interpret what my palate discerns. Sensory and attitudinal pleasures thus intermingle and reinforce one another, and I discover more to enjoy in this steak than a non-connoisseur would. Many of the pleasures documented for the ancient Cyrenaics admit similar varieties of augmentation through connoisseurship, including scented body oil,[42] wine (Plut. *Mor.* 750d–e = *SSR* 4a.93), the services of courtesans,[43] and fish—the ultimate luxury food in Greek culture.[44] And Marius's experiences obviously make room for discrimination as well, as a priest of Aesculapius explains when diagnosing the "duties" to which Marius's disposition obliges him: "To keep the eye clear by a sort of exquisite personal alacrity and cleanliness, extending even to his dwelling place; to discriminate, ever more fastidiously, select form and colour in things from what was less select; to meditate much on beautiful visible objects . . ." (*ME* I.33).

It is not clear to what extent the ancient Cyrenaics recognized and valued this sort of connoisseurship as a tool for making each moment enjoyable. One place we might expect to find references to this art of active enjoyment is under the heading of "education" (*paideia*), but this topic receives little explicit attention from the Cyrenaic doxographies after the anecdotal material for Aristippus. Aristippean "education" and "instruction" (*hupotithemai*) seem to combine the learning of principles and arguments with "training" (*askēsis*) in the application of those arguments and principles to life.[45] The mainstream Cyrenaic doxography speaks of bodily "training" in the pursuit of certain virtues (D.L. 2.91), and the Annicerean doxography speaks of "habituation" as a complement for pure reasoning (D.L. 2.96).[46] All of these modes of education pertain rather to the transformation of beliefs and emotions about what is good and bad than to the development of refined tastes.

Only two anecdotes permit us to think of Aristippean education as refinement of the capacity to enjoy. According to the first, "[Aristippus] said it was better to be a beggar than to be uneducated, since the former lack money, but the latter lack culture" (D.L. 2.70). Aristippus's point is that it is better to require financial support, as he does, than to require whatever is gained through education, as his patrons do. "Culture" (*anthrōpismos*) obviously names the product of education, which may include all those arts which make up a complete human being (*anthrōpos*). Among these could be the ability to appreciate and participate in refined leisure activities, such as those at a symposium.[47] But we must be wary of reading too much into the word "culture." It appears only three times in ancient and Byzantine Greek,[48] and may well be a translation of the Latin word *humanitas*.[49] Given the exceptional fluidity of the anecdotal tradition, this wording could easily have been introduced hundreds of years after this anecdote's birth. And even if it goes all the way back to Aristippus, its relevance to the art of connoisseurship is far from clear.

The second anecdote at issue is more promising: "When he was asked by someone in what respect his son would be better if he were educated, 'If nothing else,' he said, 'he won't sit in the theater like a stone on a stone'" (D.L. 2.72). On the one hand, Aristippus may simply mean that theater-going is a waste of time; his students will devote themselves to more edifying pursuits. However, it is tempting to infer instead that Aristippus is advocating *educated* theatrical enjoyment; his students will have a finer appreciation for acting, staging, music, dancing, and all the elements of dramatic festivals, and therefore enjoy them more.[50]

An Aristippean interest in drama would dovetail with a report in which Plutarch uses a Cyrenaic position to criticize the Epicureans (Plutarch himself is speaking):

> "We've had the same experience with spectacles. We look without discomfort at dying and sick people [i.e., in drama], and we feel pleasure and amazement when seeing the painting of Philoctetes or the sculpture of Jocasta. This," I said, "my Epicurean friends, is an important piece of evidence against you for the Cyrenaics, who argue that when we take pleasure in sounds and spectacles, it is not in the sight or the hearing, but in the thought. A hen constantly crowing[51] or a raven is an unpleasant sound, but if someone imitates a crowing hen or a raven, he delights us. We're upset when we see people with consumption,[52] but we're pleased when we see statues or images of people with consumption, because our thoughts are moved agreeably and naturally by the imitations." (*Mor.* 674a–b = *SSR* 4a.206; cf. D.L. 2.90)

The point at issue here is whether we enjoy sounds and spectacles (*akousmata* and *theamata*) through direct sensation or through thinking (*dianoia*). Plutarch cites the Cyrenaics as authorities for the latter position, which he supports by arguing that we enjoy imitations *as such*. In the larger context he explains that both adults and children enjoy what is "artfully and intelligently done" (*tekhnikōs kai logikōs prattomenon*) or "subtle and versatile" (*glaphuron kai panourgon*). In other words, in order to enjoy fictional depictions we have to recognize both that they are not real and that they have been skillfully executed.[53] Plutarch believes it is human nature to take pleasure in recognizing these things, which is why he asserts that skillful imitations move us "agreeably and naturally" (*kata to oikeion*). Plutarch's ultimate source for this entire line of reasoning may be the Cyrenaic Aristoteles, who reportedly, like his more famous namesake, wrote a *Poetics* (D.L. 5.35). If so, then we have here a constellation of evidence that points to an enduring Cyrenaic interest in a particular sphere of connoisseurship. The Aristippean anecdote hints at the pleasures of educated theater-going, the doctrinal point from Plutarch articulates how technical knowledge leads to pleasure, and the book title from Aristoteles testifies to a larger Cyrenaic effort to generate this knowledge.

Still, all in all, this amounts to very thin evidence for an acknowledged and theoretically grounded interest among the ancient Cyrenaics in cultivating the capacity for refined enjoyment. Moreover, in the Cyrenaics' case there is no recorded connection between the refinement of these powers and other areas of ethics. For a clear commitment to connoisseurship as an important tool for getting the most out of every moment, which leads naturally into morality, we must turn back to *Marius*.

After accepting Heraclitean metaphysics, Aristippean epistemology, and the imperative to enliven each passing moment, Marius's thought continues as follows:

> Conceded that what is secure in our existence is but the sharp apex of the present moment between two hypothetical eternities, and all that is real in our experience but a series of fleeting impressions:—so Marius continued the sceptical argument he had condensed, as the matter to hold by, from his various philosophical reading:— . . . then he, at least, in whom those fleeting impressions—faces, voices, material sunshine— were very real and imperious, might well set himself to the consideration, how such actual moments as they passed might be made to yield their utmost, by the most dexterous training of capacity. (*ME* I.146)

Here Marius shifts the emphasis in Cyrenaic education away from the removal of regrets and anxieties, which impede the sensation of pleasure, and the development of social versatility, which helps minimize annoyances and generate opportunities for enjoyment, to the development of an active "capacity" for enjoyment. "With this point in view," the narrator goes on, "he would demand culture, *paideia*, as the Cyrenaics said . . . directed especially to the expansion of the power of reception; of those powers, above all, which are immediately relative to fleeting phenomena, the powers of emotion and sense" (*ME* I.147). He goes on to call this an "aesthetic education," since it involves the sharpening of his powers of sensory, emotional, and moral perception (Greek *aisthēsis*). Notwithstanding Pater's continuing use of the word "reception," what he has in mind is far from passive receivership. His Marius will not only "meditate much on beautiful visible objects," as the priest of Aesculapius suggested, but also study "music, in that wider Platonic sense" (*ME* I.147). This "wider music" includes all the arts—dancing, singing, playing instruments, civic and religious rituals, military exercises, mathematics, and philosophy—by which a society attempts to create a beautiful orderliness in its individual and collective life.[54]

Understanding all these disciplines will permit him "an exquisite appreciation of all the finer traits of nature and of man," not unlike how understanding the cuts and cooking of beef permits an exquisite appreciation of steak.

This aesthetic education will not only help Marius to capture the "energy" of each passing moment, it will also (eventually) lead him away from the vulgar Cyrenaicism of Flavian to the more respectable ethics of Marcus Aurelius and, finally, of his Christian friend Cornelius. For the ancient Cyrenaics, we recall, temperance and justice are matters of prudence. Once they have understood how easy it is to acquire true goodness and avoid true badness, they should be able to reduce their desires—they should become temperate, albeit in their own idiosyncratic way. Moreover, once they have learned that the just person generally lives more pleasantly than the unjust one, Cyrenaics should "do nothing out of place." But for Marius, temperance is a key precondition for both education and vivid appreciation of each moment. The priest of Aesculapius had advised him "to keep the eye clear by a sort of exquisite personal alacrity and cleanliness," and now he understands why: only in this way can he clearly "see" and "feel" the beauty and ugliness in both experiences and systems of knowledge. Moreover, only through temperance can he accurately perceive his own moral reactions to phenomena, "a body of inward impressions, as real as those so highly valued outward ones" (*ME* I.156). Hence the questions ancient Cyrenaics might subordinate to prudence become, for Marius, questions of immediate perception. Some time after Flavian's death in Pisa, for example, Marius moves to Rome, where he witnesses a slaughter of animals and gladiators in the amphitheater.[55] Repulsed by the senseless bloodshed, he reflects:

> His chosen philosophy had said,—Trust the eye: Strive to be right always in regard to the concrete experience: Beware of falsifying your experiences. And its sanction had at least been effective here, in protesting— 'This, and this, is what you may not look upon!' (*ME* I.243)

In other words, Marius is able to *see* what the narrator calls the "evil" and the "sin" in these spectacles, and so perceive directly that it is wrong for him to "look upon" them. To put it another way, we might say that "not-to-be-looked-upon" is a quality he perceives in the bloodbath, rather than infers by applying moral rules or prudential calculations.

This direct moral perception does more than lay down prohibitions as to what Marius should not see or do. Marius also receives aspirations and positive injunctions in this way, for example in Fronto's oration in the Temple of Peace. Addressing "The Nature of Morals" from a Stoicizing perspective,[56] Fronto "seemed to Marius to be speaking directly to him" (*ME* II.7). He muses that Fronto

> supposed his hearer to be, with all sincerity, in search after some principle of conduct . . . which might give unity of motive to an actual rectitude, a cleanness and probity of life, determined partly by natural affection,

partly by enlightened self-interest or the feeling of honour, due in part even to the mere fear of penalties; no part of which, however, was distinctively moral in the agent himself as such. (*ME* II.7)

In denying that this "principle of conduct" is "distinctively moral in the agent himself," Marius means that it is not based on commitment to any doctrinal system such as Aurelius's dogmatic Stoicism or Cornelius's Christianity.[57] It is the *beauty* of Fronto's vision of "a select communion of just men made perfect" (*ME* II.10) rather than its intellectual rigor that appeals to Marius, distrustful as he is of abstraction and systematicity. The very idea of such a community, united both by customary standards of "good taste" and by moral compunctions, is justified for Marius by its immediately perceptible grace. Hitherto he has doubted the compatibility of his Cyrenaicism with traditional morality, but at this moment he realizes that he can embrace parts of the latter without admitting any "first principles" discordant with the former's skeptical epistemology (*ME* II.6). It is a matter simply of "perceiving" that many of these time-sanctioned customs are "like a music, to which the intercourse of life proceeds—such a music as no one who had once caught its harmonies would willingly jar" (*ME* II.10). Fronto helps him to grasp this through his use of the Panaetian Stoic concept of "seemliness" (*to prepon*), the aesthetic resonances of which would have been familiar to Pater both from Cicero's translation of the Greek into Latin *decorum* and from Horace's use of *decens* and *decet* in both his ethics and his poetics. This ethical-cum-aesthetic concept, Marius decides, can serve someone like him as a "comprehensive term for duty" (*ME* II.10). "Duty" is, of course, a central term in many ethical systems, so Pater implies here that Marius's vision of morality as perceptible appeal can replace doctrinal scaffolds such as Stoic *kathêkonta* or Kantian *Pflicht*.

Thus Marius joins more tightly what had only been loosely connected in our evidence for ancient Cyrenaicism, the issues of enjoying each moment and of education, and makes their interaction a vehicle for incorporating traditional morality more tightly into his new Cyrenaic ethics. He brings both education and morality under the heading of "music," because for Pater this connotes whatever imposes order and beauty on both the parts of an individual character and the interaction of individuals in social life. In this way Pater fleshes out the doxographical framework of ancient Cyrenaicism, adding the art of connoisseurship to the arts of tranquility and social mastery as the goals of philosophical education. Furthermore, Marius's pursuit of a well-informed, poised, and tasteful appreciation of whatever is "choice and fine" in every sort of human and natural phenomenon greatly clarifies what it means to be receptive to each moment's enjoyment. At the same time, Pater completes his response to his hostile reviewer. He not only attempts to show how Cyrenaicism can be compatible with traditional morality, he even suggests that it can defuse the objections to which morality is otherwise vulnerable. By dispensing with "first principles," aesthetic morality renders itself safe from reasoned attacks on the metaphysically grounded moralities of the church, the Stoics, or Kant.

Of course, those critics could respond that the devil, too, can take on a beautiful form. And the danger of consigning morality to aesthetic perception is multiplied by making each individual the arbiter of moral beauty. Perhaps Pater, in implying that traditional morality will be more beautiful to well-educated people than vulgar hedonism, ruthless self-advancement, or the cruel will to power, is simply an optimist. But his optimism seems no more implausible than the ancient Cyrenaic insistence that justice is always the most prudent strategy for the hedonist.

9.5. The Hedonic "Economy"

The previous two sections outline the key points in Pater's new Cyrenaicism, but it is worth commenting briefly on two further doxographical details that *Marius* develops. The first concerns a mysterious phrase in Diogenes Laertius's doxography, which I present here with some relevant context:

> Bodily pleasures are actually much better than psychical ones, and bodily disturbances are worse. Hence it is by these that criminals are more often punished. For they held that experiencing bodily pain is harder, and experiencing ⟨bodily⟩ pleasure is more natural for us. *Hence they exercised more management concerning one of these two.* [ἔνθεν καὶ πλείονα οἰκονομίαν περὶ θάτερον ἐποιοῦντο.] For this reason, although pleasure is choiceworthy in itself, the sources of some pleasures are opposed because they are disturbing. For this reason, the accumulation of pleasures, which does not produce happiness, appears to them very troublesome. They think that the wise man generally lives pleasantly, and the vulgar one generally lives painfully, but not in every detail. It's enough if someone pleasantly [*text corrupt*] as each one happens. (D.L. 2.90, italics mine)

The vital word here is the one I have translated "management," which in Greek is *oikonomia*. It is hard to say exactly what this management entails for the ancient Cyrenaics, since several links in the sequence of thought in this passage are obscure. Probably it refers either to prudential planning or to husbandry of resources ("economics" in the technical sense) in order to manage pleasures and pains.[58]

Pater appropriates the word *oikonomia* in this passage somewhat differently, demonstrating once again that he has read the Cyrenaic evidence both carefully and creatively. Although he must be aware of the connotations of the Greek word, he chooses to transliterate rather than translating, and so activates the resonances of English "economics." Thus as Marius thinks through the consequences of what he perceived in Fronto's speech, he returns critically to the details of Cyrenaic theory. "What really were its claims as a theory of practice?" he asks himself.

> It had been a theory, avowedly,[59] of loss and gain (so to call it) of an economy. If, therefore, it missed something in the commerce of life, which some other theory of practice was able to include, if it made a needless sacrifice, then it must be, in a manner, inconsistent with itself. (*ME* II.14–15)

In addition to the word "economy," note the other elements of economic language: "loss and gain," "commerce of life." Rather than thinking about an individual Cyrenaic planning for her own contingencies, Marius is thinking about the advantages and disadvantages of Cyrenaic ethical theory in general. He is able to occupy an evaluative position *outside* that theory, and to accuse it of making a "needless sacrifice," because he has always couched his own goals in extremely vague terms. From within the evaluative framework of Cyrenaic pleasures and pains, it makes little sense to say that focusing exclusively on pleasures and pains entails a sacrifice.[60] But we have seen that Marius declares himself interested in

> energy, variety, and choice of experience, including noble pain and sorrow even, loves such as those in the exquisite old story of Apuleius, sincere and strenuous forms of the moral life, such as Seneca and Epictetus—whatever form of human life, in short, might be heroic, impassioned, ideal. (*ME* I.151–52)

Marius's Cyrenaicism contains a romantic element missing from ancient Cyrenaicism's more sober perspective, so we are not surprised to find the narrator calling Cyrenaicism "the special philosophy . . . of the young" and the product of "that *Sturm und Drang* of the spirit" (*ME* II.19). Thus while ancient Cyrenaicism reckons its "gains and losses" in the ostensibly homogenous currency of pleasures and pains, Marius's new Cyrenaicism proceeds experimentally and enthusiastically in discovering new units for "energy, variety, and choice of experience." Previously Marius has followed Flavian's example in concentrating on the currency of visual and auditory pleasure. He must be aware that ancient Cyrenaicism focuses on even more "vulgar" pleasures than these, prominently including those of the symposium and the bedroom, although he (or Pater) is strikingly coy about acknowledging this.[61] After coming to appreciate the "music" of tradition, however, he has the powerful impression that Aristippean Cyrenaicism, by rejecting religion and reducing morality to prudence, is missing a vital resource for reaching what he takes to be its primary goal—enlivening each moment. He concludes:

> Some cramping, narrowing, costly preference of one part of his own nature, and of the nature of things, to another, Marius seemed to have

detected in himself, meantime,—in himself, as also in those old masters of the Cyrenaic philosophy. If they did realize the *monochronos hēdonē*, as it was called—the pleasure of the "Ideal Now"—if certain moments of their lives were high-pitched, passionately coloured, intent with sensation—if, now and then, they apprehended the world in its fullness, and had a vision, almost "beatific," of ideal personalities in life and art, yet these moments were a costly matter: they paid a great price for them, in the sacrifice of a thousand possible sympathies, of things only to be enjoyed through sympathy, from which they detached themselves, in intellectual pride, in loyalty to a mere theory that would take nothing for granted, and assent to no approximate or hypothetical truths. In their unfriendly, repellent attitude towards the Greek religion, and the old Greek morality, surely, they had been but faulty economists. (*ME* II.21–22)

Marius admits that focusing on superficial pleasures can produce *some* moments that are "high-pitched, passionately coloured, intent with sensation," but he denies that the traditional Cyrenaic lifestyle is the best way of pursuing their "Ideal Now." Since he has discovered a new way of specifying what can make each moment "beatific," and since that way is incompatible with the Cyrenaics' way of looking at morality and religion, he accuses them of being "faulty economists."[62] In the "commerce" of each moment, their balances—as it were—could be increased by sharper trading. Were they to admit the beauty of tradition (while still denying its metaphysical grounding or absolute truth), they could both remain faithful to their epistemology and put each moment's ledger further into the black.

In sum, when Marius reads that the Cyrenaics "exercised more *oikonomia* concerning one of these two," he takes it primarily to indicate that Cyrenaic theory involved a reckoning of "gains and losses"—an "economy"—for each moment. But Marius interprets the currency of this economy very loosely, because Pater, like his critical reviewer, chooses to think of Cyrenaicism as a recurrent, transhistorical phenomenon. "Let the reader pardon me," the narrator excuses himself, "if here and there I seem to be passing from Marius to his modern representative—from Rome, to Paris or London" (*ME* II.14). Whereas Pater's critic casts this transhistorical Cyrenaicism as the outlook of effete seagull-watchers who are too languid for manly aspirations or principles, Pater makes it the insight of "the strong young man in all the freshness of thought and feeling, fascinated by the notion of raising his life to the level of a daring theory" (*ME* II.16). His new Cyrenaicism is precisely an expression of "strength," "freshness," and "daring." Its fault is actually to have gone too far in this direction, because in its "intellectual pride" it becomes one-sided. Hence Pater thoroughly repudiates his critic's implied charges about the effeminacy of aesthetic philosophy.

Pater has not been scrupulously faithful to the ancient evidence in this area, but his thoughtful recombination of the doxographical elements reveals how

Cyrenaicism can be more flexible than we might otherwise suspect. The *oikono-mia* of Diogenes' testimony clearly involves some sorts of pleasures and pains, as I discussed above. And notwithstanding the narrator's quibbles about the proper meaning of "hedonism," there is little reason to think the pleasures of the ancient Cyrenaics focused on Marius's ultra-refined appreciation of sensory beauty. (It's hard to imagine Aristippus, for example, "keep[ing] ever by him if it were but a single choice flower, a graceful animal or seashell" [*ME* I.33].) Nor is there any evidence that ancient Cyrenaics would have ascribed much value to Marius's satisfaction in attuning himself to the "harmonies" of classical Greek and Roman tradition. (This classicism is typical of Marius's and Pater's times, but not—as far as we know—of that of the ancient Cyrenaics.) But in moving the emphasis from bodily pleasure to the issues of "economy" and "the ideal now," Pater remains within the framework of Cyrenaic theory. More importantly, he gives us a practical interpretation of this theory that is surprisingly dynamic, pluralistic in its criteria of value, and adaptable to individual styles.

9.6. The Fear of Death

This brings me to the last noteworthy aspect of Pater's reception of Cyrenaicism, which is his handling of the fear of death. We read in Diogenes Laertius's doxography that, according to the Cyrenaics, "Whoever has thoroughly learned the account of what's good and what's bad . . . can be free from superstitious dread and escape the fear of death" (D.L. 2.92). We have heard Hegesias declare that death is indifferent and seen Theodorus display his courage in the face of death. But it is not clear how someone could dissolve the fear of death by meditating on the mainstream Cyrenaic "account of what's good and bad." Probably the Cyrenaics had a battery of arguments based on their formulation of the end and related doctrines, like those of the Epicureans, which "proved" that death is no evil.[63] However, these Cyrenaic arguments have not been preserved.[64]

For Marius, too, the "superstitious dread" and the fear of death converge in his "vague fear of evil."[65] In the very first pages of the novel we read that:

> A sense of conscious powers external to ourselves, pleased or displeased by the right or wrong conduct of every circumstance of daily life—that conscience, of which the old Roman religion was a formal, habitual recognition, was become in him a powerful current of feeling and observation. (*ME* I.5)

Here "conscience" is not merely an internalized awareness of right and wrong, but a bridge between such rights and wrongs and external agents of reward and punishment. The narrator elaborates in the following chapter:

> The function of the conscience, not always as the prompter of gratitude for benefits received, but oftenest as his accuser before those heavenly

masters, had a large part in it [i.e., in his old Italian religion]; and the sense of some unexplored evil, ever dogging his footsteps, made him oddly suspicious of particular places and persons. (*ME* I.23)

We will see below that articulating the identity and intentions of his shadowy watchers—whether "heavenly masters" or "particular places and persons"—is the key to overcoming his fears. But the problem is complex, and Marius first confronts it from another angle. As I suggested in 9.2, one component of this sense of "unexplored evil" is his painful and frightening experience of mortality, which he confronts most vividly in Flavian's untimely death. His Cyrenaicism represents an initial attempt to resolve this problem, so it is not incidental that the problem forcefully reasserts itself in the chapter immediately following the one entitled "New Cyrenaicism."

In this chapter Marius is making his way from Pisa to Rome, and the invigorating effects of the journey aid his new Cyrenaic aspiration to perceive what is finest in each moment crisply and cleanly (see esp. *ME* I.164). But on the seventh day "mere bodily fatigue," the onset of darkness, and an unexpected rock-fall combine to challenge his composure. The rocks fall close—too close!

That was sufficient, just then, to rouse out of its hiding-place [*sic*] his old vague fear of evil—of one's "enemies"—a distress, so much a matter of constitution with him, that at times it would seem that the best pleasures of life could but be snatched, as it were hastily, in one moment's forgetfulness of its dark, besetting influence. (*ME* I.166)

Theoretically Marius's Cyrenaicism should free him from any "distress" at the prospect that "the best pleasures of life could but be snatched," since he has supposedly embraced the flux of everything precious and committed himself to the evanescent moment. But obviously this proves too much to ask of philosophical exercises and aesthetic attention: Marius cannot escape the fear of evil in this fashion. "A sudden suspicion of hatred against him," he continues,

of the nearness of his "enemies," seemed all at once to alter the visible form of things. . . . His elaborate philosophy had not put beneath his feet the terror of mere bodily evil; much less of "inexorable fate, and the noise of greedy Acheron."[66] (*ME* I.166)

Not only do the fears of bodily damage and extinction overwhelm the pleasures of aesthetic contemplation, they actually corrupt them by "alter[ing] the visible form of things." So Marius's new Cyrenaicism is imperfect, not only because it is "uneconomical" (see the previous section), but also because it does not address this fundamental sentiment of evil in a satisfactory way.

What Marius in fact requires is a way of experiencing the world that will transform these unseen enemies into friends. He finds this during a quiet moment of reflection on the paths his life has taken, when he realizes that

"Companionship, indeed, familiarity with others . . . had been, through one or another long span of it, the chief delight of his journey" (*ME* II.67). From here he passes to the "fantasy" of "some other companion, an unfailing companion, ever at his side throughout," whom he proceeds to associate with the providential deity "in his old philosophic readings—in Plato and others, last but not least, in Aurelius" (II.68). Strengthened by this hopeful intuition, suddenly Plato's theory of a demiurgic intelligence,[67] and Aristotle's of an unmoved mover, become plausible to Marius. "It was easier," he decides,

> to conceive of the material fabric of things as but an element in a world of thought—as a thought in a mind, than of mind as an element, or accident, or passing condition in a world of matter, because mind was really nearer to himself. (II.69–70)

This hypothesis is not only "permissible" and compatible with Marius's native idealism, it is also appealing and life-sustaining. And so, just as he has committed ethics to perception, embracing whatever regulations can beautify and enliven his passing moments, so now Marius commits theology to an analogous criterial faculty.[68] He embraces the beautiful vision of a providentially sustained cosmos, and thus creates a powerful resource against his fear of evil. For on the one hand, he now conceives of a being "to whose boundless power of memory he could commit his most fortunate moments, his admiration, his love, Ay! the very sorrows of which he could not bear quite to lose the sense" (II.70). In other words, he mitigates the sorrow he feels for the mortality of both feelings and external beings by "committing" them to this unperishing companion. And on the other, he transforms the entity watching him from a punisher into a friend:

> And again, the resultant sense of companionship, of a person beside him, evoked the faculty of conscience—of conscience, as of old and when he had been at his best, in the form, not of fear, nor of self-reproach even, but of a certain lively gratitude. (*ME* II.71)

Whereas Marius's "conscience" had occupied itself with fear rather than gratitude under "the old Italian religion," and during his early Cyrenaicism those fears had floated loose, attaching themselves to unknown "enemies," he now—finally—replaces fear with gratitude. For if the deity is with Marius, who can be against him?

This epiphany will eventually bring Marius into sympathy with the Christian church of Cornelius and Cecilia, where strong human fellowship reinforces the sentiment of divine company and oversight. (Whether this amounts to a conversion or merely another stage in his aesthetic journey is a vexed question.[69]) But that development lies outside this inquiry. The point is that Pater's narrative denies what our doxography asserts, that the Cyrenaic "account of what is good and what is bad" can liberate someone like Marius from superstitious dread and the fear of death.[70] To the contrary, these are precisely the anxieties that a narrowly Cyrenaic philosophy, one based on the lifestyles of Aristippus and Flavian, cannot eliminate. Marius requires strong feelings of companionship in order both to stabilize the ubiquitous flux, which he has not entirely succeeded in accepting, and to give his sentiment of being watched a positive coloration. The Cyrenaics' unremitting, principled skepticism tends rather to isolate him than to unite him with gods or humans, so it cannot meet his needs.

On the other hand, once again Cyrenaicism—and thus, by implication, Pater's aestheticism—provides the theoretical mechanisms for its own expansion and evolution. When Marius acquiesces to his intuitive belief in a divine companion, and uses this new belief to secure each moment's satisfaction, he is building on the epistemological and ethical principles he developed out of Cyrenaic thought. Unlike the ancient Cyrenaics, he had always included every sort of immediate perception, sensation, or emotion among his epistemic foundations, so he has as good a reason for this belief as for his adherence to traditional morality. In provisionally accepting this divine companion's existence, he does not assent to any dogmatic argument. The narrator stipulates that "no mysterious light, no leading hand from afar reached him" (*ME* II.65). In other words, he does not conclude that divine grace has enlightened him. Even at the moment of his death, he will retain "the consciousness of some profound enigma in things," the feeling that his perceptions and intuitions may always evolve (*ME* II.220). For now, he follows the lodestone of his intuitions to the surest apparent source of satisfaction, the best available bargain in terms of "gains and losses." But as a proponent of aesthetic—and thus, by implication, Cyrenaic—philosophy, he preserves the capacity to change his opinions as he accumulates learning and experience.

CHAPTER 10

Conclusion:
The Birth of Hedonism

The primary goal of this monograph has been to argue for a new understanding of ancient Cyrenaic ethics, including the development of the movement from Aristippus through to the mainstream Cyrenaics, Hegesiacs, Annicereans, and Theodoreans. I said in the introduction that such a comprehensive study would need not only to reconstruct the surviving doctrines and arguments, but also to understand the behavioral and cultural contexts within which Cyrenaic theories seemed both cogent and attractive, at least to certain individuals. In fact I have argued that these projects are intricately connected: unless we have some grasp of Cyrenaic ethics as a whole, we are in danger of misunderstanding the significance and interrelations of its doctrines and arguments.

My secondary goal has been to illuminate the philosophical significance of Cyrenaic ethics. As I also noted in the introduction, this significance is sometimes spelled out by making the Cyrenaics the originators of the hedonistic tradition in Western philosophy. Given what I have just said about the importance of holistic interpretation, it should now be apparent that this historical claim is problematic. While all hedonists organize their beliefs around the high valuation of pleasure, those beliefs are also shaped by many other contexts, among them intellectual history, popular ethics, and the practices and institutions which define "philosophy" in any given era. The upshot is that comparing chronologically distant hedonisms becomes very complex.

For example, methodologically speaking, it would be relatively easy to compare Cyrenaicism with Epicureanism.[1] Epicurus's hedonism not only possesses the same life-shaping breadth as those of his predecessors, it also situates itself against some of the same traditions in popular and philosophical ethics. The interpreter could therefore compare like to like in tracing the sympathetic and polemical lines of influence among Aristippus, the mainstream Cyrenaics, Hegesias, Anniceris, and the early Epicureans.

It is quite another matter to compare Cyrenaicism with modern hedonisms. In the introduction I highlighted Fred Feldman and Michel Onfray as two contemporary writers who treat the Cyrenaics as early precursors. I have already revisited Feldman's reconstruction of "Aristippean Hedonism" in section 5.4.

There I criticized his attempt to isolate and formalize Cyrenaic doctrines. Here I want to emphasize that Feldman and the Cyrenaics are simply engaged in different philosophical endeavors. Feldman is "searching for a suitably general statement of necessary and sufficient conditions for a life's being good in itself for the one who leads it."[2] More than that, he

> would like to find a principle that would yield a ranking of lives—a principle that would tell us when one life is better in itself for the one who lives it than some other life would have been. I would like to find a theory that would locate the fundamental sources of value in lives. Ideally, I would like the theory to assign specific (perhaps numerical) values to those elements, and then to give a systematic way of aggregating those values so as to yield a value for the whole life.[3]

Feldman believes that several varieties of what he calls "intrinsic attitudinal hedonism" are strong candidates for such a principle. He proposes that his argument may have implications for other philosophical questions, such as the nature of rationality or of excellence of character. It may also have implications for practical "quality of life" questions, such as in medical ethics. "But," he admits, "then again it might not."[4] At the end of the book he suggests that his "favored forms of intrinsic attitudinal hedonism" are compatible with ethics as diverse as those of Aristotle, Seneca, John Stuart Mill, or the contemporary philosopher of religion Robert Adams.[5] Perhaps the sort of thing which produces attitudinal pleasure depends on an individual's temperament.[6] In any event, practical consequences do not concern Feldman in this book; he takes axiology to be "intrinsically worthy of our attention" and "independent."[7]

Pigeonholing either Feldman or the Cyrenaics as members of the same "hedonistic tradition" obscures important parts of their philosophies. Of course, the Cyrenaics *do* attempt to describe what makes a life good in itself for the person living it. This is one goal of their epistemology and their formulations of the end. To this extent they share common ground with Feldman. But it is not coincidental that they do not attempt a quantitative axiology. They are not interested in comparing one life with another. Far less could they be motivated, like some of Feldman's more recent work, by the desire to clarify the terms of empirical happiness psychology.[8] Rather, their primary concern is to give theoretical shape to their inchoate visions of the good life. These visions cannot stop at axiology; they necessarily interlink theories of value with all the domains of thought and action. The merit of this system is in its capacity to justify and shape ways of thinking, feeling, and behaving, whereas the merit of Feldman's axiology is in its capacity to describe and evaluate those same ways. Focusing too much on their common hedonism obscures the profound differences between them.

Even greater complications appear in the case of Michel Onfray. The biographical genesis of Onfray's philosophy curiously resembles that of the Cyrenaic Dionysius the Turncoat, who joined the Cyrenaics after a painful illness. As

Onfray relates in *L'art de jouir* (*The Art of Enjoyment*[9]), "The doctor diagnosed a heart attack. I was about to turn 28, and this Monday the 30th of November my body underwent the experience of a wisdom that would turn into hedonism."[10] Part of what Onfray realizes is that the badness of pain is deeper than any argument. He thinks of Lucretius and longs for the solace of painlessness.[11] To this extent we can immediately understand why he speaks of hedonism.

But Onfray's hedonism involves far broader commitments. At least as important as understanding the badness of pain is the conviction that bodily experience must henceforth be the foundation for all healthy thought and behavior. "Everything was inundated by a cruel, pitiless light," he says, "which relegates to indifference everything but the echo of the metaphysical experience which the body had just come to know."[12] The body's experience is "metaphysical" because it discloses being and truth. Exquisite suffering and the approach of death have revealed the farcical nature of conventional meanings and values. While in the hospital Onfray sees the world as "ridiculous," "absurd," and "senseless";[13] he describes visits from well-wishers as "social comedy in its most caricatured theatricality."[14] In short, he begins to believe that conventional etiquette is a way of masking reality. In fact, he eventually concludes that modern Western culture is built on the repression of bodily truth:

> The repressed body produces our civilization in the form of a historically sublimated neurosis: the Platonic hatred of the body, the Christian cultivation of the death drive, the general neglect of the earth, and the tendency to make desires and pleasures anathema. . . .[15]

In other words, Onfray sees "our civilization" as a network of institutions and habits of thought and action, principal among which are those encapsulated by the labels "Platonism," "Christianity," and "German idealism" (i.e., Kantian and Hegelian ethics).[16] All three of these derive their energy from the repression of desire, frustration of enjoyment, and refusal to perceive the real evils of suffering and mortality. This energy is then "sublimated" into an ethics of self-denial and transcendental escapism.

Onfray's solution is to "reconcile the flesh and the intelligence."[17] In other words, he advocates directing self-awareness toward bodily experience, which must become the touchstone for beliefs about what is good and bad. This too is labeled "hedonism":

> The individual who pays attention to hedonism will no longer think of his body as a strangeness, a stranger, certainly, but he must also consent to these flashes of brilliance that inhabit it. . . . Consciousness informs the vital potentialities of the body in order to focus them in behaviors, actions, and conduct. . . . Consciousness is the instrument with which one may produce a style, display an original and unique manner of giving form to possibilities.[18]

The ethics of bodily awareness extends well beyond pursuit of pleasure and avoidance of pain. Embodied hedonism encompasses all the aesthetic subtleties of intuition and inclination, as Onfray signals here by speaking of "a style, . . . an original and unique manner of giving form to possibilities." Elsewhere he writes,

> The morality which the pleasure imperative makes its own calls for the production of a style, the opposite of uniformity and conformity to the masses. . . . We must finally understand what Nietzsche means when he says in *The Will to Power*, "Art has more value than truth."[19]

In other words, "the pleasure imperative" not only tells Onfray to pursue pleasure and avoid pain, it also directs him to stylize his "behavior, actions, and conduct" through minute attention to the "flashes of brilliance" and "vital potentialities of the body."

Although Onfray enlists Aristippus and the Cyrenaics precisely as "an anti-Platonic war machine"[20] in his campaign against idealism, their projects differ in important ways. Essential to Onfray's project are the rewriting of history (especially philosophical history), liberation from repression and ideological blindness, and the courage to will new values into being. These concerns are obviously both post-Nietzschean and post-Freudian.[21] There exist some similarities between them and aspects of Cyrenaic ethics. For example, the Cyrenaics are certainly interested in liberating themselves from unjustified conventions. Moreover, bodily experience is an important element in this liberatory project. One source even calls the choice to pursue non-hedonistic goals a "perversion" (*diastrophē*; D.L. 2.89). However, Onfray's premise of historically entrenched individual and civilizational neurosis does little work in our Cyrenaic evidence. In particular, the Cyrenaics do not share with Onfray the hydrodynamic model of psychical energy, which postulates that frustrated drives tend to find alternative outlets. There is thus little impetus in Cyrenaic philosophy toward rewriting the history of personal and civilizational values, since they foresee no possibility of thereby "desublimating" and reclaiming misdirected forces.

Onfray's ideal of individual self-styling also finds little correspondence in the Cyrenaic evidence.[22] On my interpretation, the closest the Cyrenaics come to this courageous and artistic exercise of the will is in the ethics of Theodorus. Like Onfray, Theodorus leaves practical ethics entirely to the discretion of the individual. Like Onfray, he dresses his sage in heroic colors. But Theodorus certainly never claims that values must be created by an act of volition. He claims instead that they must be discerned by the sage's extraordinary sensitivity to each situation. The sage excels in perspicacity, not in creativity or willfulness.

The point of these brief discussions of Feldman and Onfray is that in many ways, ancient and modern hedonisms are like apples and oranges. Any interpretation of "the hedonistic tradition" which traces similarities across time will therefore be partial and tendentious. This does not mean we should avoid making such comparisons. Dialogues with past philosophers have often inspired new theories, and should continue to do so. It merely means that we should be aware of how isolating and recontextualizing doctrines, arguments, and anecdotes changes their meaning. For example, the Cyrenaics would look rather different in a history of virtue ethics, as would Feldman in a history of analytical axiology, or Onfray in a history of continental genealogies of morals.

I will therefore conclude with the suggestion that the philosophical significance of the Cyrenaics depends to a substantial degree on the concerns of the interpreter. One person may be interested in the possible relations of Socrates' dialectic to hedonism. Another will want to examine the cogency of Anniceris's critique of eudaimonism. A third will be interested in the compatibility of Hegesias' and Theodorus's egoistic individualism with genuine commitment to caring personal relationships. And a fourth might be intrigued by Matson's suggestion that hedonism "smooths the slope suicide."[23] The Cyrenaic evidence can be mobilized in different ways at different times, as Pater's appropriation displays. For this reason I have focused on giving an account that, while pointing out internal inconsistencies, is on the whole sympathetic. I leave it to readers to determine the external standards against which they judge the Cyrenaics' ideas.

The Sources

1. Introduction

One of the greatest obstacles to the historically accurate treatment of Cyrenaic philosophy is the treacherous nature of the evidence. Giannantoni's recent collections have finally made that evidence broadly available (at least for those comfortable with ancient Greek and Latin), but by excerpting these hundreds of sayings, anecdotes, and doxographical notices from dozens of authors and anonymous compilers, who were writing for diverse audiences and purposes, and lived anywhere from Aristippus's own time to 1,400 years later,[1] these collections make it very difficult for non-specialists to use the information provided critically. This problem is exacerbated by the morselization, common to collections of this type, of even continuous blocks from the original sources. Finally, it must be acknowledged that the reliability of many of these sources is simply difficult to evaluate under any circumstances, so that much research has been devoted to uncovering their biases and organizing principles.

The aim of this appendix is to provide a concise point of reference regarding some of the key sources for Cyrenaic ethics. I am particularly interested here in two sorts of sources: those about whom scholars have raised interpretive questions, which it is not convenient to address elsewhere in this book, and those who provide testimony about a broad range of Cyrenaic topics. To my knowledge no such survey, informed by the last century's research in English, Latin, German, French, and Italian, is currently available. I hope it will therefore prove useful to readers coming to Cyrenaic ethics from a range of different backgrounds. It may also be of interest to scholars working on other minor Socratic philosophies. The authors are handled in alphabetical order with the exception of Aristocles (who is discussed under Eusebius) and Hesychius (who is discussed under Diogenes Laertius).

2. Aristotle

Aristotle's near silence regarding Aristippus and the Cyrenaics has sometimes been taken as a pregnant one: either there existed no Cyrenaic doctrines at this time (384–322 BCE), it is thought, or they were not known outside of Cyrene.[2] I mention Aristotle here primarily to correct this impression. In fact he explicitly mentions Aristippus twice. First, in the *Rhetoric*, he uses something Aristippus said to

Plato as an example of an *argumentum ad auctoritatem*: "Like Aristippus ⟨said⟩ to Plato when he thought he had said something rather peremptory: 'Well, our friend' (meaning Socrates) '⟨said⟩ nothing like this'" (1398b29–31 = SSR 4a.16). Second, in the *Metaphysics*, he reports the attack on mathematics by "some of the sophists like Aristippus," according to which all other arts concern themselves with what is better or worse, whereas mathematics is not concerned with the good and the bad (996a32–b1 = SSR 4a.170). Without naming Aristippus again, he confronts this argument several books later (1078a31–34 = 4a.171). Aelian also preserves in his discussion of nightingales what may be an otherwise lost Aristotelian reference to Aristippus's daughter and grandson, who helped establish the Cyrenaic school; but it is unclear from Aelian's wording whether Aristotle mentioned these Cyrenaics, or only the associated observation about nightingales: "Most people praise the son of Arete, the sister [*sic*[3]] of Aristippus, as a someone taught by his mother. Aristotle says that he himself has witnessed young nightingales being taught to sing by their mother" (*AH* 3.40 = SSR 4b.6). Finally, many passages in Aristotle's works could have been inspired by Aristippean behavior, writings, or anecdotes. But here I confine myself to clearly attested references.

The principal point I wish to make is that even these two unambiguous references already put Aristotle's recognition of Aristippus at the level he accords to other non-Academic contemporaries. For while Aristotle consistently takes account of the opinions of Plato and the pre-Socratics in many of his works, and occasionally mentions contemporary Academics like Speusippus and Eudoxus, he discusses his other philosophical contemporaries very sparingly. The most frequently cited is Antisthenes, whose pithy sayings are employed in Aristotle's *Politics* and *Rhetoric*, and whose arguments about contradiction and definition are confronted in the *Metaphysics* and *Topics*. In total, he receives five explicit references.[4] But Diogenes of Sinope is mentioned only once, in the *Rhetoric*, for his use of metaphor (1411a24–25 = SSR 5b.184).[5] And the Megarics receive notice only as a group and only in a cluster of related passages in *Metaphysics* B (=SSR 2b.15), where Aristotle disagrees with what they say about potentiality and actuality. Aeschines of Sphettus also appears to receive a single notice—if indeed the "Aeschines" of *Rhet.* 1417b1 (= SSR 6a.92) is the Socratic—for his use of emotional characterization in rhetorical narratives. Phaedo of Elis never appears in Aristotle's works at all, unless we count references to Plato's *Phaedo*. From all of this it is clear that we cannot read any significance at all into Aristotle's taciturnity regarding Aristippus and his followers.

3. Cicero

The philosophical works of Marcus Tullius Cicero (106–43 BCE) preserve doxographical and anecdotal information on all topics and periods in the Cyrenaic movement. Although he was an influential Roman statesman, orator, and oratorical theorist, his philosophical knowledge was also extensive. He studied with Philo of Larissa and Antiochus of Ascalon, the two premiere Academics

of his day; with Posidonius of Rhodes, the most eminent Stoic; with the leading Epicureans Zeno and Phaedrus; and he was acquainted with many others.
Of course, he also read widely, and had access to doxographical compilations.[6]

For these reasons it is rarely possible to be certain about Cicero's immediate
or ultimate sources, although there is at least one exception that interests us. He
repeatedly asserts or implies that the Aristippean or Cyrenaic end is "pleasure"
or "obtaining pleasure."[7] Several of these passages appear as part of or in close
proximity to what is called the "Carneadean articulation" (*divisio Carneadea*),
which derives from the Academic skeptic Carneades (214/3–129/8 BCE). Carneades directed much of his philosophical effort toward criticizing the doctrines of his contemporaries. In order to facilitate this he created a scheme for
categorizing all possible positions about the ethical end. This "articulation"
starts from the premise that practical wisdom must concern something "con-
cordant with nature, which by itself elicits desire" (Cic. *Fin.* 5.16). Carneades
identifies three initial candidates: pleasure, absence of pain, and "the primary
natural things." These three generate the first three ends: obtaining pleasure,
obtaining absence of pain, and obtaining primary natural things. Next Carneades acknowledges that virtue may also elicit desire by itself, but adds that
virtue must be spelled out in terms of one of the three initial candidates: "the
principle of what is right and virtuous" is to do whatever is possible in order to
obtain pleasure, or absence from pain, or primary natural things, even if you
do not succeed. This generates three further ends: doing whatever you can to
obtain pleasure, doing whatever you can to obtain the absence of pain, and
doing whatever you can to obtain the primary natural things (ibid. 5.19). Carneades now has six "simple" ends. To these he adds three "complex" ends, each
of which combines two simple ends: virtue and pleasure, virtue and absence
from pain, or virtue and primary natural things. Each of these involves both
doing whatever you can to obtain something *and* obtaining it.[8]

Cicero's use of Carneades—probably via Clitomachus or Antiochus of
Ascalon—explains two features of his reports of the Cyrenaic end. First, he
indifferently assigns this doctrine to the Cyrenaics, the Cyrenaics and Aristippus, or (most often) simply to Aristippus. This anachronism is not surprising,
given that Cicero's reports of the articulation show a preference for assigning
an innovative figurehead to each slot in the grid. Either Epicurus or Aristippus
is usually given the position of honor for hedonism. Second, it explains the
precise form the doctrine takes. The "simple" end of obtaining pleasure (often
just abbreviated as "pleasure") is a fixed position in the scheme, so we should be
skeptical about its exact correspondence to the Cyrenaics' own wording.

4. Clement of Alexandria

Clement of Alexandria (died ca. 215 CE) preserves both anecdotal and doxographical information on all periods and figures in the Cyrenaic movement
except Hegesias. Most of this information appears either in his *Pedagogue*,

which is a work of moral instruction for Christians, or more often in the *Stromata*, which is an esoteric miscellany of pagan and Christian texts and topics intended to produce a higher level of Christian "gnosis."[9] He reports that he travelled the Mediterranean in his youth sampling various teachers, including an Ionian Greek in Greece, a Syrian and an Egyptian in southern Italy, an Assyrian and a Jew in the Middle East, and finally the Christian Stoic Pantaenus in Egypt (*Strom.* 1.1.11; Eus. *HE* 5.10). Later tradition held that Pantaenus was the founder of a "catechetical school of Alexandria," to the leadership of which succeeded Clement, Origen, and five other men before its termination around 400 CE. There has been controversy about the existence and nature of this "school,"[10] but there is no doubt that there was an Alexandrian tradition of eclectic Christian scholarship. What is important for us is that these Alexandrians were broadly educated, had access to good library resources, and believed in the use of pagan literature to reveal Christian truth.

The effort to identify Clement's principal sources has not encountered much success. One thing worth noting, however, is that like Cicero, his account of the Cyrenaic end appears to go back to Carneades. This emerges from the fact that *Strom.* 2.21.127.1–128.2, which includes two pieces of information about the Cyrenaics (= *SSR* 4a.198–99), also includes a series of philosophers and ends corresponding to Cicero's reports of the Carneadean articulation: Epicurus and Aristippus propose the simple end of pleasure, Hieronymus the simple end of absence of pain, Dinomachus and Callipho the complex end of virtue and pleasure, Diodorus the complex end of virtue and absence of pain (compare Cic. *Fin.* 5.20–21, *Tusc.* 5.84–85, *Luc.* 131). Moreover, the end attributed to Callipho by Clement is strikingly Carneadean: "to do everything in one's power to pursue pleasure and to obtain it." Here Carneades' definition of virtue as "doing everything in one's power to obtain [the primary object of desire]" is distinctly recognizable.[11] Third, this passage and the Carneadean passages in Cicero are the *only* times Callipho is mentioned in the whole corpus of ancient Greek and Latin literature. In fact Cicero reports that Carneades "frequently used to defend the position of Callipho with such zeal that he appeared to approve of it, although Clitomachus affirmed that he had never been able to understand what Carneades approved of" (*Luc.* 139). These three points place Clement's reliance on a Carneadean source beyond any reasonable doubt.

This casts a certain amount of light on what Clement says about the Cyrenaics and Epicurus:

> For ⟨we know⟩[12] that both the Cyrenaics and Epicurus belong to those who make pleasure their starting point, because these say expressly that living pleasantly is the end, and that only pleasure is an endlike good. But Epicurus says that the removal of hurt is also a pleasure, and that whatever draws ⟨people⟩ to itself by itself is choiceworthy . . .

The Carneadean articulation begins with the premise that every philosophy is defined by the basic material toward which practical wisdom is oriented (Cic.

Fin. 5.16–17). It is this which Clement's source is after when he says that the Cyrenaics and Epicureans "make pleasure their starting point." He then explains the basis for this claim, which is that "these say expressly that living pleasantly is the end, and that only pleasure is an endlike good." The next question for a Carneadean is whether the Cyrenaics and Epicureans have a simple end, which would be formulated as "pleasure" or "obtaining pleasure," or a complex end, which would combine virtue and pleasure. Clement addresses precisely this question only a paragraph later: "Now, Epicurus and the Cyrenaics say that the first thing belonging to us is pleasure, but that excellence, which has emerged for the sake of pleasure, produces pleasure." Although Clement does not report it, from this the Carneadean source undoubtedly inferred that the Cyrenaic and Epicurean end is simple rather than complex (as reflected also in Cicero, see above).

5. Diogenes Laertius

The lives of Aristippus and Theodorus in Diogenes Laertius's *Lives and Opinions of the Eminent Philosophers* constitute by far our most important source for Cyrenaic ethics. This single block (2.65–104) begins with a fairly typical life for Aristippus: a few biographical details (2.65–66) merge into a series of sayings and anecdotes (2.66–83), which are followed by a list of homonyms (i.e., famous people with the same name, 2.83) and different authorities' lists of his writings (2.84–85). A single, out-of-place doctrinal position then intrudes (2.85) before Diogenes announces, "Since we've written his life, let's go through the Cyrenaics derived from him, some of whom also called themselves Hegesiacs, Annicereans, or Theodoreans" (2.85 = *SSR* 4a.160). After a more detailed succession (i.e., a who-taught-whom list of Cyrenaics, 2.85–86), there follow doxographies of the orthodox Cyrenaics (2.86–93), of the Hegesiacs (2.93–96), and of the Annicereans (2.96–97). Finally, a complete life of Theodorus, which includes biography, doxography, anecdotes, and homonyms, concludes Diogenes' material on the Cyrenaics (2.97–104).

The issues raised by this text and its use of sources are so complex that I can only touch upon the most prominent and germane to our discussion. I will consequently begin with a few words about manuscripts, modern editions, and Diogenes' relation to other existing sources for the Cyrenaics. Next I will briefly address the authors and genres on which Diogenes' doxographical sections draw. Finally, I will discuss the anecdotal tradition inside and outside Diogenes' text and the challenges it creates for scholarship.

a. Diogenes, Hesychius, and the Suda

Regarding Diogenes and other sources, the most important relation to clarify is that between his text and those of Hesychius of Miletus, pseudo-Hesychius, and the tenth-century Byzantine encyclopedia called the Suda. Hesychius probably wrote his *Onomatology or Table of Those Renowned for Learning* in the sixth century CE. Although this work is lost, many entries in the Suda, including those on Aristippus, Anniceris, and Theodorus, rely on it heavily.[13] Hesychius and Diogenes seem to have shared a principal source for biographical material, as Mannebach, following Schwartz, has demonstrated by close comparison of D.L. 2.65–66 with the Suda's entry on Aristippus.[14] For this reason the Suda's confirmation of reports in Diogenes regarding Aristippus does not constitute independent evidence.[15] This is especially true because Diogenes himself is also among the Suda's sources, so that it is sometimes hard to determine whether the Suda reflects the common source of Diogenes and Hesychius or simply draws directly from Diogenes. But it does sometimes preserve significant information missing in Diogenes, so that we may infer that it is drawing on Hesychius, and moreover on a passage in which either Hesychius is using an alternate source, or Diogenes has neglected the source he shares with Hesychius. This is most strikingly true for Anniceris and Theodorus (*SR* 4g.2, h.2).[16]

The works *SSR* ascribes to "Hesychius Milesius," by contrast, have no evidentiary value at all. The first is Flach's 1882 edition of the fragments of Hesychius, the relevant parts of which are drawn entirely from the Suda.[17] The second is pseudo-Hesychius's *On Famous Men*, which is a Byzantine forgery compiled from Diogenes and the Suda.[18] The earliest manuscript of this forgery is of significant philological value for Diogenes' text, however, to which I will now turn.

b. Manuscripts and Editions of Diogenes

Since the different manuscripts of Diogenes give different readings at several points in our evidence, it is worthwhile concisely to address their relative merits and those of modern editions derived from them. The most detailed and well received treatment of the history of Diogenes' text is that of Knoepfler,[19] which is not as widely available as it should be. The most important manuscripts of Diogenes are those listed as B, P, and F in *apparatus critici*. These three derive from a lost common ancestor, but Knoepfler argues that contamination of the Italian tradition represented by these three occurred between this ancestor and the corrected versions of P and F we now possess. B is thus the best complete manuscript still existing, although the readings of P and F are still occasionally preferable. But a fourth manuscript, Vaticanus Graecus 96, which contains pseudo-Hesychius (φ) as well as excerpts from Diogenes (Φ), appears to have diverged from the tradition before the common ancestor of BPF. Φ therefore offers an important complement to BPF wherever its excerpts overlap with the complete text, as they do for most of the passages that concern us. Unfortunately, Long takes almost no cognizance of Φ in his 1964 Oxford Classical Text of Diogenes, which has been broadly condemned for this and other reasons.[20] Reviews of Marcovich's 1999 Teubner edition, which relies heavily on Φ, have been lukewarm.[21] But Marcovich's reasonably full listing of the readings of BPF, as well as his edition of Φ in his second volume, will at least allow us to make up our own minds about the text.[22]

c. Diogenes and Ancient Historiography of Philosophy

I must now say a word about the authors and genres on which Diogenes draws. When Diogenes cites a specific author and work, such as Panaetius's and Clitomachus's works *On the Sects* and Meleager's *On Doctrines* in his orthodox Cyrenaic doxography (2.87 and 2.92), we may be tempted to infer that these are his primary sources of information. But two centuries of *Quellenforschung* have led to the conclusion that we can rarely determine Diogenes' sources, and that he comfortably cites authorities at any number of removes.[23] His work draws especially on two related genres as well as on what we might more loosely call the doxographical mode of writing: works *On the Sects* apparently gave systematic accounts of particular philosophers' doctrines, focusing on post-Socratic schools; *Successions of Philosophers* focused on biographical details, including who-taught-whom particulars (many of which were invented), lists of works, and noteworthy sayings or anecdotes; and doxographical compilations sometimes collected various philosophers' opinions on the same topics, while at other times they proceeded philosopher by philosopher.[24] An example of the last mode of writing is the excerpt from Epiphanius discussed later in this chapter. No pure examples of the first two genres survive, but it is clear that Diogenes draws upon all of these categories, preserving references he finds in his sources and adding new ones in a somewhat aleatory fashion. Although we can occasionally detect where he has stitched together notes from various texts, he does not consistently mark these boundaries for us.[25] In many places, therefore, we can neither say what his sources were nor even where he passes from one source to another.

d. Diogenes and the Anecdotal Tradition

The anecdotal tradition forms an important component of Diogenes' lives of Aristippus and Theodorus. Tsouna McKirahan is right that because ancient philosophy was conceptualized as something permeating all aspects of behavior, anecdotes could reveal "the philosophy in action." For this reason, she argues, they can be valuable resources for both historical and philosophical interpretation.[26] In fact, among the works attributed to Aristippus are three books of "useful sayings" (D.L. 2.85). But we should also observe Kindstrand's cautionary note on anecdotal collections in his important article on "Diogenes Laertius and the 'Chreia' Tradition":

> But it was a literature with no firm tradition and lacking a good reputation, being instead generally anonymous and highly variable in character. Moreover we may assume that there was a constant exchange of material between originally different collections, and that new ones were constantly appearing, as almost every scribe would try to improve upon his immediate predecessor. The same element of frequent change would also

apply to single items, where an anecdote could be abbreviated into a pure saying or a saying developed into an anecdote, not to mention changes of attribution.[27]

To Kindstrand's cautionary notes we should add Goldhill's discussion of how the creative manipulation of anecdotes was an essential conversational skill for anyone claiming to be "educated" in late antiquity.[28] In the earliest surviving handbook on rhetorical education, for example, we read that

> Chreias [i.e., sayings] are practiced by restatement, grammatical inflec-
> tion, comment, and contradiction, and we expand and compress the
> chreia, and in addition (at a later stage of study) we refute and confirm.[29]

Later authors give examples of how a short saying attributed to someone famous can be expanded in numerous ways into entire paragraphs during this process of "elaboration."[30] We can immediately perceive the fluidity of which Kindstrand and Goldhill speak by comparing variants of the same Aristippean anecdotes in Diogenes and the so-called *Gnomologium Vaticanum*, which was an independently circulating anecdotal collection.[31] It is important to keep in mind that ancient authors not only neglected the precise wording of anecdotes, they developed great sophistication in altering them according to their rhetorical needs.

Kindstrand also mentions "changes of attribution." Many anecdotes were ascribed both to Aristippus and to other philosophers or "sages" generally. Their content was doubtless felt loosely to cohere with the personalities of more than one figure, which raises questions about both their original ascription and the modifications their content may have undergone while being adapted to different authorities. It will suffice to list these in a note.[32] A special sub-division of this class involves the substitution of Aristippus for lesser-known Cyrenaics.[33] The reliability of each of these deserves particular scrutiny, although in some cases they are not without evidentiary value.

In sum, I agree with Tsouna McKirahan that the anecdotal tradition is a valuable resource for *philosophical* interpretation: it shows us how the personality and—to a lesser extent—the theories associated with a philosopher like Aristippus might find expression in behavior. But because of the fluidity of the tradition, which allowed compilers far removed from any knowledge of Aristippus to rework these imaginative "enactments of philosophy," I believe we must be cautious in ascribing *historical* value to this evidence. To put it another way, these anecdotes often communicate the sort of thing Aristippus might say, but rarely indicate precisely what he did say.

6. Epiphanius

Saint Epiphanius of Salamis began his encyclopedic heresiology in 374/5 CE and hastily completed it within about three years.[34] Those working on the Cyrenaics will find three separate excerpts from what Giannantoni calls *Adversus haereses* in *SSR* (4a.177, 4f.2, 4h.15). These are written consecutively in Epiphanius's text, which appears *in extenso* in Giannantoni's source, Diels' *Doxographi Graeci*.[35] Anyone trying to pursue the references further will want to know that recent editors and translators generally use Epiphanius' preferred title, *Panarion*, rather than *Adversus haereses*, and that Diels' and Giannantoni's "*Adv. haer.* III 2,9 (III 25)" is "*De fide* 9" in the standard edition of the *Panarion* by Holl and Dummer, or "*Panarion* VII *De fide* 9" in the English translation by Williams.[36] Epiphanius says in *De fide* 3 that the eighty heresies he has refuted in the foregoing correspond to the eighty concubines contrasted with the one beloved (i.e., the true church) in Song of Songs 6: 8–9. Beginning with *De fide* 9.1, he sketches forty-four Greek philosophies as a gesture toward the "numberless maidens" also contrasted with the beloved in that scriptural passage. Our three excerpts come from this sketch, and resemble bowdlerized summaries of Diogenes Laertius's lives of Aristippus, Theodorus, and Hegesias. The convergence is striking enough to support the proposition that Epiphanius and Diogenes share an important source. But Epiphanius's entries also contain formulations of Aristippean and Theodorean doctrines otherwise unattested, and introduce a variant of a Hegesiac doctrine. It is therefore important to carefully consider their reliability, especially since prior scholarship on Cyrenaicism, though it has occasionally emphasized Epiphanius's formulations (especially for Aristippus),[37] has neglected to inspect his working methods and background.

The first thing we must note is that Epiphanius, who received a monastic rather than a classical education,[38] is not generally knowledgeable about Greek philosophy. This, combined with his haste and probably also with defects in his source, has produced both subtle and spectacular errors in his information. Hence when addressing Epiphanius's preservation of the doctrines of the physicists, Diels protests, "In vain you'll torture yourself asking what on earth made this numbskull confuse such matters! But it isn't worth it."[39] Diels thinks that the fullness of the list of forty-four philosophers suggests Epiphanius's source had a "sharp and learned mind,"[40] but points out numerous errors in the information Epiphanius gives under these names.[41] For example, he ascribes to Parmenides the Anaximandrean doctrine that "the unlimited" is the cosmic principle (*De fid.* 9.14) and makes the Stoics Cleanthes, Chrysippus, and Diogenes of Babylon hedonists (*De fid.* 9.41–44). These and other reports are so spectacularly and inexplicably wrong that it's hard to imagine they did not already appear in Epiphanius's source. (The work of Diels' "sharp, learned mind" may have been jumbled through several intermediaries before Epiphanius read it!) Other entries are more subtly erroneous, as when he attributes to Chrysippus the opinion that "sons should sleep with their mothers and daughters with their fathers" (*De fid.* 9.43). In fact Chrysippus chose these conventionally outrageous actions as examples of things the Stoic sage, whose understanding of cosmic order is incommensurable with that of normal people, might under extraordinary circumstances judge appropriate.[42]

While Epiphanius's information on the Cyrenaics does not contain spectacular errors, it does contain what, in the light of these and other examples, we can now identify as characteristic distortions. His report that Theodorus "advised everyone to steal, forswear themselves, and rape and pillage" (*De fid.* 9.28), for example, is much like his distortion of Chrysippus. Theodorus did challenge conventional notions of justice, but his point was far more nuanced. This much would be obvious even without the foregoing exploration of Epiphanius. But Epiphanius and Diogenes Laertius differ over a less obvious point regarding Hegesias. Epiphanius says, "He said living was profitable for the fool, but dying was profitable for the sage" (*De fid.* 9.29 = *SSR* 4f.2), whereas Diogenes says, "living is profitable for the fool, but indifferent for the wise person" (2.95 = *SSR* 4f.1). This is not the place to go into Hegesias's opinion regarding the choiceworthiness of death and life, which I address in chapter 7; but given what we have learned about Epiphanius, we should be predisposed to expect precisely this sort of distortion from him.

7. Eusebius and Aristocles

Eusebius of Caesarea wrote his *Preparation for the Gospel* between approximately 310 and 330 CE.[43] His testimony in book 14 primarily concerns Cyrenaic epistemology, regarding which I have relatively little to say in this book. But it is introduced by two paragraphs about the distinct contributions made by Aristippus and the Metrodidact to the theoretical formulation of Cyrenaic ethics (*Praep. Ev.* 14.18.31–32 = *SSR* 4a.173 + 4b.5). Since no other source explicitly addresses this issue, and since Eusebius appears to use language that is relatively uncontaminated by the anachronistic terminology that characterizes most of our other evidence, this passage is crucial to any interpretation of early Cyrenaic thought.[44] It is therefore important to establish how reliable Eusebius's report is.

It is clear, to begin with, that Eusebius's source for his critique of Cyrenaic epistemology is the Peripatetic Aristocles of Messene, whose book *On Philosophy* he quotes verbatim in book 11 and throughout books 14 and 15 of this work. Eusebius's agenda is polemical: he aims to show that whatever truth resides in Greek philosophy was borrowed by Pythagoras and Plato from "the Hebrews," and subsequently dissipated in debates among philosophical schools due to the contentious nature of "the Greek race."[45] Book 8 of Aristocles' *On Philosophy*, which scholars tentatively assign to around the beginning of the Common Era,[46] furnishes Eusebius with attacks on the epistemology of the Cyrenaics, the Pyrrhonean skeptics, Protagoras and Metrodorus, the Eleatics and Megarics, and Epicurus.[47] Scholars have generally considered Aristocles an excellent source, noting that he shows an unusual preference for primary sources himself, and appears to use good secondary sources where primary ones were unavailable.[48] The work *On the Sects* by the second-century BCE

Academic Clitomachus has been proposed as Aristocles' source for (parts of his exposition of) Pyrrho, the Megarics, and the Cyrenaics, but in each case this remains only a plausible conjecture.[49]

It is debated whether Eusebius has also drawn his two-paragraph introduction to the Cyrenaics from somewhere in Aristocles' work. Chiesara has persuasively argued that, since these paragraphs interrupt Aristocles' transition from his attack on Pyrrhonism to that on Cyrenaicism, which otherwise fit together seamlessly, Eusebius must have found it elsewhere.[50] Comparison with Eusebius's introductions to his other excerpts from Aristocles suggests that he adapts material from the excerpts themselves, but also draws both on other authors and on compilations such as *On the Sects* or *Successions of the Philosophers*. It is thus impossible to tell whether Eusebius found the information he includes in the crucial two paragraphs about Cyrenaic ethics elsewhere in Aristocles, and subsequently inserted it before his quotations from Aristocles' book 8, or found it in another author's work. But whatever its provenance, we have good reason to be confident about what Eusebius says. Heir to the Alexandrian scholarship of Clement and Origen (and probably to part of Origen's library), Eusebius was a pioneering librarian and scholar of both Christian and pagan texts. His use of other important doxographical sources—e.g., pseudo-Plutarch's *On the Physical Doctrines of the Philosophers*—shows that he applied his learning and books judiciously.[51]

8. Plato

We have every reason to think that Plato was well acquainted with Aristippus both during their shared cultivation of Socrates in Athens and at the court of the tyrants of Syracuse. It is thus disappointing that Plato only mentions Aristippus once in his voluminous corpus, when Phaedo tells Echecrates that Aristippus and Cleombrotus were not present at Socrates' execution, because they were in Aegina (*Phd.* 59c3–4 = *SSR* 4a.14).[52] Plato would be a particularly valuable witness for Aristippus's thought, because he could help us clarify to what extent Aristippus in fact anticipated later Cyrenaic theories. But the lack of explicit citations has not stopped scholars from extrapolating Aristippean positions from numerous passages in Plato's dialogues.

The influence of Aristippus on Plato's dialogues has been a hotly debated question since at least the latter half of the nineteenth century, at which time most scholars accepted that theories promulgated in the *Theatetus* and *Philebus* derived from Plato's fellow Socratic.[53] At that time it was usually assumed that Aristippus already held the positions attributed to the Cyrenaics, so that resemblance between Cyrenaic ideas and those in these dialogues could serve as evidence for the dialogue's reliance on Aristippus. This assumption came under attack in scholarship of the early twentieth century.[54] Then, following Giannantoni's carefully researched, cogently argued, and exhaustive treatment of scholarly arguments for and against Aristippean influence on every Platonic dialogue for which it had been suggested,[55] the consensus shifted decisively against the possibility of learning about Aristippus from Plato. Döring's attempt to reassert the feasibility of attributing Cyrenaic epistemology to Aristippus, and supplementing it with Plato's *Theaetetus*, has made very little impact.[56]

I have no intention of reopening the complex questions regarding Aristippus's influence on Plato here, since I am broadly in agreement with Giannantoni and with those who have responded critically to Döring. While we cannot with certainty deny that any of the ethical and epistemological positions in Platonic dialogues reflect Aristippean influence, neither do independent sources for Aristippus confirm that he held positions like these. Moreover, there are some significant divergences between Cyrenaic doctrine and the putatively Aristippean passages in Platonic dialogues. For this reason, we cannot take positions in the *Theaetetus* and *Philebus*, which are never ascribed to Aristippus, as evidence for what Aristippus thought.

9. Xenophon

There is no question that Xenophon, unlike Plato, is an important source for Aristippus's thought. He makes Aristippus Socrates' interlocutor in *Memorabilia* 2.1 (= *SSR* 4a.163), where Socrates sets out to show his self-indulgent companion the value of self-control, and in order to do so argues for the necessity of acquiring the qualities of a good household manager, friend and family member, and—above all—political leader. Aristippus, with considerable independence and vivacity, denies any inclination toward political involvement, and questions whether it is any better to impose deprivations on oneself than to suffer their imposition by others. Aristippus is also Socrates' interlocutor in *Memorabilia* 3.8 (= *SSR* 4a.165), where Xenophon tells us that he hopes to avenge his earlier refutation: he asks Socrates "if he knew anything good" or "anything beautiful," intending to show that whatever Socrates answered, it could also be bad or ugly in some circumstances. But Socrates defines goodness and beauty in a fashion that dodges Aristippus's eristic trap.

These passages are extremely important, both because Xenophon must have known Aristippus personally, and because his testimony predates any possible confusion between Aristippus and his Cyrenaic successors. Nevertheless, we must keep in mind that Xenophon's primary intention is not to expound and refute Aristippus's positions, but rather to defend Socrates' memory by showing that, contrary to the accusations against him of "impiety" and "corrupting the youth," he tried to help his young companions become better family members, friends, and citizens. Where he failed, as with Alcibiades, Critias, and (in Xenophon's opinion) Aristippus, he was not responsible. Vivienne Gray has shown how 2.1 completes an "architectural block" that began with 1.4, in which Socrates shows his concern to persuade his followers of the importance of piety, the benefits of self-control, and the dangers of imposture.[57] At the same time, 2.1 looks forward toward another block dealing with correct relationships with family, friends, and polis.[58] The structural function of 3.8 is less clear, but it seems both to bookend the previous block with the recurrence of Aristippus from 2.1, and to anticipate the series of Socratic definitions in 3.9.[59]

Taking account of the purpose behind Aristippus's appearances in the *Memorabilia* and their integration into the work's structure helps clarify their evidentiary value. First, it makes it very unlikely that Xenophon was doing his best to record actual conversations. Although they surely reflect Xenophon's basic understanding of Aristippus's lifestyle and thought, the dialogues may very well be fictional in most of their details. Second, von Fritz's thesis that 2.1 does not fit at this juncture, was not written for the *Memorabilia* at all, and originated as a response to a work by Aristippus, is generally implausible.[60] Erbse and Narcy have persuasively answered von Fritz's specific arguments, which build on those of Gigon, about the internal incoherence of 2.1 and its inappropriateness for this location in the *Memorabilia*.[61] Thus we should take Xenophon's testimony as our best guide to the overall impression made on his contemporaries by Aristippus's behavior, but we must keep in mind that Xenophon's own agenda is to package Socrates as an admirable mentor and citizen. This involves cleanly distinguishing him from any objectionable followers like Aristippus. We must therefore be wary in accepting specific formulations Xenophon puts into Aristippus's mouth.[62]

APPENDIX 2

Annicerean Interpolation in D.L. 2.86–93

1. Introduction

Diogenes Laertius clearly distinguishes "those who stuck with the way of Aristippus" (οἱ μὲν οὖν ⟨ἐπὶ⟩ τῆς ἀγωγῆς τῆς Ἀριστίππου μείναντες, 2.86), whom throughout this book I have called the "mainstream Cyrenaics," from "the Annicereans" (οἱ δ᾽ Ἀννικέρειοι, 2.96). He purports to give the mainstream doctrines at 2.86–93, and the Annicerean doctrines at 2.96–97. This apparently clean distinction between orthodoxy and Annicereanism is repeated by Clement of Alexandria. Clement first gives the Cyrenaic end and several Cyrenaic doctrines at *Miscellanies* 2.21.127.1–2.21.128.2 (= *SSR* 4a.198–99). He then returns at 2.21.130.7–8 to give a significantly different Annicerean end and several Annicerean doctrines (= *SSR* 4g.4). We know that this arrangement goes far back in the doxographical tradition. For example, Diogenes tells us that the early doxographer Hippobotus recognized nine philosophical sects in his book *On the Sects*: "first Megaric, second Eretric, third Cyrenaic, fourth Epicurean, fifth Annicerean, sixth Theodorean, seventh Zenonian or Stoic, eight Academic (i.e., Old), ninth Peripatetic" (D.L. 1.19–20).[1] Strabo's testimony also suggests that Anniceris established a distinct body of new doctrines, saying that Anniceris "seems to have rectified the Cyrenaic sect and introduced the Annicerean one in its stead" (18.3.22 = *SSR* 4g.1).

Unfortunately, there are strong reasons to believe that the mainstream doxography at Diogenes Laertius 2.86–93 is thoroughly mixed up with Annicerean evidence. Schwartz saw this as early as 1903. In his article on Diogenes Laertius in the *Real-Encyclopädie der Classischen Altertumswissenschaft*, he states,

> The excerpts concerning Cyrenaic doctrine (II 187ff.) are also a desolate rubble field, the chaos of which has been exacerbated by the harmonizing tendency of modern historians of philosophy. We can't rely on D[iogenes'] apparent ordering of Cyrenaics (II 86–93), school of Hegesias (93–96), Annicereans (96–97), Theodoreans (97–99). For example, several Annicerean theorems have been crammed into the Cyrenaic teachings . . .[2]

Various other scholars have addressed this difficulty since Schwartz, either attempting to excise the Annicerean from the mainstream Cyrenaic material, or attempting to deny that Diogenes Laertius 2.86–93 is in fact interpolated with Annicerean doctrines.[3] However, none of these efforts are entirely satisfying. Clearly not *all* parts of 2.86–93 are Annicerean. To give just one example, the mainstream doctrine concerning friendship reported at 2.91 is incompatible with the Annicerean doctrine on the same topic at 2.96–97. The first says that "a friend is for the sake of usefulness," while the second clearly intends to correct and refine this doctrine: "It is not only for usefulness that ⟨the wise man⟩ embraces his friend." On the other hand, there are signs of Annicerean influence throughout the ostensibly mainstream passage. While some of these can be explained by the perseverance of mainstream beliefs in Annicereanism, this defense does not fully explain the breadth and variety of evidence for interpolation.

In this appendix I will therefore be arguing for two conclusions. First, there are compelling reasons to believe that parts of 2.86–93 are Annicerean. Although these reasons are not uniformly clear or strong, and none is completely persuasive on its own, as a group they make it difficult to sustain Diogenes Laertius's explicit attributions. Second, it is impossible to identify the boundaries of the Annicerean intrusions with any degree of confidence.

2. The Convergence between D.L. 2.86–89 and Clement *Strom.* 2.21.130.7–8

The most important evidence for interpolation is the convergence between a text explicitly mentioning the Annicereans in Clement of Alexandria and a passage in Diogenes Laertius's mainstream doxography.[4] For ease of reference, I begin by printing the texts side by side below and numbering the points at which they correspond. Since the text of Diogenes is much longer, I have underlined the parts in it that correspond to elements in Clement's report.

Diogenes Laertius, 2.86–89 = SR IV A 172	Clement of Alexandria, *Strom.* 2.21.130.7–9 = SR IV G 4
[1] *They also think that the end differs from happiness, since the particular pleasure is an end, but happiness is the composition of particular pleasures, among which are numbered both those that have gone by and those that are to come.* The particular pleasure is choiceworthy for itself; happiness is not choiceworthy for itself, but for particular pleasures. A proof that pleasure is the end is that we are favorably inclined to it	[1] Those called the Annicereans from the Cyrenaic succession put no definite end in place for the whole of life, but ⟨said⟩ that the pleasure arising from each action is the proper end of that action.

without deliberate choice from childhood, and when we have attained it, we avoid nothing so much as pain (which is opposed to it). Pleasure is good even if it comes from the most unseemly sources, as Hippobotus says in his *On the Sects*. For even if the action is out of place, still the pleasure is choiceworthy for itself and something good.

[2a] And *"the removal of what hurts,"* *as has been said by Epicurus, seems to them not to be pleasure.* Nor is lack of pleasure pain. For both are in motion, and neither lack of pain nor lack of pleasure is a motion, (2b) *since lack of pain is the state of someone sleeping.* They say that some people are able not to choose pleasure, due to perversion.

[2a] These Cyrenaics reject Epicurus's definition of pleasure, viz.: "the removal of what hurts";

[2b] and they call it the state of a corpse.

[3] *But not all mental pleasures and hurts supervene on bodily pleasures and hurts. For joy occurs also for the simple well-being of the fatherland, as for our own.*

[3] For we feel joy not only because of ‹bodily› pleasures, but also because of other people's company and the love of public distinction. But Epicurus thinks that all joy in the soul supervenes on previous bodily experience.

Obviously the points made at [1], [2a–b], and [3] in the two passages do not correspond exactly. While Diogenes specifies the relation between happiness and the end at [1], Clement merely insists that there is no comprehensive end for an entire life, and that each action takes a definite pleasure as its own end. Diogenes uses the example of someone sleeping at [2b], Clement uses that of a corpse. At point [3], Diogenes and Clement give different occasions for independent mental pleasures: Diogenes cites the prosperity of ourselves or our countries, Clement cites company and public distinction. These divergences are strong enough that if we took the points individually, each similarity would bear little evidentiary weight.

However, there are also strong reasons for positing a shared source for the two passages. First, notwithstanding divergences in detail, the passages' similarities are striking, especially when taken as a group. Since "happiness" generally names the "end for the whole of life," Diogenes and Clement are saying much the same thing at [1]. This is particularly noteworthy because the doctrine reported there is so unusual in the history of ancient philosophy. At points [2a–b] both texts quote the same doctrine of Epicurus in exactly the same words, and then proceed to refute it by similar examples. At point [3] they again make the same anti-Epicurean point, and reinforce it with similar examples. And not only do these three points of similarity appear in close proximity in the two texts, they appear *in the same order*.[5] These are the simplest and most powerful reasons to believe that the passages share a common origin.

Next it should be remarked that some parts of Clement's testimony are unclear, but can be clarified by reference to Diogenes. For example, Clement does not explain how the example in [2b] justifies the claim in [2a]: "[2a] These Cyrenaics reject Epicurus's definition of pleasure, viz.: 'the removal of what hurts'; [2b] and they call it the state of a corpse." The example of the corpse is rhetorically powerful, but leaves the reader to infer exactly how it invalidates Epicurus's definition of pleasure. But Diogenes fills in the missing premise:

> [2a] "the removal of what hurts," as has been said by Epicurus, seems to them not to be pleasure. Nor is lack of pleasure pain. *For both are in motion, and neither lack of pain nor lack of pleasure is a motion,* [2b] since lack of pain is the state of someone sleeping.

The sequence of thought has now become clear: pleasure is "in motion," but "lack of pain" is not a motion, so there is no pleasure in it. Our source clearly believes that "lack of pain" and "the removal of what hurts" are synonyms. Therefore, there is no pleasure in "the removal of what hurts." Notwithstanding the misleading conjunction "since" (*epei*) beginning [2b], the example of the sleeping person is not a further argument. Rather, it is a persuasive redescription of what the "removal of what hurts" actually looks like. Clement's "corpse" executes the same persuasive maneuver.

Comparison of Clement with Diogenes is even more helpful at the juncture between [2b] and [3], since Clement's ordering of the clauses makes the sequence of thought enigmatic. Here is Clement's version:

> [2a] These Cyrenaics reject Epicurus' definition of pleasure, viz.: "the removal of what hurts"; [2b] and they call it the state of a corpse. [3] For we feel joy not only because of ⟨bodily⟩ pleasures, but also because of other people's company and the love of public distinction. But Epicurus thinks that all joy in the soul supervenes on previous bodily experience.

By beginning [3] with the word "for" (*gar*), Clement implies that [2a–2b] follows from [3]. It is very hard to see how this is so: the dependence of joy on bodily pleasure is not obviously pertinent to Epicurus's definition of pleasure or the Cyrenaics' objection to that definition.[6] Fortunately, Diogenes' ordering of the clauses in [3] eliminates this confusion: "[3] But not all mental pleasures and hurts supervene on bodily pleasures and hurts. For joy occurs also for the simple well-being of the fatherland, as for our own." Diogenes has simply swapped the conjunctions with which the two sentences in section [3] begin. With this change it becomes clear that the logical connection marked by the word "for" is internal to section [3]. This makes much better sense: it is easy to grasp how the examples of joy are supposed to disprove the thesis that all mental pleasures supervene on bodily pleasures.

The capacity of Diogenes' text to clarify what remains incomplete or enigmatic in Clement's text is the second compelling reason to believe they share a common source. Taken together with my first argument, this makes it probable that the two authors share a common source (at however many removes), which they both communicate in an abbreviated form. Clement generally gives us a more abbreviated version of what was in that source than Diogenes.[7]

This shared source was probably Annicerean rather than mainstream. While Diogenes attributes points 1–3 to the mainstream Cyrenaics, Clement explicitly attributes point 1 to the Annicereans. Where such a disagreement occurs, it is more likely that the original source attributed the material to the Annicereans than the mainstream Cyrenaics. There are two reasons for this. First and most importantly, it is plausible for an Annicerean doctrine to be described using the generic term "Cyrenaic," but unlikely that a mainstream doctrine would be labeled with the specific term "Annicerean." (To employ the jargon of textual criticism, "Annicerean" is the *lectio difficilior*.) Second, Anniceris claimed to have "rectified" the Cyrenaic school, and may therefore have represented his as the "correct" Cyrenaic philosophy. So the Annicereans might have put these forward as "Cyrenaic" positions themselves, which could easily confuse doxographers.

This initial argument about Annicerean derivation is corroborated by one of the details in point 3. Although Diogenes ascribes this material to the mainstream Cyrenaics, the example he uses strongly recalls the Annicereans instead. "Joy occurs also for the simple prosperity of the fatherland [*patridos*]," he reports, "as for our own." As I discuss in section 6.6, the Annicereans "correct" Hegesias by emphasizing the importance of our personal and civic relationships to our enjoyment of pleasure. Aristippus presumably set the tone for mainstream Cyrenaic perspectives on civic participation when he made statements like those Xenophon attributes to him in *Memorabilia* 2.1.13. There Aristippus prefers being "a stranger everywhere" to accepting political obligations. By contrast, the first sentence of the Annicerean doxography at D.L. 2.96 ends, "they left friendship in life and gratitude and honor towards parents and willingness to take action for one's fatherland [*patridos*]." Not only does this statement reject earlier Cyrenaic quietism in general, it also concludes with the same example as point 3 in Diogenes. We therefore have a plausible reason to connect point 3 with Anniceris. This argument dovetails with what I have just said regarding point 1 and strengthens the overall case regarding points 1–3 as an Annicerean grouping.

3. Formulations of the End and Demotion of Happiness

We have just seen that there are good reasons to believe the strikingly unusual doctrine of the end at Diogenes Laertius 2.87–88 is an Annicerean interpolation. According to this doctrine happiness is not the end. Rather, particular pleasures are ends. This position differs from the formulation of the end attributed to Aristippus's grandson, the Metrodidact. According to Eusebius, the Metrodidact "clearly defined the end as living pleasantly [*to hēdeōs zēn*]" (*PE* 14.18.32 = *SSR* 4b.5). I discuss these two formulations at length in section 4.6, so it suffices here to observe that we cannot make them compatible without claiming that Eusebius is either confused or speaking vaguely. Both are unlikely, since he is an excellent source and presents this as the Metrodidact's "clear definition." Taking the definition at D.L. 2.87–88 as Annicerean dissolves the contradiction.

We should next observe that the only other statement about "happiness" and "living pleasantly" in D.L. 2.86–93 appears to harmonize with the formulation of the end proposed by Anniceris, not the one by the Metrodidact. Once again I have discussed this passage at length elsewhere in the book,[8] so I will merely summarize in brief the results of that analysis. The passage runs as follows:

> . . . although pleasure is choiceworthy in itself, the sources of some pleasures are opposed because they are disturbing. The result is that the accumulation of pleasures, which does not produce happiness, appears to them very troublesome. They think that the wise man generally lives pleasantly, and the vulgar one generally lives painfully, but not in every detail. It's enough if someone pleasantly [*text corrupt*] as each one happens. (D.L. 2.90–91)

The tone of the passage toward "happiness" and "living pleasantly" is skeptical. First, it says that "the accumulation of pleasures, which does not produce happiness, appears to them very troublesome." This sounds like a good reason to avoid trying to "produce happiness." An Annicerean can simply focus on the pleasures arising from each action instead. Second, the passage says that "the wise man generally lives pleasantly, . . . but not in every detail." If even the sage cannot "live pleasantly in every detail," the implication may be that we should not make "living pleasantly" our aim. Once again, this is precisely the Annicerean doctrine. Third, the passage concludes with the admonition, "It's enough if someone pleasantly [*text corrupt*] as each one happens." What is missing here seems to be an alternative to the Metrodidact's end of "living pleasantly." Whatever verb has fallen out, the phrase "as each one happens" recalls the particular ends of Anniceris.

The convergence between the formulation of the end at 2.87–88 and the comments about happiness and living pleasantly at 2.90–91 significantly expands the domain of likely interpolation in 2.86–93 as a whole.

4. Anti-Epicurean Arguments

The third and last sign of Annicerean interpolation in D.L. 2.86–93 is a series of anti-Epicurean positions. Epicurus probably began teaching in Mytilene in 311/10 BCE, then migrated to Lampsacus, and finally settled and established the Garden at Athens around 307/6 BCE. There he continued to write and teach until his death around 270 BCE. It is therefore unlikely that his newer form of hedonism became influential enough to attract Cyrenaic criticism before the very end of the fourth century BCE. But the last mainstream Cyrenaics named in our evidence are the Metrodidact and Paraebates. The former was probably born before 370 BCE, and so would have been extremely old by the time Epicurus began to make an impact. The latter was probably born before 355 BCE,[9] so it is just possible that he authored the Cyrenaic criticisms of Epicurus. Moreover, there may have been later mainstream Cyrenaics whose names have been forgotten, who could have produced these anti-Epicurean arguments. But rather than hypothesizing their existence, it is more parsimonious to argue that Paraebates' student Anniceris authored this material, especially as this argument dovetails with the other signs of Annicerean influence investigated in this chapter.

We should not leap to the conclusion that every comparison with Epicurus amounts to an anti-Epicurean argument formulated by the Cyrenaics themselves. Some may very well be doxographical intrusions. These could arise in two fashions. First, a doxographer has introduced the comparison on his own initiative, without any basis in polemics between Epicurus and the Cyrenaics. Second, Epicurus has attempted to distinguish his position from that of the Cyrenaics, and a doxographer has injected Epicurus's distinction between the two schools back into the Cyrenaic material.

The first explanation is compatible with the contrast between Cyrenaic and Epicurean positions at D.L. 2.86, for instance:

⟨They mean⟩ pleasure of the body, which is also the end, as Panaetius says in his *On the Sects*, not static pleasure from the elimination of hurts or something like freedom from disturbance, which Epicurus admits and says is the end.

Nothing in this report indicates that either the Cyrenaics or Epicurus had the other in mind when formulating these positions. Panaetius or a later doxographer may have made this comparison on his own initiative.

The second explanation is compatible with what may be an implied comparison at D.L. 2.90: "Bodily pleasures are actually much better than mental ones, and bodily disturbances are worse. Hence it is by these that criminals are more often punished." This passage clearly recalls a passage in Diogenes' life of Epicurus:

Also with reference to the Cyrenaics: they say that bodily pains are worse than mental ones, since criminals are punished in the body. But

[Epicurus] says mental ones are worse, since the flesh is only disturbed by what is present, but the soul by what is past, what is present, and what is to come. (D.L. 10.137 = *SSR* 4a.200)

This could be another doxographical invention, since neither the Cyrenaics nor Epicurus engages with the other's argument. In other words, it may be Diogenes or one of his predecessors who has juxtaposed these two positions and their supporting arguments. On the other hand, Diogenes' way of presenting this material subtly suggests that the Cyrenaics elaborated their position first, and then Epicurus clarified how his position differs from the Cyrenaics' and why it is preferable. Either way, there is no need to postulate that the Cyrenaics had Epicurus in mind when they offered the explanation at D.L. 2.90 for why they believe bodily pleasures are better than mental pleasures, and bodily pains are worse.[10]

Yet after we have set aside these dubious cases, there remain five arguments against Epicurean positions that appear to originate with the Cyrenaics themselves. I have dealt with most of these elsewhere in this book, so here I will be brief. Four of them appear in succession at 2.89–90 (numbering mine):

[1] And "the removal of what hurts," as has been said by Epicurus, seems to them not to be pleasure. Nor is lack of pleasure hurt. For both are in motion, and neither lack of pain nor lack of pleasure is a motion, since lack of pain is the state of someone sleeping. They say that some people are able not to choose pleasure, due to "perversion."[11] [2] But not all psychical pleasures and hurts supervene on bodily pleasures and hurts. For joy occurs also for the simple prosperity of the fatherland, as for our own. [3] But they also deny that pleasure is perfected by the memory or anticipation of good things, as Epicurus thought. For the movement of the soul is dissipated by time. [4] They say that pleasures don't occur through mere seeing or hearing, since we listen with pleasure to people mimicking songs of mourning, but with displeasure to those really singing them.

I discussed arguments 1 and 2 earlier in this appendix, where we saw that they correspond to anti-Epicurean arguments associated by Clement with the Annicerean definition of the end. Here my emphasis is slightly different: in order to show that these arguments were made by Cyrenaics themselves, and not introduced by doxographers, I want to highlight that they are not simple comparisons like that attributed to Panaetius in the last paragraph. Diogenes presents them as direct Cyrenaic attacks on well-known Epicurean positions. In each case the Cyrenaics first deny the Epicurean thesis, and then offer an argument against it. Drawing on both D.L. 2.89 and Clement's presentation of the same material, we can summarize the first two anti-Epicurean arguments as follows:

[1] Contrary to what Epicurus believes, "The removal of what causes hurts" is not a pleasure.[12] All pleasures are "in motion," but "the removal of what

causes hurts" does not involve motion. It is a static condition—the condition of someone sleeping, or of a corpse. Therefore it cannot be a pleasure.

[2] Contrary to what Epicurus believes, not all joy in the soul supervenes on bodily experience.[13] Our own prosperity and that of our fatherland, other people's company, and ambitious pride have nothing to do with prior bodily experience. But each of these is a source of joy. Therefore not all joy in the soul supervenes on prior bodily experience.

Argument 3 takes us beyond the zone of interpolation already identified by comparison with Clement, but the pattern remains the same. First the Cyrenaics deny Epicurus's position, then they provide an argument against it. That argument is missing a premise (which I have supplied in brackets below), but appears to run something like this:

[3] Contrary to what Epicurus believes, pleasure is not perfected by the memory or anticipation of good things.[14] [Only the presence of good things can generate the motion in which pleasure consists.] Therefore anticipation of good things cannot generate the motion of pleasure. Moreover, this motion is dissipated by the passage of time. Therefore the memory of good things cannot generate the motion of pleasure.

Argument 4 is not labeled as an attack on Epicurus by Diogenes, but parallel evidence from Plutarch suggests it was intended as such:

"This," I said, "my Epicurean friends, is an important piece of evidence against you for the Cyrenaics, who argue that when we take pleasure in sounds and spectacles, it is not in the sight or the hearing, but in the thought. A hen constantly crowing or a raven is an unpleasant sound, but if someone imitates a crowing hen or a raven, he delights us. We're upset when we see people with the wasting sickness, but we're pleased when we see statues or images of people with the wasting sickness, because our thoughts are moved agreeably and naturally by the imitations." (*Mor.* 674a–b = *SSR* 4a.206)

Based on both Diogenes' point 4 and this parallel evidence from Plutarch, we can summarize the fourth argument something like this:

[4] Contrary to what Epicurus believes, pleasures don't occur through mere seeing or hearing. The example of theatrical enjoyment shows that the pleasure or displeasure we take in seeing or hearing has a cognitive dimension.[15]

Diogenes' point 4 gives this argument without any hint of polemical context. But the fact that [4] comes immediately after three explicitly anti-Epicurean arguments in Diogenes combines with the evidence of Plutarch to make it probable that this was an anti-Epicurean point in Diogenes' source as well.

The last anti-Epicurean claim appears about a page later, near the end of the doxography. The passage reads as follows:

> Meleager in the second book of his *On Doctrines* and Clitomachus in the first book of his *On the Sects* say that [the Cyrenaics] consider both physics and dialectic to be useless parts of philosophy. For whoever has thoroughly learned the account of what's good and what's bad can speak well and be free from superstitious dread and escape the fear of death. (D.L. 2.92)

Several points have been compressed into these two sentences, and not all of them are anti-Epicurean. For example, Epicurus agrees with the Cyrenaics in repudiating dialectic (D.L. 10.31). However, physics—the understanding of nature—is absolutely central to Epicurean philosophy. One intended effect of the Cyrenaics' rejection of physics may therefore be to impugn Epicurus. The second sentence confirms that the Cyrenaics have Epicurus in mind, since it promises that one can achieve characteristically Epicurean goals even without physics. The goals in question are liberation from both superstitious dread and from the fear of death.[16] The fifth anti-Epicurean argument, which is implied by this passage, thus goes something like this:

> [5] Contrary to what Epicurus believes, one does not need to study nature in order to escape the fear of supernatural beings and of death. One can achieve these things simply by studying [the Cyrenaic account of] what is good and what is bad.[17]

At the end of this section I have identified five probable anti-Epicurean arguments in D.L. 2.86–93, which stretch from the first word of 2.89 to the last word of 2.92. Two occur in passages that I have already, on unrelated grounds, argued to be Annicerean interpolations. These two occur in a single cluster with the second pair, which suggests that these four share the same source. Hence if the first two are Annicerean, the latter two are likely to be Annicerean as well. The fifth is widely separated from the other four, and could therefore have a different source. But the breadth of other evidence for Annicerean influence on this doxography makes the Annicereans the most plausible suspects.

5. Conclusion

It goes without saying that we must employ caution when denying an author's explicit attributions and replacing them with others. As I anticipated at the beginning of this chapter, not all of the foregoing arguments have been equally compelling, and none has been compelling enough on its own to justify positing widespread interpolation in D.L. 2.86–93. But it is not on the basis of any one argument that we must assess the possibility of interpolation. Rather, we must decide this question on a holistic basis, which proceeds from arguments about individual pieces of evidence toward hypotheses about the provenance of larger blocks of text, then returns from that larger picture to reassess individual pieces. In this way the strong arguments in section 2 raise the possibility of interpolation elsewhere in the doxography, which illuminates the otherwise puzzlingly late criticisms of Epicurus in section 4; and attributing those criticisms to Annicereans, in turn, corroborates the arguments in sections 2 and 3. At the end of this hermeneutic oscillation I have come to believe that Schwartz, Mannebach, and Döring were correct: it is very likely that many parts of D.L. 2.86–93 are Annicerean.

In fact I think it is possible that the confusion goes even further than this. When Sextus Empiricus and Seneca tell us that the Cyrenaics divide philosophy into five parts (Sen. *Ep.* 89.12, SE *M* 7.11 = *SSR* 4a.168), should we not once again think of the Annicereans? For by the testimony of Seneca and Sextus these five parts, though they purport to be subdivisions of ethics, actually cover the normal terrain of any Hellenistic philosophical system:

> According to some those from Cyrene appear only to accept the ethical part [of philosophy] and to dismiss physics and logic as contributing nothing to living happily. But some have thought that they reverse themselves inasmuch as they divide the ethical part into the topic of choice-worthy and avoidance-worthy things, that of experiences and also that of actions, then too that of causes, and finally that of proofs. Of these people say that the topic of causes comes from the part of physics, while that of proofs comes from the part of logic. (SE *M* 7.11)

Here we are dealing with a philosophy that is both highly systematized and comprehends the parts expected of any Hellenistic system. As Seneca says immediately before reporting this Cyrenaic evidence, "The best and largest number of authorities have said that there are three parts of philosophy: ethics, physics, and logic" (*Ep.* 89.9). That would suggest that we are dealing with a late recension of Cyrenaicism, perhaps from the first half of the third century BCE. Thus we could once again be looking at Annicerean evidence.

This uncertainty would be troubling if the primary aim of this book were to give a well-rounded analysis of the philosophy of each of the major figures in the Cyrenaic movement. I have gone some way toward providing such an analysis for Hegesias and Theodorus. However, my focus has generally been on the evolution of themes rather than the breadth and depth of individual thinkers. For some important themes, such as personal and civic relationships, it has been possible to distinguish with some degree of confidence the individual contributions by Aristippus, the mainstream Cyrenaics, Anniceris, and Hegesias. Elsewhere I have made no effort to say who thought what, since our evidence does not allow any clear discriminations. Overall the flexibility of my approach has permitted me to respect the inexactitude and even confusion which we should admit the evidence presents.

NOTES

Chapter 1. Introduction

1. See DK A 167; B 4, 71, 146, 194, 207, 211, 235 with Gosling and Taylor 1982, 27–37; Warren 2001, 29–72.
2. See Arist. *EN* 10.2 with Gosling and Taylor 1982, 255–83.
3. Our only source for Polyarchus "the Voluptuary" is Ath. 545a–546c, who says he is excerpting from Aristoxenus' (lost) *Life of Archytas*.
4. 2002, 19.
5. 2002, 11.
6. 2002, 30–33. Compare Onfray 1991, 234–43; 2006, 109–33.
7. Derrida 1998 explores this "archive fever" with his typical mixture of evocative brilliance and obfuscation.
8. Gouirand 2005. Zilioli 2012 only came into my hands as I was making the final revisions to this book, and has relatively little to say about ethics. My thoughts about Zilioli's bold metaphysical thesis will appear in Lampe forthcoming A.
9. Antoniadis 1916, Döring 1988.
10. Giannantoni 1958, Mannebach 1961. See also Giannantoni 1983–85 and 1990.
11. See especially Tsouna-McKirahan 1994; Wolf 1997, 67–71; Long 1999, 632–39; and Brunschwig 2001.
12. On Aristippus and Plato, see especially Natorp 1890; Zeller 1910; Philippson 1925, 465–73; Mauersberger 1926; Diès 1941, liii–lxxx; Mondolfo 1953; Giannantoni 1958, 116–69; Döring 1988, 27–32; and Brunschwig 2001, 472–75. On Aristippus and Xenophon, see Gigon 1953, 1–84; Classen 1958; von Fritz 1965; Erbse 1980; and Narcy 1995. On Aristippus and other Socratic authors generally, see Dümmler 1889, 166–88.
13. Irwin 1991, Annas 1993, 227–36, Graver, 2001, 155–77, Warren 2001, 164–74, Tsouna 2002, O'Keefe, 395–416.
14. Winiarczyk 1981, Laks 1993.
15. The works listed in the last few notes are of course not limited to the narrow rubric under which I have classified them. Numerous other articles are potentially relevant here, and will appear at the appropriate place in this book's references.
16. See also Burnyeat 1982, 27–28; Fine 2003, 192–206; Giannantoni 1997; Brunschwig 2001.
17. The best general introduction to all aspects of the Cyrenaic movement remains Giannantoni 1958, 13–115. Also worth reading, although with greater caution, are Zeller 1868, 287–331; Gomperz 1905, 209–45; and Humbert 1967, 250–72. For concise, recent overviews in English, see the online encyclopedia article by O'Keefe 2006 or combine Long 1999, 632–39 with Brunschwig 1999, 251–59 (both in the same volume).

18. 2006, 19.
19. 1995, 59.
20. The term "spiritual exercises" belongs to Hadot 1995, 81–125 and *passim*; 2002, 172–233. In this Hadot is sometimes followed by Foucault 2005, who more often refers to "techniques of the self" (e.g., 46–51). Sellars 2003, 107–66 comments critically on both Hadot and Foucault, and systematically develops this approach with reference to Stoicism. Nussbaum 1994 does not use the term "spiritual exercises" and is critical of Foucault (353–54), but she covers similar ground.
21. 2002, 3.
22. Hadot 2002 attempts to describe the "fundamental choice" represented by each philosophical school. This may be useful in an introduction to ancient philosophy, but it also threatens to obscure the complexity Hadot himself brings out elsewhere. Saying that an ethical system constitutes an intelligible existential whole does not entail claiming that it can be conveniently summarized. For this reason I will not try to reduce any of the Cyrenaic schools to a "fundamental choice."
23. In his edition of Aeschines of Sphettus, Dittmar 1912, 60–62 suggests this passage derives from a lost text by that author. The evidence for this is that Diogenes Laertius tells us that Aristippus "came to Athens, *as Aeschines says*, because of Socrates' fame" (2.65). However, Giannantoni 1986, 212–13 notes that the passage shares some generic features of scenes of philosophical conversion. Whatever its historicity, it illustrates how those sympathetic to Aristippus depicted his turn to philosophy.
24. Long 2006, 27.
25. Representative discussions are in Taylor 1989, 25–52; Rorty 1991, 23–43; Ricoeur 1991, *passim* (esp. 139–269).
26. On Socrates, see Eisner 1982; Seeskin 1987, 73–95; White 2000; Hobbs 2000. On Athenian law, see Cohen 1995, 61–118; Lanni 2006, 25–31.
27. This approach to reception is unusual in the history of philosophy, but bears a strong resemblance to Charles' Martindale's seminal theorization of reception for scholars working on Latin literature (1993).

Chapter 2. Cyrene and the Cyrenaics: A Historical and Biographical Overview

1. See Kahn 2001, 39–85.
2. See Warren 2002, 160–92.
3. Pyrrhonean skepticism has been very thoroughly studied. See chapter 7 n. 30.
4. "Schools of thought" (αἱρέσεις) rather than institutions with established buildings, successions of "scholarchs," etc. On the Greek terminology, see Glucker 1978, 159–92. On the dangers of accepting at face value the teacher–pupil relationships recorded by ancient historians of philosophy, see Kienle 1961. On the Socratic successions particularly, see Giannantoni 1990, vol. 4, 41–50, 167–71, 223–33.
5. It is debated whether the Megarics and Dialectics were genuinely separate schools. See Sedley 1977, Döring 1989.
6. These twenty are: Aithiops of Ptolemaïs, Anniceris of Cyrene, Antipater of Cyrene, Arete of Cyrene, Aristippus of Cyrene, Aristippus "the Metrodidact" of Cyrene, Aristoteles of Cyrene, Aristoxenes of Cyrene, Bion of Borysthenes,

Clitarchus (of Alexandria? [*FGrHist* II.B p. 741–52]), Dionysius "the Turncoat" of Heraclea, Epitimides of Cyrene, Hegesias of Cyrene, Lysimachus (city unknown [Athen. 6.252c]), Nicoteles of Cyrene, Paraebates of Cyrene, Posidonius (city unknown [Suda A 2466]), Simmias (of Syracuse? [D.L. 2.114]), Menedemus of Eretria, and Theodorus of Cyrene. Most of these are discussed further elsewhere in this book.

7. Based on archeological surveys and demographic models, Laronde estimates that Hellenistic Cyrene had a population of around 100,000, with as many as 628,000 living in the region (1987, 340–42).

8. There are chronological problems with this toponym, however, as I discuss below.

9. Eshlemen 2007/2008.

10. The three from elsewhere in the Mediterranean of whom we are certain are Menedemus of Eretria, Dionysius of Heraclea, and Bion of Borysthenes (who came from Olbia on the coast of the Black Sea). Dionysius may have met his Cyrenaic teacher in Athens, where he was studying with Zeno; Bion certainly met Theodorus there. The two students lost by Aristoteles to Stilpo (Clitarchus and Simmias) may be from Alexandria and Syracuse. Posidonius is not given a toponym, but epigraphical evidence suggests he was not from Cyrenaica.

11. See Herodotus, 4.150–68. An alleged copy of the founding decree is included in a fourth-century Cyrenaic inscription granting citizen rights to Thereans (Meiggs and Lewis 1969, no. 5, p. 5–9).

12. Gomperz 1905, 209–10. The glossy photographs in Di Vita, Di Vita-Evrard, Bacchielli and Polidori 1999, 184–239 give a good impression of what so impressed him.

13. On the monarchical period see esp. Herodotus 4.150–67, 199–205, and Pindar's *Pyth.* 4–5 and 9 with Chamoux 1953. On the civil war of 401 BCE, see Diod. Sic. 14.34 and Arist. *Pol.* 1319b11–26 with Laronde 1987, 249–56. My account in this section draws heavily on the magisterial histories of Chamoux and Laronde. For a more concise overview, see Goodchild 1971, 17–63.

14. The identity of this lucrative spice remains unknown. See Chamoux 1953, 246–63.

15. Laronde 1987, 147 (treasury), 30–33 (grain).

16. Laronde 1987, 199–218.

17. Laronde 1987, 41–84, 356–58. Extensive parts of the oligarchical constitution established by Ptolemy in Cyrene survive in *SEG* IX.1, and are discussed and partly re-edited by Laronde (1987, 95–128).

18. On Magas' reign, see Chamoux 1956.

19. Ibid. 32 n. 3–4.

20. For the list of Cyrenean philosophers in this paragraph I rely on Crönert 1965, 94–97. For their dates, I rely on the relevant entries in *DPhA*.

21. Laronde 1987, 140–47; Elrashedy 2002, 109. For Pindar, cf. n. 13 above.

22. D.L. 3.6 suggests that Plato visited Theodorus in Cyrene, but this may be a fiction inspired by Plato's dialogues.

23. D.L. 3.20. Laronde locates this ransomer of Plato—not to be confused with the Cyrenaic philosopher of the same name—in an aristocratic lineage traceable through inscriptional evidence (1987, 118).

24. In fact names in Καρν- are unique to Cyrene, as is the name "Anniceris." See Robert 1967.

25. *SEG* IX and XX contain numerous inscriptions from Cyrenaica. Chamoux 1953 and Laronde 1987 are both carefully based on archeological data.

26. See n. 4 above, Giannantoni 1958, 96.

27. The date is based entirely on conjectures about how old he must have been when he met Socrates and other datable individuals in his life. See Giannantoni 1958, 16.

28. Laronde 1987, 129–31 suggests that names indicating excellence (beginning Ἀριστ- or Ἀρειατ-) or containing references to the military, especially to cavalry and chariots, were common for the aristocracy of Cyrene. The name "Aristippus" appears frequently in inscriptions from *SEG* IX and XX.

29. In fact the Cyrenaic form of his name was certainly "Aratades." The Cyreneans used a Doric dialect, whereas by convention we use a Latinized transliteration of the Attic dialect. (See Giannantoni 1990, vol. 4 p.137; Crönert 1965, 94.)

30. Cf. Giannantoni 1958, 14 n. 4. This conjecture is based on Socratic Epistle 27 (= *SSR* 4A.226.8, 35).

31. This is an important omission, since scholars have sometimes wanted to connect Cyrenaic epistemology with Protagorean relativism via Aristippus. See Giannantoni 1958, 19–21.

32. See Pl. *Phd.* 59c3–4; Xen. *Mem.* 2.1, 3.8; D.L. 2.47.

33. Hermodorus of Syracuse said that "Plato and the other philosophers went to [Euclid of Megara] after Socrates' death, because they feared the savagery of the tyrants" (D.L. 2.106; cf. 3.6). One anecdote does place Aeschines and Aristippus in Megara (D.L. 2.62).

34. See esp. Dümmler 1889, 166–88 and Giannantoni 1986, 211–14; 1990, vol. 4, p. 147–54.

35. This emerges from many sources, which are gathered at *SSR* 4a.15–26.

36. Giannantoni 1958, 26–35.

37. D.L. 2.65, 2.72, 2.74–75, Suda A 3908, Plut. *Mor.* 4f, Gnom. Vat. 743 n. 24 (these and other sources at *SSR* 4a1–9).

38. The son is mentioned in an anecdote presented by D.L. 2.81 and three other sources (= *SSR* 4a.135–36). Regarding his daughter see the following section.

39. Giannantoni 1958, 16–18; 1990, vol. 4 p. 137–38.

40. Wilamowitz-Moellendorf 1965, 48–53.

41. For thorough discussions of Aristippus's writings, see Mannebach 1961, 76–84; Giannantoni 1958, 55–73; Giannantoni 1990, vol. 4 p. 155–68.

42. The historiographer Sotion and the Stoic philosopher Panaetius credit these compositions to him at D.L. 84; Panaetius elsewhere denies the authenticity of Aristippus's dialogues (D.L. 2.64). (On Sotion see Kienle 1961, 79–91; Mejer 1978, 62–74.) *Pace* Giannantoni 1990, vol. 4 p. 155–56, the historian Theopompus' accusation that Plato stole his dialogues from Aristippus does not strike me as convincing evidence for Aristippus having left written works (Athen. 508c–d): by parity of reasoning one could conclude, since Menedemus accuses Aeschines of stealing Socrates' dialogues, that Socrates left written works (D.L. 2.60). Giannantoni's argument from the letter of Epicurus preserved in Philodemus is also dubious (1990, vol. 4 p. 156), since Angeli revises the interpretation of the papyrus on which it is based in her recent edition of Philodemus' *To the Friends of the School* (1988, 166–67, 238–40). Where Giannantoni reads οἴ]δα[μεν εἶναι] πισ[τ] ὁ[ν] Κράτη[τ]ος [καὶ Ἀρ]ιστίππου τὰς πε[ρί τινων το]ῦ Πλάτωνος [διατριβ]ά[ς,

Angeli's new text reads, [5---].A.[. . . . . . τὸ περ]ὶ [Σω]κράτ[ους τοῦ Ἀρ]ιστίππου [κ]αὶ Σπευ[σίππου το]ῦ Πλάτωνος [ἐγκώμιον].

43. On the genre of *chreiai* see Kindstrand 1986, 221–25.

44. For example, it looks like Aelian has some work—spurious or authentic—in mind in *SSR* 4a.110, and Aristotle's report of Aristippus's argument concerning the uselessness of mathematics may also derive from a written source (*SSR* 4a.170).

45. Dillon 2003, 35.

46. *Pace* Classen 1958, 185 n. 5. See Mannebach 1961, 85–86, who also gives parallels for the phrase μένειν ἐπί; Giannantoni 1990, vol. 3 p. 169–71; Döring 1988, 34–35.

47. At this point Diogenes and the Suda probably rely on the same source. See appendix 1.5a.

48. The principal collections of inscriptions are *SEG* IX and XX.

49. Ptolemaïs would eventually be founded at the old port of Barca, a rival of Cyrene which went into mysterious decline around 375 BCE.

50. D.L. 2.72, 2.83; Strab. 17.3.22; Clem. Al. *Strom.* 4.19.122.1; Themist. *Orat.* 21 244b; Eus. *PE* 14.18.32; Ael. *NA* 3.40 = *SSR* 4b.

51. Theodectes studied with Aristotle and Isocrates in Athens.

52. No evidence places Menedemus in Cyrene, although political responsibilities—admittedly from later in his life—place him all over the Greek-speaking Mediterranean (*SSR* 2f.8, 16).

53. See Jacoby 1916, esp. 2278. Clement explicitly attributes *SSR* 4e.2 to Istrus' *On the Special Nature of Contests*, and Jacoby notes that two passages in Aelian overlap with other material Clement attributes to this work.

54. D.L. 7.166, Athen. 281d, Cic. *Fin.* 5.94, *Tusc.* 2.60.

55. To which add now Philodemus *Academicorum Historia* col. XX (ed. Dorandi 1991) and Athenaeus 437f (von Arnim 1893 gives 437e, but oddly leaves out 437f). Much of this evidence probably derives from the *Life of Dionysius of Heraclea* by his near-contemporary Antigonus of Carystus (see Wilamowitz-Moellendorf 1881, 123–26).

56. Cf. Crönert 1965, 95 and *DPhA* A 417.

57. On the genre *On the Sects* and Diogenes' usage of it, see appendix 1.5c.

58. Kienle 1961, 77–78; Mejer 1978, 45.

59. White 1994, 143.

60. Valerius Maximus also records this anecdote (*SSR* 4f.5), but given his heavy reliance on Cicero, he is probably not an independent source.

61. Laks 1993, 35.

62. Epicurus began teaching in Mytilene and Lampsacus around 311/310 BCE, and in Athens in 307/306.

63. The principal Cyrenean inscriptions: in SEG IX and XX, Meiggs and Lewis, 1969, no. 5, p. 5–9; Laronde 1987, 95–128. On the family of the Annicerides, see Laronde 118.

64. The name Ποσειδώνιος first appears in SEG IX.102.

65. More exactly the name Θεύδωρος (the normal form in the dialect of Cyrene) appears: e.g., SEG IX.1.77, 49.17–18, 50.44, XX.735 *passim*.

66. On the prosopography suggested by fourth-century inscriptional evidence, see further in Laronde 1987, 95–128.

67. D.L. 2.103, Plut. *Mor.* 606b, Philo *Quod omn. prob.* 127–30 = *SSR* 4h.9, 13.
68. Cf. Winiarczyk 1981, 66.
69. See Döring 1972, 157–64; Giannantoni 1990, vol. 4. p. 107–13.
70. So Giannantoni 1990, vol. 4. p. 111–12, following Suda Σ 829, P 3238.
71. Brancacci 1982, 57–58.
72. Cf. von Fritz 1934, 1829; Winiarczyk 1981, 71–72; Brancacci 1982, 59–61.
73. Regarding Theodorus' influence on Bion, see Kindstrand 1976, 67–70.
74. On the period of Demetrius' rule in Athens, see Habicht 1997, 53–66.
75. Philo *Quod omn. prob. lib.* 127–30, D.L. 2.101–2 = *SSR* 4h.9, 13.
76. Cf. Winiarczyk 1981, 67–68.
77. Cic. *Tusc.* 1.102, 5.117; Seneca *Tranq.* 14.3; Plut. *Mor.* 499d, 606b; Stob. 3.2.32; Gnom. Vat. 743 n. 352 (= *SSR* 4h.7–9).
78. So Winiarczyk 1981, 70.
79. Not to be confused with Lysimachus, king of Thrace. Hermippus calls this Lysimachus a student of Theophrastus, Callimachus calls him a Theodorean. Studying with one does not preclude studying with the other, as Bion demonstrates.

Chapter 3. Knowledge and Pleasure

1. Cic. *Luc.* 131, *Fin.* 2.18–20, 2.34–41, 5.17–20 = *SSR* 4a.178, 183–85, 187.
2. On the *divisio Carneadea* and Cyrenaic formulations of the end, see appendix 1.3–4.
3. 1982, 40–43.
4. 1998, 3; cf. 53.
5. See especially Giannantoni 1997, Tsouna 1998, Brunschwig 2001, Fine 2003.
6. See Long 2006, 70–95.
7. The word τρυφή frequently has negative moral connotations.
8. Athen. 544b, Tatian *Orat.* 2.1, Maxim. Tyr. *Phil.* 1.9, Lucian *Vit. Auct.* 12, D.L. 2.76, Clem. Al. *Paed.* 2.8.68.4–69.1, Sen. *Ben.* 7.25.1 = *SSR* 4a.53–54, 58–59, 63–66.
9. D.L. 2.67, 2.69, 2.81, 2.74–75; Athen. 544d, 588c, 588e–f, 599b; Jo. Chrys. *Hom. in Mt.* 33.4; Plut. *Mor.* 750d–e; Clem. Al. *Strom.* 2.20.117.5–118.1 = *SSR* 4a.86–96, 99.
10. Fish was the premiere luxury food for the ancient Greeks. See Davidson 1997.
11. Cf. Suda A 3908, Hor. *Serm.* 2.3.99–102, Auson. *Opusc.* 3.1.10, Gnom. Vat. 743.39, Cic. *Inv.* 2.176, *Off.* 1.148 = *SSR* 4a.79–83.
12. Plut. *Mor.* 469c, Stob. 4.15.32 = *SSR* 4a.74, 84.
13. Stob. 3.20.63, Ael. *VH* 7.3 = *SSR* 4a.109–10.
14. D.L. 2.68, 2.79–80; Gnom. Vat. 743 n. 36, 743 n. 43–44; Apul. *Flor.* 2; Scholia in Apoll. Rhod. Argon. 2.77; Schol. in Hom. *Il.* E 2 = *SSR* 4a.104, 107–8, 149.
15. Compare von Arnim 1893, 23; Natorp 1895, 904; Classen 1958; Giannantoni 1958, 23, 42–54, 70–73; Mann 1996; all of whom (in different ways) call into doubt the analytical rigor or systematicity of Aristippus's way of thinking. On the other side of this question, see Mannebach 1961, 88, 107 and Döring 1988, 62–70.
16. Many of these also appear in Xenophon's other works. Even the Socratic emphasis on "knowing oneself" as a prerequisite for statesmanship, for example, appears in *Cyropaedia* 7.2.20–24 in a form strikingly reminiscent of *Memorabilia* 4.2.
17. Nor does Diogenes Laertius mention a single doctrine in his life of Aeschines (2.60–64).

18. As Tsouna-McKirahan 1994, 380 argues.
19. The hypothesis of Classen 1958, that Xenophon had a decisive influence on the later tradition regarding Aristippus, is unnecessary.
20. See p. 139.
21. Gosling and Taylor 1983, 38; Tarrant 1994, 122.
22. Of course the extent to which Socrates commits himself to the argument here is controversial. See also Tarrant 1994 for detailed arguments about the hedonistic implications of arguments in Plato's *Gorgias* and the Platonic *Hippias Major*. Stenzel 1927, 887 calls attention instead to *Resp.* 505b–6c.
23. Zeller 1868, 211; Stenzel 1927, 877–78 and 887; and (most forcefully) Tarrant 1994. More guardedly, see Guthrie 1969, 498.
24. 1868, 211; cf. Guthrie 1969, 490.
25. The literature on the historical Socrates is vast. A representative sample of studies from different perspectives includes Montuori 1984, Vlastos 1991, Danzig 2010, Dorion 2011.
26. While it is Aspasia rather than Socrates who interrogates Xenophon and his wife at this point in Aeschines' *Aspasia*, this appears to be reported by Socrates for his own purposes (rather like Socrates' report of Diotima's speech in Plato's *Symposium*).
27. Compare Wolff 1997, 60–71, whose loosely similar suggestion requires far more definite assumptions about the historical Socrates: Socrates' project was to unify "the good" and "the beautiful" in a single "end"; each of his followers inherited this project; and Aristippus reasoned "pleasure" was good, beautiful, and the end.
28. [Plut.] *Strom.* 9, Eus. *PE* 854c, Them. *Or.* 34.5, D.L. 2.92; possibly Diog. Oen. fr. 3 col. 2-fr. 4 col. 1, Galen *PHP* 9.7.13–16 = *SSR* 4a.166–67, 69. It should be noted these authors are late and many are unreliable. Nevertheless, they carry some weight as a group.
29. This was a bone of contention among Socrates' followers. The clarity, rigor, and transmissibility of number theory, plane and solid geometry, astronomy, and harmonics provided an attractive model for ethical "science." These disciplines became increasingly prominent in Plato's later dialogues (e.g., *Resp.* 522a–531d, *Laws* 746d–747a, *Tim.* 36a–d, 53b–57d, *Phlb.* 23c–27c, 56d–57a). According to Xenophon, however, Socrates recommended learning only enough geometry to measure land for distribution or usage, enough astronomy and astrology to make intelligent decisions in matters requiring understanding of daily, monthly, and yearly cycles, and only enough arithmetics for utilitarian purposes (*Mem.* 4.7.2–8).
30. See Roochnik 1996. Nehamas 1998, 75–77 suggests that crafts were the historical Socrates' primary models for ethical knowledge.
31. The accuracy of the positions Xenophon ascribes to Aristippus is controversial. See Gigon 1953, 1–37; Fritz 1965; Erbse 1980; Narcy 1995. Certainly the *Memorabilia* are historical fictions; Xenophon is not recording an actual conversation. But this at least looks like the sort of argument Aristippus would have made.
32. As Gigon 1953, 37 notes, this position may have generated an anecdote at *SSR* 4a.102: "When Aristippus was asked, 'So you're everywhere?' he answered, 'Well then I wasted my fare on this passage!'" The enigmatic question "So you're everywhere" may follow the unexpressed claim, "I'm *a stranger* everywhere."
33. Gigon 1953, 35–36; Holmes 1979, esp. 123–24.

34. I choose the translation "experience" rather than "affect" for two reasons: first, like Greek πάθος and unlike English "affect," it is a common noun; second, the grammar of "experience" as both noun and verb maps neatly onto the grammar of the Greek noun πάθος and verb πάσχω. However, it should be noted that "experience" lacks the strong connotations of passivity which πάθος possesses.

35. Against the position that Aristippean epistemology predates and influences Plato's *Protagoras*, see appendix 1.8. Mannebach 1961, 115–17 reviews the evidence and scholarship for attributing the theory to Pyrrho's influence on the Metrodidact. On Pyrrho and the Cyrenaics, see also sections 7.4, 8.3.

36. Eusebius twice ascribes the doctrine that "only the experiences are apprehensible" to "those following Aristippus" (τοὺς κατ᾽ Ἀρίστιππον) *PE* 14.2.4, 14.18.31 = *SSR* 4a.216–17. But this appears simply to be a periphrasis for "the Cyrenaics."

37. The phrase ἡδονὴν ἐντάττων τὴν κατὰ κίνησιν is difficult to translate, since ἐντάττω almost always means "inserting among." Hence Laks gives "insérer" (1993, 32 n. 56) and Brunschwig, "intercalant" (2001, 466 n. 29). In his edition of Eusebius, des Places offers "en précisant qu'il s'agissait du plaisir en mouvement" (1987, 165). In her edition of Aristocles, Chiesara gives "enjoining" (2001, 33), which certainly makes better sense. But the only place I could find where ἐντάττω means this is the papyrus cited by LSJ (s.v. ἐντάσσω def. III). Nowhere in his voluminous writings does Eusebius use ἐντάττω with this meaning.

38. On the physiological element of Cyrenaic descriptions of experiences, see Everson 1991, 128–35; Tsouna 1998, 9–20.

39. However, Brunschwig 2001, 469–71 makes a case that "these experiences" should refer only to pleasure and pain. See also Laks 1993, 26 n. 31.

40. In a well-known article, Burnyeat 1982 denies that Greek philosophers ever ascribe truth or falsity to mental states. For the Greeks, he argues, truth and falsity always concern representations of external reality. Everson 1991, 128–35 attempts to buttress this position with the argument that Cyrenaic "experiences" refer to physiological conditions, not subjective states. However, Tsouna 1998, 31–61 and Fine 2003 compellingly rebut these arguments.

41. I borrow Tsouna's translation of κινεῖται as "stirred" (1998, 154–56).

42. Sextus says, "Someone who pushes on his eye is stirred as if by two, and a madman sees two Thebes and fantasizes a double sun" (*M* 192). At this point the Cyrenaic neologisms appear to break down, but if they are consistent, their intention must be to rephrase the content of their vision as an aspect of their phenomenal consciousness rather than a representation of any external reality.

43. Mannebach 1961, 116 n. 1; Giannantoni 1997, 189; Tsouna 1998, 31; Brunschwig 2001, 460–61. Giannantoni, Tsouna, and Brunschwig all note that the word "perception" recurs in one of the Cyrenaic formulations of the end, which is anachronistically attributed to Aristippus: "He said that smooth motion which is delivered to perception is the end" (D.L. 2.85).

44. It is possible that late Cyrenaics themselves adopted this Stoic term.

45. LSJ s.v. ἐναργής.

46. This gets the Cyrenaics into tricky territory, as Aristocles already observes (F5 = *SSR* 4a.218). See Tsouna 1998, 42–45, 63–68.

47. As Tsouna 1998, 75–88, 96–98 cogently argues, the Cyrenaics never appear to have called into doubt the existence of either the external world generally or other minds in particular.

48. This is the fourth Neopyrrhonean mode. Testimony is conveniently collected and analyzed by Annas and Barnes 1984, 78–98.

49. This is the first Neopyrrhonean mode. See Annas and Barnes 1984, 31–65.

50. Cf. Brunschwig 2001, 462–63.

51. For different reconstructions of the argument implied by this passage see Tsouna 1998, 100–11.

52. Regarding this enigmatic clause and the manuscript issues underlying it see pp. 131 and 236 n. 34.

53. Döring 1988, 60–61. This is not to imply that a state of stillness contains no informative experiences, such as "being yellowed." The relation of purely informative experiences to the typology of motions is left completely undetermined by our evidence.

54. Cf. Pl. *Grg.* 492e5–6.

55. The adjective εὐδοκητός, like the noun εὐδόκησις, is derived from the verb εὐδοκέω. The examples of this verb cited in LSJ all take a personal subject (unlike the verb δοκέω). Usually they take a dative of the thing with which the subject is pleased or satisfied. Two examples will suffice: καὶ τότε μὲν ἐπὶ τούτοις διέλυσαν τὸν σύλλογον, οὐδαμῶς εὐδοκήσαντες ἀλλήλοις ("At that time and on those conditions they dissolved the meeting, though they were by no means satisfied with one another," *Plb.* 18.52.5); τῇ τε αἱρέσει τῶν ἀνδρῶν, οὓς Ἄππιος ἠξίου ὁριστὰς γενέσθαι τῆς δημοσίας γῆς, πάνυ εὐδοκῶ ("I am entirely satisfied with the men whom Appius deemed fit to become officers in charge of land boundaries," D.H. 8.74.3).

56. Cf. Mannebach 1961, 112.

57. In Hellenistic philosophy, this debate will be elaborated in terms of what Brunschwig 1986 has called the "cradle arguments" of the Epicureans and Stoics.

58. I consistently (if somewhat awkwardly) translate ἀλγηδών as "hurt" in order to distinguish it from πόνος, which I translate "pain," and λυπή, which I translate "distress."

59. Both of these find echoes in later Epicurean arguments for the goodness of pleasure, which they may have influenced. See Cic., *Fin.* 1.29–31 and D.L. 10.137 with Brunschwig 1986, 115–28 and Sedley 1996.

60. It is harder to reconstruct how a Cyrenaic could claim to know anything about non-human animals' experience!

61. Translating ἐν μόναις αὐτὸ [scil. τὸ κριτήριον] ταῖς ἐνεργείαις καὶ τοῖς πάθεσι ὁρίζουσιν. Tsouna 1998, 156 apparently takes the καὶ to be epexegetic, for she translates "to the *energeiai*, i.e. to the *pathê.*"

62. In her commentary on Aristocles, Chiesara 2001, 141–42 cites Arist. *De An.* 3.11–12.

63. Note that there have been intense scholarly debates about precisely how to construe the Neopyrrhonist position. See, for example, the articles conveniently assembled and reprinted in Burnyeat and Frede 1997.

64. See S.E. *PH* 1.25–30 and *M* 11.110–67 with Nussbaum 1994, 280–315. See also Sedley 1983 on tranquility as the prime motivator for Greek skepticism.

65. LSJ s.v. ζῶ def. I.2.

66. It is debated how the Cyrenaics' experiences permit them to speak about external objects. See Plut. *Mor.* 1120b–21c = *SSR* 4a.211 with Tsouna 1998, 81–88. Fine 2003, 206 plausibly argues that some examples of Cyrenaic

experiences—especially that of seeing two suns or two Thebes—"have represen-
tational content."

67. The Greek text runs as follows: τινὲς δὲ τέ[λ]η τὰ πάθη τῆς ψυχῆς ἐχθέμενοι καὶ
μὴ προσδεόμενα τῆς ἐπ᾽ ἄλλων κρίσεως, πᾶσιν ἐξουσίαν ἀνυπεύθυνον ἔδοσαν
ἐφ᾽ ὅτῳ βούλονται λέγειν χαίρειν καὶ τὰ πρὸς τοῦτο συντείνοντα πράττειν.

68. Translation adapted from the edition of Indelli and Tsouna-McKirahan 1995, 103.

69. 1995, 124-25, with references to earlier scholarship. Cf. Tsouna 1998, 71.

70. See the following section.

71. Indelli and Tsouna read, οὐδ᾽ [ἔφασκον] τινες ε̣ἶν̣α̣ι δυνα[τον γ]ινώσκειν οὐδέ[ν].

72. 1998, 70.

73. Indelli and Tsouna-McKirahan 1995, 125, Tsouna 1998, 71.

74. Here I preserve the reading of all the principal manuscripts (BPFΦ), which is:
ἀνῄρουν δὲ καὶ τὰς αἰσθήσεις οὐκ ἀκριβούσας τὴν ἐπίγνωσιν, τῶν δ᾽ εὐλόγως
φαινομένων πάντα πράττειν. Reiske and Madvig suggest the attractive emenda-
tion, τῷ δ᾽ εὐλόγως φαινομένῳ πάντα πράττειν. In this case we could translate,
"They rejected perceptions since they don't permit accurate discernment, and
said it is by reasonable appearance that they perform every action." This would
make the connection between the two clauses clearer: reasonable appearance
would obviously be a supplement for feeble sensory perceptions. However, it
is hard to see how the corruption from dative to genitive could have occurred,
since the two words in question are not contiguous, and the genitive is the
lectio difficilior. Hence if either τῷ or φαινομένῳ were corrupted from dative
to genitive, it is unlikely the other would have been corrupted to match. It is
the difficulty of making sense of the sentence with these words in the genitive
that leads Goulet-Cazé et al. to write, "il faut d'abord mèttre une ponctuation
forte dans le grèc avant τῶν δ᾽ εὐλόγως" (1999, 303 n. 2). In that case we would
no longer need to ask what the weakness of sensory perception has to do with
"doing whatever appears reasonable." But this punctuation would eliminate the
epistemologically important contrast between "perception" and "appearance"
that the sentence seems to communicate. Marcovich emends the second clause
to τῶν δ᾽ εὐλόγως φαινομένων ⟨παντὶ⟩ πάντα πράττειν ("[they said] they do
whatever appears reasonable to everyone"), but this does not even address the
problem.

75. This is best taken as a repudiation of the Epicurean position that perceptions
always tell the truth (LS 16).

76. 1998, 56.

77. *M* 7.194, discussed by Tsouna 1998, 54-57.

78. Tsouna 1998, 70-71.

79. Compare Arcesilaus's argument, which he elaborate against Sphaerus's teacher
Zeno, that "the reasonable" is an adequate standard of judgment for action (S.E.
M 7.158). Britain 2008 cogently argues that this is not Arcesilaus' own doctrine,
but rather a dialectical position adopted for the sake of argument.

80. So Döring 1988, 18-19, following Mannebach 1961, 111. See also Antoniadis
1916, 35-37.

81. See Tsouna 1998, 12 n. 12, who clarifies (via personal communication) that the
intermediate experience "could be simply the completion of the process of, e.g.,
'being yellowed' or acquiring a *pathos* of yellow." Cf. Brunschwig 2001, 465-68.

82. This passage may actually be an Annicerean interpolation, as I discuss in appendix 2.
83. Döring 1988, 44. In response, see Laks 1993. Döring goes on to imply that the innovation was not introducing mental pleasures, but introducing "alongside sensual [pleasure] a pleasure of the soul that is independent from sensual pleasure and autonomous" (ibid. 52).

Chapter 4. Virtue and Living Pleasantly

1. Tsouna 1994, 377–82 and 2002, 470–72 has laid particular emphasis on this point.
2. However, in one anecdote Aristippus humorously explains, "Socrates did it too! People sent him bread and wine, and he took a little and sent the rest back. His provisions were overseen by the leading men of Athens, but mine by my slave Eutychides" (D.L. 2.74).
3. von Arnim 1898, 26–28; Giannantoni 1958, 36–38.
4. Compare Aristotle's infamous passage on "natural slaves" in *Politics* 1.4–7 and Foucault's influential discussion of internal "freedom" as a prerequisite for mastery over women, foreigners, and slaves (1985, 78–93 with Winkler 1990).
5. As Giannantoni notes in *SSR*, the same anecdote is ascribed to Anacharsis. The confusion is easy to explain: in collections of sayings, Anacharsis would be abbreviated to Aν, Aristippus to Aρ. If five sayings by the latter followed five by the former, one belonging to Aristippus could easily be reassigned. A saying about horses would naturally migrate to the legendary Scythian horsemen. But Cyrene was also renowned for horses, as Mannebach 1961, 67 recalls. And unlike Aristippus, Anacharsis never existed!
6. The root meaning of πλείων is simply "more," but it is often unidiomatic to translate it as such in English. In any event, Aristippus clearly conceives of "more" as "more than what is necessary." See LSJ s.v. πλείων def. II.1.
7. These Epistles seem to have been written in the second or third century CE. See Sykutris 1931, 1933; Lampe forthcoming B. *Pace* Crönert 1936, 150–51, I am neither persuaded that Epistle 27 is the "Letter to His Daughter Arete" ascribed to Aristippus at D.L. 2.84 nor that "the letter-writer will have possessed a firm knowledge of the familial relationships of Aristippus" (ibid. 151). Sykutris 1933, 115–16 had already noted that *Ep.* 8–27, 28, and 30–34 all abound in the picturesque details Crönert notes in 27. On grounds of style and dialect Sykutris argues that the same author penned all of these. Clearly these both demonstrate erudition and create a "reality effect." But nothing prevents the author from having fabricated some of the details. At the very least, it must be noted that the "garden in Berenice" (*Ep.* 27.2) cannot have existed, since the polis of Euhesperides was not renamed "Berenice" until Berenice, daughter of Magas, married Ptolemy III and thus reunited the kingdom of Cyrene with Ptolemaic Egypt. This happened after 249 BCE, around a century after the fictional date of this letter.
8. Actually he is on the island of Liparos, which is north of Sicily and therefore not on the way to Cyrene. Unless the authors are geographically confused, this may be a satirical play on words: one meaning of the Greek word *liparos* is "rich, comfortable, easy," just like Aristippus (LSJ s.v. λιπαρός, def. III).
9. Reading ὥστε τὸ ἐμὸν συμβούλευμα τοῦτο συμφέρειν with Sykutris for συμφέρον. Even still this sentence is very awkward and may be corrupt.

10. Concerning the etymology and diverse meanings of σωφροσύνη, see North 1966. Classic discussions include Plato's *Charmides* and Euripides' *Hippolytus*, each of which explores multiple ways of understanding this intriguing Greek virtue.

11. Compare Philodemus' detailed comments about the suffering associated with greed in *On Property Management* (esp. 14.5–17.2).

12. For example, Callicles in Plato's *Gorgias*.

13. The anecdote appears in slightly different versions in the Suda, Athenaeus, Sextus Empiricus, Stobaeus, the Gnomologium Vaticanum, and Gregory of Nazianz (all at *SSR* 4a.31–34).

14. Compare a phrase sometimes appended to his famous saying about Laïs (see below): "What's best is to control and not be controlled by pleasures, not to avoid pleasures" (D.L. 2.75; cf. Stobaeus 2.17.17 = *SSR* 4a.98).

15. The allusion, of course, is to the "judgment of Paris," who was asked to preside over a beauty contest between Hera, Athena, and Aphrodite. This caused the Trojan War, Paris' death, and the destruction of Troy.

16. On Cyrenaics and courtesans see section 6.3.

17. *SSR* 4a.104 gathers the other testimonia for this anecdote. The Gnomologium Vaticanum gives two different versions (743 n. 36 and n. 44), as does John of Salisbury (*Policr.* 5.17 and *Ep.* 191). Apuleius gives just one (*Flor.* 2).

18. *SSR* 4a.50 lists eleven sources in which this anecdote appears. However, many of these are unquestionably interdependent, since they are identical. Significant variations are given by Galen, Cicero, and the Gnomologium Vaticanum.

19. Compare the philosophical "journey" of Lucretius' Epicurus, who surveys the universe and "reports" his findings to "us" (1.72–77).

20. By "ontological" I mean to indicate, first, the difference in kind between heroes like Achilles with divine parents and men with mortal parents, and second, the more generalized divine underpinning of the role-and-class hierarchy in archaic Greek literature. For a thought-provoking general discussion of the latter, see Détienne 1996. For specific examples, see Pindar's first *Pythian* with the interpretation of Segal 1998, 1–24, or his second *Pythian* with the interpretation of Most 1985, 60–132.

21. Hobbs 2000; see also Eisner 1982; Seeskin 1987, 73–95; White 2000.

22. On the cultivation of Epicurus and the other founding Epicureans as heroes see Clay 1999, 75–102. I am not aware of any literature on Stoic heroism, although Barnouw 2004 and Sherman 2005 are at least tangentially relevant.

23. First, Aristippus's reply is far less pointed with this wording. Second, as a general rule we should put little faith in the exact wording of anecdotes. See appendix 1.5d.

24. The adjective "presentist" is borrowed from Graver 2001.

25. See Wilson 1997, 10, which cites Rudolph 1894.

26. This is very difficult to perceive in *SSR*, which splits this continuous passage into the following snippets: 4a.174, 53, 36, 20, 96, 31, 9.

27. The Greek text runs, πάνυ σφόδρα ἐρρωμένως ἐῴκει λέγειν ὁ Ἀρίστιππος, παρεγγυῶν τοῖς ἀνθρώποις μήτε τοῖς παρελθοῦσιν ἐπικάμνειν μήτε τῶν ἐπιόντων προκάμνειν· εὐθυμίας γὰρ δεῖγμα τὸ τοιοῦτο καὶ ἵλεω διανοίας ἀπόδειξις. If Aelian had wanted to impute the final clause to Aristippus, he would probably have written ἀπόδειξιν.

28. On Cyrenaic arguments against Epicurus, see appendix 2.4.

29. The closest I have found are several occurrences of τὸ φθάνον with infinitives. For example, κάμπτεται γὰρ τὸ φθάνον ἐκτετάσθαι ("What has previously been extended bends" [Galen, *De motu musculorum* ed. Kühn 4.387.9]); τὸ φθάνον γεγονέναι ὕδωρ ἐν αὐτῇ ("the water that has already been created in it" [Alexander of Aphrodisias, *In Aristotelis meteorologicorum libros commentaria,* ed. Hayduck p. 55.25]).

30. It may be for this reason that Mannebach 1961, 96 concludes, "It cannot be doubted that here we have the philosopher's own words." It is curious that another citation by Aelian, at *VH* 7.3 = *SSR* 4a.110, also suggests that Aelian is looking at a more extended Aristippean document than he actually quotes.

31. A very similar argument appears at Arist. *Ph.* 217b32–34, as Warren 2001, 169 has also noted. Rather than refuting it directly, Aristotle demonstrates its naïveté through his subsequent discussion of time. Cf. Sext. *M* 10.197–202 with Warren 2003.

32. Here I am deliberately echoing Hume, who articulates a similar intuition: what distinguishes among sensory impression, memories, and figments of the imagination is simply the decreasing "force" and "vivacity" of the ideational content (*Treatise of Human Reason* I.I.1–3, I.III.5 = 1978, 1–10, 84–86). Of course, Hume suspends judgment about the cause even of sensory impressions and memories (ibid. I.III.5 = 84).

33. Warren 2001, 161–79 and Feldman 2004, 31–34 read the evidence this way. Concerning their interpretation, see section 5.4.

34. LSJ s.v. μονόχρονος, ov. The word elsewhere appears only in much later metrical and grammatical texts (Mannebach 1961, 96), with the exception of a papyrological fragment attributed to Aristoxenus (P. Oxy. 1.9 col. 3). I borrow the translation "unitemporal" from Tsouna 1998, 15–16.

35. Mannebach 1961, 96. LSJ s.v. ἡδυπάθεια gives "pleasant living, luxury."

36. E.g., Arist. *EN* 1098a18–20, Pl. *Grg.* 500c1–4, *Resp.* 352d5–6, *Phlb.* 11d4–6. Cf. Annas 1993, 27–46.

37. Cf. Eur. *Ba.* 902–11, *Hec.* 623–28.

38. 1995, 221–22.

39. Part of this is quoted by Hadot 1995, 228, as is Marcus Aurelius 12.3.1–4.

40. Many of these passages are cited by Goldschmidt 1969, 39 n. 6.

41. For a more thorough analysis of Marcus Aurelius' efforts to "circumscribe the present" see Hadot 1998, 131–37. On the Stoic theory of the "retrenchable present" which underlies this effort, see Schofield 1988.

42. In fact Marcus is extraordinarily prone to stepping even further back and situating his life in the entire universal nexus of Fate, God, and Law, as Hadot 1998, 137–63 discusses. By my count, the word "entire" (ὅλος) appears a staggering 102 times in the *Meditations.*

43. Nevertheless, Athenaeus' version suggests much the same exercise.

44. It is worth recalling that πόνος becomes the "end of evils" or *summum malum* for the Cyrenaics.

45. See Détienne and Vernant 1978.

46. One relevant value which will not appear here is friendship, which I defer for independent consideration in chapter 6.

47. The contrast with Antisthenes was occasionally drawn in antiquity (Suda A 3909 = *SSR* 4a.19, Aug. *Civ. Dei* 18.41 = *SSR* 5a.70), but tended to be replaced by comparison with Diogenes of Sinope (*SSR* 4a.44–48). See also Antoniadis 1916, 116–28; Tsouna-McKirahan 1994, 382–87.

48. This is the first line of Pindar's fifth *Pythian Ode*, which he wrote for Arcesilaus, the last king of Cyrene, in 462 BCE.
49. This position was probably articulated, either by the Cyrenaics themselves or by later doxographers, in response to the Stoic admission that their ideal sage was unbelievably rare.
50. Clement's report almost certainly derives from a Carneadean source, and Cicero's report probably does as well (especially given that both pair Epicureanism and Cyrenaicism). See appendix 1.3–4.
51. cf. Phld. *Rh.* col. 12.41 = *SSR* 4a.11. This anecdote clearly belongs to the controversy about Socrates' failure to defend himself effectively at trial, regarding which see Danzig 2011.
52. Lanni 2006, 41–64.
53. An obscure collection of anecdotes supplies an alternate version: "When [Aristippus] was asked what he got from philosophy, he replied, 'Doing without instruction what some do through fear of the laws" (*SSR* 4a.105).
54. Compare Epicurus' doctrine that no custom is intrinsically just, but that "natural justice" is the contract in any community neither to harm nor be harmed (*RS* 31–33; cf. the other texts collected at LS22).
55. For example, Xenophon says this is why Critias and Alcibiades sought out Socrates (*Mem.* 1.2.14–16). In the pseudo-Platonic *Theages*, which is probably from the late fourth century BCE, the ability to speak with witty people is precisely the product of Socratic philosophizing which Aristides values (*Thg.* 130b8–c6).
56. Epicureans' concern with the fear of death is well documented by the texts assembled in LS 24. For the disturbance caused by incorrect beliefs about the gods, see LS 23A–D and 23I. For the use of physics to eliminate the fear of death and the gods, see Epic. *Rat. Sent.* 11–12. For a fuller treatment of Cyrenaic arguments against Epicurus, see appendix 2.4.
57. For an attempt to do so see Graver 2001, 161–70. Cf. Döring 1988, 46–47.
58. The phrase "empty belief" is associated with Epicureanism, so this may not be the Cyrenaics' own wording. The notion that even the sage will experience distress, because it occurs "naturally," also recalls Epicurus. See Tsouna 2007, 32–51.
59. It is evident from the simplistic and repetitive way Cicero discusses this Cyrenaic belief at *Tusc.* 3.28–76 that he has only the scantiest doxographical notice in front of him.
60. Compare Philodemus' comments on "natural" distress associated with dying: when someone capable of progressing in philosophy is dying prematurely (*De Morte* 17.33–36); when someone is leaving behind close relatives, who will experience serious hardship because of one's death (ibid. 25.2–10); or when someone is dying in a foreign country, especially if one leaves behind relatives back at home (ibid. 25.37–26.3). See also the discussion by Tsouna 2007, 41–51.
61. Compare the Stoic theories at D.L. 7.111–13, Andronic. Rhod. 1–3, Arius Didymus *Epit.* 10b with Brennan 2005, 89–113; Graver 2007, esp. 35–60.
62. For Hegesias's position on the value of death, see section 7.3–5. For Walter Pater's creative supplementation of this lacuna in his "new Cyrenaicism," see section 9.6. For the Cyrenaics and religion, see the following note.
63. We have disappointingly little evidence about Cyrenaic theology. According to the Gnomologium Vaticanum, Aristippus opines that "praying for good things

and asking god for anything is laughable. For doctors don't give food or drink when the invalid asks for them, but when they think they'll be beneficial" (743 n. 32 = *SSR* 4a.132). Similarly, Clement tells us that the Cyrenaics consider prayer unnecessary (*mē dein eukhesthai*), though he does not give the reason (*Strom.* 7.7.42.2–3 = *SSR* 4a.220). But very similar thoughts are attributed to Socrates, Stilpo, and espectially Diogenes of Sinope, so their authenticity and exactitude is dubious (Mannebach 1961, 99; cf. Kindstrand 1976, 231–32). Still, a certain skepticism about conventional religion was widespread in the period, is consistent with Cyrenaic ethics generally, and helps to explain how Theodorus arrived at his more radical critique of religion (for which see section 8.5).

64. These laws are transcribed, translated, and discussed in Robertson 2010. For this particular rule, see column B 97–105.

65. Notwithstanding their skepticism about conventional religion, I suspect that Cyrenaics would normally obey the sacred laws—not because of any Pascalian wager, but because of the guideline not to do anything "out of place" (D.L. 2.93).

66. The word for "school" here is *diatribē*. On the meaning of this word see Glucker 1978, 162–66.

67. Sellars 2003, 118–21.

68. Cf. D.L. 6.70 on Diogenes of Sinope's bodily training, although the authenticity of this passage has been challenged.

69. 2001, 161.

70. The Stoics popularized the term "progress" by denying that the philosophical learner becomes progressively less vicious and more virtuous (LS 61I, S-U). This Cyrenaic position is either adopted in opposition to the Stoics or—more likely, given the chronology—reformulated by doxographers in order to put Cyrenaic thinking into dialogue with Stoicism.

71. See the following chapter.

72. This does not imply any position on the *degree* of foresight Cyrenaics recommend. Their lifestyle may permit them to get by with a minimum of planning.

73. The exception is Laks 1993, 33–34, who suggests that "management of pleasures" names the condition on the basis of which a Cyrenaic can be called "happy."

74. The *Oeconomica* ascribed to Aristotle is probably by Theophrastus. On the genre and philosophical topic in general, see Natalie 1995. On Philodemus' *Oeconomica* see Tsouna 2007, 163–94.

75. Οὐδεμία ἡδονὴ καθ᾽ ἑαυτὸ κακόν· ἀλλὰ τὰ τινῶν ἡδονῶν ποιητικὰ πολλαπλασίους ἐπιφέρει τὰς ὀχλήσεις τῶν ἡδονῶν. The diction is so similar as strongly to suggest influence in some direction. The doxographer may have Epicurus in mind when paraphrasing the Cyrenaic position.

76. On adultery in Athenian culture and law, see Cohen 1991, 98–170; Todd 1993, 276–79. Much of what Cohen says will apply to other Greek cites as well.

77. The first issue which leads to disagreement is whether or not to read μὴ before ποιοῦντα. Three of our four best manuscripts read μὴ (ΒΡΦ), and the one which does not is the least reliable of the group (F). So we ought to retain the μὴ unless it does not make sense. Laks 1993, 34 n. 65 rightly argues that it does make sense. He translates, "l'accumulation des plaisirs [est] la chose la plus pénible, quand elle ne produit pas la bonheur." Goulet-Cazé et al. 1999, 298 more or less follows him, translating "l'accumulation des plaisirs, ne produisant pas dans ce cas le bonheur,

leur semblait fort désagréable." The second reason for disagreement is also one of the reasons why some scholars read without μή. This is the implications of this sentence for interpretations of Cyrenaic presentism. Those who want to insist that Cyrenaics are consistently and narrowly focused on the present, and eschew all prudential planning and care for their future lives, are naturally tempted to remove the μή. Two clear examples of this are Annas and Warren: "However, the Cyrenaics are unenthusiastic even about this limited role of happiness, considering it a bore and a nuisance to collect together the pleasures which make up happiness" (Annas 1993, 231); "it appears to them that the collection of pleasures which produce happiness is a most difficult thing" (Warren 2001, 166). (Döring 1988, 41–42 and Graver 2001, 165 offer similar translations, though they do not have the same interpretive agenda). Finally there are those who want to argue that the Cyrenaics do in fact care about their future lives. They retain the μή and construe δυσκολώτατον in a rather strained fashion. Examples include Mannebach and Tsouna: "difficillima iis videtur esse voluptatum collectio vitam beatam non efficiens; vel melius sensu consecutivo: ita ut ea (voluptatum collectione) beatitudo non efficiatur" (Mannebach 1961, 93–94); "It seems virtually impossible to them that the collection of pleasures would not amount to happiness" (Tsouna 2002, 488). While I strongly agree that Cyrenaics care about their lives as a whole, I do not think we need this strained translation in order to defend that position.

78. κατὰ μίαν. . . ἐπανάγῃ ΡΦ: ἐπανάγει BF : κατωμίδα coni. Madvig : ἐπαναλάβῃ coni. Emperius. Madvig 1871, 13 is surely right that the object of the main verb has dropped out of this sentence. However, his suggestion that κατὰ μίαν should be κατωμίδα cannot be right. First, κατὰ μίαν makes good sense in this context. Second, κατωμίδα ("cape") may not even be a Greek word: it is itself a conjectural correction for κατωτίδες, which appears only in one passage of the Byzantine lexicographer Hesychius. Third, even if κατωμίδα were a Greek word, Madvig's attempt to make sense of it in this sentence is desperate. Emperius' revision of ἐπανάγῃ to ἐπαναλάβῃ is hard to justify on philological grounds, and in any event will not solve the problem.

79. Cf. Annas 1993, 39–42, though I employ slightly different terms than she. Note that these criteria are introduced already in Pl. *Phlb.* 20d, suggesting that they are the product of cooperative thinking in the mid-fourth-century BCE Academy.

80. See Tsouna 2002, 472; O'Keefe 2002, 402.

81. Perhaps the closest Epicurus comes to explicitly saying this in his surviving writings is at *Men.* (= D.L.) 10.128: "We say that pleasure is the beginning and the end of living blissfully."

82. O'Keefe 2002, 402–3 n. 24, following a hint in Irwin 1991, 55. O'Keefe is right to question the exactitude of Clem. Al. *Strom.* 2.21.127.1–2, but wrong to claim that in Eusebius' case "the author's main concern is simply to assert that the Cyrenaics are hedonists." In fact Eusebius' purpose very clearly encompasses differentiating Aristippus's hedonistic formulations (or lack thereof) from those of his grandson.

83. Clement actually ascribes this to "those around Aristotle."

84. This may be the kernel of the Cyrenaics' argument against the fear of death.

85. See section 3.4.

86. However, this puts a lot of weight on a brief phrase. This may simply be an argument *for* pleasure as the end, not an argument *against* "living pleasantly" as the

end. In that case we would have only two arguments here against the endlikeness of happiness.

87. 1993, 39.
88. On the "meditation on death" see Hadot 2002, 190–98.
89. Note that we know nothing at all about the Cyrenaic theories of logic and causation other than that they existed.
90. We do not know that Posidonius was an exile, only that he was not Cyrenean. I use this scenario simply as a thought experiment.

Chapter 5. Eudaimonism and Anti-Eudaimonism

1. The starting point for this scholarly trend appears to be Annas 1993, 38–39, 227–36 (reprised in Annas 2007, 44–46). Tsouna 2002 and Sedley 2013 (which I heard as I was finalizing this manuscript for publication) are important exceptions. Laks 1993 and Graver 2001 also offer more nuanced readings.
2. Irwin 1991.
3. O'Keefe 2002, 408.
4. Warren 2001, Feldman 2004.
5. Skinner 1969, 28, cited by Rorty 1985, 50.
6. Rorty's 1985, 51. He exemplifies, "Somebody who thinks that the question of whether all words are names, or some other semantical thesis, is the sort of question which is decisive for one's views about lots of other topics will have a quite different imaginary conversation with Plato than somebody who thinks that philosophy of language is a passing fad, irrelevant to the real issues which divide Plato from his great modern antagonists (Whitehead, Heidegger, or Popper, for example). The Fregean, the Kripkean, the Popperian, the Whiteheadian, and the Heideggerian will each re-educate Plato in a different way before starting to argue with him" (1985, 54).
7. Rorty actually refers to "the mighty mistaken dead" (1985, 51).
8. Irwin 1991. Responses include Tsouna 1998, 130–35 and 2002, 482–89; Warren 2001, 167; Graver 2001, 163; and O'Keefe 2002, 398–401; all of which have influenced my discussion.
9. However, he disavows in a footnote any intention to take a position on debates about which Cyrenaic introduced which theory (1991, 79 n. 2).
10. So does Epicharmus at D.L. 3.10–11, as Irwin notes (ibid. 66); but as Irwin also notes, the evidence for Epicharmus is unreliable.
11. Tsouna 1998, 130–35 and 2002, 482–89; O'Keefe 2002, 398–401.
12. 1998, 132. I do not agree with Tsouna's arguments at 2002, 487–88, to the effect that Cyrenaic references to memory and the statement about happiness at D.L. 2.91 confirm this point. Taken in isolation, Irwin's interpretation of the statements about memory are equally persuasive; and the translation of the sentence at D.L. 2.91 is too controversial to support any particular interpretation.
13. O'Keefe 2002, 199.
14. 1991, 77. A similar problem arises with Irwin's claim that "Epicurus . . . seems not to have learned all he ought to have learned from the Cyrenaics" about the resources of sensationalist epistemology for arguing about eudaimonism and hedonism (ibid. 78). It's unsurprising that Epicurus didn't learn these lessons if the Cyrenaics never made these arguments.

15. *SSR* 4a.174, discussed in section 4.3.
16. 2001, 163.
17. 2002, 403–5.
18. Ibid. 406.
19. Ibid. 408.
20. Pp. 87–90, 97–98.
21. Ibid. 408.
22. On the syntax of the verb εὐδοκέω see chapter 3 n. 56.
23. Pp. 77–80.
24. Pp. 91–96.
25. Warren 2001, 161–79; Feldman 2004, 31–34.
26. 2001, 136 n. 2; 142 n. 13; 154–55; 158 n. 35; 161 n. 42. Warren is by no means responding to Parfit alone; he has ready widely in the modern debate.
27. Ibid. 135–36 and *passim*.
28. He admits that various phases of Cyrenaic thought are entangled in the evidence, but (implicitly) chooses to focus on trends throughout that evidence rather than attempt to disentangle it (ibid. 165).
29. Ibid. 173.
30. Ibid. 168–69.
31. Ibid. 175.
32. Ibid. 172.
33. 2004, 30. Feldman's sources seem to be Diogenes Laertius and O'Keefe's article in the *Internet Encylopedia of Philosophy*.
34. Ibid. 31.
35. Ibid. 32.
36. Feldman 2004, 33.
37. Warren quotes Athenaeus' version of *SSR* 4a.174 at p. 168 and Aelian's at p. 172, which could give the misleading impression that we have two sources for this position (rather than two reports sharing a common origin). I discuss these two passages at length in section 4.3.
38. Chapter 4 n. 77.

Chapter 6. Personal and Political Relationships

1. See Konstan 1997, 6–11. Note, however, that Konstan's claims have been very controversial (e.g., Herman 1998, Flaig 2000). Material on Greek friendship in general is gathered by Dover 1974, 180–84 and Dillon 2004, 78–100.
2. On "benefaction" as a topic in philosophical ethics, see Inwood 2005, esp. 65–68.
3. LSJ s.v. χάρις IV.
4. LSJ s.v. χάρις II.2.
5. LSJ s.v. χάρις III. One may also φέρειν or τίθεναι χάριν.
6. Hence Epicurus says that "someone who is always looking for more help is not a friend," because "he trades χάρις for exchange" (*Sent. Vat.* 34 = LS 22F).
7. LSJ s.v. χάρις I. For a good introduction to the semantic range of χάρις, see MacLachlan 1993, 3–12. On χάρις in Pindar's *Pyth.* 2 see Hamilton 2003, 56–73 and especially Most 1985, 60–132. See also Millett 1998, 230–33.

8. This is the anthropological terrain of "gift exchange," the classic exposition of which is Mauss 1990 (originally published 1923/1924).

9. 1974, 181.

10. These and many other passages are cited by Dover 1974, 180. Blundell 1989 analyses how Sophocles' plays instantiate and interrogate this rule.

11. On this entire complex of values in Homeric epics (the most influential texts of Greek antiquity), see Finley 1956, 125–64; Adkins 1960, 30–60; Redfield 1975, 99–127; Williams 1993; Cairns 1993, 48–146; Zanker 1994. On Classical Athens as a "feuding culture," see Cohen 1995, 61–142. On Plato's handling of these values, see Hobbs 2000.

12. Testimony collected by Dover 1974, 273–75.

13. Millet 1998, 230–33.

14. 1993, 229. This claim implies an opposition between "self-concern" and "other-concern" which, as Gill 1998 has compellingly argued, is often unhelpful in approaching ancient Greek ethics, in which the master terms are mutuality and reciprocity.

15. Golden 1981. We cannot say whether it was accepted also at Cyrene, but we do not, in any event, know where this anecdote is supposed to take place.

16. Golden 1981, 330–31.

17. Testimony collected by Dover 1974, 274.

18. *Cri.* 45c8–d6, 54a1–b1. I return to this comparison in section 7.5.

19. On Aristippus and Arete see section 4.3. Note that Callimachus *Ep.* 20 (ed. Pfeiffer) about the death of "Aristippus's children" Melanippos and Basilo, which Onfray 2002, 78 and Gouirand 2005, 226–27 take to concern our philosopher, almost certainly pertain to a different and later Cyrenean. Epigraphical evidence shows that Aristippus was an extremely common name in Cyrene.

20. On this relationship see Giannantoni 1986, 213.

21. On the provenance of these spurious epistles see chapter 4 n. 7.

22. This recalls the ludicrous accusation by Menedemus of Eretria that these dialogues were written by Socrates and passed to Aeschines by Xanthippe (D.L. 2.60).

23. Discussed at length in chapter 3.

24. 1993, 229.

25. With the following see especially Reinsberg 1989, esp. 80–125; Davidson 1997, 109–36; Kurke 1999, 175–219; and McClure 2003A and 2003B.

26. Section 4.2.

27. Hence the proverb, "Not every man can go to Corinth" (home of Laïs and other legendary courtesans), which Horace *Ep.* 1.17.26 associates with Aristippus.

28. At *Od.* 21.152 the suitor Leodes is the first to try to string Odysseus' bow, and when he fails, he says, "Friends, I'm not stretching it, let someone else take it."

29. Athenaeus cites Antigonus of Carystus for the first anecdote, but Nicias' *Successions* for the second.

30. "Laïs" was the name of at least two and possibly three Corinthian courtesans. See Geyer in *RE* 12, 513–16; McClure 2003A, 187–88.

31. "Denial of autonomy" and "inertness" are two of the seven overlapping notions Nussbaum 1995 identifies in sexual objectification. I also make use of some of her other analytical categories, including "denial of subjectivity" and "fungibility."

32. See n. 28.

33. Note that in the Laïs anecdote Aristoteles breaks his own rule!

34. I say "friendly love" rather than "friendship" because in the *Lysis* φιλία clearly encompasses a broad array of relationships: between friends, parents and children, and even (arguably) the aspiration toward lovable Forms.

35. This is set out most clearly in *EN* 8.2, but usefulness remains a recurrent theme in Aristotle's analysis of φιλία throughout books 8 and 9.

36. This claim is explained further in *EN* 9.9 and 9.12, where Aristotle explains why the good man, despite being self-sufficient, still needs friends.

37. Later Epicureans are divided about how to interpret this position, as Cicero *Fin.* 1.66–70 = LS 22O testifies.

38. Plato's *Lysis* is aporetic, so we cannot say that Socrates actually approves of usefulness as an element of friendship.

39. Annas's way of fleshing out the metaphor is prejudicial: "An absent friend is thus like an amputated toe . . ." (1993, 231). We could just as well say, "An absent friend is like an amputated leg," which would give a very different impression.

40. Annas 1993, 231–32.

41. Winiarczyk 1981, 77 compares this with Cynic beliefs, but it could just as well have come from the Megarics, Dialectics, or Cyrenaics themselves.

42. I take "self-sufficiency," as in Aristotle or Epicurus, to be less than total. We are not dealing with desert hermits.

43. Aristotle is concerned to counter arguments of this kind in *EN* 9.9 and *EE* 4[7].12. Epicurus attacks Stilpo in particular for maintaining such a position (Sen. *Ep.* 9).

44. Aristotle makes more or less this claim about "friendships" based on narrowly conceived usefulness: "Usefulness [*to khrēsimon*] is not enduring," he says; "it comes and goes. So if the cause of their friendship is dissolved, the friendship too is dissolved, since the friendship exists with regard to those things" (*EN* 1156a21–24; cf. 1157a14–16).

45. Theodorus may also derive this argument from his Dialectic or Megaric teachers, since Epicurus imputes such a position to the Megaric Stilpo (Sen. *Ep.* 9).

46. I address the obvious objection to this argument—that the sage can be friends with other sages—in the following chapter.

47. Clearly, then, Hegesias does not think benefiting oneself qualifies as "benefaction."

48. ἔλεγον τὰ ἁμαρτήματα συγγνώμης τυγχάνειν codd. Marcovich (following Casaubon) writes ⟨δεῖν⟩ after τυγχάνειν.

49. The Greek does not give a subject: καὶ μὴ μισήσειν, μᾶλλον δὲ μεταδιδάξειν ΒΡΦ. The confusion created by this lack of subject is reflected in F, which clarifies by amending to μισήσεις and μεταδιδάξεις. But this would be an odd idiom in doxographical Greek, and we know that F is our least reliable manuscript. We can supply the main verb ἔλεγον from the previous sentence. When the indirect speech clause has the same subject as the main clause, that subject is not expressed. Hence I have supplied the subject "they" for the verbs "hate" and "teach." Another possibility is to supply "the wise person" (τὸν σοφὸν) as the unexpressed subject. The very next sentence begins τόν τε σοφὸν. Thus if this sentence originally ended with τὸν σοφὸν, the words could have fallen out because of the duplication.

50. Precise interpretation of this sentence will depend on whether we take πάθει in τινι πάθει κατηναγκασμένον to mean "passion" (as I have translated it) or "experience" (in the technical Cyrenaic sense). Either way the doctrine recalls Socrates' insistence that no one errs voluntarily, as noted by Zeller 1868, 328–29; Gomperz 1905, 221; and Tsouna 2002, 482.

51. *Pace* Goulet-Cazé 1999, 195–96.

52. The phrase is often used of marching out in battle, but is also used by the Stoics in their discussions of suicide. On Theodorus' criticism of the Stoic doctrine of suicide see pp. 159–60.

53. See section 2.6.

54. Laronde 1987, 41–84, 356–58. Laronde also suspects that the Cyrenean conquest of the the Macae and the Nasemones took place between 330 and 325 BCE (ibid. 211). Cyrene probably fought with Carthage some time in the earlier fourth century as well, but precise dating is impossible.

55. 1993, 234.

56. Pp. 88–91.

57. Laks 1993, 34–36; Annas 1993, 234.

58. The Greek lacks an explicit subject: τόν τε φίλον μὴ διὰ τὰς χρείας μόνον ἀπο-δέχεσθαι ὧν ὑπολειπουσῶν μὴ ἐπιστρέφεσθαι ἀλλὰ καὶ παρὰ τὴν γεγονυῖαν εὔνοιαν, ἧς ἕνεκα καὶ πόνους ὑπομενεῖν. καίτοι τιθέμενον ἡδονὴν τέλος καὶ ἀχθό-μενον ἐπὶ τῷ στέρεσθαι αὐτῆς ὅμως ἑκουσίως ὑπομενεῖν διὰ τὴν πρὸς τὸν φίλον στοργήν. I have carried over the subject ὁ σοφός from earlier in the doxography for three reasons. First, this makes good sense in context. Second, the participle τιθέμενον indicates that we are dealing with a singular masculine subject. Third, it is plausible that the sentences about reasoning and habituation which intervene have been inserted into what was originally a continuous discussion of how the Annicerean sage handles friendship.

59. Aristotle goes on to add that this reciprocal good will must be recognized. At *EN* 9.5 Aristotle argues that good will is merely the starting point of friendship, and that it is inadequate to motivate action. But this is of questionable consistency with his invocation of good will in other places in *EN* 8–9, and looks like an at-tempt to draw sharper distinctions than exist in common usage.

60. Cf. Zeller 1868, 330; Annas 1993, 233–35.

61. See the examples given at LSJ s.v. στέργω def. I.1.

62. 1993, 234.

63. 1905, 225. The following is indebted to Gomperz 1905, 223–25, which is the lon-gest discussion of which I am aware concerning "social feelings" in Cyrenaicism.

64. This resembles what Mitsis 1988, 104–9 calls the "associationist" interpretation of the Epicurean doctrine of friendship, where a similar problem arises. Moreover, both Gomperz 1905, 228 and Mitsis draw inspiration from John Stuart Mill.

65. In fact the verb ἀχθόμαι is much broader than the English "be annoyed," com-prehending various forms of mental discomfort. The active ἀχθέω means to load or burden. For the middle ἀχθόμαι LSJ gives "mostly of mental oppression, *to be vexed, grieved.*"

66. Annas 1993, 235. This is a specific manifestation of the general problem with the Annicerean end I discussed in section 4.6, pp. 158–63.

Chapter 7. Hegesias's Pessimism

1. §11, trans. Johnson.

2. *BoT* §3.

3. "Those illuminated illusory pictures of the Sophoclean hero, briefly put, the Apollonian mask, are . . . necessary creations of a glimpse into the inner terror

of nature, bright spots, so to speak, to heal us from the horrifying night of the crippled gaze" (*BoT* §9).

4. "For who can fail to recognize the *optimistic* element in the heart of dialectic, which celebrates a jubilee with every conclusion and can breathe only in cool brightness and consciousness, that optimistic element which, once it has penetrated tragedy, must gradually overrun its Dionysian regions and necessarily drive them to self-destruction—right to their death leap into middle-class drama. Let people merely recall the consequences of the Socratic sayings 'Virtue is knowledge; sin arises only from ignorance; the virtuous person is the happy person': in these three basic forms of optimism lies the death of tragedy" (*BoT* §14).

5. Nussbaum 1986.

6. It is unclear on what basis Annas 1993, 233 claims that "Hegesias did cling to the orthodox insistence that our end is particular pleasures. . . ."

7. The argument continues, "First of all half the time, in which I'm asleep, is indifferent. Next, the first part, childhood, is painful. When the kid is hungry, his nurse puts him to bed. When he's thirsty, she bathes him. He wants to go to sleep, and she shakes his rattle. If he escapes the nurse, the slave attendant, the trainer, his teachers for writing, music, and painting receive him. His age increases: there is also the mathematician, the geometer, the horsebreaker. He gets up early; he has no leisure. He's an ephebe. He fears the ephebic magistrate, the trainer, the fighting instructor, the superintendent of the gymnasia. By all of these he's whipped, watched, and rough-handled. He's twenty years old, no longer an ephebe. Now he fears and watches the superintendent of gymnasia and the general. If it's necessary to do a night watch, these young men do the night watch; if it's necessary to stand guard and stay awake, these stand guard. Now he's a man in his prime. He serves as a soldier and ambassador for the polis, he participates in politics, he leads the troops, he equips a chorus, he presides at the games. He thinks the life he lived as a child was bliss. He's past his prime and coming to old age. Once again he endures being treated like a child and longs for his youth: 'To me youth is lovely, old age is heavier than Aetna.' So I don't see how anyone will have lived a happy life, if we must measure it by the abundance of pleasures."

8. Mannebach 1961, 109.

9. 1998, 554.

10. Ibid. 555. Matson's entire reconstruction of the argument leading to Hegesiac pessimism appears on this page. I have expanded Matson's argument here in order to strengthen it.

11. Ibid. 555.

12. Ibid. 555. "Whatever is rational should be done" appears to be Matson's paraphrase of the clause in D.L. 2.95 that I translate "they do whatever appears reasonable" (discussed at length in section 3.5).

13. Ibid. 553.

14. Ibid. 556.

15. 1998, 556. At 2006, 113–25 Matson argues that Rawls' "celebrated book *A Theory of Justice* is not about justice" at all (113). His critique of Rawls continues in 2006, 126–48.

16. 1998, 557.

17. Matson might respond that no one is born a sage, and that any agent's preenlightenment existence would be more painful than pleasant. Thus the hedonic

calculus for anyone's life as a whole would still be negative. But it is not clear that Hegesias would agree that every childhood and adolescence is more painful than pleasant, even in the absence of wisdom. Moreover, Hegesias is not interested in the choice one would make if one were given the option of either living or never being born. The Hegesiac agent does not consider suicide from behind a "veil of ignorance" somewhere outside of life itself. The choice of dying or continuing to live is embedded in a life that includes a past that can no longer be changed and a concrete set of possibilities for the future.

18. The evidence of Valerius Maximus (*SSR* 4f.5) is without independent value, since he is almost certainly wholly dependent on Cicero.

19. While Cicero gives Ἀποκαρτερῶν as the title, I assume that the full Greek title is ὁ Ἀποκαρτερῶν. Minor corruption in the Greek text of a Latin manuscript, which would have been copied by scribes without knowledge of Greek, is hardly surprising.

20. Compare the Stoic doctrine at Cic. *Fin.* 3.60–61 = LS 66G.

21. καὶ τῷ μὲν ἄφρονι τὸ ζῆν λυσιτελὲς εἶναι, τῷ δὲ φρονίμῳ ἀδιάφορον. Epiphanius reports that Hegesias believes "Living is advantageous for the fool, but dying is advantageous for the wise man" (*De fide* 9.29 = *SSR* 4f.2). But this is the sort of uncharitable distortion we expect from Epiphanius.

22. Compare the Stoic position at Plut. *Mor.* 1042a–b, 1064e.

23. One possibility is that our doxography is speaking loosely when it says it is "advantageous" for fools to live. The point may be that the fool cannot be trusted to determine whether, in his current circumstances, death is advantageous. Fools are liable to be motivated by irrelevant factors such as patriotism, honor, or unrequited love.

24. On the mythopoetic impulses behind the stories about the deaths of Heraclitus, Empedocles, and Democritus see Chitwood 2004.

25. See the fascinating exploration of the legend of Cleombrotus by White 1994, who suggests Callimachus may intend an allusion to Hegesias.

26. Also noted by Zeller 1868, 328; Gomperz 1905, 221.

27. 2006, 36.

28. E.g., *The Gay Science* §45: "Only someone who is continually suffering could invent such happiness—the happiness of an eye before which the sea of existence has grown still and which now cannot get enough of seeing the surface and this colourful, tender, quivering skin of the sea: never before has voluptuousness been so modest." For further references, along with a concise but sensitive analysis of Nietzsche's complex relationship with Epicurus, see Caygill 2006.

29. The meaning of this sentence may rather be, "rich people do not experience more pleasure than poor people," but I have kept in the English root "different" in order to reveal its continuity in the passage.

30. I adopt the translation of ἀδιάφορα καὶ ἀστάθμητα καὶ ἀνεπίκριτα from Chiesara's edition of Aristocles. The interpretation of this passage, like the position of the historical Pyrrho more broadly, is an object of unending controversy. I share the opinion of Long 2006, 95 that "Timon is not only our best guide [to Pyrrho's philosophy] but also a guide who largely forecloses any reliably independent access to his hero." However, I find the arguments of Bett 2003, 14–59 persuasive, if not decisive. Sedley 1983 and Warren 2002, 86–128, are also good on the motivational foundations of Pyrrhonean philosophy, although I am not

convinced by Warren's restriction of Pyrrho's skepticism to ethics. For more up-to-date bibliography see Bett 2010.

31. The indifference/impassivity complex was widespread in fourth-century BCE philosophy, with some Cynics, Megarics, and the Stoic Aristo adopting variations on the position that everything *except virtue and vice* is indifferent, and therefore expecting to achieve self-mastery. Brancacci 1982 argues that Pyrrho influenced Theodorus, as I discuss in the following chapter.

32. This theory is superficially similar to Plato's "repletion" theory of pleasure (e.g., *Grg.* 493d5–94a5, *Phlb.* 31d4–36c1). However, note that the terminology of our passage is very different, suggesting that Diogenes preserves Hegesias' own terms at this point.

33. Brancacci 1982, 71 notes the similarity of this theory and skeptic theories reported at D.L. 9.82, 87, which invoke the different perceptions created by "lack [or] fullness" (ἔνδειαν πλήρωσιν) or "because of strangeness or scarcity" (παρὰ τὸ . . . ξένον ἢ σπάνιον).

34. Reading ἥδιόν with manuscripts B, P, and F, where the first corrector to B and Φ have ἴδιον. The reading ἴδιον can be explained as a corruption of ἥδιόν at which B¹ and Φ independently arrived through itacism and because the meaning of the sentence with ἥδιόν is obscure. I have considered proposing that the correct reading is ἡδίω (fem. acc. sg.). I would then say that ω could just possibly be corrupted to ον, leading to the variation between ἥδιόν and ἴδιον in our primary witnesses. But this solution, unlikely in any script, is almost impossible in uncials. And the immediate ancestor of B was still in uncials (Knoepfler 1991, 132, 154). For my translation compare Laks 1993, 26–27 and Goulet-Cazé 1999.

35. Keeping Cyrenaic epistemology in mind, perhaps we had better take this to mean that pleasure is not reliably connected with *our experiences of* any particular sources. For example, pleasure is not reliably connected with the experiences of stickiness, viscosity, and color (that we collectively call "honey"); pain is not reliably connected with the experiences of light, heat, and warmth (that we collectively call "fire").

36. In Xenophon's Anabasis 4.8.20–21 the soldiers are reduced to vomiting and delirium by the honey of Trebizond.

37. "Septic drugs" were designed to promote the production of pus, which was considered good for healing. In his notes to book 9 of the 1999 Goulet-Cazé edition of Diogenes, Brunschwig notes that these drugs may have had anaesthetic properties.

38. See Morgan 1994, 97 and Bussanich 2006, 210. On Empedocles as a shaman, see Kingsley 1995. This is not to say that Socrates was a shaman, only that some of the symbolic vocabulary of shamanism was inherited by classical philosophers.

39. See Finley 1956, 125–64; Adkins 1960, 30–60; Redfield 1975, 99–127; Williams 1993; Cairns 1993, 48–146; Zanker 1994.

40. 2000 *passim*. Hobbs provides a useful thumbnail sketch of "the *thumos* as a coherent whole" at 30–31.

41. This is the song of Demodocus.

42. 1999, 48–49.

43. With the proviso that Sophocles' Ajax estimates his worth higher than it really is, which is one of the causes of his tragedy.

44. Regarding the textual issues in this quotation see chapter 6 n. 47–49.

45. Zeller 1868, 328–29; Gomperz 1905, 221; and Tsouna 2002, 482.

46. Compare *EN* 9.7, where Aristotle explains that benefactors love the recipients of their beneficence like craftsmen love their artifacts: both love the products of their own activity.

47. Prudential motives could also be adduced for this behavior. For example, in this way the sage might avoid the sort of escalation that would culminate in injuries which are *not* indifferent to him.

48. First edited by Gronewald 1985 (whose edition appears in *SSR*), who also provides a German translation, commentary, and historical interpretation. Further discussion by Barnes 1987 and Spinelli 1992, with Spinelli also re-editing part of the text.

49. This translation is based on the text by Gronewald 1985, taking into account also some of the conjectures of Spinelli 1992.

50. Each line fits approximately 15–20 letters.

51. Several words are legible in fragment a, which *SSR* prints immediately following column III, including "disturb," "persuasive," "release" (twice), "nothing good," and "bad." But it is not certain where in the dialogue this fragment belongs.

52. Gronewald 1985, 33–34, 46; cf. Barnes 1987, 365. Parts of Xenophon's *Memorabilia* and *Apology* also reflect this tradition.

53. 1987, 366.

54. 1985, 49–53.

55. Compare the perennial controversy regarding whether Socrates believes in the hedonistic positions he expounds in Plato's *Protagoras*.

56. These are *Callias, Axiochus, Aspasia, Alcibiades, Telauges,* and *Rhino* (Diog. Laert. 2.61 = *SSR* 6a.22). Fragments and testimonia are collected at *SSR* 6a.41–90.

57. Suda AI 346 = *SSR* 6a.25. The other "headless" dialogues are *Polyaenus, Draco, Eryxias, On Virtue, Erasistratus,* and *The Leather Cutters.* Nothing survives from these dialogues. Diogenes Laertes reports that according to Perseus, a Stoic of the third century BCE, they were actually written by the Eretrian philosopher Pasipho (regarding whom we know even less than regarding Aeschines; testimonia at *SSR* 2c).

58. The substantial fragments of Aeschines' *Aspasia* and *Alcibiades* are largely concerned with caring for oneself, through loving relationships, in order to become better. See Kahn 1994.

59. Note that mu for nu preceding mu or beta is common in papyri.

60. Here Socrates asks Callicles whether he agrees with the earlier conclusion of Polus and Socrates that whenever people act, what they "really want" is not what they choose to do, but that good for the sake of which they ultimately make that choice and take that action (467c5–68b8). He recapitulates this point here by saying, "the good is the end of all actions, and one should do everything else for its sake" (τέλος εἶναι ἁπασῶν τῶν ἀγαθῶν τὸ ἀγαθόν, καὶ ἐκείνου ἕνεκα δεῖν πάντα τἄλλα πράττεσθαι). Plato uses *telos* with the same sense at *Prt.* 354b7–c2, as Gronewald notes (1985, 43).

61. Cf. Spinelli 1992, 12. τέλος here may also mean "the ultimate term of goodness (or of badness)," a meaning which it also sometimes has in Cyrenaic sources.

62. Socrates and his interlocutors set out to discuss "the condition and disposition of the soul . . . that can make life happy for all people" (*Phlb.* 11d4–6). The closest he comes to introducing the term τέλος in our sense is at 22b4–6, where he and Protarchus agree that neither pleasure nor cognition is "sufficient and complete

(ἱκανὸς καὶ τελεὸς) and choiceworthy for all plants and animals, who could always in this way live out their lives."

63. See Lear's description of what Aristotle does here as an "inaugural instantiation" of the concept of a single unifying principle for life (2002, 6–25). Cf. Antoniadis 1916, 30 n. 1, 32–40, Mannebach 1961, 110–11, Giannantoni 1983–85, vol. 3, 167–68, Annas 1993, 31–42.

64. To this period we can almost certainly date some of the following: *Alcibiades* I and II, *Hipparchus*, *Minos*, *Epinomis*, *Lovers*, and *Theages*.

65. See section 3.6.

66. 1992.

67. The lacuna here makes precise interpretation difficult, but Gronewald 1985, 45 and Spinelli 1992, 10–11, 14 n. 22 agree on the gist of its meaning. See the following note.

68. "[τί λέγεις;] ἢ ἐπιλυπότερος;" "οὐ γὰρ δή, μ[ὰ τὸν Δ]ία." "οὔτ' ἄρα τ[άδ' ἐκεῖ]να [ἢ]ττον ἡδ[έα ὄντα κα]ταλείπειν λυπ[οῖ]τ' ἂν ὁ νοῦν ἔχω[ν] εἰ μέλλοι ἀποθ[νήισ]κειν.

69. Suggested by the anecdote about Ptolemy prohibiting him from teaching.

70. 2000, 59–74.

71. In some cases there were legal guidelines for the penalties. See Todd 1993, 133–35; Laani 2006, 39–40.

72. According to both Plato and Xenophon, Socrates claims that a daemonic sign or voice sometimes intervenes in his decisions. Of course, this was among the reasons why he was charged with impiety. See especially Pl. *Ap.* 31c4–36, Xen. *Mem.* 1.1.4–5.

73. In fact it is *just* possible that our papyrus invokes old age as one of the factors in Socrates' pessimism about a pleasant life. The phrase ἐπὶ γήρως would fit neatly into the lacuna in col. II.13, although the more common ἐν τῶι γήραι would not. It could then be translated, "So up until now we haven't in any part of our discussion been able to find that the life of a sensible person [during old age] is more pleasant than it is distressing?"

74. Chapter 6 n. 45.

75. The closest Greek philosophy comes to this may be in the sophistry of Hippias of Elis, who reportedly made all his own clothes (Pl. *Hp. Ma.* 368b). Nothing in our evidence for Hegesias hints at any such practical polymathy.

76. 2000, 210.

77. All remaining translations of the *Iliad* in this chapter are from Lattimore. Hobbs 2000, 211 also cites these famous lines.

78. Nussbaum makes a closely related point with a different passage from Pindar: some of the beauty and value of human life is premised on its vulnerability (1986, 1–2).

79. The parallelism, which extends to many details of the two scenes, is frequently noted by critics.

80. Knox has spoken eloquently about the isolation of Sophoclean protagonists: "To those who face him, friends and enemies alike, the hero seems unreasonable almost to the point of madness, suicidally bold, impervious to argument, intransigent, angry; an impossible person whom only time can cure. But to the hero himself the opinion of others is irrelevant. His loyalty to his conception of himself, and the necessity to perform the action that conception imposes, prevail over all other considerations" (1964, 28).

81. As Hobbs 2000, esp. 210–61, and Nussbaum 1986, 87–233 both argue with respect to Plato, although both rightly note that Plato's works implicitly recognize the cost of this elimination of tragedy.
82. Plato says nothing about Xanthippe's fate after Socrates' death.

Chapter 8. Theodorus's Innovations

1. Regarding both practical wisdom and justice see sections 4.2 and 4.4a–d.
2. Gomperz 1905, 244; Winiarczyk 1981, 76–78; Long 1999, 636. No Cynics are named among Theodorus' teachers, whom I discuss in section 2.6. His interactions with the Cynics Hipparchia and Metrocles are combative (D.L. 2.102, 5.97–8). (The anecdote about Theodorus and Metrocles is more often but less plausibly attributed to Aristippus and Diogenes.)
3. For these senses of "end" see pp. 53–54; and pp. 85–86.
4. For the tripartition, see LS 58A. The Stoics most often use the word μέσα to distinguish what they call "intermediate obligations" from "righteous actions." The former are technically indifferent, although if performed with the right intention and understanding they become righteous actions and therefore good (LS 59B, D, F–I). For μεταξύ see LS 59G, 59l, and SVF 3.115, 118, 181.
5. E.g., Zeller 1868, 325–6; von Fritz 1934, 1829; Winiarczyk 1981, 80–1.
6. See section 6.5–6.
7. 1981, 73, 80–1, 83.
8. Winiarczyk 1981, 77–78; Zeller 1868, 325–26; von Fritz 1934, 1827–30. Von Fritz and Winiarczyk argue that Theodorus' motivation is to compete more effectively with Epicurus' promise of a more stable and well-rounded joy than the Cyrenaics can offer. This is possible but unlikely: notwithstanding their superficial similarity at the level of hedonism, the sober and pragmatic quietist Epicurus is an unlikely competitor for the flamboyant and provocatively public Theodorus. As an existential option Theodorean philosophy is closer to Cynicism and possibly some forms of Megaric/Dialectic philosophy.
9. On Theodorus' self-sufficiency, see section 6.5.
10. Section 7.3.
11. Brancacci 1982, 57–72.
12. Clearly this makes him a Pyrrhonist like Pyrrho, not a (neo)Pyrrhonist like Sextus Empiricus. Regarding the debates about Pyrrho's philosophy, see chapter 7 n. 30.
13. Ibid. 63, 66–67.
14. Ibid. 63, 66.
15. Ibid. 70.
16. Ibid. 69.
17. Ibid. 63.
18. Ibid. 68.
19. Ibid. 63.
20. Ibid. 63.
21. In fact Brancacci prints τὴν ὑπόληψιν φυλάττοντες, but I am not sure on what authority. Pohlenz 1952 does not list any such alternate reading in his apparatus criticus.
22. Ibid. 66.

23. See the following section.
24. Ibid. 70.
25. Ibid. 69.
26. A scholarch of the Old Academy, not to be confused with the Cynic Crates.
27. Kindstrand 1976, 164 takes this as a sarcastic question: Surely putting on Cynic clothes was enough to give him a Cynic character? This may be correct, as Diogenes' life of Bion is notably hostile.
28. See Kindstrand 1976, 67–70.
29. Strabo actually names the Peripatetic Aristo of Ceos, not the Stoic Aristo of Chios, as the emulator of Bion. However, Kindstrand 1976, 79–82 persuasively argues that here, as often, the two Aristos have been mixed up.
30. See section 2.8.
31. The evidence is so fragmentary, indeed, that in order even to produce this generalization one must combine the testimony for Euclid, Stilpo, and the Megarics as a group. Moreover, one must assume that the Dialectics espouse more or less the same ethical positions as the Megarics (assuming these really were separate schools: see Sedley 1977, Döring 1989). One may then note that both to the Megarics and to their notional founder Euclid is ascribed the position that the good is unitary, and the virtues (practical wisdom is the only one named) are among its aspects (D.L. 2.106, 7.161, Cic. Luc. 129 = SSR 2a.30–32). A rather imprecise source tells us that according to the Megarics, "freedom from disturbance" (ἀοχλησία) is the "primary appropriate thing" (πρῶτον οἰκεῖον, Al. Aphr. De An. p. 150 = SSR 2o.34). Finally, Stilpo's commitment to impassivity is well attested (Teles fr. 7, Sen. Ep. 9.1–3 = SSR 2o.32–3).
32. This criticism seems to go back to Chrysippus, who successfully defended Zeno's positions against the challenges of Aristo and his followers. For a thorough discussion of Aristo's position see Ioppolo 1980, esp. 142–243; for a rather uncharitable analysis see Striker 1991, 14–24; for more sympathetic interpretations, Boys-Stones 1996, Porter 1996.
33. Ioppolo 1980, 125.
34. There are obviously limits to the explanatory power of this analogy. For example, linguistic convention determines which sounds express which meanings, but what determines which actions express justice? Such puzzles, fortunately, are beyond the scope of my investigation.
35. Boys-Stones 1996, 87–94.
36. Boys-Stones 1996 suggests that Plut. Mor. 1045b represents the same Aristonean position. There Chrysippus attacks "some philosophers" who recognize an "adventitious motion in the ruling part" of the mind, which "becomes apparent above all in the case of indistinguishables." This motion frees these philosophers from external determination. Boys-Stones argues that the determination in question is by false beliefs, and the "adventitious motion" in the face of "indistinguishables" is what "occurs" to the sage in Cicero's testimony.
37. The attack on conventional values is widespread in the fifth and fourth centuries BCE, as Winiarczyk 1981, 75–76 rightly notes. In particular it should be observed that the approval of theft, sacrilege, disregard of marriage conventions, and cosmopolitanism are all attributed to Diogenes of Sinope at D.L. 6.72–73. All of these positions may have appeared in Diogenes' Republic, which Theodorus could well have read.

38. Ioppolo 1980, 142–46.
39. Winiarczyk 1981, 81–82; Long 1996, 637 n. 43.
40. We know the Stoic Sphaerus was in the court of Ptolemy, while the Stoics Persaeus and Philonides were in the court of Antigonus with Bion of Borysthenes. Others may have been elsewhere.
41. See the succinct and authoritative presentation of the evidence on this doctrine by Griffin 1986, 70–75.
42. Compare Plutarch's spirited attack on the same Stoic position (*Mor.* 1063c–65a).
43. Discussed on pp. 113–15.
44. See D.L. 7.130 and the numerous other texts collected at *SVF* 3.757–68.
45. Of course, orthodox Stoics recognize exceptions to these generalities "according to circumstance." But Theodorus, like Aristo, seems critical of every general norm.
46. E.g., Phil. *Quod omn. bon. lib.* 127, Plut. *Mor.* 467b = *SSR* 4h.9–10.
47. See Winiarczyk 1981, 84–85, with references to earlier literature.
48. This is not to say that Epicurus really *was* influenced by Theodorus, which is likely to be a doxographical fabrication. See Winiarczyk 1981, 85.
49. This strongly resembles a coda added to one version of the Lysimachus anecdote (discussed in the following section): "The steward of Lysimachus, Mithres, was there and said, 'It seems it's not only gods but also kings of which you have no knowledge.' 'How do I have no knowledge,' he said, 'when I believe that you're hateful to the gods?'" (D.L. 2.102).
50. Plut. *Mor.* 1075a, Aët. 1.7.1, [Gal.] *Hist. Phil.* 35, Cic. *ND* 1.2, 1.63, 1.117 = *SSR* 4h.16–19. The only possible exception, Clem. Al. *Protrept.* 2.24.2 = *SSR* 4h.24, obviously has an ax to grind.
51. See section 2.8.
52. Ibid.
53. Sedley 2002, 41–83; Dillon 2003, 159–77.
54. See Winiarczyk 1981, 77 n. 60 and the note by Goulet-Cazé in her edition of D.L.
55. Compare Diogenes the Cynic, who "recognized no convention of marriage, but said that people should have sex when they persuade one another" (D.L. 6.72).
56. See section 6.3.
57. Reading κάλλος for καλὸς in the manuscripts, a change which M. Patillon has also suggested (as noted in the edition of Goulet-Cazé et al.).
58. Reading χρήσιμον to agree with κάλλος rather than χρήσιμος with the manuscripts.
59. See especially Winkler 1990, with some criticism by Davidson 1997.
60. See especially the speech of Diotima in the *Symposium* and the palinode of the *Phaedrus*.
61. See D.L. 4.19–22 and Phld. *Academica* 13.10–11, 14.37–45, 15.31–46 with Tarrant 2005, 141–45.
62. See Fiasse 1999; Nussbaum 2002, 76–86.
63. See especially D.L. 2.137 with the sexual innuendo of Crates at D.L. 6.91.
64. See my earlier discussions of the heroism of Aristippus (pp. 111–13) and especially Hegesias (pp. 235–41).
65. On Lysimachus see Lund 1992, who assesses the sort of anecdote involved here at 10–12.
66. The *cantharis* beetle or "Spanish fly" is highly caustic when ground up, and so was often used in poisons.

67. Pp. 62–63.
68. Socrates adds that they owe something to the polis they represent, but this is not relevant to Theodorus.
69. Here Theodorus's condemnation is clearly conflated with that of Socrates, who was accused of denying the civic gods, introducing new divinities, and corrupting the youth (Pl. *Apol.* 24b8–c1, Xen. *Mem.* 1.1.1).
70. Halliwell 2008, 19–38 and *passim*.

Chapter 9. The "New Cyrenaicism" of Walter Pater

1. Aristippus also plays some role in the *Epistles* of Horace (see Préaux 1977, Gigante 1993, and Traina 1991 and 1994), in the spurious Socratic epistles (see Lampe forthcoming B), and in the multi-volume epistolary novel of Christoph Wieland, *Aristipp und einige seiner Zeitgenossen* (published 1800–1802). More recently, Michel Onfray has repeatedly invoked them as predecessors for his radical philosophy (see chapter 10).
2. Later to be renamed *The Renaissance: Studies in Art and Poetry*.
3. 1987, 139.
4. Pater's Marius will later detect "the taint of a graceless 'antinomianism'" in his own youthful philosophy, which resembles that of the Conclusion (*ME* II.6).
5. For broader contexts for these necessarily brief and selective remarks see Jenkyns 1980, Dellamora 1990, Dowling 1994, Prettejohn 2007, and Evangelista 2009.
6. For example, S. Colvin at Seiler 1980, 54; M. W. Oliphant at Seiler 1980, 90–91; and even the anonymous reviewer who accuses Pater of a "new Cyrenaicism" (Seiler 1980, 74–77; discussed further below). John Morley attempts to meliorate what he calls Pater's "Hedonism" at Seiler 1980, 67–70.
7. Seiler 1980, 54.
8. Inman 1984, 110. The relevant excerpt from Mackarness's lecture is reprinted by Seiler 1980, 95–96.
9. For a concise summary, with references to sources and scholarship, see Evans 1970, xx–xxii.
10. Monsman 1967, 65; Inman 1998, 15.
11. Here a passage from "Diaphaneitè [*sic*]" (*MS* 255), slightly reworked in "Winckelmann" (*R* 194), is noteworthy. Of Winckelmann's writings Pater says, "It is as if the mind of one, lover and philosopher at once in some phase of pre-existence—φιλοσόφησας πότε μετ᾽ ἔρωτος—fallen into a new cycle, were beginning its intellectual career again, yet with a certain power anticipating its results." The Greek phrase here is an expurgated version of the philosophical lover of the *Phaedrus*, whom Plato describes as παιδεραστήσαντος μετὰ φιλοσοφίας, "who has loved *a boy* philosophically" (249a1–2). On Pater's homoeroticism, see Dellamora 1990, 58–68, 102–116, 167–92; Evangelista 2009, 23–54. On "Socratic eros" at Victorian Oxford, see Dowling 1994, 67–103.
12. For the details of this affair see Inman 1998.
13. Seiler 1980, 73–78.
14. He uses the phrase twice at Seiler 1980, 75. His source—and that of Pater—may have been Zeller 1868, 303, where the texts of both Athenaeus and Aelian are given in the original Greek. See Shuter 1997, 132 n. 27.

15. Seiler 1980, 76.
16. Ibid. 77.
17. On Pater's absorption and transformation of "Victorian masculine poetics and technologies of the male self," see Sussman 1995, 173–202 (quotation from 173).
18. E.g., Heraclitus, *Homeric Problems,* 70.
19. On Pater's "aesthetic historicism," see especially Williams 1989, from whom I borrow the term "transfiguration."
20. See especially the reviews of E. Pattison and M. Oliphant (Seiler 1980, 71–73, 85–91).
21. See especially Shuter 1997, 39–60 on Pater's evolving religious views.
22. The unfinished *Gaston de Latour* was intended to be the second part.
23. On Marcus Aurelius and Stoicism in Pater and Victorian literature generally, see Behlman 2004 and forthcoming. Behlman 2004, 141–46 rightly notes that what Pater calls "Epicureanism" loosely combines Cyrenaicism with aspects of Apuleius's literary "euphuism," Heraclitean metaphysics, and incubatory "Aesculapian" medicine at various points in *Marius*. Platonism also overlaps with Stoicism in many parts of the novel. However, it retains distinctive elements in Marius's interview with Apuleius (*ME* II.87–91), which strongly recalls Pater's own interpretation of Platonic idealism (*PP* 134–5, 168–72). On Pater's Platonism, see Varty 1994.
24. To the best of my knowledge, no one has remarked that *On Obligations* is the most likely inspiration for the aestheticized vision of Stoicism Fronto gives in chapter 25. This is suggested not only by the pervasively aesthetic language of Cicero's text, but also by the fact that *On Obligations* 1.93–151 is the primary source for the Panaetian doctrine of τὸ πρέπον mentioned by Fronto at *ME* II.10.
25. See especially Monsman 1967, 65–97; Miller 1976; Iser 1987, 129–52; and Williams 1989, 169–234; all of whom have influenced the analysis which follows.
26. Seiler 1980, 75.
27. For an extended analysis of this passage, see section 4.3.
28. "Idealism" is Pater's own recurrent term, although its meaning changes throughout the novel. On Pater's engagement with English empiricism, see Williams 1989, 18–25 and (less persuasively or clearly) Loesberg 1991, esp. 16–27.
29. Marius himself never speaks in the novel, which is entirely free from dialogue, though he often focalizes the narration. Conspicuously anachronistic comments reveal that the narrator possesses Pater's own transhistorical perspective. On this narratological strategy, see Williams 1989, 184–93.
30. More particularly, they read the Cupid and Psyche story within the *Golden Ass,* which provides the allegorical key for a Christian reading of *Marius* as the search for salvific love. Flavian's poem is the anonymous *Pervigilium Veneris,* also about love. See Monsman 1967.
31. The connection between Marius's moral intuitions (which encompass religiosity, intellectual integrity, and everything that falls under the notion of "conscience") and the deaths of his father and mother is suggestively explored by Miller 1976, 98–101.
32. He also calls him the "sensible exponent" of this philosophy (ibid.), as Cornelius will later be the sensible exponent of Christianity.
33. The reason for this belief is undoubtedly that he identifies "the subtler philosophers" of Plato's *Theaetetus* with Aristippus and his followers. On the history of this debate, see appendix 1.8.

34. There is no evidence that Aristippus or any other Cyrenaic held any Heraclitean beliefs about the instability and indeterminacy of reality. For a spirited attempt to argue otherwise, see Zilioli 2013. For a rebuttal, see Lampe forthcoming A.

35. Pater's argument from "peculiarities in the instruments of cognition" (*ME* I.138) can easily come from either Plutarch *Mor.* 1120b–21c or Sextus *PH* 1.215, *M* 7.190–200 (= *SSR* 4a.211–13), and the argument against "common experience" and the "fixity of language" unambiguously reflects Sextus *M* 7.195–96. Pater may have read these and other passages, all quoted in Greek, in the footnotes to Zeller 1868, 287–323.

36. Pater goes on to compare the Parmenidean strain in Plato with "modern metaphysicians" (*PP* 32).

37. A third series of programmatic statements about philosophy (beside those in *R* and *ME*), which I cannot analyze here, occurs in *Plato and Platonism*. For example: "To realise unity in variety, to discover *cosmos*—an order that shall satisfy one's reasonable soul—below and within apparent chaos: is from first to last the continuous purpose of what we call philosophy" (52; cf. 35–36). Roberts 2008, whose intelligent and critical analysis of Pater's philosophical method is a refreshing counterweight to the laudatory stance elsewhere in the scholarship, seems to miss this evolution in Pater's perspective. Moreover, though he is right to object that Pater's criterion of truth is under-argued (and vulnerable to objections from twentieth century philosophies of truth), he himself fails to give adequate emphasis to the erotic and transformative dimensions of Pater's philosophy.

38. In fact this passage looks like an amalgamated paraphrase of the complementary reports of Athenaeus and Aelian grouped by Giannantoni at *SSR* 4a.174.

39. See Williams 1989, 26–37.

40. See especially sections 4.3, 4.5.

41. Here the narrator is quoting from Pascal's comment on Montaigne, which Levey (in a note to his edition of *Marius*) traces to Pascal's "Interview with M. de Saci concerning Epictetus and Montaigne."

42. D.L. 2.76, Clem. Al. *Paed.* 2.8.64.1, 2.8.68.4–69.1, Sen. *Ben.* 7.25.1 = *SSR* 4a.63–66.

43. See section 6.3.

44. Wine, fish, and courtesans (along with boys) constitute the triad of "consuming passions" of ancient Greece analyzed by Davidson 1997. On Aristippus's enjoyment of fish see Athen. 544c–d, D.L. 2.75, Plut. *Mor.* 750d–e = *SSR* 4a.36, 69, 93.

45. See section 4.2.

46. Both of these are discussed in section 4.4c.

47. Compare Plato's discussion of sympotic drinking in *Laws* book 1.

48. The other two occurrences are in scholia to the *Iliad* and in a letter by Michael Gabras (twelfth/thirteenth century CE).

49. Giannantoni 1990, vol. 4, 175–76.

50. Of course, the Athenian dramatic festivals were much more than series of plays. On their civic and religious contexts, see Winkler and Zeitlin 1992.

51. The Greek has ἀλεκτορὶς. . . βοῶσα, where ἀλεκτορὶς must be a female chicken. βοῶσα should indicate a louder noise than "clucking" or "cackling," and hens do sometimes crow in the absence of roosters.

52. I.e., pulmonary tuberculosis.

53. Compare Gorgias' observation that "tragedy is deceit in which the one who deceives is juster than the one who does not deceive, and the one who is deceived is wiser than the one who is not deceived" (DK B23 = Plut. *Mor.* 348c).

54. See Pater's discussion of Sparta, juxtaposed with his discussion of Plato's *Republic*, at *PP* 197–266 (brought under the heading of μουσική at *PP* 200).

55. Primarily it is animals, but the narrator relates that the gladiatorial contests also, despite the "buttons" Aurelius mandates for their swords, have "the efficacy of a human sacrifice" (*ME* I.240).

56. This chapter is entitled "Stoicism at Court," but Fronto does not appear to be a dogmatic Stoic either here or in his preserved letters to Marcus Aurelius.

57. These are the examples Marius himself gives. He makes the same point slightly later by saying he "admits . . . no moral world at all" (*ME* II.8).

58. See section 4.4a.

59. This "avowedly" is the strongest hint that Pater is reading our passage. Compare *ME* II.24: "[Aristippus] professed above all things an economy of the moments of life." The words "economy" and "economists" appear with reference to Marius's Cyrenaicism at least five times in *Marius*, at II.15, 22, 24, 28, and 219.

60. More precisely: from within Cyrenaic axiology this would amount to a different claim, that focusing on pleasures and pains actually obstructs their effective pursuit. Marius's point is more complex: in order to challenge the "economy" of Cyrenaic ethics, he first challenges their interpretation of what he calls "the Ideal Now" (see below).

61. Though it has plenty of erotic tension (e.g., with Flavian, Cornelius, and Cecilia), *Marius* is completely free from explicit references to the pleasures of sex or eating.

62. Compare Pater's thoughts on Goethe, Greece, and the goal of modern intellectual culture at *R* 228–29.

63. For the Epicureans, see esp. Warren 2004.

64. See my speculative reconstruction in section 4.4b.

65. These issues are discussed in all major analyses of the novel. I have found those of Monsman 1967, 66–97 and Miller 1976, 98–101 especially helpful.

66. The quotation, as Levey notes in his edition, is from Virgil's praise of Lucretius at *Georgics* 2.491–92: "inexorabile fatum / subiecit pedibus strepitumque Acherontis avari."

67. The narrator does not actually mention the demiurge of Plato's *Timaeus*, but rather refers elliptically to "the 'World of Ideas,' existent only because, and in so far as, they are known, as Plato conceived" (II.69). This looks like a Neoplatonic interpretation of the relation between the demiurge and the Ideas.

68. The narrator explains this by saying that "the will itself" is "an organ of knowledge, of vision" (II.65). In other words, Marius's desire to believe—indeed, his *need* to believe (II.64)—is one form of perception.

69. Whether this amounts to a conversion or merely another non-committal stage in his aesthetic journey is a vexed question. Contrast Monsman 1967, 85–97 with Iser 1987, 139–52.

70. Pater apparently had the much more well-documented Epicurean arguments against the fear of death at least as much in mind as this passing assertion in the Cyrenaic doxography, as his quotation of Lucretius (see n. 66 above) suggests.

Chapter 10. Conclusion: The Birth of Hedonism

1. Of course, the comparison would still be philosophically complex. To the best of my knowledge, it has never been undertaken in any detail. See appendix 2.4 for Annicerean arguments against Epicurus. The best discussion of Epicurus's reaction to the Cyrenaics is in Sedley 2013, which I had the good fortune to hear just as I was finalizing this book for publication.

2. 2004, 13.

3. Ibid.

4. 2004, 14–15. But note that in his newest book Feldman employs these results to criticize ("in a respectful, collegial way"; 2010, 272) research on "happiness" by empirical psychologists (2010, 231–67).

5. 2004, 203.

6. "As a result, the Stoic sage might be living the Good Life, and then again he might not. It depends upon whether he enjoys his style of life. . . . Similarly for the Aristotelian scholar, deeply engaged in philosophical wisdom. If he takes substantial intrinsic attitudinal pleasure in the fact that he is engaging in this sort of thing, then his life is going well for him" (2004, 203–34).

7. 2004, 15.

8. See n. 4 above.

9. The title is an homage to Julien Offray de la Mettrie, who wrote a treatise of the same title in 1751. At the same time, Onfray probably intends the modern connotations of *jouir* (which now means "come" in the sexual sense) to be available.

10. 1991, 15. He discusses the experience in detail at 15–23.

11. Ibid., 16.

12. Ibid., 22.

13. Ibid., 19.

14. Ibid., 21.

15. 2002, 19.

16. Onfray frequently attacks Hegel and especially Kant. For this triumvirate of repressive forces, see 2006, 26: "The ocean we must cross? Idealist philosophy in its triple form, Platonic, Christian, and German."

17. 1991, 23.

18. 1991, 215. Compare Onfray's suggestion that philosophies arise through bodily experience: "Tension occupies the flesh for a long time. The body is a strange place where influxes and intuitions, energies and forces circulate. Sometimes the resolution of conflicts and mysteries, the solutions for deflecting shadows and confusions appear in a moment of exceptional density, which opens a gap in existence and inaugurates a perspective rich in possibilities. So the body of a philosopher presents itself as a crucible where existential experiences are developed, and later called to take form in logical and rigorous structures" (ibid., 31–32). Onfray's *Contre-histoire de la philosophie*, in which Aristippus and the Cyrenaics feature (2006, 109–33), is intended as "a history of philosophy that isn't established *against* the body, despite it or without it, but *with* it. . . . I contend that the question, *What can the body do?* hasn't yet been truly explored" (2006, 25).

19. 1991, 306. Cf. 238.

20. 2002, 30–33; 2006, 117–20.

21. Onfray's "counter-history" obviously takes its starting point from Nietzsche's genealogy of morals, as his will to power is explicitly Nietzschean. This is not to deny that he can be critical of Nietzsche (see 1991, 74–81). The language of "repression," "neurosis," and "sublimation" is Freudian. Herbert Marcuse's *Eros and Civilization: A Philosophical Inquiry into Freud* and *One-Dimensional Man* are among the last works Onfray discusses in *L'Art de jouir* (1991, 297–300). Although he does not discuss Jacques Lacan there, he alludes to the famous phrase from Lacan's *The Ethics of Psychoanalysis*—"don't give way on your desire"—in his discussion of Sade (1991, 285). The most recent volume of Onfray's *Contre-histoire de la philosophie*, which I have not had a chance to see, appears to be devoted to the psychoanalysts Otto Gross, Wilhelm Reich, and Erich Fromm (2013).
22. Contra Onfray 1991, 238; 2002, 21.
23. 1998, 554; discussed in section 7.3.

Appendix 1. The Sources

1. The most recent appears to be John of Salisbury (= *SSR* 4a.104), who died ca. 1180 CE.
2. See Giannantoni's overview of scholarship on this topic, 1958, 87–95.
3. Arete was Aristippus's daughter, not his sister.
4. *Met.* 1024b32–34 =*SSR* 5a.152, *Top.* 104b20–21 = *SSR* 5a.153, *Met.* 1043b23–28 = *SSR* 5a.150, *Pol.* 1284a15–17 = *SSR* 5a.68, *Rhet.* 1407a10–11 = *SSR* 5a.50.
5. In fact Aristotle ascribes this passage to "the dog" (ὁ κύων).
6. For an excellent introduction to his biography and sources see *DPhA* C 123.
7. *Luc.* 131, 139, *Fin.* 1.23–6, 1.39, 2.18–20, 2.35, 2.39–41, 2.114, 5.20 = *SSR* 4a.178–87.
8. The key sources for the *Carneadea divisio* are Cic. *Fin.* 5.16–21, *Tusc.* 5.83–85, *Luc.* 130–32.
9. On Clement and his works see the summary in *DPhA* C 154 with Osborn 2005.
10. See the summary of the controversy by Itter 2009, 7–15.
11. As Stephen White has suggested to me.
12. A verb is missing from the text, but I follow Giannantoni in reading ἴσμεν.
13. *DPhA* III, 678–79.
14. 1961, 101–104. Cf. Schwartz 1903, 753–58.
15. E.g., *SSR* 4a.20, 31, 37, 51, 160, and parts of 4a.1.
16. See also *SSR* 4a.19, 52, 79 and parts of 4a.1.
17. *DPhA* III, 679–80.
18. Ibid. 680.
19. 1991, 13–154, summarized by Decleva Caizzi 1994 and Dorandi 1999b. Decleva Caizzi's review is cautiously positive. Dorandi, in his review of Marcovich 1999, is more emphatic in his praise of Knoepfler: "il libro di Knoepfler resta il punto di partenza imprescindibile per ogni ricerca ulteriore" (2002, 334). Barnes also compares Knoepfler favorably to Marcovich (2002, 9). Dorandi 2013 appeared too late for me to draw on its insights for this book.
20. See Knoepfler 1991, 111–38, with exhaustive references to earlier responses to Long at p. 111 n. 2. More recently, compare the casual disparagement of Long's edition by Dorandi and Barnes (2000, 331; 2002, 11).

21. Dorandi 2002, Barnes 2002.
22. Marcovich claims that he records these readings *exhaustively* (1999, xvii), but Barnes objects that Marcovich has not recorded anywhere near all the variants of either F or P for the section Barnes has inspected (2002, 9).
23. Mejer 1978, 7–29; Goulet 2001.
24. For *Successions* and their relation to biography, see Kienle 1961, 79–96. For relations among these genres and modes of writing, see Mejer 1978, 60–95 and 2006. Giusta's argument that all ethical doxography derives from a *Vetusta Placita* by Arius Didymus (as physical doxography from Theophrastus) has not been well received, but his remarks on the relations among the Cyrenaic testimony of Cicero, Clement, Eusebius, and Diogenes merit consideration (1964, 252–65, 414–19).
25. See Goulet's cautionary note regarding the feasibility of separating primary sources from later additions by identifying stylistic "interruptions" (2001, 85–87).
26. 1994, 387–91. Cf. Mann 1996, 105–12; Mansfeld 1994, 179–91.
27. 1986, 231–32.
28. Goldhill 2009 and see the sections on *khreiai* in the progymnastic exercises assembled and translated in Kennedy 2003.
29. Aelius Theon, *Exercises* 101 (ed. and trans. Kennedy).
30. Hermogenes of Tarsus, *Preliminary Exercises* 7–8; Aphthonius *Preliminary Exercises* 23–25 (both ed. and trans. Kennedy).
31. Mannebach 1961, 105–106; Kindstrand 1996, 234–35. The *Gnomologium Vaticanum* can be consulted in full in the edition by Sternbach 1963.
32. For ease of navigation I have placed the SSR numbers in bold. Many but not all of the following are listed in the upper band of the app. crit. of *SSR*. See also the further anecdotes Giannantoni calls into question at vol. 4, 174–77. An anecdote that features the same conclusion as SSR **4a.5**, which concerns the high (but merited) price of Aristippus's tutelage, is also attributed to Isocrates ([Plut.] *Mor.* 838a, noted by *SSR* ad loc.). SSR **4a.42**, in which Aristippus spits on an uppity slave, is also ascribed to Diogenes of Sinope (D.L. 6.32, noted by Humbert 1967, 257, *SSR* ad loc., and Marcovich 1999 ad loc.). SSR **4a.50** regards a shipwreck, after which Aristippus is reassured by geometrical signs in the sand that he is among civilized folk. On returning to Cyrene, he advises people to take on a journey only what can swim away with them. The first part of this probably belongs originally to Aristippus precisely because he is the *lectio difficilior* (he was not interested in mathematics), although Cicero is tempted to ascribe it to Plato (ibid.). The second part seems to be tacked on, and is also ascribed to Antisthenes (D.L. 6.6). Humbert claims that SSR **4a.88**, in which Aristippus denies responsibility for a courtesan's pregnancy, is also attributed to Diogenes of Sinope (1967, 257–58). But I have not been able to follow his references. (The Aristippean anecdote, for which he gives D.L. 2.75, occurs at 2.81. For Diogenes of Sinope he gives 5.81, but neither at 5.81–90 nor at 6.81–90 have I found the anecdote in question.) Witticisms very similar to those at SSR **4a.106**, which explain why philosophers frequent the powerful rather than vice versa, are also ascribed to Simonides, Socrates, Antisthenes, and others (e.g., at *Gnom. Vat.* 6, Arist. *Rhet.* 1391a8–12, as noted by Mannebach 1961, 69; Sternbach 1963, 7; and others). The second half of SSR **4a.107**, which compares those whose education does not include a thorough course in philosophy to Penelope's suitors, is also attributed to Aristo of

Chios. (Diogenes himself notes this; Mann adds that the abbreviation "Ar" could lead to this confusion [1996, 112].) Opinions very similar to that Aristippus gives about prayer at SSR **4a.132** are ascribed to Socrates and especially to Diogenes of Sinope (Mannebach 1961, 99; cf. Kindstrand 1976, 231–32, cited by SSR ad loc.) SSR **4a.133** is clearly lifted from the spurious Socratic letter from "Simon the Cobbler" to Aristippus, in which it is the last sentence (SSR III A 16). Either Arsenius or his source has mistakenly ascribed it to the addressee rather than the author. SSR **4a.137–39** are misogynistic witticisms attributed to a range of other figures (references given by Mannebach 1961, 72).

33. For example, SSR **4a.131**, in which Aristippus responds to a slur regarding his exile from Cyrene, is clearly copied from a famous family of anecdotes regarding Theodorus's well-attested exile (SSR 4h.9, 13.45–7, as SSR notes ad loc.). In SSR **4a.44–45, 47–48** Aristippus and Diogenes of Sinope exchange words about the relative merits of washing vegetables (the humble life) and cultivating kings (the luxurious life). SSR **4a.46**, presumably attempting to restore historical plausibility, replaces Diogenes with Antisthenes. (It is also possible that Antisthenes originally featured in the anecdote, but was replaced by the more famous Diogenes.) SSR **4a.13.52–56**, which may well be the original version, transfers the incident to Theodorus and the Cynic Metrocles.

34. Williams 1987, xvi.

35. 1879, 589–93 at 591.

36. Holl and Dummer 1980–1985, 505–9 at 507; Williams 1994, 646–51 at 648–49. Williams numbers the chapters of the *Panarion* continuously, so that all of the *De fide* is headed "*De fide* VII" because it follows "*Panarion* VI."

37. For example, Mannebach goes so far as to say, "Quales fuerint Aristippi λόγοι περὶ ἡδονῆς, de quibus mentionem facit Eusebius (fr. 155 [= SSR 4a.173]), ex hoc loco intellegitur, ubi genuina philosophi verba servata esse videntur" (1961, 93).

38. Williams 1987, xi.

39. 1879, 175. The whole of Diels' discussion of Epiphanius is suffused with apoplectic indignation (ibid. 175–78).

40. Ibid. 175.

41. Ibid. 176–77.

42. Vogt 2008, 20–64, esp. 39.

43. Sirinelli and des Places 1974, vol. 1, 8–14.

44. On this passage's preservation of what may be the Cyrenaics' original epistemological language, see Mannebach 1961, 115–16; Tsouna 1998, 11.

45. Johnson 2006, 126–49.

46. Chiesara 2001, xiv–xxiv.

47. Ibid. fr. 4–8.

48. Ibid. xxiii–xxiv.

49. Ibid. 96, 137–38, 156. Our one and only reference to this Clitomachean work is D.L. 2.92, where it is cited for the Cyrenaic rejection of physics and dialectic.

50. 2001, xxxviii–xxx, with references to earlier scholarship (to which add Döring 1988, 58). Note that if Chiesara and Döring are correct, then Giannantoni is wrong to list these testimonia under the name "Aristocles" rather than "Eusebius." But Carriker agrees with Giannantoni and the prior consensus that Eusebius found this information elsewhere in Aristocles (2003, 81–82).

51. On Eusebius' use of pseudo-Plutarch, one of the key witnesses to Aetius, see Diels 1879, 5–10; Mansfeld and Runia 1997, 130–41. On his use of an unnamed doxographical compendium that, like Aetius, goes back to Aristotle's pupil Theophrastus, see Diels 1879, 169–74. On Eusebius's library at Caesarea, see Grafton and Williams 2006, 178–232. On his extensive acquaintance with specific philosophical works, see Carriker 2003, 75–130.

52. The ancient tradition took this as a veiled attack on Aristippus (*SSR* 4a.14–15), which was confirmed by further anecdotes (4a.16–18).

53. Sustained investigation of how Plato's fellow Socratics found expression in his dialogues goes back at least to Schleiermacher, who detected Aristippean influence in the *Grg.* and *Tht.* (1818, 183–85 = 1836, 201–2; cf. Giannantoni 1958, 116). The controversy over this topic among German historians of philosophy in the 1880s and 1890s is documented in the first volumes of *Archiv für Geschichte der Philosophie* (=Zeller 1910 [orig. 1888] and Natorp 1890) and in Dümmler 1889, all of whom give further references to contemporary discussions of the issue.

54. See the exchanges among Antoniadis 1916, 31–49; Philippson 1925, 465–73; Mauersberger 1926; Diès 1941, liii–lxxx; and Mondolfo 1953.

55. 1958, 117–69.

56. Döring 1988, 27–32; rebutted by Brunschwig 2001, 472–75. Tsouna does not respond to Döring's arguments, but does reject one position for which he argues, namely that we can supplement Cyrenaic epistemology with Plato's *Tht.* (Döring 1988, 30–32; Tsouna 1998, 124–37). Giannantoni recognizes the challenge Döring raises, but in response repeats his arguments from 1958 more or less without modification (1997, 190–203). The only favorable responses to Döring's conclusions on this point of which I am aware are Göbel 2002, 134 n. 32, and Zilioli 2013 (regarding which see Lampe forthcoming A).

57. 1998, 124–30. That Xenophon's Socrates, unlike that of Plato, is undeniably a teacher, see Morrison 1994.

58. Gray 1998, 130–42.

59. Ibid. 142–44. Delatte 1933, 92–107, which is the only sustained analysis of 3.8 of which I know, has nothing substantial to say about Aristippus.

60. von Fritz 1965.

61. Erbse 1980; Narcy 1995; Gigon 1953, 1–84.

62. Hence I disagree with Classen's argument that the best way to find the real philosophy of Aristippus, uncontaminated by later Cyrenaic thought, is to go to Xenophon and Aristotle (1958, 185–86). Xenophon is obviously free of such contamination, but the biases in his testimony can only be corrected by critical reliance on later sources.

Appendix 2. Annicerean Interpolation in D.L. 2.86–93

1. On Hippobotus (including Diogenes' use of his work), see Kienle 1961, 77–78; Mejer 1978, 45.

2. 1903, 741.

3. For attempts to excise the Annicerean material, see von Fritz 1934, 1827–28; Mannebach 1961, 107–10; Döring 1988, 42–57. For an attempt to deny

interpolation, see Laks 1993, 40–49. Goulet-Cazé 1999, 188–94 largely agrees with Döring, but attempts to incorporate some of Laks' insights.

4. For other discussions of this convergence, see especially Döring 1988, 49–57; Laks 1993, 39–49.

5. Laks 1993, in his otherwise subtle and persuasive article, seems to underemphasize this important point.

6. Cf. Döring 1988, 51. Laks' explanation of the sequence of thought in Clement's testimony is unnecessarily ingenious (1993, 43–45).

7. We can see that Diogenes' text is also abbreviated because he does not include the same examples as Clement, and omits to label 3 as an anti-Epicurean point.

8. Section 4.5.

9. Since Menedemus of Eretria (ca. 345/4–261/60) considered studying with him (D.L. 2.134). (On the dating of Mendemus see Dorandi 1999a: 52.)

10. Döring 1988, 52–57 believes the Cyrenaics developed their theory of mental pleasures almost entirely in response to the Epicurean challenge, but Laks 1993, 36–41 offers persuasive counter-arguments.

11. This is not an anti-Epicurean point, but there is another reason to date it very late. The word "perversion" (διαστρόφη) is a technical one in the Stoa, as Mannebach 1961, 112 notes. The Stoics became influential even later than Epicurus.

12. Epicurus espouses this position in almost exactly these words at *Rat. Sent.* 3.

13. The key evidence for this Epicurean position includes Plut. *Mor.* 1089d = LS 21N and Cic. *Tusc.* 3.41 = LS 21L. For its interpretation see Nikolsky 2001, esp. 448–50 and Woolf 2009.

14. Important evidence for this Epicurean position includes Cic. *Tusc.* 5.55 = LS 21T, *Tusc.* 3.33, and D.L. 10.22.

15. For a more thorough analysis of Plutarch's testimony, see pp. 182–83.

16. Epicureans' concern with the fear of death is well documented by the texts assembled in LS 24. For the disturbance caused by incorrect beliefs about the gods, see LS 23A–D and 23I. For the use of physics to eliminate the fear of death and the gods, see *Rat. Sent.* 11–12.

17. For a more thorough analysis of Cyrenaic thinking about emotions, see section 4.4b.

BIBLIOGRAPHY

Adkins, Arthur W. H. 1960. *Merit and Responsibility*. Chicago: University of Chicago.

Angeli, A. 1988. *Filodemo: Agli Amici di Scuola (PHerc. 1005)*. Naples: Bibliopolis.

Annas, Julia. 1993. *The Morality of Happiness*. Oxford: Oxford University Press.

Annas, Julia and Jonathan Barnes. 1985. *The Modes of Scepticism: Ancient Texts and Modern Interpretations*. Cambridge: Cambridge University Press.

Antoniadis, Evangelos. 1916. *Aristipp und die Kyrenaiker*. PhD dissertation, Göttingen, Dieterische Univ.-Buckdruckerei.

Arnim, Hans von. 1893. *Leben und Werke des Dio von Prusa. Mit einem Einleitung: Sophistik, Rhetorik, Philosophie in ihrem Kampf um die Jungendbildung*. Berlin: Weidmann.

Barnes, Jonathan. 1987. "Editor's Notes." *Phronesis* 33: 365–66.

———. 2002. Review of *Diogenes Laertius: Vitae Philosophorum*, ed. M. Marcovich. *Classical Review* 52.1: 8–11.

Barnouw, J. 2004. *Odysseus, Hero of Practical Intelligence. Deliberation and Signs in Homer's Odyssey*. Lanham, MD: University Press of America.

Behlman, Lee. 2004. "Burning, Burial and the Critique of Stoicism in Pater's *Marius the Epicurean*." *Nineteenth-Century Prose* 31.1: 133–69.

———. Forthcoming. "The Victorian Marcus Aurelius and the Appeal of the Quasi-Christian." *The Journal of Victorian Culture*.

Bers, Victor, trans. 2003. *Demosthenes, Speeches 50–59*. Austin: University of Texas Press.

Bett, Richard. 2003. *Pyrrho, His Antecedents, and His Legacy*. Oxford: Oxford University Press.

———. 2010. "Pyrrho." In *The Stanford Encyclopedia of Philosophy (Winter 2010 Edition)*, ed. Edward N. Zalta. Accessed 25 May 2012. http://plato.stanford.edu/archives /win2010/entries/pyrrho/.

Blank, David. 2003. "Atomist Rhetoric in Philodemus." *Cronache Ercolanesi* 33: 69–88.

Blundell, Mary Whitlock. 1989. *Helping Friends and Harming Enemies: A Study in Sophocles and Greek Ethics*. Cambridge: Cambridge University Press.

Boys-Stones, George. 1996. "The ἐπελευστικὴ δύναμις in Aristo's Psychology of Action." *Phronesis* 41: 75–94.

Brancacci, A. 1982. "Teodoro l'Ateo e Bione di Boristene fra Pirrone e Arcesilao." *Elenchos* 3: 55–85.

Brennan, Tad. 2005. *The Stoic Life: Emotions, Duties, and Fate*. Oxford: Oxford University Press.

Britain, Charles. 2008. "Arcesilaus." In *The Stanford Encyclopedia of Philosophy (Fall 2008 Edition)*, ed. Edward N. Zalta. Accessed 8 March 2012. http://plato.stanford .edu/archives/fall2008/entries/arcesilaus/.

Brunschwig, Jacques. 1986. "The Cradle Argument in Epicureanism and Stoicism." In Schofield and Striker 1986, 113–44.

———. 1999. "The Beginnings of Hellenistic Epistemology." In *The Cambridge History of Hellenistic Philosophy*, ed. Keimpe Algra, Jonathan Barnes, Jaap Mansfeld, and Malcolm Schofield, 229–59. Cambridge: Cambridge University Press.

———. 2001. "La théorie Cyrénaïque de la connaissance et le problème de ses rapports avec Socrate." In *Socrate et les Socratiques*, ed. Gilbert Romeyer Dherbey and Jean-Baptiste Gourinat, 457–77. Paris: Vrin.

Burnyeat, Myles. 1982. "Idealism and Greek Philosophy: What Descartes Saw and Berkeley Missed." *The Philosophical Review* 91.1: 3–40.

Burnyeat, Myles and Michael Frede, eds. 1997. *The Original Sceptics: A Controversy*. Indianapolis: Hackett.

Bussanich, John. 2006. "Socrates and Religious Experience." In *A Companion to Socrates*, ed. Sara Ahbel-Rappe and Rachana Kamtekar, 200–13. Oxford: Wiley Blackwell.

Cairns, Douglas. 1993. *Aidos: The Psychology and Ethics of Honour and Shame in Ancient Greek Literature*. Oxford: Clarendon Press.

Carriker, Andrew James. 2003. *The Library of Eusebius of Caesarea*. Leiden: Brill.

Caygill, Howard. 2006. "Under the Epicurean skies." *Angelaki* 11.3: 107–15

Chamoux, F. 1953. *Cyrène sous la monarchie des Battiades*. Paris: E. de Boccard.

———. 1956. "Le roi Magas." *RHist* 216: 18–34.

Chiesara, Maria Lorenzo, ed. and trans. 2001. *Aristocles of Messene: Testimonia and Fragments*. Oxford: Oxford University Press.

Chitwood, Ava. 2004. *Death by Philosophy: The Biographical Tradition in the Life and Death of the Archaic Philosophers Empedocles, Heraclitus, and Democritus*. Ann Arbor: University of Michigan Press.

Clarke, Michael. 2004 "Manhood and Heroism." In *The Cambridge Companion to Homer*, ed. Robert Fowler, 74–90. Cambridge: Cambridge University Press.

Classen, Carl Joachim. 1958. "Aristippos." *Hermes* 86: 182–92.

———. 1996. "Aristipp und seine Anhänger in Rom." In Keimpe A. Algra, Pieter W. van der Horst, and David T. Runia, eds. *Polyhistor: Studies in the History and Historiography of Ancient Philosophy*, 206–19. Leiden: Brill.

Clay, Diskin. 1999. *Paradosis and Survival: Three Chapters in the History of Epicurean Philosophy*. Ann Arbor: University of Michigan Press.

Cohen, David. 1991. *Law, Sexuality, and Society: The Enforcement of Morals in Classical Athens*. Cambridge: Cambridge University Press.

———. 1995. *Law, Violence, and Community in Classical Athens*. Cambridge: Cambridge University Press.

Crisp, Roger, trans. 2000. *The Nicomachean Ethics*. Cambridge: Cambridge University Press.

Crönert, Wilhelm. 1936. Review of *Die Briefe des Sokrates und der Sokratiker*, J. Sykutris. *Gnomon* 12.3: 146–52.

———. 1965. *Kolotes und Menedemos: Texte und Untersuchungen zur Philosophen- und Literaturgeschichte*. Amsterdam: Hakkert.

Danzig, Gabriel. 2010. *Apologizing for Socrates: How Plato and Xenophon Created Our Socrates*. Lanham, MD: Lexington Books.

Davidson, James. 1997. *Courtesans and Fishcakes: The Consuming Passions of Classical Athens*. London: Harper Collins.

Decleva Caizzi, Fernanda. 1994. Review of Knoepfler 1991. *Classical Review* 44.1: 31–32.

Dellamora, Richard. 1990. *Masculine Desire: The Sexual Politics of Victorian Aestheticism*. Chapel Hill, NC: University of North Carolina.

Derrida, Jacques. 1998. *Archive Fever: A Freudian Impression*. Trans. E. Prenowitz. Chicago: University of Chicago Press.

Détienne, Marcel and Jean-Pierre Vernant. 1978. *Cunning Intelligence in Greek Culture and Society*. Trans. Janet Lloyd. Atlantic Highlands, NJ: Humanities Press.

Diels, Hermann, ed. 1879. *Doxographi Graeci*. Berlin: G. Reimer.

Diès, Auguste, ed. and trans. 1941. *Platon: Oeuvres complètes. Tome IX–2e Partie*. Paris: Les belles lettres.

Dillon, John M. 2003. *The Heirs of Plato: A Study of the Old Academy, 347–274 B.C.* Oxford: Clarendon Press.

———. 2004. *Salt and Olives: Morality and Custom in Ancient Greece*. Edinburgh: Edinburgh University Press.

Dittmar, H., ed. 1912. *Aischines von Sphettos: Untersuchungen und Fragmente*. Berlin: Weidmann.

Di Vita, Antonio, Ginette Di Vita-Evrard, Lidiano Bacchielli. 1999. *Libya: The Lost Cities of the Roman Empire*. With photographs by R. Polidori. Cologne: Könnemann.

Dorandi, Tiziano. 1991. *Storia dei filosofi: Platone e l'Academia: (PHerc. 1021 e 164)*. Naples: Bibliopolis.

———. 1999a. "Chronology." In *The Cambridge History of Hellenistic Philosophy*, ed. K. Algra, J. Barnes, J. Mansfeld, and M. Schofield, 31–54. Cambridge: Cambridge University Press.

———. 1999b. "La tradition manuscrite." In *Diogéne Laërce: Vies et Doctrines des Philosophes Illustres*, 33–39.

———. 2002. Review of *Diogenes Laertius: Vitae Philosophorum*, ed. M. Marcovich. *Phronesis* 45.4: 331 40.

———. 2013. *Diogenes Laertius: Lives of Eminent Philosophers*. Cambridge: Cambridge University Press.

Döring, Klaus. 1988. *Der Sokratesschuler Aristipp und die Kyrenaiker*. Mainz: Akademie der Wissenschaften und der Literatur.

———. 1989. "Gab es eine Dialektische Schule?" *Phronesis* 34: 293–310.

———. 1972. *Die Megariker: Kommentierte Sammling der Testimonien*. Amsterdam: Grüner.

Dorion, Louis-André. 2011. "The Rise and Fall of the Socratic Problem." In *The Cambridge Companion to Socrates*, ed. D. R. Morrison, 1–23. Cambridge: Cambridge University Press.

Dover, K. J. 1974. *Greek Popular Morality in the Time of Plato and Aristotle*. Oxford: Blackwell.

Dowling, Linda C. 1994. *Hellenism and Homosexuality in Victorian Oxford*. Ithaca, NY: Cornell University Press.

Dümmler, Ferdinand. 1889. *Akademika: Beiträge zur Litteraturgeschichte der Sokratischen Schulen*. Giessen: J. Ricker.

Eisner, Robert. 1982. "Socrates as Hero." *Philosophy and Literature* 6: 106–18.

Elrashedy, Faraj Mohmoud. 2002. *Imports of Post-Archaic Greek Pottery into Cyrenaica*. Oxford: Archaeopress.

Erbse, Hartmut. 1980. "Aristipp und Sokrates bei Xenophon (Bemerkungen zu Mem. 2,1)." *Würzburger Jahrbücher für die Altertumswissenschaft* 6: 7–19.

Eshleman, Kendra. 2007/2008. "Affection and Affiliation: Social Networks and Conversion to Philosophy." *Classical Journal* 103.2: 129–40.

Evangelista, Stefano. 2009. *British Aestheticism and Ancient Greece: Hellenism, Reception, Gods in Exile.* Basingstoke, U.K.: Palgrave Macmillan.

Evans, Lawrence, ed. 1970. See Pater, Walter.

Everson, Stephen. 1991 "The Objective Appearance of Pyrrhonism." In *Companions to Ancient Thought 2: Psychology,* ed. S. Everson, 121–47. Cambridge: Cambridge University Press.

Feldman, Fred. 2004. *Pleasure and the Good Life: Concerning the Nature, Varieties, and Plausibility of Hedonism.* Oxford: Oxford University Press.

———. 2010. *What Is This Thing Called Happiness?* Oxford: Oxford University Press.

Fiasse, Gaëlle. 1999. "La problématique de l'amour-éros dans le stoïcisme: Confrontation de fragments, paradoxes et interprétations." *Revue Philosophique de Louvain* 37.3–4: 459–82.

Fine, Gail. 2003. "Subjectivity, Ancient and Modern: The Cyrenaics, Sextus, and Descartes." In *Hellenistic and Early Modern Philosophy.* J. Miller and B. Inwood, eds. Cambridge: Cambridge University Press, 192–231.

Finley, M. I. 1956. *The World of Odysseus.* Harmondsworth: Penguin.

Flaig, Egon. 2000. Review of Konstan 1997. *Historische Zeitschrift* 270.3: 716–17.

Foucault, Michel. 1985. *The History of Sexuality, Volume 2: The Use of Pleasure.* Trans. R. Hurley. Harmondsworth: Viking.

———. 2005. *The Hermeneutics of the Subject: Lectures at the College de France 1981–1982.* Ed. F. Gross, trans. G. Burchell. New York: Palgrave MacMillan.

Fritz, K. von. 1934. "Theodoros." *RE* 5A.2: 1825–31.

———. 1965. "Das erste Kapitel des zweiten Buches von Xenophons Memorabilien und die Philosophie des Aristipp von Kyrene." *Hermes* 93: 257–79.

Giannantoni, Gabriele. 1958. *I Cirenaici: raccolta delle fonti antiche.* Florence: G. C. Sansoni.

———. 1983–85. *Socraticorum Reliquiae.* Naples: Bibliopolis.

———. 1986. "Socrate e i Socratici in Diogene Laerzio." *Elenchos* 7.2: 183–216.

———. 1990. See *SSR* in the List of Abbreviations.

———. 1997. "Il concetto di αἴσθησις nella filosofia cirenaica." In *Lezione Socratiche,* ed. G. Giannantoni and M. Narcy, 181–203. Naples: Bibliopolis.

Gigante, M. 1993. "Quel che Aristippo non aveva detto." *Parola del Passato* 48: 267–80.

Gigon, Olof. 1953. *Kommentar zum ersten Buch von Xenophons Memorabilien.* Basel: Friedrich Reinhardt.

Gill, Christopher. 1998. "Altruism or Reciprocity in Greek Philosophy?" In *Reciprocity in Ancient Greece,* ed. Christopher Gill, Norman Postlethwaite, and Richard Seaford, 303–28. Oxford: Oxford University Press.

Giusta, Michelangelo. 1964–68. *I dossografi di etica 1–2.* Torino: Università di Torino.

Glucker, John. 1978. *Antiochus and the Late Academy.* Göttingen: Vandenhoeck & Ruprecht.

Göbel, Christian. 2002. "Megarisches Denken und seine ethische Relevanz." *Classica et Mediaevalia* 53: 123–39.

Goldhill, Simon. 2009. "The Anecdote: Exploring the Boundaries Between Oral and Literate Performance in the Second Sophistic." In *Ancient Literacies: The Culture of Literacy in Greece and Rome,* ed. W. A. Johnson and H. N. Parker, 96–113. Oxford: Oxford University Press.

Goldschmidt, Victor. 1969. *Le système stoïcïen et l'idée de temps*. Paris: Vrin.

Gomperz, Theodor. 1905. *Greek Thinkers: A History of Ancient Philosophy*, vol. 2. Trans. G. G. Berry. New York: Scribners.

Goodchild, R. G. 1971. *Kyrene und Apollonia*. Zurich: Raggi.

Gosling, J. C. B. and C. C. W. Taylor. 1982. *The Greeks on Pleasure*. Oxford: Clarendon Press.

Gouirand, Pierre. 2005. *Aristippe de Cyrène: le chien royal. Une morale du plaisir et de la liberté*. Paris: Maisonneuve & Larose.

Goulet, Richard. 2001. "Les références chez Diogène Laërce: Sources ou authorités?" In *Études sur les vies de philosophes dans l'antiquité tardive: Diogène Laërce, Porphyre de Tyr, Eunape de Sardes*, 79–96. Paris: Vrin.

Goulet-Cazé, M.-O. 1999. "Les Socrates et leurs disciples." In *Diogéne Laërce: Vies et Doctrines des Philosophes Illustres*, 172–208.

Goulet-Cazé, Marie-Odile, J.-F. Balaudé, L. Brisson, J. Brunschwig, T. Dorandi, R. Goulet, M. Narcy, and M. Patillon, ed. and trans. 1999. *Diogène Laërce: Vies et Doctrines des Philosophes Illustres*. 2nd ed. Paris: CNRS.

Grafton, Anthony and Megan H. Williams. 2006. *Christianity and the Transformation of the Book: Origen, Eusebius, and the Library of Caesarea*. Cambridge, MA: Belknap Press.

Graver, Margaret. 2001. "Managing Mental Pain: Epicurus vs. Aristippus on the Pre-rehearsal of Future Ills." *Proceedings of the Boston Area Colloquium in Ancient Philosophy* 17: 155–77.

———. 2007. *Stoicism and Emotion*. Chicago: University of Chicago Press.

Gray, Vivienne. 1998. *The Framing of Socrates: The Literary Interpretation of Xenophon's Memorabilia*. Stuttgart: Steiner.

Griffin, Miriam. 1986. "Philosophy, Cato, and Roman Suicide." *Greece & Rome* 33: 64–77; 192–202.

Gronewald, M. 1985. See PKöln in the list of abbreviations.

Gulick, Charles Burton, trans. 1927–41. *Athenaeus: The Deipnosophists*. 7 vols. London: William Heinemann.

Guthrie, W. K. C. 1969. *A History of Greek Philosophy, Vol. 3: The Fifth-Century Enlightenment*. Cambridge: Cambridge University Press.

Habicht, Christian. 1997. *Athens from Alexander to Anthony*. Trans. Deborah L. Schneider. Cambridge, MA: Harvard University Press.

Hadot, Pierre. 1995. *Philosophy as a Way of Life: Spiritual Exercises from Socrates to Foucault*. Ed. Arnold Davidson, trans. Michael Chase. Oxford: Blackwell.

———. 1998. *The Inner Citadel: The Meditations of Marcus Aurelius*. Trans. Michael Chase. Cambridge, MA: Harvard University Press.

———. 2002. *What Is Ancient Philosophy?* Trans. Michael Chase. Cambridge, MA: Belknap Press.

Halliwell, Stephen. 2008. *Greek Laughter: A Study of Cultural Psychology from Homer to Early Christianity*. Cambridge: Cambridge University Press.

Hamilton, John T. 2003. *Soliciting Darkness: Pindar, Obscurity, and the Classical Tradition*. Cambridge, MA: Harvard.

Hense, O., ed. 1909. *Teletis Reliquiae*. 2nd ed. Tübingen: Mohr.

Herman, Gabriel. 1998. Review of Konstan 1997. *Journal of Roman Studies* 88: 181–82.

Hobbs, Angela. 2000. *Plato and the Hero: Courage, Manliness, and the Impersonal Good*. Cambridge: Cambridge University Press.

Holl, Karl and Jürgen Dummer, eds. 1980–1985. *Epiphanius*. 3 vols. 2nd ed. Berlin: Akademie Verlag.

Holmes, Stephen Taylor. 1979. "Aristippus in and out of Athens." *The American Political Science Review* 73: 113–28.

Humbert, Jean. 1967. *Socrate et les petits socratiques*. Paris: Presses universitaires de France.

Hume, David. 1978. *A Treatise of Human Nature*. Ed. L. A. Selby-Bigge and P. H. Niddith. 2nd ed. Oxford: Clarendon.

Indelli, G. and V. Tsouna-McKirahan, ed. and trans. 1995. *On Choices and Avoidances*. Naples: Bibliopolis.

Inman, Billie Andrew. 1984. "The Emergence of Pater's Marius Mentality: 1874–75." *English Literature in Transition, 1880–1920* 27.2: 100–23.

———. 1998. "Estrangement and Connection: Walter Pater, Benjamin Jowett, and William H. Hardinge." In *Pater in the 1990s*, ed. L. Brake and E. Small. Accessed 31 October 2010. http://www.eltpress.org/pater/tablec.htm.

Inwood, Brad. 2005. *Reading Seneca: Stoic Philosophy at Rome*. Oxford: Clarendon Press.

Ioppolo, Anna Maria. 1980. *Aristone di Chio e lo Stoicismo antico*. Bibliopolis: Naples.

Irwin, Terence. 1991. "Aristippus against Happiness." *Monist* 74.1: 55–82.

Iser, Wolfgang. 1987. *Walter Pater: The Aesthetic Moment*. Trans. D. H. Wilson. Cambridge: Cambridge University Press.

Itter, Andrew C. 2009. *Esoteric Teaching in the* Stromateis *of Clement of Alexandria*. Leiden: Brill.

Jacoby, F. 1912. "Hegesandros." In *RE* 7: 2600–2602.

———. 1916. "Istros 9." In *RE* 9.2: 2270–82.

Jenkyns, Richard. 1980. *The Victorians and Ancient Greece*. Oxford: Basil Blackwell.

Johnson, Aaron P. 2006. *Ethnicity and Argument in Eusebius' Praeparatio Evangelica*. Oxford: Oxford University Press.

Kahn, Charles H. 1994. "Aeschines on Socratic Eros." In Vander Waerdt 1994, 87–106.

———. 2001. *Pythagoras and the Pythagoreans: A Brief History*. Indianapolis: Hackett.

Kennedy, George A., trans. 2003. *Progymnasmata: Greek Textbooks of Prose Composition and Rhetoric*. Atlanta, GA: Society of Biblical Literature.

Kienle, Walter von. 1961. *Die Berichte über die Sukzessionen der Philosophen in der hellenistischen und spätantiken Literatur*. PhD diss., Freie Universität Berlin. Kindstrand, Jan Fredrik. 1976. *Bion of Borysthenes: A Collection of the Fragments with Introduction and Commentary*. Ed. J. F. Kindstrand. Upsala: Almqvist & Wiksell.

———. 1986. "Diogenes Laertius and the 'Chreia' Tradition." *Elenchos* 7: 220–43.

Kingsley, Peter. 1995. *Ancient Philosophy, Mystery, and Magic: Empedocles and Pythagorean Tradition*. Oxford: Clarendon Press.

Knoepfler, Denis. 1991. *La Vie de Ménédème d'Érétrie de Diogène Laërce: Contribution à l'Histoire et à la Critique du Texte des Vies des Philosophes*. Basle: Friedrich Reinhardt.

Knox, Bernard M. W. 1964. *The Heroic Temper: Studies in Sophoclean Tragedy*. Berkeley: University of California Press.

Konstan, David. 1997. *Friendship in the Classical World*. Cambridge: Cambridge University Press.

Kurke, Leslie. 1999. *Coins, Bodies, Games, and Gold: The Politics of Meaning in Archaic Greece*. Princeton: Princeton University Press.

Laks, André. 1993. "Annicéris et les plaisirs psychiques. Quelques préalables doxographiques." In *Passions and Perceptions: Studies in the Hellenistic Philosophy of*

Mind, ed. Jacques Brunschwig and Martha Nussbaum, 18–49. Cambridge: Cambridge University Press.

Lampe, Kurt. Forthcoming A. Review of *The Cyrenaics*, U. Zilioli. *Classical Review* 64.1.

———. Forthcoming B. "The Life of Aristippus in the Socratic Epistles: Three Interpretations." In *Creative Lives*, ed. J. Hanink and R. Fletcher. Cambridge: Cambridge University Press.

Lanni, Adriaan. 2006. *Law and Justice in the Courts of Classical Athens*. Cambridge: Cambridge University Press.

Laronde, André. 1987. *Cyrène et la Libye Hellénistique: Libyai Historikai*. Paris: CNRS.

Lear, Jonathan. 2002. *Happiness, Death, and the Remainder of Life*. Cambridge, MA: Harvard University Press.

Loesberg, Jonathan. 1991. *Aestheticism and Deconstruction: Pater, Derrida, and de Man*. Princeton: Princeton University Press.

Long, A. A. 1999. "The Socratic Legacy." In *The Cambridge History of Hellenistic Philosophy*, ed. K. Algra, J. Barnes, J. Mansfeld, and M. Schofield, 617–41. Cambridge: Cambridge University Press.

———. 2006. *From Epicurus to Epictetus: Studies in Hellenistic and Roman Philosophy*. Oxford.

Long, H. S., ed. 1964. *Diogenis Laertii Vitae Philosophorum*. 2 vols. Oxford: Clarendon Press.

Lund, Helen S. 2002. *Lysimachus: A Study in Early Hellenistic Kingship*. London: Routledge.

MacLachlan, Bonnie. 1993. *The Age of Grace: Charis in Early Greek Poetry*. Princeton: Princeton University Press.

Madvig, J. N. 1871. *Adversaria critica ad scriptores graecos*, vol. I. Copenhagen.

Mann, Wolfgang-Rainer. 1996. "The Life of Aristippus." *Archiv für Geschichte der Philosophie* 78: 97–119.

Mannebach, Erich, ed. 1961. *Aristippi et Cyrenaicorum Fragmenta*. Leiden: Brill.

Mansfeld, Jaap. 1994. *Prolegomena. Questions to be Settled Before the Study of an Author, or a Text*. Leiden: Brill.

Mansfeld, Jaap and David T. Runia. 1997. *Aëtiana: The Method and Intellectual Context of a Doxographer. Volume One: The Sources*. Leiden: Brill.

Marcovich, M., ed. 1999. *Diogenes Laertius: Vitae Philosophorum*. 2 vols. Leipzig: Teubner.

Mársico, C. Forthcoming. *Los filósofos socraticos: Testimonios y fragmentos*. Buenos Aires: Losada.

Martindale, Charles. 1993. *Redeeming the Text: Latin Poetry and the Hermeneutics of Reception*. Cambridge: Cambridge University Press.

Matson, Wallace I. 1998. "Hegesias the Death-Persuader; or, the Gloominess of Hedonism." *Philosophy* 73: 553–58.

———. 2006. *Uncorrected Papers: Diverse Philosophical Dissents*. Amherst: Humanity Books.

Mauersberger, A. 1926. "Plato und Aristipp." *Hermes* 61: 208–30.

Mauss, Marcel. 1990. *The Gift: The Form and Reason for Exchange in Archaic Societies*. Trans. H. D. Walls. Forward by M. Douglas. London: Routledge.

McClure, Laura. 2003A. *Courtesans at Table: Gender and Greek Literary Culture in Athenaeus*. London: Routledge.

———. 2003B. "Subversive Laughter: The Sayings of Courtesans in Book 13 of Athenaeus' *Deipnosophistae*." *American Journal of Philology* 124: 259–94.

Meiggs, R. and D. Lewis, ed. and trans. 1969. *A Selection of Greek Historical Inscriptions to the End of the Fifth Century B.C.* Oxford: Clarendon.

Mejer, Jorgen. 1978. *Diogenes Laertius and his Hellenistic Background.* Wiesbaden: Franz Steiner.

———. 2006. "Ancient Philosophy and the Doxographical Tradition." In *A Companion to Ancient Philosophy*, ed. Mary-Louise Gill and Pierre Pellegrin, 20–33. Oxford: Blackwell.

Miller, J. H. 1976. "Walter Pater: A Partial Portrait." *Daedalus* 105.1: 97–113.

Millett, Paul. 1998. "The Rhetoric of Reciprocity in Classical Athens." In *Reciprocity in Ancient Greece*, ed. Christopher Gill, Norman Postlethwaite, and Richard Seaford, 227–53. Oxford: Oxford University Press.

Mitsis, Phillip. 1988. *Epicurus' Ethical Theory: The Pleasures of Invulnerability.* Ithaca: Cornell University Press.

Mondolfo, Rodolfo. 1953. "I Cirenaici e i raffinati del Teeteto platonico." *Rivista di Filosofia* 44: 127–35.

Monsman, Gerald C. 1967. *Pater's Portraits: Mythic Pattern in the Fiction of Walter Pater.* Baltimore: Johns Hopkins University Press.

Montuori, Mario. 1981. *Socrates: Physiology of a Myth.* Trans. J. M. P. and M. Langdale. Amsterdam: J. C. Gieben.

Morgan, Michael L. 1990. *Platonic Piety: Philosophy and Ritual in Fourth-Century Athens.* New Haven: Yale University Press.

Morrison, Donald R. 1994. "Xenophon's Socrates as Teacher." In Vander Waerdt 1994, 181–208.

Most, Glen W. 1985. *The Measures of Praise: Structure and Function in Pindar's Second Pythian and Seventh Nemean Odes.* Göttingen: Vandenhoeck & Ruprecht.

Narcy, Michel. 1995. "Le choix d'Aristippe." In *La tradizione socratica: seminario di studi*, ed. G. Giannantoni, M. Gigante, E. Martens, M. Narcy, A. M. Ioppolo, and K. Döring, 71–87. Naples: Bibliopolis.

Natali, Carlo. 1995. "*Oikonomia* in Hellenistic Political Thought." In *Justice and Generosity*, ed. André Laks and Malcolm Schofield, 95–128. Cambridge: Cambridge University Press.

Natorp, P. 1890. "Aristipp in Platons Theätet." *Archiv für Geschichte der Philosophie* 3.3: 347–62.

———. 1895. "Aristippos." In *RE* 2.1: 902–906.

Nehamas, Alexander. 1998. *The Art of Living: Socratic Reflections from Plato to Foucault.* Berkeley: University of California Press.

Nietzsche, Friedrich. 2009. *The Birth of Tragedy out of the Spirit of Music.* Trans. I. Johnston. Arlington: Richer Resource Publications.

Nikolsky, Boris. 2001. "Epicurus on Pleasure." *Phronesis* 46.4: 440–65.

North, Helen F. 1966. *Sophrosyne: Self-Knowledge and Self-Restraint in Greek Literature.* Ithaca: Cornell University Press.

Nussbaum, Martha. 1986. *The Fragility of Goodness: Luck and Ethics in Greek Tragedy and Philosophy.* Cambridge: Cambridge University Press.

———. 1990. *Love's Knowledge: Essays on Philosophy and Literature.* Oxford: Oxford University Press.

———. 1994. *The Therapy of Desire: Theory and Practice in Hellenistic Ethics.* Princeton: Princeton University Press.

———. 1995. "Objectification." *Philosophy and Public Affairs* 24.4: 249–91.

———. 2002. "Eros and Ethical Norms." In *The Sleep of Reason: Erotic Experience and Sexual Ethics in Ancient Greece,* ed. M. Nussbaum and Juha Sihvola, 55–94. Princeton: Princeton University Press.

O'Keefe, Tim. 2006. 2002. "The Cyrenaics on Pleasure, Happiness, and Future-Concern." *Phronesis* 47: 395–416.

———. "Cyrenaics." 2006. In *The Internet Encyclopedia of Philosophy*, ed. J. Fieser and B. Dowden. Accessed 13 June 2009. http://www.iep.utm.edu/c/cyren.htm.

Onfray, Michel. 1991. *L'art de jouir: Pour un matérialisme hédoniste.* Paris: Grasset.

———. 2002. *L'invention du plaisir: Fragments cyrénaïques.* Paris: Livre de poche.

———. 2006. *Contre-histoire de la philosophie 1: Les sagesses antiques.* Paris: Grasset & Fasquelle.

———. 2013. *Contre-histoire de la philosophie 8: Les freudiens hérétiques.* Paris: Grasset.

Osborn, Eric. 2005. *Clement of Alexandria.* Cambridge: Cambridge University Press.

Padel, Ruth. 1992. *In and Out of Mind: Greek Images of the Tragic Self.* Princeton: Princeton University Press.

Parfit, Derek. 1987. *Reasons and Persons.* Corrected paperback ed. Oxford: Clarendon Press.

Philippson, R. 1925. "Akademische Verhandlungen uber die Lustlehre." *Hermes* 60.4: 444–81.

Pohlenz, M., ed. 1952. *Plutarchus: Moralia.* Vol. VI.2. Leipzig: Teubner.

Porter, James. 1996. "The Philosophy of Aristo of Chios." In *The Cynics: The Cynic Movement in Antiquity and its Legacy*, ed. R. Bracht Branham and Marie Odile Goulet-Cazé, 156–89. Berkeley: University of California Press.

———. 2002. "ΦΥΣΙΟΛΟΓΕΙΝ. Nausiphanes of Teos and the Physics of Rhetoric: A Chapter in the History of Greek Atomism." *CErc* 32: 137–86.

Préaux, J. 1977. "Horace et Aristippe." In (editor unnamed), *Mélanges offerts à Léopold Sédar Senghor. Langues, littérature, histoire anciennes,* 395–400. Dakar: Les nouvelles ed. africaines.

Prettejohn, Elizabeth. 2007. *Art for Art's Sake: Aestheticism in Victorian Painting.* New Haven: Yale University Press.

Redfield, James. 1975. *Nature and Culture in the Iliad: The Tragedy of Hector.* Chicago: University of Chicago Press.

Reinsberg, Carola. 1989. *Ehe, Hetärentum und Knabenliebe im antiken Griechenland.* Munich: Beck.

Ricoeur, Paul. 1991. *Oneself as Another.* Trans. Kathleen Blamey. Chicago: University of Chicago Press.

Robert, L. 1967. "Sur le nom d'un proxène d'Épidaure en Cyrénaïque." *Revue des études grecques* 80: 31–39.

Roberts, Gabriel. 2008. "'Analysis Leaves Off': The Use and Abuse of Philosophy in Walter Pater's *Renaissance.*" *The Cambridge Quarterly* 37.4: 407–25.

Robertson, Noel. 2010. *Religion and Reconciliation in Greek Cities: The Sacred Laws of Selinus and Cyrene.* Oxford: Oxford University Press.

Roochnik, David. 1996. *Of Art and Wisdom: Plato's Understanding of Techne.* University Park: Pennsylvania State University Press.

Rorty, Richard. 1985. "The Historiography of Philosophy: Four Genres." In *Philosophy in History: Essays on the Historiography of Philosophy,* ed. R. Rorty, J. B. Schneewind, and Quentin Skinner, 49–75. Cambridge: Cambridge University Press.

———. 1989. *Contingency, Irony, and Solidarity.* Cambridge: Cambridge University Press.

Rudolph, F. 1894. "Zu den Quellen des Aelian und Athenaios." *Philologus* 52: 652–63.

Schleiermacher, Friedrich. 1818. *Platons Werke.* Zweiten Teil erster Band. 2nd ed. Berlin: Realschulbuchhandlung.

———. 1836. *Schleiermacher's Introductions to the Dialogues of Plato.* Trans. William Dobson. Cambridge and London: Pitt Press and John William Parker.

Schofield, Malcolm. 1988. "The Retrenchable Present." In *Matter and Metaphysics: The Fourth Symposium Hellenisticum,* ed. Jonathan Barnes and Mario Mignucci, 329–74. Bibliopolis: Naples.

Schofield, Malcolm and Gisela Striker, eds. 1986. *The Norms of Nature: Studies in Hellenistic Ethics.* Cambridge: Cambridge University Press.

Schwartz, E. 1903. "Diogenes Laertios." In *RE* 5.1: 738–63.

Sedley, David. 1977. "Diodorus Cronus and Hellenistic Philosophy." *Proceedings of the Cambridge Philological Society* 203 n.s. 23: 74–120.

———. 1983. "The Motivation of Greek Skepticism." In *The Skeptical Tradition,* ed. Myles Burnyeat, 9–29. Berkeley: University of California Press.

———. 1996. "The Inferential Foundations of Epicurean Ethics." In *Epicureismo Greco e Romano,* ed. Gabriele Giannantoni and Marcello Gigante, vol. 1, 313–39. Naples: Bibliopolis.

———. 2013. "Epicurean versus Cyrenaic Happiness." Paper presented at "On the Psyche: Studies in Literature, Health and Psychology," Exeter, United Kingdom, July 4–7.

Seeskin, Kenneth. 1987. *Dialogue and Discovery: A Study in Socratic Method.* Albany: State University of New York Press.

Segal, Charles. 1998. *Aglaia: The Poetry of Alcman, Sappho, Pindar, Bacchylides and Corinna.* Lanham: Littlefield and Row.

Seiler, R. M. 1980. *Walter Pater: The Critical Heritage.* London: Routledge & Kegan Paul.

Sellars, John. 2003. *The Art of Living: The Stoics on the Nature and Function of Philosophy.* Aldershot: Ashgate.

Sherman, Nancy. 2005. *Stoic Warriors: The Ancient Philosophy Behind the Military Mind.* Oxford: Oxford University Press.

Shuter, William F. 1997. *Rereading Walter Pater.* Cambridge: Cambridge University Press.

Sirinelli, Jean and Edoard des Places, ed. 1974. *Eusèbe de Césarée: La préparation évangélique.* Paris: Éditions du cerf.

Skinner, Quentin. 1969. "Meaning and Understanding in the History of Ideas." *History and Theory* 8.1: 3–53.

Spinelli, Emidio. 1992. "P. Köln 205: Il 'Socrate' di Egesia?" *Zeitschrift für Papyrologie und Epigraphik* 91: 10–14.

Stenzel, J. 1927. "Sokrates (Philosoph)." In *RE* 3A.1: 811–90.

Sternbach, L., ed. 1963. *Gnomologium Vaticanum e Codice Vaticano Graeco 743.* Reprint. Berlin: De Gruyter.

Striker, Gisela. 1991. "Following Nature: A Study in Stoic Ethics." *Oxford Studies in Ancient Philosophy* 9: 1–73.

Sussman, Herbert. 1995. *Victorian Masculinities: Manhood and Masculine Poetics in Early Victorian Literature and Art.* Cambridge: Cambridge University Press.

Sykutris, Johannes. 1931. "Sokratikerbriefe." In *RE* Suppl. 5.981–87.

——. 1933. *Die Briefe des Sokrates und der Sokratiker*. Paderborn: F. Schöningh.

Tarrant, Harold. 1994. "The *Hippias Major and Socratic Theories of Pleasure*." In Vander Waerdt 1994, 107–26.

——. 2005. "Socratic *Synousia*: A Post-Platonic Myth?" *Journal of the History of Philosophy* 43.2: 131–55.

Taylor, Charles. 1989. *Sources of the Self: The Making of the Modern Identity*. Cambridge: Cambridge University Press.

Todd, Stephen. 1993. *The Shape of Athenian Law*. Oxford: Clarendon.

Traina, A. 1991. "Orazio e Aristippo: le Epistole e l'arte di convivere." *RFIC* 119: 285–305.

——. 1994. "In Aristippi praecepta relabor." *Eikasmos* 5: 243–46.

Tsouna, Voula. 1998. *Cyrenaic Epistemology*. Cambridge: Cambridge University Press.

——. 2002. "Is There an Exception to Greek Eudaemonism?" In *Le style de la pensée: Recueil de textes en hommage à Jacques Brunschwig*, ed. Monique Canto-Sperber and Pierre Pellegrin, 464–89. Paris: Les Belles Lettres.

——. 2007. *The Ethics of Philodemus*. Oxford: Oxford University Press.

Tsouna-McKirahan, Voula. 1994. "The Socratic Origins of the Cynics and Cyrenaics." In Vander Waerdt 1994, 367–391.

Vander Waerdt, Paul A., ed. 1994. *The Socratic Movement*. Ithaca: Cornell University Press.

Varty, Anne. 1994. "Flux, Rest, and Number: Pater's Plato." In *Platonism and the English Imagination*, ed. Anna Baldwin and Sarah Hutton, 257–67. Cambridge: Cambridge University Press.

Vlastos, Gregory. 1991. *Socrates: Ironist and Moral Philosopher*. Cambridge: Cambridge University Press.

——. 1994. *Socratic Studies*. Cambridge: Cambridge University Press.

Vogt, Katja M. 2008. *Law, Reason, and the Cosmic City: Political Philosophy in the Early Stoa*. Oxford: Oxford University Press.

Warren, James. 2001. "Epicurus and the Pleasures of the Future." *Oxford Studies in Ancient Philosophy* 21: 135–79.

——. 2002. *Epicurus and Democritean Ethics: An Archaeology of Ataraxia*. Cambridge: Cambridge University Press.

——. 2003. "Sextus Empiricus and the Tripartition of Time." *Phronesis* 48: 313–343.

——. 2004. *Facing Death: Epicurus and His Critics*. Oxford: Clarendon.

Watson, John. 1895. *Hedonistic Theories from Aristippus to Spencer*. Glasgow: James Maclehose and Sons.

White, S. 1994. "Callimachus on Plato and Cleombrotus." *Transactions of the American Philological Society* 124: 135–61.

——. 2000. "Socrates at Colonus." In *Reason and Religion in Socratic Philosophy*, ed. Nicholas D. Smith and Paul Woodruff, 151–75. Oxford: Oxford University Press.

Wilamowitz-Moellendorf, Ulrich von. 1965. *Antigonos von Karystos*. Reprinted from the 1881 edition without change. Berlin and Zürich: Weidmann.

Williams, Bernard. 1993. *Shame and Necessity*. Berkeley: University of California Press.

Williams, Carolyn. 1989. *Transfigured World: Walter Pater's Aesthetic Historicism*. Ithaca NY: Cornell University Press.

Williams, Frank, trans. 1987. *The Panarion of Epiphanius of Salamis*. Leiden: Brill.

Wilson, Nigel G., ed. and trans. 1997. *Aelian: Historical Miscellany*. Cambridge, MA: Harvard.

Winiarczyk, Marek. 1981. "Theodorus Ὁ ἌΘΕΟΣ." *Philologus* 125: 64–94.

Winkler, J. 1990. *The Constraints of Desire: the Anthropology of Sex and Gender in Ancient Greece*. New York: Routledge.

Winkler, John J. and Froma I. Zeitlin, eds. 1992. *Nothing to Do with Dionysus? Athenian Drama in Its Social Context*. Princeton: Princeton University Press.

Wolff, Francis. 1997. "Être disciple de Socrate." In *Lezioni socratiche*, ed. Gabriele Giannantoni and Michel Narcy, 31–79. Naples: Bibliopolis.

Woolf, Raphael. 2009. "Pleasure and Desire." In *The Cambridge Companion to Epicureanism*, ed. James Warren, 158–78. Cambridge: Cambridge University Press.

Zanker, Graham. 1994. *The Heart of Achilles: Characterization and Personal Ethics in the Iliad*. Ann Arbor: University of Michigan.

Zeller, Eduard. 1910. "Zu Aristippus." In *Eduard Zellers Kleine Schriften*, ed. O. Leuze, H. Diels, and K. Holl, vol. I pp. 419–24. Berlin: Georg Reimer.

———. 1868. *Socrates and the Socratic Schools*. Trans. O. J. Reichel. London: Longmans, Green, and Co.

Zilioli, Ugo. 2012. *The Cyrenaics*. Durham: Acumen.

INDEX

The following names appear with such frequency that they have not been indexed: Anniceris, Aristippus, Diogenes Laertius, Hegesias, Socrates, Theodorus.

Milton Keynes UK
Ingram Content Group UK Ltd.
UKHW010645101123
432313UK00002B/77

9 780691 176383